The

Liberal's

Guide To

Conservatives

J. Scott Wagner

Summerborne Books

Praise for
The Liberal's Guide to Conservatives

An important book that should be read by people everywhere along the political spectrum. J. Scott Wagner has brought together a variety of research in neuroscience and cognitive psychology that helps to explain political ideology. He has done an excellent job of explaining these results in language that non-experts can understand. I find the title of the book a little misleading, because he has explained the factors leading to liberal ideology as well as he has explained the factors leading to conservative ideology. You can learn about yourself while learning about others!
– Dr. Anthony Stahelski, author of *Statistics for the Statistically Challenged*

J. Scott Wagner shows a remarkable knack for navigating a course through social science theories and empirical findings, and extracting clear, practical lessons. Although framed as an instruction manual to help liberals better understand conservatives, the book's observations about psychology and citizenship extend well beyond that objective.
– Dr. Jeffrey Mondak, author, *Personality and the Foundations of Political Behavior*

The Liberal's Guide to Conservatives is well-written, entertaining, and insightful. I enjoyed the broad perspective on the subject.
– Charles Brack, neuropolitics.com

J. Scott Wagner exemplifies the liberal ideals of openness to new ideas and the search for empirical truth unclouded by political bias or agenda. He makes great progress in building a bridge across the partisan divide.
– Theindependentwhig.com

J. Scott Wagner reviews and clearly explains a wide range of cutting-edge research. A enjoyable read for anyone interested in learning more about the science of political psychology.
– Dr. Chris Sibley, Editor of *The Cambridge Handbook of the Psychology of Prejudice*

This book makes a well-researched argument for why 'the other side' isn't stupid, evil or crazy, delving into the very real psychological and experiential differences that shape our opinions. It left me feeling that I not only understand conservatives better, but myself as well.
– Samuel Mills, writer, *An Examined Life*

Requests for permission to reproduce portions of this work should be sent to Permissions, care of Reach the Right at the address below, or via email to permissions@reachtheright.com.

Published by:
Summerborne Books, a division of Reach the Right,
POB 839, Cotati CA 94931

ISBN: 0998157414
ISBN-13: 9780998157412

This book was composed in Baskerville, Cambria, Arial, and Helvetica Neue.

Internal design: Jimmy Peacock and Heather Jansen.

Cover: Designed by Monkeys, designedbymonkeys.com

To my mother, Maureen "Monte" Wagner–

filled with curiosity, impelled by love.

Table of Contents

Introduction

*I am often mad, but I would hate
to be nothing but mad.*
-E.B. White

WHEN DONALD TRUMP stormed in from nowhere to capture the 2016 Republican Presidential nomination, and spent about fifteen bucks doing it, a handful of ideology researchers weren't nearly as surprised as the rest of us. They'd been watching a bubble form in their statistical image of conservatives for about fifteen years, and the picture had recently lurched into focus.

As The Donald worked that scintillating ascent of the first half of his supernova of a candidacy, I was finishing up the research for this effort. I'd started in early 2010. That year, Dr. Jeff Mondak published an influential book that showed the difference between conservatives and liberals to be very much a matter of two, key personality traits. His work, along with a completely maddening lack of accessible basic information about what makes conservatives tick, got me doing a series of articles, which quickly turned into a book effort. It turned out to be a perfect time to get involved, as many scholars have been expanding and clarifying work on personality, genetics, language, biases, and the social side of ideology since then.

I have a near-perfect combination of cross-ideological skills and experience to make this science coherent, so I thought this would be quick. Raised conservative, in a religious home (now horribly lapsed); former naval officer; liberal activist (police brutality, land use, general whatnot); educated in psychology, engineering, business, and sociology; executive and consultant in corporate America, with extensive cross-cultural international experience. In graduate school, I'd focused on *qualitative research*, which is climbing all up into people's individual lives (as opposed to quantitative research, which means larger scale experiments and questionnaires, which the field emphasizes).

I seemed ready. But by three years in, I'd become quite frustrated at the pace of progress toward getting a clear, succinct, helpful guide together for you. It wasn't just my personal weaknesses, or problems with interviewing and working with conservatives; it was the zigging and zagging between different buildings on different campuses. I had to make connections people weren't making, or, if they were, it was the usual scholarly mumble job, with treasure stuffed in musty journals, the cryptological academic overlay.

Anyone doing interdisciplinary work has this problem of finding out who's worked on the angles on reality that you're trying to clarify; that's one reason why so little of such work gets done. Ideology is so interdisciplinary that it can't be thought of as primarily political, or individual psychology, or social psychology, or genetic, or anthropological, or cognitive science, or anything in particular. Which makes insights hard to gather and hard to apply− even hard to see in the first place. I'd try to dig up a root of an idea in political psychology, and it would've burrowed over from parent ideas in a dozen nearby fields.[1] Politics kept having little to do with it. I became a victim of a problem of scholarship confirmed by Erin Leahey, in a study of academics, that researchers get slow because there's not one learning curve, but many ("unproductive," she had said, unkindly).

Unfortunately, Dr. Leahey also showed with others that being vigorously interdisciplinarian makes for little funding, especially if you're working on squishy psychology ideas, or if you're not looping in some-thing that makes someone corporate-sized money quickly. This is a tragedy, because connections aren't getting made like they should. But it had an odd upside for someone like me: small, far-flung piles of great work lying around on ideology that helped form the picture. It has been a thrill throughout this project to be one of a handful of people in the world holding up some Hope Diamond of an insight, grinning and taking notes. You'll see− there are dozens of gems in here that provide a handhold on these people, and ourselves. Throughout the entire effort, I've been like one of those old guys out on the beach at sunrise, swinging a metal detector, picking up hair pins and quarters− except that I'd find a fistful of gold every month or so. There were a handful of bug-eyed Australian academics, or retirees in Cameroon who led me down ratholes, but that was rare; mostly, I've struggled simply to learn enough to do ideology up for you fairly and clearly, while testing the work out in the field.

Who would've guessed, for instance, that information theory, an arcane computer-ish affair, was perfect for getting across the hopelessness of our communication challenge; that theater arts was palming the single best technique for tough political conversations; or that desperate epileptic patients would provide us the key insight into our single, core, ideological psychological difference?

We needed air on this subject in the various psychology fields involved, in particular– badly. Until recently, the findings there almost uniformly painted conservatives essentially as jackasses, with zero offsets that justify their existence. It was as if all we could ask ourselves was exactly how screwed up conservatives were, and we were set to do it up in marble.

It's true that some fishy things are involved with conservatives, if you ask me; otherwise, we'd be over there rooting for their ideas alongside them. But we've been mapping out conservative fishiness quite enthusiastically, and not doing much else on ideology psychology (*political* psychology does many useful things, don't get me wrong; in an odd way, the psychology of ideology isn't exactly their thing). It isn't that all the studies were wrong; they were just one-sided. They seemed like exactly half the story. The questions felt wrong.

The most annoying political conversations I have to endure with liberals and conservatives have a grinding, half-correct, all-knowing characteristic; much of the research feels the same. Let's have "The Big Lebowski" drive the point home. Early on, Walter, a mildly insane character, gets excited and scary in the bowling alley; later, he justifies his behavior with a rant that he ends with "AM I WRONG?! AM I WRONG?!" And the Dude, the hero of the story, retorts, "You're not wrong, Walter, you're just an asshole." And Walter says, "Alright then."

One can be quite right in this life, and still be clueless.

In 2012, Jon Haidt published *The Righteous Mind: Why Good People are Divided by Politics and Religion*, which makes a powerful case for benefits to certain conservative perspectives. The book is somewhat uncomfortable for us liberals in places, and it received decidedly mixed reviews among liberal academics– but street conservatives jumped right in the water and flapped around happily in it. Jon's work is nice to them; more than that, it takes a tough, vague concept– morality– and breaks it down in a way that may not be perfect, but feels natural and commonsense for about half the nation. With a handful of colleagues, Jon tries to paint the other side of the canvas for us, so we aren't as narrow-mindedly focused on how great our own world view is. His work aligns well with the completely no-brainer results from Dr. Mondak's personality science that had gotten me started: that liberals aren't angels, and conservatives aren't Satan's little minions. Not full-time, anyway.

At one level, everyone knows that; the worst ideologue could tell me that, on their worst day. But our *unconscious* minds, including those of our overwhelmingly liberal-soaked academic friends, know no such thing. We have tremendous unconscious resistances to seeing anything good, or neutral, or mixed, or complicated about these people, no matter what we say– and that's a huge problem. Not because we all need to learn about the Dark Side so we'll agree with them, or because we should like them, or appreciate them. The problem is more basic. There's a whole sector of reality we're purposefully ignoring or dismissively twisting, because we're prejudiced. That gap in our world view hurts us, as we'll see, and not just a little.

Here are some reasons why we might want to learn about conservatives more truthfully than we have. I'm going to save you the impassioned essay, and flip you the quick list version; let's throw out the notion early that this guide is a sentimental work, here to make you love these people, or hide their sins, or get across any one thing about them, for that matter. Think more basic; think science, or commonsense. You don't have to believe and use all the below reasons actively, like I have to; take your pick as a motivator. Some are antagonistic, some are new-age nice, some are commonsensical, and some are spy vs. spy:

Reasons to Understand Conservatives

Know your enemy.
Find the good in everyone.
We all have to live together.
Everyone wants the same thing.
Hey, let's copy that, we suck at that.
We all have weaknesses and strengths.
Keep your friends close, and enemies closer.
How do we minimize the damage they're causing?
Let's persuade them effectively that our ideas will work.

Not one of those goals is served by ignoring basic aspects of the nature of conservatives, the way our unconscious mind demands of us.

We should all be clear-eyed about the kinds of nastiness possible among our friends on the right; I'll assume I don't have to do a lot of railing for you; that you're bought off, like I am, how dangerous and predictably wrong they can be policy-wise; that we don't have to stroke each other's fur over their evilitudes. But a numbing, repetitive simplicity of our common themes, and the caricatures of stupid, evil, and crazy conservatives are like one of those little robot vacuum cleaners with old ice cream covering its infra-red eye, stuck in a corner, spinning and lurching over the same patch of parquet.

Work since 2012, by Colin DeYoung, Elizabeth Suhay, Stanley Feldman and many others, has expanded and clarified aspects of conservative personality, genetics, and social influences dramatically, so that we've started to get great insights that go far beyond the black-hat, stick-man versions of conservatism that we've painted for each other for decades. In the meantime, I've done a few tours of the Midwest, South, and Southwest, observing individual lives, to try to breathe some life into great papers like "The Openness/Intellect Trait Domain as a Paradoxical Simplex." Tried to get some nice clothes on these ideas, and push them down the runway for you. Get us asking the right questions about them, or at least better ones.

Here in the seventh year of building this guide, with a tremendous amount of help from a great team of academics and experts, we've only made a good start of it. But it pleases me greatly to get you something that isn't a thousand pages long, that doesn't sound like many of those academic papers, yet still gets you a useful handle on these people. There are still gaps, and soft spots that don't bear weight, which we'll step around together, here and there: it isn't the most elegant and neatly-trimmed of subjects, this picture of conservatives we can paint right now. But it's useful and clear enough to hand to you, for all the arm wrestling and charm offenses you're destined for.

There's another reason why I spent gobs of time confused and frustrated while doing research. The work of understanding ideology is painfully personal sometimes, to do right; like looking in a mirror, to look into another mirror, to see if you have a psychic bald spot out of sight that's making you read the terrain wrong. While you're getting upset at some conservative in a bar in Hoboken, who keeps politely saying the same silly-sounding thing to you in different ways.

There's no getting around the fact that ideology is near the center of what makes us human– that it lurches into the painting unpredictably, and colors our perception without us realizing when, or how, or why it did. **If you're liberal, you can't separate out understanding conservatives from understanding yourself**. That's why so much of 60 years of ideology research sounds like a bad political ad.

The most popular question at my appearances is, "Isn't all this useful for conservatives, too?" It's a reasonable question, though usually, their irritation and body language hints that the person is really asking something like "why'd you just splat all this at *me*? I don't need it; I'm an incredibly open-minded liberal. Conservatives are the jackasses– how come you're not out there making a *real* difference, with the evil guys?"

Try to not to be that fellow. But to answer the question: sure, almost every word is technically useful for conservatives. But I don't care nearly as much about educating *them* to be effective; I'm a liberal activist watching *us* go down in flames– individually, in government, in elections– for lousy reasons. And anyway, most conservatives are much more interested in a different kind of political book, with quick answers, slathers of sarcasm, and ready enemies.

I'm not preaching outside of a McDonald's in Tulsa because of those reasons just listed. And you're only going to listen to a liberal. A guide for liberals needs to reveal them from our perspective. After all, there are a hundred million American conservatives out there dying to tell you what you get wrong about them, and they don't do you any good. That's an old lesson the linguistics people quietly proved early last century, and quickly buried in their unfathomable texts: perspective drives words and ideas like a cowgirl drives cattle– and their cowgirl ain't heading to our barn.

Our mind wants to run, then, with thinking that the whole reason for a guide of this kind, liberal to liberal, is to help us shift that vile viewpoint of theirs over to ours. You know– dumb to smart, evil to good, scary to fun-loving.

It's a reasonable wish. It could happen. If that's your focus, though, there's some good and bad news. The bad news: you bought the wrong book. We're trying to understand conservatives and work well with them. I don't have a damn thing in here about making great arguments, even though the last three chapters are about talking with them successfully. This is a broader affair.

The good news is that, thanks to the miracles of materialism, self-interest, and money, persuasion science is much, much further along than ideological studies. If you'd like to hotwire your way to conservative soft spots and funny bones, or eek that last 1.5% of the election battle your way, borrow some scrap paper and make notes as you skim the last two chapters; better, buy the liberal scholar/consultant Drew Westen's *The Political Brain*, or, even better, the conservative go-to political hack Frank Luntz's *Words that Work*. Or just admit that you're wanting sales advice, and mainline it: read Gerry Spence's extravagantly titled, but excellent and apropos, *How to Argue and Win Every Time*.

Those are great books to move on to, once we understanding these principles we'll cover. What we're after is finding ways to appreciate conservatives, talk sensibly with them, learn from them (wha?!), stay calm around them, get things done with them, be good friends or partners to them, and at least be able to pass a multiple-choice quiz on their main motivations and perspectives. We're trying to get into ingroups (be part of the "in" group with them), worm our way out of outgroups, build and deepen personal relationships, and understand how real conservatives differ from the TV versions. Because we can't learn about them without learning about ourselves, we'll also look at what's going on unconsciously behind the words we're both speaking, so that we can make educated guesses about what's really happening in a conversation.

We have a huge advantage as we focus on conservatives one at a time: because the world is a big, beautiful place, statistical truths usually melt graciously away for us with each specific conservative, so that these somewhat abstract differences of ours aren't nearly as crucial after the first little bit, when it usually becomes obvious which ones are pertinent and which aren't. Because our whole selves are usually so much broader than our ideological selves, we can also get along seamlessly with many conservatives because other personality fits, or the situation, lets you cram ideology in the cooler for as long as it takes to find out that they're pretty great.

Conservatives are better at getting along smoothly than we usually give them credit for, because they're typically such social creatures, used to keeping their heads down to keep it from getting chopped off. They burrow easily into liberal charity organizations and elsewhere, blending in, rolling with insults, keeping their opinions to themselves; making sincere friends of their political enemies, in a way we liberals often find surprising, or impossible. Some of the advice in this guide is to try to be as good as they are at some things; that's one of those things. They don't reach out as naturally, but they can be pretty darn great at the getting along part, once we've done the reaching out successfully.

There are many odd and cool ways around the personality and belief conflict problems. There's even a kind of opposites-attract tendency present in many professional, romantic and political relationships. Shared goals, or warmth, or shared hobbies, or the jigsaw puzzle of compatible strengths and weaknesses can easily make ideology a sideshow. For years, I accosted conservatives in bars, at AA meetings, in churches, at political offices, neighborhood events, and in coffee shops all across the U.S. to suss that out for you. You probably would've had fun if you'd come along, as I did, with warm, often spectacularly polite people.

It won't always go well, though. It didn't for me. Sometimes, especially with conservative political leaders, I discussed politics directly, usually right after meeting them, as a kind of finishing school on some pieces of this work. Sometimes, it veered into what felt like trying to be polite while throwing knives at each other, especially if I was tired. I didn't always escape those conversations with friendship and respect intact. But most talks, especially those just touching upon the political here or there, were more instructive and positive. When they were hard,

I discovered early that it was almost always my fault. Not that their shotgun wasn't often at the ready; and many didn't make it easy. But the point of this guide is that we have much more control over the quality of our time with conservatives than we think. That's why I've been so motivated to get this guide to you: I can tell you how your side of the conversation can control 95% or so of the potential for disaster.

Not to imply that one should always be Jesus-like, or polite, or always be anything in particular; that depends on what you're trying to get done, and who you're working with. Usually, we need to be better at being polite, curious, and clear with conservatives. Sometimes, being blunt, or angry, or civilly disobedient can be enormously helpful– call it extreme clarity. We don't do enough of either the niceties or the bluntness, but choose instead to fret and waste our moments in the mushy middle, being distant, or entitled, or resentful. This guide is about understanding and working with conservatives *effectively*, which can take many forms.

Most of the biggest problems we get into one-on-one involve losing our tempers when we shouldn't with conservatives, misunderstanding them, or making an error that leads to people being mad that shouldn't be. These are all mistakes that are avoidable, with a little study and practice. This is a remarkably difficult point to grasp for some, especially those of us who are very liberal; we tend to assume that any problems we have with conservatives are miraculously due solely to their personal faults or nasty views; that there's no need to treat the affair as worthy of study or practice, because it can't make a difference.

You can probably understand, having read this far, why I've named our nonprofit Reach the Right (to facilitate understanding and working with conservatives). But I can't tell you how many times I've had to explain the name of the company to liberals whose gut reaction is "why would you want to reach the right?" There's often a suspicion that I'm a conservative plant, or at least under the spell of the Dark Side. Or they think the whole affair is a waste of time, that conservatives are hopeless.

That's an understandably human, moral reaction, but dangerous anyway. Ignorance, standoffish attitudes, and demonization are best left to conservatives to use, if they like; as we'll see, they have much better psychological rationalizations for such. As Stephen Stills once said of liberals, "We're supposed to be some kind of different." We *are* different, and the tools and assumptions behind polarization aren't our bailiwick, no matter how horrified we are by their ideas.

We also have to recognize the strength of that impulse to polarize within ourselves, by acknowledging a conflicting truth about our nature: that mankind is *generally* conservative, only more or less so, for both healthy and unhealthy biological and evolutionary reasons.[2] In that sense, think of being liberal as just being less conservative; when we panic or get angry, we often fight to climb into the same telephone booth with them to get tough, or overreact. Think of how liberals got us into Vietnam, for instance, and kept us there; how most liberals ended up wanting to invade Iraq. That means that we're not that different, so our own biases, prejudices, misunderstandings, and typical reactions as liberals give us a clear, mirror-image laboratory for understanding those who seem to be on earth for a different purpose than us, but who share our human flaws.

A bit of housekeeping, and then we're off. This guide is meant to be direct and useful, and as straightforward as possible. Footnotes (endnotes, actually) provide background. There are the usual reference notes, but there are also clarifying explanations. If something sounds a little too tidy, or confusing, dig a bit deeper in the endnotes. Publishers discourage footnotes in books that aren't for experts: all them little numbers on the page whisper to your unconscious self all along the way how boring it must be. Publishers have writers use the opposite approach: speak breathlessly, make a snazzy, open-and-shut case, and go dark on references. Or notes are hidden in the back, with no link between the mumbling and dissembling going on, front or back. I can't get past the first wingding of a story in those kinds of books without feeling like I've been blindfolded, and am being led by the elbow. In this guide, you and I couldn't do that; there's too much at stake in getting it right, and having you buy in to the underlying science.

Even so, there's nothing more malleable than scientific data. A footnote doesn't necessarily mean the point made is a fact; it often just means someone else believes it, too, someone who wrote more about it, on a nice letterhead. Something about putting a tiny number after a statement says much more to our unconscious mind than it should. It should mean something along the lines of, "If you're interested in this, or have questions, read more about it here." Until you read a reference, it should be thought of more like one of a chestful of Russian military medals, not a halo hovering over an idea.

I didn't use notes if the research or source referred to is easily found on the web with an intuitive search phrase. Unless there is an explicit statement otherwise, the studies used are high-quality, well-constructed studies.[3] Many studies commonly bandied about on the subject, some of which are famous, had to be ignored.[4]

If what I've written isn't backed with good studies, or enough of them, or I've learned it on the road in interviews, I've said "I think" or "I believe" somewhere in there. If I say "seems," it's either my opinion or the opinion of others I respect; it's not necessarily a fact. Much of what I bring to the table personally through interviews and my background is "seems" material. I think those are some of the most useful points of the guide, so I'm hoping you turn them over in your mind, despite the lack of an appended Russian campaign medal, to see if you can use them.

A few apologies. The first to the world of science, for using the word "ideology." Ideology is a beautiful, useful, much more general concept than ours, encompassing a realm of psychology that involves what happens when people grab *a limited set of ideas* around a subject– any subject, from butterfly collecting to race car driving– and who run enthusiastically with their chosen subset. It turns out that there are certain tragedies and dead ends that happen in patterns when we lop off conveniently what we run with as facts, no matter what the field.

Using an ideology isn't generally a great idea, but we humans can't help ourselves. Like Winnie the Poo, we are bears of very little brain, and can't hold two somewhat conflicting ideas in our hands at the same time, the way all fields force good scientists to do. Ideology lets us stick with one side of the argument the whole way through, so nothing conflicts– unlike reality, which we're usually trying to avoid right then, without realizing it. In that sense, political ideology is the obvious child of its parent, ideology. What we'll be talking about isn't *political* ideology, though, because that's far too specialized, as we'll address in Chapter One. Because I'm not enough of a marketeer to make up and trademark a new word for what we'll be talking about, we've followed the crowd– you and I will abuse the word ideology together.

Something worse: I haven't applied that more general and powerful science of ideology to this guide, outside of a few snide swipes, because I promised my mommy and my publicist that I wouldn't try to get liberals to stop being so ideological, in a guide about conservatives. Instead, I poured that into the Ideology Appendix, because I couldn't live with myself without making clear somewhere how bad it is to be too ideological. You can be very liberal, by the way, like me, and still not be ideological; that's what the Appendix covers. It's short: if you're feeling particularly mature today, I'd recommend it as a start on this affair.

Another apology has to do with libertarians. It would be wonderful to address them completely, but we can't; there's too much ground to cover as is, in a practical guide of conservatism. They're very tricky, and clever, and contrary. Things would get mixty-mixed easily, vaulting us from having fun to something else. The good news is that most of the libertarians we don't cover are the easiest conservatives to get along with. And we do cover the mean ones. So when they sucker-punch you in conversations, and you're bent over with the wind knocked out of you,

you'll know why they did it, and how.

A final apology, though not a heartfelt one, is for divvying up people into conservatives and liberals, as if they were apples and oranges, or Hatfields and McCoys. Most of the studies used in this guide had their test subjects call themselves liberal or conservative, and took them at their word. Different part of the country, and different kinds of people, have widely varying opinions on what's liberal or conservative. Being conservative is surprisingly hip in the heartland among Democrats (the opposite is less common, but happens). I've met dozens of people who were quite liberal politically who called themselves conservative Republicans. They're about one in ten conservatives. I call them "the confused." They learned as kids that liberals, whoever they are, are evil. If you tell them they're liberal, they get very sad.

But any alternatives we use to labeling our own ideology is worse. Some studies go by people's positions on things like climate change, but there aren't enough of those studies to be useful. Many issue approaches get confusing or worthless, especially with international studies, or over time, because our issues vary so much.

The only other way of trying to break us up into two useful groups would be to go by political parties: though that makes some research useful and straightforward, it creates problems for us. As of now, about 40% of people consider themselves politically independent, so we'd be discussing only a little over half the people if we talk about the parties. The political parties themselves are misleading. According to years of Pew studies, most Democrats don't consider themselves liberal, about a third of Republicans don't consider themselves conservative, and most independents consider themselves conservative.

People have private ideas of what ideology means, too, and it varies wildly across location, race, and income. Conservatives oppose each other all over the country, in sometimes bitter battles. Most of my liberal activist work in California involves facing off against my fellow liberals (the label LINO's, or liberal in name only, gets tossed around by the meanies among us). The whole business is a mess, actually: the person who is a pure conservative, in terms of what they believe, the programs they support politically, and their personality characteristics, is rare. Almost everyone is an ideological mulatto. One has to tread carefully when trying to slice down the middle of America– through families, regions, races, and economic groups– to get at something of use.

Yet we must try. Powerful insights into how ideology affects us matter. They matter more than almost anything, notwithstanding all the whining about putting people in boxes unfairly. And there's great news: it turns out that self-styled conservatives and liberals have clear personality differences which researchers have documented, that turn out to be very helpful to know.[5]

We have two huge advantages in this effort, too, which is why my apology about pigeonholing us as liberals and conservatives isn't wholehearted. First, we're not trying to describe people at all perfectly; and secondly, modern statistics is extremely powerful, and takes care of many of the most pressing concerns that problems with definitions create.

This guide is a set of templates you can hold up to a person in good light, and either toss out or use, as seems fit. You can confidently start with the stereotypes we wrestle into being here if you're trying to work with someone, just as you might wisely avoid dangerous neighborhoods at night, or use the more formal "vous" instead of "tu" to address a shopkeeper in France. If a person is fairly conservative in personality, you will find these principles help you immensely. If they're strongly conservative, these principles can be make-or-break. And if you're wrong, the price you pay is almost always modest.

The poet Robert Frost once wrote[6] about a fellow who was trying to grow peach trees in New Hampshire, to make the point that "there are roughly zones" in life: zones where we stand in good company, where fears are well-founded, and where certain ideas for how to work together make sense. Our task is just to gather great, looming truths, the kind of thing I couldn't miss on the road, into a useful toolkit; the rest can await our kids to be uncovered.

These zones, or generalizations, about ideological personality and other differences are more easily seen the more ideological a person is. This should make sense, since they're ideological characteristics. Many of my activist friends are particularly good fits with liberal traits; conservative stereotypes also fit better with far-right conservatives. The closer we get to the center, the less the characteristics tend to hold, though they're usually quite helpful at beginnings.

Also, the further someone is from us ideologically, in any direction, the harder it is to get along with them, and the more need we have for preparation and care. This is another way of saying the same thing, of talking about zones; the ideological characteristics are very powerful in determining who we engage with, and how close we get. I think this also explains most of the conflict between liberals, or between conservatives, because our ideological comfort zones are smaller than many people think; the borders have to be respected even between the center-left or center-right and their more ideological cousins within their same ideology. That's how powerful these tendencies are.

I tried to spend time on the road thinking of a world where there were no conservatives, where we liberals have to put our money where our mouths are. A world where we can't just tug and tug on our side of the rope, complaining about stupidity and dishonesty; where we have to actually plan and execute on our fantasies as the tug rope magically slides our way. It is surprising how hard this kind of thinking is, and how little we actually do it. If we're realistic, it's not easy to envision how we want things to be; what we'd argue about, or do poorly, if we sweep away the constraints the right throws at us. It's much easier and more natural, more knee-jerk, to frame the purpose of our political life as a kind of death-spiral with conservatives, like Sherlock Holmes wrapping himself around his nemesis, Moriarty, before falling with him to their deaths.

We even think that having the right notion of how things should be (national health care; ending wars; equality; tiny militaries) automatically means that if we get to do what we want, we'll do it right. That's silly. All those things are insanely difficult to pull off, even without political resistance. Beating conservatives is a good goal, but it most assuredly isn't our main job description. Letting go of that mindset is a part of understanding them.

It's not even true that we need to get the laws we want to make big, healthy change common and transformative in America. Our individual job is to be good liberals, living by our playbook, and governing well whatever's in our purview. Unafraid to question our assumptions, and eager to correct for our blind spots. Living liberal ideals, and healthily questioning our ability to do things right, could utterly transform our society without a single new law in our favor, without converting a single conservative to our cause. We create many of our own problems.

If we can keep that in mind, the self-satisfied, uncurious perspective we usually protect and shore up can be shed long enough to at least understand why conservatives think and act the way they do.

Let's take that pause now. And let's forget about politics awhile; let's learn about conservatives as people. When we're done together, you'll make fewer mistakes, and the ones you make won't be as deadly. The questions you'll ask will have changed, too: they'll be more interesting, and more useful.

Chapter One

IDEOLOGY ON THE BRAIN

Everything that irritates us about others can lead us to an understanding of ourselves.
-Carl Jung

O UR CAT is a perfect coal black, a model of feline mystery. She has a grating meow, a screech, really, that she uses to be let out in the mornings. She becomes strident and scolding with any delay. When I can't stand it anymore, I unearth myself from my layers and shuffle to the door, as she skitters behind and before me. As I reach for the doorknob, she crouches, tense, readying a spring into the pre-dawn killing spree. I open the door in a rush. But instead of leaping into the wan light, as she advertises will happen, she freezes, then slowly lowers herself into a crouch. Only part of her head is outside. Sniffs a bit, while my robe flaps in the breeze. I consider gently pinching her neck with the door at these moments, in a half-asleep, impromptu attempt to train the untrainable. She rises again, no longer in a hurry, then slowly lowers her haunches. Watches a faraway bird. Glances at my feet. The cold seeps up my robe. We look out together. Today may not be a hunting day, after all.

Studies show that liberals put up with this nonsense much more often than conservatives, who are more likely to have an obedient, loving, relatively uncomplicated dog. Makes sense, doesn't it, somehow? One of my friends, a liberal, finds dogs annoying– the undying, mindless loyalty, the devotion bought with no coin whatsoever. All that simplicity and consistency seems shallow and boring to her. We liberals are much more statistically likely to mollycoddle a cat, this fiercely independent, unpredictable animal, whose version of love borders suspiciously on flagrant self-interest.

1

There's a whole ragtag gaggle of these contrasts between liberals and conservatives. One study found liberals tend to have more fashionable offices at work, and that we surround ourselves with more color there. There's evidence that conservatives have quite a few more cleaning products at home. Certain little parts of our brains measure out significantly smaller or larger, on average. Liberals are almost twice as likely to claim they never eat fast food. Conservatives watch team sports much more, and individual ones less; many even consider the quality and location of major sports teams in the area when deciding where to live, which is an odd notion for almost all of us liberals.

My favorite statistic of this kind is one of many surprising findings about smell and ideology: in a large, online survey, very conservative women liked the scent of newborn babies a bit more than they liked the scent of coffee– but liberal women liked the smell of coffee three times as much as the smell of newborns![1]

This innocent-seeming cavalcade of contrasts between liberals and conservatives extends right down through to the roots of who we are; for many of us, it results in an oil-and-water discomfort with each other. Ideology makes it hard to even agree on many of the basics of good and evil,[2] so it shouldn't come as a surprise that it affects where we choose to live, and who we interact with. It's been creating two separate nations right under our noses. In the '70's, as our society became mobile for the first time, the rural and urban differences in ideology really got going, and are now very prominent.[3] States, counties, suburbs, neighborhoods, and even specific blocks have been clumping along liberal and conservative lines for decades,[4] which is one of many cascading reasons we have so much more polarization.

Politics are a detail in the story of what we call ideology. Politics just don't matter that much for most of us, typically lagging far behind family, work, and religion as life drivers. Over half of us don't even bother to vote in a typical election, and even if we do, many vote out of a sense of duty, as made clear by research that shows how spectacularly uninformed most voters are.

As liberals, most of us can appreciate many conservative individuals; we also usually feel a need to get along with them, if we can, and work with them. But if you're as political as I am, you're probably a bit bipolar on the subject, because you're also convinced that conservatives can run us and the rest of the world right off a cliff with dangerous or dastardly ideas. Quite a swirly personal philosophy, if you think about it, holding these two notions of conservatives at the same time: tough-but-worth-it, and Hitler's little handmaidens.

An interview I had with one state's Democratic Party Executive

Director highlights how fundamental and unsolvable this problem is. The first part of our talk, she mapped out her model of bipartisan fellowship, and recounted various techniques and attitudes– respect, patience, clarity– that have helped her succeed in striking compromises and making strong relationships with conservatives. She clearly believed that working well with conservatives was essential and entirely possible, given a good attitude and enough effort. And she was smooth. Convincing. She'd probably talked that schtick a thousand times. It certainly sounded less hollow than it usually does.

When I asked her how she became an involved liberal, though, the tenor shifted remarkably. She had lived in a southern state in the '90s– I'm not going to say which one to protect the guilty, but for many liberals, the state's name rhymes with Mordor. One day, a teacher's aide rapped her daughter's knuckles with a ruler for reading on the school bus after school, while waiting for the other kids to get on the bus to be taken home. The rule had been that the waiting children were to sit up straight, look forward, and stay silent until the bus left. Her daughter was very upset when she got home, and her mother was furious all night, going to the school first thing the next day to talk to the principal.

His response was a shock to her. He politely and consistently refused to discuss the appropriateness of the policy with her, and told her repeatedly that the teacher was well within her authority to punish the girl the way she did. He tried to explain patiently, in as many different ways as he could, that what mattered for both the girl and her mother was that a rule had been violated, and that the child had received the standard, long-approved punishment. He felt that was all he needed to get across at the meeting; even more, he thought it essential to his point that cruelty or appropriateness *not* be discussed, so that focus could be kept on the real issue at hand– disobedience– as a lesson to the mother. No change of policy happened, nor an apology– "not even close," she told me. The frustration she felt from not being able to protect her child prompted her to seek volunteer work with the Democratic Party; that led eventually to her career in politics.

There was a dramatic change in her voice and attitude when she shifted from talking about the importance of compromise to her personal story. She had sounded so even-handed and generous toward conservatives before that story, but didn't touch the core of herself or her beliefs until she told me the story of her daughter. It had been decades, yet she was still enraged.

As I've toured the Midwest, South, and Southwest interviewing political and non-political conservatives and liberals, I've experienced this irreconcilable duality I saw in her many times within myself, and I've seen it in others. Every year now, as polarization begins to gain ground in our hearts, we all get a little more chicken-brained about conservatives. We want to be effective and useful, but we're liberals because we believe liberalism is the right *moral* choice. We're not playing a game, here: there are conservative behaviors and ideas that outrage us because we see them as morally wrong– as evil. When those subjects are involved, compromise or getting along can sometimes be far from our minds. And this problem isn't just within politics: on a personal basis, we can have this same kind of conflict, even if we're a mix of genius and saint with them.

I think all those feelings are entirely appropriate. Yet, where you and I may see moral lines being clearly crossed, with visual and audible alarms clanging, conservatives may see nothing at all. I suspect the school principal was probably not particularly different from many conservatives that the Executive Director tried to work with every day. His behavior was predictable and ordinary. They cannot see our limits, and sometimes can't even imagine those limits being where we say they are. Usually, at about the same time, we're stepping over a moral limit of theirs, without appreciating how it affects them. From the principal's standpoint, it would have been immoral for the daughter to *not* be punished for breaking a known rule; the punishment details didn't matter. He saw her mother's protests as immoral as well.

I must've said the word "moral" a dozen times in the last two paragraphs. Calling our differences moral helps us understand how fundamental and huge they feel, but it doesn't explain *why* we have the feeling; it's like saying somebody's evil because they do bad things. Research shows that the word morality is almost magic: just calling something moral makes us take the issue way more seriously than we would otherwise, and makes us more easily persuaded.[5] I just did that, and it probably made a difference to you. It means we're thinking in terms of good and evil about something humans have a choice about, like rapping a little girl's knuckles. But if we wipe away the cobwebs, and move the statue of an old Greek fellow or two out of the way, we're actually saying we really, really, reallyreallyreeelly **value** ending the hitting of little girls, forever; we value that so much that we want to promote the effort, and put a medal on its chest; we want a word that can help us turn what we value into a sacred reference.

As the moral psychologist Jon Haidt likes to say, morality *binds* and *blinds*; it brings us closer to our friends, and makes it difficult or impossible to relate to some others. There are some great, complicated definitions of morality that are good for scientists, but we're going to try to tie our morals back to what we value the most, so we understand a little about the whys of these differing ideological moralities. Where do they come from? And why do they vary so much– why do they seem almost like polar opposites for liberals and conservatives?

To find out, we have to delve to the basic human drives behind those morals. We'll look at some astounding, powerful evidence from human neurology about conservative values, which helps us start with a simple, single reference point, from which much of the rest unfolds. We'll then look at conservatives and ourselves from the standpoint of personality, where we are able to turn that reference point into great focus on specific parts of who we are.

Our personalities have to get the job done for each of us through snarls of biases that we filter everything through. Looking in some detail at a few example cases will help us recognize the patterns of them in ideology. That'll help make us humble about our personal skill at carving out an efficient reality, because we'll see how each of us insert goofiness and problems into our affairs– and it'll help us be much more patient with conservatives, who have a whole golf bag full of biases they wheel around with them.

That's the basic theory we need, which will prepare us for the section that explains conservative politics– the two types of conservatives, and the extremists that cause us and the rest of conservatives so many headaches. We'll be ready then to circle back to morality, to see how to avoid the anger and disgust that morality is designed to bring to the party. In the final section, we put all that together, and get into the nuts and bolts of working with them well, by focusing on good conversation.

These angles on the affair– neurology; personality; cognitive biases; politics; morality; and communication– will give you an approach that'll be useful with the individual conservatives you come across in your life, whether they be family members, friends, your partner, people at work, or politicians. It'll help you fathom the TV versions and bigwig politicians much better as well, as long as you keep in mind all the theater and posing and blusterfussing involved in their worlds.

We're going to be developing two statistical versions of conservatives, blobs of humanity who can never come into sharp focus. These mostly male, 90% white, mildly overweight, fairly happy American[6] conservatives don't exist in real life, but they have certain very useful similarities to my Uncle Donald, and to Donald Trump, who do exist.

We're going to be building *stereotypes*, or generalizations. These stereotypes will be troublesome to certain folks, because they will occasionally sound prejudiced, or too complimentary, or prejudiced and complimentary and weird all at once. Here's the thing, though: psychologists that study people in a social setting *generalize for a living*. We build stereotypes, hopefully good ones, and then, if we have enough information, we also look into the ways that exceptions apply.

So we'll be saying things like, "conservatives are xxx" over and over; behind that statement, we are saying something like:

> Based on good-to-great evidence from multiple studies, people who label themselves conservatives have a statistically significant [probably real] tendency to be xxx. However, some conservative individuals may be a kind of opposite, and others may have the xxx tendency far more than the average, so buyer beware, use common sense, and your mileage will vary; because your Uncle Donald, or whoever you're working with, isn't a statistic.[7]

The few times we have good information on any important exceptions to those statistical blobby people, we'll discuss it. But usually the tendencies themselves are extremely helpful on their own. I hope you can see that our stereotypes aren't the same as the one a long-dead relative of mine once graced me with, with the introduction, "Lemme tell you about them blacks," before revealing his keen sense of social science for ten minutes. There are good and bad stereotypes, or generalizations– the words are synonyms– but the power and accuracy of good stereotyping is one of the strongest, most repeated findings of social science.[8] And we're fortunate compared to most of psychology, because great work done in ideology in the last ten years allows us to build **excellent stereotypes** (now there's a phrase you've never heard before). They don't free us from having to remember that humans vary wildly– even conservatives. But they give us a *huge* leg up when working with them, especially at beginnings.

Let's noodle around inside the conservative mind now, without asking. We'll need to start with a mild bit of neurology.

The Brain in Two Acts

Nearly every animal bigger than a bug has a split-brain structure, and we all share many of the same basic communication patterns between the brain hemispheres.[9] Virtually all major brain processes– the senses, speech, metaphor interpretation and use, and emotions– involve various parts of both brain hemispheres actively. Each of these processes require separate stages (sometimes over 20), and there is strong evidence for negotiation and comparative processes that do incredibly complicated tasks. We know that the split-brain structure takes advantage of *deliberately isolated strengths*. As one celebrated neuroscientist wrote, "except in the light of lateralization [two hemispheres] nothing in human psychology/psychiatry makes any sense."[10]

We usually think of the brain's halves as mirror-images of each other, but they're quite different. Like grocery bags filled with different products, the right one is normally bigger than the other, usually with an overlap on one side, and a mild twist to the whole affair. The sides make use of different mixes of neurotransmitters, the chemicals involved in all brain processes, and have a contrasting mix of cell types. Data is processed on both sides at the same time, or nearly so, and often pours both ways across the divide between them in multiple streams during even many simple acts, often with a fading glow of cross-town traffic, a ghosting audit trail.

The original brain hemispheres formed over 400 million years ago, in the ocean. Many birds will watch prey with the left eye, which means their right hemisphere is "watching" it (most parts of the right side are controlled by the left hemisphere, and vice versa). Crows will focus on close work with tools using their right eye; toads shift the focusing hemisphere once they get used to a new sight or experience. The split takes advantage of groupings of tools that are different for each hemisphere, to alter the "point of view," and to compare and contrast quickly and consistently, so that one approach doesn't inappropriately dominate.[11] The two sides have separate reasons for existing; all animals sort out how to use the different impulses and strengths of the modules on both sides to arrive at our interpretation and reactions. Humans tend to use more of their right hemisphere when learning things, and more of their left once they have learned the action. That general move from more right to more left-side activity is seen across human lives; one prominent neuroscientist thinks we shift this way gradually as our lives trend toward more established routine.[12]

Until the late 1960's, people suffering from certain types of severe epilepsy got relief from the problem by cutting a certain part of the neural bridge between the hemispheres, so the hemispheres couldn't communicate as well with each other anymore. Researchers accidentally discovered that the surgery usually revealed two seemingly-complete, separate personalities in each individual, especially right after surgery. Researchers could talk to one personality by standing on one side or speaking into one ear, and then switch to the other personality. The many useful discoveries eventually led to a Nobel Prize for Dr. Roger Sperry, who directed much of the research.

Incredibly, almost every one of the many distinctive traits of the left hemisphere's "personality" correspond remarkably to statistical findings about Americans who label themselves conservatives. The same statistical connection can also be seen between the right hemisphere and American self-styled liberals[13] (for a list of each of those 19 traits, and a more detailed explanation of how they relate to ideology, see the Ideology and the Brain Appendix).

We all use both sides of our brain as we do almost everything. But for reasons we don't fully understand, most of us rely more on one of the two *perspectives*, or philosophies, of these brain hemisphere "sub-personalities" when we interpret the world and act in it. That choice seems to dictate our ideological viewpoint. It's also seen in our personalities, and so it's strongly inherited. This makes sense in light of one prominent research team's findings: "Several distinct lines of evidence indicate that each hemisphere plays a unique role in inference making," or in interpretation of the world around us.[14] Since ideology involves some of humanity's most vital inference making, we shouldn't be surprised to see it involved in the divided structure of our brain.

This is a large claim. Many people, even some scientists, think any kind of talk about hemispheres is forbidden because of popular misunderstandings of the science, as if that meant that there's nothing to be learned from the most fundamental division of any organ in biology. There's a whole roving squadron of people on the web who gleefully call anything a myth if it has to do with the brain hemispheres. They ignore some of the most respected neuroscientists in the field, though, some of whom have specialized in hemispheric difference. Several have spent most of their lives exploring the reasons for the split, and its implications. One of them has a great metaphor that will help us begin to understand the most fundamental schism between us and conservatives, so deeply rooted in our basic biology.

The General and the Scout

Dr. V.S. Ramachandran, Director of the Center for Research on Brain and Cognition in San Diego, California, is slightly stooped, and dark-featured: he gesticulates energetically, and paces often while he talks. He uses a simplifying metaphor of the left hemisphere of the brain, the one statistically associated with conservative traits. He says it's like a general assigned to fight a battle using conventional weapons. The right hemisphere (that's us liberals) is like a scout, who gives an update to the general just before battle.[15] As the general prepares to attack, the scout comes back from over the hill and tells him that the enemy has nuclear weapons. This forces the general to change his plan, and to make a new one, because there's far too much risk of failure if the scout is right:

The coping strategies of the two hemispheres are fundamentally different. The left hemisphere's job is to create a model and maintain it at all costs. If confronted with some new information that doesn't fit the model, it relies on...defense mechanisms to deny, repress or confabulate [make up fables]; anything to preserve the status quo. The right hemisphere's strategy, on the other hand, is fundamentally different. I like to call it the 'anomaly [exception] detector', for when the anomalous information reaches a certain threshold, the right hemisphere decides that it is time to force the left hemisphere to revise the entire model.[16]

This analogy shows the left hemisphere trying to get an important process (the battle) done, and the right hemisphere trying to provide crucial exceptions to the plan to improve the process (bad guys have nuclear weapons).

There's a big difference between easy and tough decisions, though. With nukes, as long as you trust the scout, all that's left is to just pack your bags and go home. But what if the scout came in at the last moment and told the general that, instead of nuclear weapons, there were 800 tanks on the enemy side, not the 500 planned for– what would the general do? Here's Dr. Ramachandran again:

A good general would ask the scout to shut up and instruct him [to] not tell anyone about what had been seen. Indeed, he may even shoot the scout and hide the report in a drawer,...[or] tell the scout to lie to the other generals and tell them that he only saw 500 tanks, which would be analogous to a confabulation [making up a fable]. The purpose of all of this is to impose stability on behavior and to avoid vacillation.

This example hints at what a mess it is inside our heads all of a sudden when the "scout" picks up information that suddenly threatens a well-laid plan by the "general." It's even worse than that: the scout might be wrong, or might exaggerate to get the general to do what he wants. These two partners worked so well together on a simple case, but now we're talking repression, confabulation, exaggeration, and who knows what.

This isn't all bad, even if it sounds like it might involve quiet metaphorical murders, or little pieces of us telling lies to other little pieces. Neurological life is a complicated business. After all, maybe the general is right: maybe they should attack anyway. Decision-making, or having to choose all of one side of an argument as the winner, often has a big downside, no matter which we do. But we can't half choose, even though the price paid might be high if we make a wrong choice. Half choosing, or vacillating, is another way of saying we do nothing, which is really just another expensive choice. There's no way to avoid messiness.

Conservatives love the general and scout story, because the boss in the tale is associated with them ("that's exactly right!"). I wish my guy was king of the story, but he ain't.[17] Michael Gazzaniga, the most experienced and celebrated hemispheric researcher, agrees with Ramachandran that the left hemisphere generally manages our life, with important exceptions; other researchers aren't so sure. It turns out to be a tough question to answer, and fortunately, it's not important for our purposes. The point for us is unmistakable: the left hemisphere[18] uses strategies and approaches that inspire the conservative orientation toward **supporting important processes**, in the spirit of the general. To borrow a phrase from a popular conservative manifesto,[19] "the conservative adheres to custom, convention, and continuity" to get things done. Exceptions to the process– anomalies, complications– are often either ignored or fought against, unless conservatives are convinced with powerful evidence that an exception needs to affect the process.

The right hemisphere uses strategies and capabilities that inspire the liberal orientation toward **supporting important exceptions**, in the spirit of the scout. This hemisphere is the exception detector, focused on things like how an individual or a minority group is being hurt by an established process. Because of this mission or attitude, it's attracted to novelty in general, to discovering interesting or useful new ways of doing things; its world is one where "exceptions," or unusual items, get most of the attention.

As we review the details of these perspectives throughout this guide, you'll be able to see many ways we've each taken direct inspiration from these contrasting viewpoints. Inside our heads, the two approaches are naturally at odds, but are also quite dependent on each other to get our affairs done correctly. We should derive some bit of comfort from knowing that these biological approaches we each key off are not only different, but sometimes even irreconcilable, for **practical** reasons. As human beings, we each have to figure out how to get our life's work done, but also how to adjust our approach when we're doing it wrong, or even figure out when we need to stop it and do something else. That simple idea turns out to be a good way of summing up a basic human dilemma that we're trying to solve with the hemispheric design.

Unfortunately, we can't run all the way from that scientific fact to a fanciful conclusion that we have a wonderful, healthy ideological conflict going on that's all for the good, so everyone smile for the camera; that it's tough, but it'll be great. We should be careful with such generalities, even if there's some truth to it, because we live in a specific time and place, with jerks and angels and geniuses and dummies working it out. Remember murderous generals, and exaggerating scouts. It matters enormously sometimes which side wins when ideologies conflict, and it matters what particular notion we each foist as truth. That's true both personally, and as a nation. Ideological competition might well be healthy in some ways, in theory, but we don't live in Theory-istan, any more than the general or scout does.

In our regular life— not the abstract one, where we're whining about world hunger or Republicans, but the one with alarm clocks, and kids, and jobs, and sore ankles— we all dash between depending more on one or the other hemisphere's perspectives. We're pretty slick at it. Think in terms of climbing a stairwell in bad light, for instance. Normally, the process or pattern of climbing stairs has you on a kind of calm, easy autopilot, because you're an expert at stairs. But if it's very dark, you may have to be struggling to see obstacles in the way, and be tentative about where you put your feet: that uses much more of a right-hemisphere (and visual) orientation, as exceptions to the normal process become important.[20] As individuals, we all have the responsibility to find ways to be a judicious general, working efficiently on vital things, and a careful scout, making sure we don't run ourselves over a cliff with too much emphasis on whatever we normally do.

We might wonder if a focus on process is actually playing out in the world of conservatives: instead of valuing a process of some kind, conservatives seem as if they're just attacking what we want all the time. For example, some attack gay marriage— in other words, they try to stop important exceptions from enjoying the right to the "process" of marriage. In their mind, they're defending something crucial. We need to remember their default perspective: that it's wrong to change the current process, *exactly* the way it is, because the exceptions we liberals are pointing out shouldn't have influence.

Did you catch that *"exactly"* part? It's like the fine print of a contract you end up in court over. If you think about it, a process of any kind is just a collection of rules for how things should happen. If someone who's focused on the process sees you lopping off a rule you don't like, it can make them crazy. Conservatives aren't going to be flexible about such things the way we are. Our version of common sense might be "just make it work, and bend the rules if you have to." Their version would be "just make it work, unless it breaks a rule." Think of it like a conversation we raise with them when we see a problem:

[You] This isn't working for him.
[Them] That's too bad. Life sucks sometimes.
[You] Well, life shouldn't suck for him this time. Adjust the rules.
[Them] Are you trying to change rules out of the blue?
[You] Yes, because they suck.
[Them] Yeah— well, my daddy made the rules. Life sucks sometimes.

It ties back to this need to preserve, to save something exactly as is, that can seem so alien to us. One Senator sponsored a bill to keep Harriet Tubman's face off the twenty dollar bill: "It's not about Harriet Tubman; it's about keeping the picture on the twenty, y'know? Why would you want to change that? I am a conservative, I like to keep what we have."[21] If something seems to work fine as is, keeping it the same becomes vital, because of an orientation far beyond politics, rooted deeply in the psyche.

Knowing why conservatives do what they do means everything. In the political world, we should almost always concentrate on our role of improving process, instead of attacking process. That view of our role has unexpected power, and it leads to odd opportunities. It lets us avoid what amounts to a *cultural misunderstanding*. Two groups of people who usually live in different worlds, and who have different values, and particular, mysterious expressions of those values, are essentially different cultures. Thinking in terms of cultural difference can be helpful; it helps us press pause on our reactions when they waylay us.

For those of use who have travelled, it's a little easier to be more careful with our judgments about motivations and meaning with conservatives. Sometimes, they're just different than us; dragging in morality every chance we get is a waste of time, and counter-productive.

Let's take an example from a cultural difference we can easily yank out of a moral frame, so we can see how this might work. Many French people commonly use insults that are brutally true with those they are close to, and even people they don't know well but whom they like.[22] It's a cultural tic, mostly among males, that happens at parties and other casual situations where most Americans would normally be pleasant as a rule, especially with a foreigner. The French are trying to say, typically while a little drunk, "our relationship is so much bigger than these weaknesses you and I have, that we can joke about them." It's a little similar to how American grade-school boys might relate to each other, in their rough-edged way. Your role in this game is to accept the insult easily and simply, maybe with a grin and a shrug, because it doesn't matter, in light of how neato the guy is– and then, later, you're supposed to insult him back in the same way, as if *his* weakness is no big deal. They *love* hearing Americans do that.

If, instead, you take their insult seriously, they get angry, frustrated, and defensive, because you're saying that their friendly little insult is more important than any relationship you might develop with them. That's when you will see the supposed French rudeness in full flower. This one French oddity is a big reason why so many Americans run screaming back home from French vacations, utterly clear on how rude French people are. Yet navigating that alien gauntlet successfully was one of the most interesting and satisfying bonding experiences of my travel life. After all, how often do people break forth in a great grin when you insult them truthfully and accurately?

I have had hundreds of similar experiences with conservatives, turning what most liberals think of as an unavoidable argument into a bonding experience. Knowing **why** one is being "attacked" is powerful enough to change a potential disaster into an opportunity.

Order in the Court

Our left hemisphere's orientation around the day-to-day processes or patterns that get our lives done makes for a kind of fixation on patterns, like useful abstractions, rules, and fundamental values.[23] It's a first-principles approach to life. We're going to go over eight values they have, most of them unconscious, that drive their lives. This will help us remember where they're coming from when they do or say something mysterious. There's nothing sacred about this list, mind you; we're still early in this game. A different researcher might well have a different list. But we're not interested in perfection; we just want a door in to these people, and this list is a great way in.

The most accepted theory of values in psychology is the Schwartz Theory of Basic Human Values. It lists ten broad values that all humans share; three of them are a group of values called "Conservation" by the theory, and they are the first three below. All the rest of the values listed are evidenced directly and strongly from the hemispheric studies, and they support the three Conservation values directly. There's some give-and-take with certain people and their values, but Donald Trump's in here, and all the Bushes, and those conservative preacher types, and my Uncle Donald. Their differences can matter, as we'll see through their personalities, but they share almost all of these same values. [24]

The Foundation Values of Conservatives

– **Security.** In the words of Dr. Schwartz, security is "safety, harmony, and stability of society, of relationships, and of self." This basic *human* value, which liberal share, colors everything for practically all conservatives, lying behind all the other values. Like all humans, valuing security bleeds over into a desire for consistency and certainty, in a very general sense.[25] If our reality's wobbling in unexpected ways, we can't feel safe.

All humans react strongly when threatened, but conservatives have been shown to be more *threat-sensitive* than liberals. This might be great sometimes, while, other times, studies have shown that they can see a threat where there isn't one. Most conservatives share a view that the world is a dangerous place; many also think of the world as a competitive jungle, ruthless and cruel.[26]

– **Hierarchy** means trusting that it's healthy for people to have limits on their capabilities and influence, depending on their place in society, their personal gifts, and chance. The traditional (and religious) version of valuing hierarchy, embraced by about two-thirds of conservatives, is knowing one's place, being obedient, appreciating the importance of conforming to tradition, and following good leaders.[27]

The other use of hierarchy is by roughly two-thirds of conservatives as well (the two types overlap, with many being both). They want to provide opportunities for wealth or influence through unlimited personal freedom, and they're comfortable with class hierarchy.[28]

Roughly half of conservatives use both these kinds of hierarchy greatly, especially "elites" like the Bushes, and virtually all politicians. They want all Americans to be limited by their traditional values, *and* they want no limits to their economic freedom, to allow strong hierarchies in society.[29]

Using strong hierarchies is a primary technique of maintaining order; they help make relationships, business, social groups, and all kinds of processes much clearer, simpler, and effective.[30] There are many statistical differences between liberals and conservatives that illustrate this appreciation of hierarchy, such as: family roles; organized religious; business attitudes; and a heightened emphasis on loyalty in a broad sense, to brands, habits, people, and groups.

–**Tradition** provides consistency, certainty, and especially order to our lives. This is probably the value that is talked about the most by social conservatives, or about two-thirds of conservatives, well over half of whom are religious; we see it in their emphasis on organized religion, lessons from history, traditional values, capitalism (which is viewed as traditional), and being extremely careful about change. The word tradition comes from the Latin *traditio*, which meant handing down something; it's a reverence for reference points that seem to have worked from the past.

–**Orderliness** is how we control and structures our lives, and it supports all the other values. Dr. Sperry's work on split-brain patients showed a strong emphasis on order in the left hemisphere.[31] ***Orderliness is the strongest conservative personality trait.***[32] Social conservatives are particularly orderly, but both kinds of conservatives, social and economic, have a zillion ways of being orderly. As Russell Kirk said at the beginning of the first of "Ten Conservative Principles," a popular conservative manifesto (see the Appendix with that name for the whole thing; italics in the original):

...order is made for man, and man is made for it... This word *order* signifies harmony. There are two aspects or types of order: the inner order of the soul, and the outer order of the commonwealth...The problem of order has been a principal concern of conservatives ever since *conservative* became a term of politics...

– you get the idea. If conservatives were hippies, order would be, like, everything, man, totally. When conservatives argue between themselves, it's usually because they disagree how to best be orderly. I'd encourage skimming "Ten Conservative Principles" keeping order in mind, and you'll see how it's behind the whole structure and emphasis.

The last four values below can be thought of as sub-values to order, because they exist to support a need for order, often in the service of safety or security. All were prominent in the studies of the left hemisphere perspective. These help us break down the conservative emphasis on orderliness into useful handles, because it takes on several basic forms. Think of these as the important *versions* of order in our lives.

-**Certainty** sounds like knowing, or being factual, but for us in this guide, certainty is a *feeling* that we know how to do things, and that we know what's going to happen. Feeling uncertain is nerve-wracking, especially when we try to do something essential, such as stay safe.[33]

-**Consistency**, a kissing cousin of certainty, provides not only a sense of control, but also helps us feel as if life is predictable, which the left hemisphere values highly. Routine is preferred to variability. Consistency in life provides a lulling that can actually feel like certainty; it can also helps us feel safer. Most of the problem conservatives have with changing rules is that it's not consistent. Liberals often have the biggest problem with the conservative demand for consistency; it can feel like the most alien form of order to us.

—**Simplicity**, which may sound like "simplistic" or "simpleton" to the liberal ear, can actually have great advantages. Explaining and understanding feel easier and more complete when explanations are kept simple. This is a kind of philosophical preference, that keeps to the old saying that when you're looking for an answer to a problem, the simplest solution is probably the best. The preference for simplicity was another strong finding from hemispheric studies, because it helps obtain certainty and order. Complexity is the opposite, and can appear suspicious.

—**Strong Boundaries** are best thought of as how order actually gets done: they're the primary tool of order. Order makes it vital to piece out life into clear categories, and boundaries do that for us. There isn't any better way of thinking about order than compartmentalizing in life, using separations or boundaries between things, people, and ideas. Conservatives have a great appreciation for definite, strong boundaries,[34] and a sense that competition (struggle across boundaries, or to maintain them) is natural and healthy in life, from the fight between good and evil all the way down to a football rivalry.

Boundaries can be extremely helpful for all of us as we puzzle out situations. Human attitudes about boundaries of all kinds seem tied up with hemispheric specialization; emphasizing important processes in life makes us want relatively "thick" boundaries, so we can organize, categorize, and separate: between disgusting and pure things; countries; one's community and everyone else; family roles; economic classes; and even between friends. The Robert Frost poem, "Mending Wall," is about New Hampshire neighboring farmers working on their wall together, and it makes the point directly: "Good fences make good neighbors."

Boundaries include hierarchy, which also separates people and things, but it goes beyond hierarchy; it's a more fundamental tendency to both enclose and separate items and groups. Our liberal emphasis on newness and exceptions, in contrast, has us emphasizing thinner or even non-existent boundaries, as we work to notice and *include*, across boundaries.

The real story of that list of values is how it secretly centers around order. It's easy to overlook the desire for order as the central, founding member of this club of fundamental conservative values– to get distracted by security, or tradition. The Senator who didn't want the twenty dollar bill changed is motivated by a need for order. I have come to realize that it's actually a difficult trait for us liberals to overemphasize about conservatives when trying to work with them, especially those who are very conservative.

To liberals, order can seem minor in the scheme of life, like a bookkeeping skill, but it's actually the primary tool that even liberals use to get safety, certainty, and consistency in our lives. We don't think in those terms, but we should try. If one's life is about trying to get things done, think about how everything needs its place: to have a schedule whenever possible; to be able to rely on rules, or laws; to categorize; to know where you're going; to think abstractly; to divide friend and foe. Everything should be either important or unimportant, sensible or doubtful, easy or complex, safe or unsafe, disgusting or acceptable. Conservatives use this universal human effort as more of a strict approach to success in life than we do, in keeping with the left hemisphere's perspective.

We all know that emphasizing order in life has a down side, though. A good summary of this guide is to call it a manual for dealing with orderly beings. Dr. Michael Gazzaniga, who worked on hemispheric studies for over 40 years, discovered what he calls **the left-brain interpreter**:

> The left hemisphere is always hard at work, seeking the meaning of events. It is constantly looking for order and reason, even when there is none—which leads it continually to make mistakes. It tends to overgeneralize, frequently constructing a potential past as opposed to a true one.[35]

In research about conservative psychology, they've been shown to want "cognitive closure," which is a fancy way to say they want to *feel* sure about everything, to "close the books" and make a decision. They engage in "motivated social cognition," which means they're biased, and can grind their way to seeing what they want to.

Now, don't be a wise guy about this tendency. From a certain angle, those research findings are perfectly reasonable. It looks bad on paper the way Dr. Gazzaniga puts it, but constructing meaning is a good thing. Meaning is *always* "constructed," or created in our mind from clues gathered in life. We just don't like seeing what a frail and goofy process it is, for all of us. Yet we'd all be lost without it, and we all make mistakes while we do it. We all have a left brain hemisphere, after all.

Those are human faults sometimes, yes, but the overall urges are in the service of some very good causes. For one thing, our *personal narratives* seem to be formed completely in the left hemisphere, and we rely on those for inspiration, and clarity about our place and purpose in life. We make those up out of thin air, and haven't got a whole lot of justification for them, but we'd be miserable or dead without them. The left-brain interpreter is where our whole brain seems to begin the notion of establishing meaning in what it sees– the why of it all. In the isolated left hemisphere of the brain studies, we're just seeing the origins of that meaning-making ideal, barricaded off from much of the brain it needs to do it correctly.

So: order is absolutely essential, and usually quite advantageous. Sure wish I had me some. But like any other tool, using order too much in life comes at a cost.

Let's look again at our list of fundamental conservative values or goals, seen in evidence from the split-brain studies, but also over and over in both general life and the narrower world of politics.

* Security
* Hierarchy (conforming, obedience)
* Tradition
  Order
  Certainty
  Consistency
  Simplicity
  Boundaries

The first three values,[36] with asterisks beside them, are the ones that conservatives speak of the most. The other values are best thought of as strong unconscious drives, though they are sometimes mentioned and championed. The desire for order is best thought of as the unconscious primary driver for all the rest of these values, even though it is rarely discussed as having that importance.[37]

Notice how talking about each of these values loops the others in naturally; how it can even be difficult to talk about them without mentioning the others. Conservatives work for safety and stability, through orderliness. The constellation of values naturally reinforce each other, which is one reason why conservatives group together so much socially, more so than liberals.

Let's look in some detail at a case of alleged police brutality, to illustrate how these values mechanically play out for those who side more with the perspective of the brain's left hemisphere. Here are some legitimate, healthy "processes" that are involved with what we see as conservative resistance to the police brutality movement, in rough order of importance. In parenthesis are the fundamental conservative values that play out in the process.

- *Public safety* (safety, order, certainty, boundaries, and hierarchy)
- *Respect for authority* (hierarchy or authority, tradition, certainty)
- *Obeying the law* (order, consistency, boundaries)
- *Saving money or time* (safety, order, consistency)

To a liberal activist working a specific case of police brutality, these four processes can usually be accepted as valuable, but they seem almost completely unrelated to the matter at hand– some innocent has been killed, or beaten, or jailed unfairly. Concern for the victim isn't listed, not because conservatives don't care, but because conservatives typically inherit the same tendency we have to focus on one side of an issue, and they choose to focus on **defending the process** of good law enforcement, in keeping with their left hemispheric orientation toward their basic values.

That makes victim concerns, or concerns about an exception to law enforcement, less visible to them (at least initially. Proof of illegal police behavior sometimes changes that). It's common that what we see as an important exception, they take to be a dangerous one; they see it threatening the process of law enforcement from being kept strong. This conflict is a natural fallout from the emphasis of our opposing perspectives, and it happens constantly in the police brutality fight.

Neglect of the victim is often all we liberals see, and it usually seems incredibly obvious to us; it can disgust or anger us. We also see a vicious irony when we think police have broken the law, or taken advantage of their authority cruelly; good guys being bad burns us up.

Conservatives, on the other hand, are quite afraid that hurting the police's reputation is dangerous to public safety, because criminals– dangerous exceptions, who don't abide by the law– will feel emboldened to break the law. Conservatives are also anxious to consistently provide positive motivation for the majority of police not involved in brutality, who they see as honest and heroic on a day-to-day basis. They despise activists emphasizing how evil the police can be, which can demoralize and shame the officers. Discussions can often focus on the police not involved in the incident, and the negative effects of the publicity on their motivation. This often confuses us liberals. We think, what could protecting the process possibly have to do with us highlighting this exception that's been hurt?

Conservatives also worry greatly about budget cuts that can occur through disrespect for what police do; they usually think police budgets are already too low, because it's a primary social safety process. Because one important process is promoting respect for authority, the evidence needed to convince a conservative of wrongdoing on the police's part has to be very strong. That high standard can be seen in the many defenses and protections of police that are built into the system through law, procedure, secrecy, and standard practice (police practices are a system generally built by conservatives, to protect conservative values).

Many of the cruel incidents and killings by the police occur to criminals during law-breaking activity, which naturally makes conservatives sympathetic to law enforcement's perspective, especially unconsciously; it looks like hero versus jackass right from the start to them, and it's tough to move their view elsewhere.

Finally, the interests of saving time and money can also enter into a specific event ("We don't have time for this," or a similar phrase, is sometimes heard on recordings or by witnesses when police brutality is committed). Police can feel overworked and overstressed, and conservatives feel that pain of their heroes far more than liberals usually do. Many police forces have budget challenges, which means less officers in the field, and a need to take less time with each incident, so the officer can get back on patrol.

Listening to a conservative talk about police brutality is to hear a swirling cocktail of those related values, intermixed and strengthening each other, as they defend the police, often as the actual victim.

I watched a nearly half-hour film multiple times with a conservative, in which Esa Wroth, an injured, inebriated, handcuffed man, later convicted of drunk driving, was held face-down on a cement floor awaiting the arrival of an ambulance. He screamed in pain most of the video, occasionally was threatening, and occasionally tried to turn to his side from his stomach, either in rebellion or in pain, as he was held down with his arms held high behind his head, pulled out of their sockets. He was tazed over two dozen times as a half-dozen deputies kept him down, cursed at him and beat him when he moved, and ignored his pleas and concerns about pain.

It seemed a straightforward case of abuse to me, but the fellow I watched the video with disagreed strongly, pointing out avidly whenever the suspect "was trying to get up" (disobedience of authority by a lawbreaker), the two times he cursed and threatened the deputies (safety, hierarchy, tradition), and the health risk the deputies were taking when Mr. Wroth may have tried to bite a deputy (safety of the hard-working officers; law-breaking criminal/exception). My conservative acquaintance told me that an officer had been head-butted by Mr. Wroth before the video started; he also pointed out repeatedly (correctly) that the deputies were following the vague local procedures for arrests. That it was a lawful arrest and per procedure was paramount to him— just like it was with the principal of the girl punished on the bus— much more important than my opinions about cruelty.

Film footage[38] was made available to the public quickly and voluntarily by the Sheriff's office involved. They usually delay such things as long as they can, but they thought, like my conservative friend, that it proved conclusively that Mr. Wroth was handled professionally. They quickly realized that their perception wasn't universally shared.

While I saw an unconscionable, risky, cruel attack on a victim, my conservative friend only saw officers who:

- obeyed the law;
- risked their health for the public's safety;
- had their authority dangerously disrespected; and who
- did their job promptly for the ambulance service.

He didn't see an attack by police: **he saw an important process being threatened by an risky exception.** The damage and risk to Mr. Wroth, my exception, was viewed as very secondary. I could tell that it felt inappropriate to even acknowledge the physical damage or pain of Mr. Wroth, the way it's often tough for humans to acknowledge the other side has a modest point to make (and the way the principal wouldn't acknowledge the mother's complaint about her daughter's punishment). He felt the process, and therefore his foundational values, were unfairly attacked.

Although I believed that Mr. Wroth's rights were grossly violated (he later received a sizable out-of-court settlement, which Mr. Wroth's lawyer felt resulted from the film we watched), my conservative friend was asking me to spend the time to focus on his justifications of the officers' actions. He did this not only to make his points, but also to see if I valued the healthy processes that he did; he was checking my moral fiber. The challenging effort of showing him that I shared many of those values, while trying hard not to veer back over to my more natural values, led to a good, practical conversation. We talked about better procedures, some of which were quite difficult to get right; equipment that should've been available; reducing the risk of expensive lawsuits; how communicating better with Mr. Wroth during the incident might've helped; and how time and money can enter into these situations. We both learned, and we respected each other more afterwards.

One of the best tools we have when relating to conservatives is to unbury our own appreciation of their values, especially safety, hierarchy, and tradition, the most conscious conservative values. Those last two, hierarchy and tradition, may be hard to find within us at first, because many of us keep those values in a storage unit in the next town over, or in the barn. We have more interesting things to pay attention to, and though we actually do value them, we don't think or speak in those terms. While conservative respect for their various values related to orderliness can be a little beyond us liberals, these three are universal human values, appreciated by everyone to some degree.

Even if we do this, though, it can be hard going. They can't understand why we can't follow them in their mostly-unconscious emphasis on certainty, consistency, simplicity, and strong boundaries—all the tools that their orderly nature uses to support safety, hierarchy, and tradition. That leads to tedious repetition, for both of us, as they try, over and over, to explain things they see as basic. We appear to them to be stupid, or at least in possession of an incredible blind spot. On my side, I sometimes experience it like being a bull rider, trying to stay alert and sensitive to clues, but liable to get bucked off at any time, because the unexpected twists of their order-driven points seem so alien to me that I fly off onto the dirt. In those moments, we're both perplexed that we can't get the basics across.

It helps enormously to struggle to see behind and around what conservatives say, to the values that drive them. It doesn't magically dissolve the conflict, but looking past what's being said to the whys will make a positive outcome much more likely.

The Dark Continent

To make progress on the most practical aspects of understanding and working with conservatives, we'll need to learn how we liberals play into the situation. To do that, we have to understand our own motivations, and how they create challenges for conservatives; we need to look at the right hemisphere perspective.

Early neuroscientists took the view that the right hemisphere was the dark continent of the brain; in the words of Dr. Roger Sperry, it was thought of as "illiterate, and relatively retarded." Until the early 1960s, it was believed to be a kind of reserve brain, like a spare tire. This ignorance of half the brain's function came about because of how the right hemisphere works with the left. Dr. Sperry's work with epileptic patients initially seemed to align with this early confusion: many commonly-present hemispheric personality traits are clear and helpful to understand left-hemisphere leanings, but, other than problems with speech and some logic, there are only a few right side traits, and they seemed a little strange. Patients were often more anxious; they were more pessimistic; and they would treat problems that they were familiar with as if they were new each time, even though they remembered how they did it before. (Actually, those symptoms don't seem strange to conservatives at all: their reaction is, "Yes! Proof that they're stupid whiners." While we liberals hear those symptoms and get a puzzled look on our face as we stroke our beards: "Mmm. How mysterious.")

Strange as it may seem, all those traits are likely symptoms of one overwhelmingly important factor: the right hemisphere emphasis on exceptions, or **novelty**. Let's see how that can be.

Children who damage their right hemisphere when very young have a very difficult time learning to speak, ever; it usually creates a permanent problem for them with language. But adults that get the same right-side damage usually have almost no problems afterwards with their speaking ability. This was confusing until quite recently, when neuroscientists hit upon the fact that the right side specialization in novelty or newness is designed for **learning**.

Here's what is happening. As we learn language, we shovel what we figure out using our right hemisphere into the parts of the left hemisphere that mostly manage and run speech permanently. In the left hemisphere, we turn those lessons learned about language into a slew of reusable routines or patterns, like words, phrases, grammar, and recognition of speech. Once those are in place, the adult can lose a large portion of their right hemisphere, and it doesn't matter, because language doesn't have much to do with the right hemisphere any more. But the child lost her training module with the damage, and language wasn't in her left hemisphere yet; she's forced to learn language with the left hemisphere, which requires tons of adjustment to its wiring to even begin to imitate what the lost hemisphere had.

This role of handling new things, of learning, explains the tendency of the right hemisphere of the split-brain patients to see everything as new. It's not designed to do half of everything; it's designed to focus on learning, and adjusting ourselves. We're so used to doing things that are new as if they were unknown, and old things as if they were known, that we don't realize that those are two *entirely* different tasks, with completely different skill sets and values.

Think of building a robot that puts a bumper on a car, versus building a robot that can *learn* how to put a bumper on a car, from scratch. Different animals, huh? Any thoughts on which would be more complicated? Which would take one software engineer a week to do, and which would take an army of software engineers years of work, just to do a decent job? That single difference can help us understand how different the worlds of the left and right hemispheres are; how specialized they are. It probably also explains why we ignored and misunderstood the right hemisphere's purpose for so long; it's a world unto itself, specialized, innovative, and complex.

An openness and exploration approach seems to be a kind of default for the right hemisphere, and no wonder. It seems as if the only reason it won't take on that specialized job of using an original approach on a problem in real life is if the left hemisphere pops in to say "never mind, I've got this," so the right hemisphere can relax while something already learned gets used.

But what if the right hemisphere never got to do that handoff– what if no signal of "never mind, I've got this" ever comes from the left hemisphere? Not having any 'stop' signals by the left hemisphere, like the patients being studied by Dr. Sperry, Dr. Gazzaniga, and their team, seems to explain part of the anxiety and pessimism in those patients: not only are the usual routines not available to solve even simple problems because of the damage, but new routines don't have a way of being established or rejected; no one is there to tell that exception engine to relax, to stop solving the problem. Nothing ever feels doable, or done.[39] Typically, these patients are left very indecisive, which is highly stressful. Even small problems sit and fester in their minds, leading a large minority of such patients to become suicidal, with various levels of depression in the rest considered normal.[40]

Another aspect of the right hemisphere provides great insight about our liberal perspective, but we have to promote Dr. Ramachandran's scout to give you a more complete story about your right hemisphere, the inspiration for your perspective on life. After all, being a scout is a pretty wimpy role in the battle, compared to the left hemisphere general. Scouting seems way too humble a role for half of our brain– until you think of it as having responsibility for finding out what's really going on out there in the world, and in ourselves.

An avalanche of evidence has shown one of the most reliable generalizations that can be made about our brain hemispheres is that the right hemisphere (scout) takes a perspective by taking a detailed *picture* of a specific event, usually at a quite specific time.

A patient who still has their right hemisphere (the scout) intact but is severely damaged on the front left side can be blindfolded and be given an object to hold in their hand, and they usually know what it is. They can guess what it looks like, about as well as you or I could. They have a 3-D image of it in their head, and they can draw a decent version of it.

Someone with just their left hemisphere remaining, though, severely damaged on the right, has no 3-D capability; blindfolded, they can describe pieces of the object (like any parts sticking out), or how the surface feels, but usually have no idea what it is, even if it's familiar to them. Their sketches of the items are hilarious, and often completely unrecognizable. Their problem was eventually shown to not just be with physical objects; they were just as bad at understanding stories. They knew details of the story, but couldn't understand the overall idea, or moral,[41] which they seemed to need to pick up from the right hemisphere that it can't access.

This difference between the hemispheres that inspire our ideological outlook has huge implications, but not necessarily the ones you'd think. Our minds want to run to "Ah, yes, we liberals get the "big picture" accurately, while conservatives are stuck in the weeds with facts, screwing it up." Nmph. No. Try to avoid thinking about any of this in terms of who's wrong and who's right, or who gets it and who doesn't. The brain has these two ways of doing things, because we need them both, quite literally all the time. They do different things, for different reasons. If one sucked at everything, evolution would've disappeared it for us, and we'd have a lovely half-head working.

The puzzle piece this picture-versus-facts difference gives us is how we prefer to build our world views. Think of it as a picture versus a thousand words, or, better, a picture versus a nicely organized, explanatory essay, with a little flow diagram included at no charge. That'd be a start. Another way is to think that the right hemisphere uses a special *inspiration* from visual sensitivity (because the right side is tied closely to more of the brain's visual processing). It longs to focus on the gist of the issue around *living, breathing, specific* examples, the same way we use our vast field of vision to focus ultimately on only the pertinent portions of what we have in our field of view. In particular, complex emotional aspects can be captured better by the right side, to help find that critical detail that matters.

The left hemisphere is, instead, quite anxious to put the facts of the situation into an overall context; it wants to categorize or break a situation into its component parts, so that it can explain them in relation to one another, and arrive at the "picture" that way. And it's better at doing that. The lack of 3-D capability is made up for with a logical and abstraction emphasis, so that certain patterns can be followed well. It's about first principles, precedents, and building a picture from them.

Imagine a right hemisphere struggling to learn how to read music, and a left one reading it later, using all the rules and structure built from all that pain of the initial learning process. The right hemisphere was invaluable as it made the link between random lines on a page and a note, or a key on the piano; the left hemisphere was invaluable later, when the note was well-known, and it rapidly and unconsciously lets us 'see' the note itself when we see those random lines on the page.

The right side doesn't care about principles and precedents nearly as much; it's living through the event it sees, not trying to make as much sense of it, or put it in context, or categorize it usefully. It's not supposed to think about patterns: that destroys the uniqueness of the experience.

In the police beating example, I looked at it as an overall carelessness about the suspect's well-being, while my acquaintance saw a series of difficult, required steps of the process of justice. Yes, he saw the category of "suspect," but it had to be factored in with other categories that make up the process of law enforcement. I saw one particular suspect, and latched onto the details of his treatment as the pertinent exception in the picture: the endless screaming; the arms wrenched at an unnatural angle; the 20+ tazings and beatings. My focus was on the cruelty. The overall process of law enforcement– the suspect's law-breaking, the procedures, risks, time pressures, and hard work–were blurred out for me.

In contrast, my conservative friend saw that overall process of justice and criminality rolling forth in great detail, and the cruelty was blurred out for him; it didn't matter as much. The list of procedural steps were happening properly; that's what mattered.

This is a common pattern of ideological interactions, even more outside of politics than in it: liberals try to get attention on only what we think needs to be fixed, based on this one particular example, while conservatives tend toward "a slavish following of the internal logic of the situation," as one neuroscientist said about the left hemisphere, to make sure that exceptions are seen as dangerous or unimportant. My conservative friend might've said, "We can't stop the world for you every time someone screams in pain, to set aside the rules we live by." For him, the whole point of rules is to follow them unquestioningly, so that the world picture he's built up continues to make sense. That entails almost preventing exceptions from being considered. That's effectively the opposite of the common saying among my activist friends that "rules are made to be broken."

Conservatives get frightened when we second-guess the rules whenever our own specific (and often emotion-driven) "picture" questions the process. Why even bother to have rules, Scott, if you're going to ignore them every time we turn around because you notice something, or feel something? This is a special drunk driver? His violence and threats are a unique case, somehow?

The neuroscientist and psychiatrist Iain McGilchrist characterizes this as the **individual-versus-category conflict**, to make clear how a *living, immediate* image of reality fights one that is *built up logically from categories*. As Dr. Sperry said when accepting his Nobel Prize, the two brain hemispheres are "mutually antagonistic modes of cognitive processing"; they work largely apart, are "antagonistic" toward each other, and only communicate and negotiate in highly specific ways, through a specialized bridge of nerves that connect those different views of reality.

That's tough enough, but there are many related complications. For instance, notice how utterly dependent the right hemisphere of an adult is on the left hemisphere, but how the left hemisphere has an easy time convincing itself it doesn't depend on the right much. I love this about the general and scout metaphor. They're both needed, but it's quite easy for a certain party to think they don't need the other much. That stilted relationship is so fundamental to both our perspectives of life that it ends up having an influence on how we have to work with conservatives, which we'll address later. That's only one of many strange, uneven aspects of our relationship: each side has its own language, its own goals, and its own challenges.[42]

None of this talk about perspectives should be taken to mean that conservatives are experts at getting processes done, or that liberals are fantastic at getting exceptions shoved into processes well; it just means we're big on those things happening. One of the knotty problems of ideology is that we each think we're soo *talented* at what we emphasize in life. But being inspired to fix injustice, or defend law enforcement, doesn't mean we do a great job defending what's important to us. That leap in logic, which most of us do about ourselves without thinking, is no more rational than assuming you're a good computer programmer because you can imagine how great it'd be to work at Google. Or that you have a green thumb because you adore walking around in pretty gardens.

This seems so small and simple a point: it isn't. It means that understanding and working with conservatives requires us to learn two quite separate things. First, we need to know what drives conservatives, which we can think of as the pure, underlying motivations and tendencies that they mostly get handed involuntarily, through inheritance and early exposure. That's what we've been covering, and we'll continue through the next three chapters. The rest of the guide after that covers the particular things they *do*, showing some of those actions as awkward, frustrating, or terrible attempts to reach their usually hidden goals like certainty, or maintaining a strong boundary, on the way to championing processes. Our own common liberal strengths and weaknesses will be factored in, since much of what they're doing is reacting to us.

By the end, we'll have learned how to keep their intentions in mind, even in the difficult cases, so their actions and words don't get in the way of you being able to see what they're really after, and what they want from you. Not that we're getting to happy outcomes every time (though it's surprising how effective this knowledge can be). The goal is simply to plan how to best work with a person by knowing them well, and then– the hard part– following through on your plan.

We've learned how conservatives have an underlying perspective that seems mysteriously inspired by basic aspects of our biology. They think of a successful life as built around **important processes**, which focuses them on safety, hierarchy, tradition, and the several ways they keep **order** in their life, to keep those established processes clicking along well. We focus on important exceptions to those processes because of our emphasis on novelty in life.

These principles provide the foundation for this guide. Fortunately, these conservative values also show up even more clearly behind our detailed **personality traits**. Thanks to the work of hundreds of hard-working psychologists, looking at conservatives through the lens of personality theory provides striking detail, to build a much clearer image of that statistical conservative of ours.

Chapter Two

PERSONALITY – THE BASICS

Tell me what you pay attention to,
and I will tell you who you are.
-José Ortega y Gasset

A N IDEOLOGY MIGHT best be thought of as 1) a shared perspective 2) of people in a certain culture, 3) who tend to have a certain clump of personality traits. There's a few pieces to that working definition, and we'll go through each, but we're going to concentrate on the last one for now, that ideology involves a group of personality traits.

This is wonderful news, for a fistful of reasons. First, personality can be roughly defined as the way humans express our values;[1] that means that those foundational conservative values we talked about in Chapter One are expressed through certain personality traits.[2] This lets us study conservative attitudes and actions through the lens of personality. Which is terrifically practical, since we know a great deal about the traits involved.

If we see liberals and conservatives as specialists in certain clumps of traits, it frees us to think of the clashes we have with each other as personality conflicts. That turns out to be an incredibly helpful overall attitude. Looking at things this way doesn't make our problems relating to one another go away, but we can be far less confused about what's happening, and why.

Perhaps most importantly, focusing on personality helps get us as far as we can from thinking that our ideology is morally good, and theirs is morally bad. That's a terrible trap. Not because it's necessarily wrong in a certain situation: we might be absolutely right about the dreadful morality of a decision to invade a country, or punish a child. The problem is that when we *habitually* see what people believe or do in terms

29

of good and evil, it cuts explanation off at the knees; people who do evil things *are* evil, you see, end of discussion, instead of expressing a personality trait that may be great at the dinner table, hideous when working in a mine shaft, and neutral the vast majority of the time. Seeing in terms of good and evil makes things simple and neat, but notice how it chokes off discussion about what to do about the issue, or about our relationship with the other person, or how to think about why they did it: we're left with a narrow list of options, mostly variations on "yell louder," or "you're fired," or one of our favorite four methods of pouting. There's nothing to understand anymore; evil won out, as usual, and all that remains is the whining and drinking.

Lobsters, then Conservatives, then Liberals

Personality counts: that's the great news. But there's also some news you might take hard, but you may as well hear it early: there's quite powerful evidence, through personality theory, that liberals and conservatives are both here for a reason, evolutionarily speaking.[3] Let's look at evidence from the field of evolutionary psychology, which looks into the past to discover how our minds developed, at why we're the way we are.

Most people think that evolution is always a matter of grinding forward, toward better– getting bigger, smarter, stronger, faster, and so forth. That our species is optimizing all the time, so that we're better equipped to succeed in the world. This happens with some species or individual traits, but is actually an uncommon version of evolution. Evolution starts out with mutations, after all, genetic mistakes that sometimes end up being used, but mostly just get weeded out, or that stick around and don't do anything. Most evolution is actually a kind of meandering based on random mutations, in keeping with all the chance involved in the process.

But there are somewhat purposeful-looking meanderings that are excellent candidates for explaining how ideology got here today, through its underlying personality traits. The first is called "frequency selection": this is the survival or thriving of a wide variety of traits in a species. In some complicated situations, species evolve fantastic variety, both physically and mentally. In our case, we know that certain conditions favor certain personality traits, and discourage others; and there are tons of different kinds of conditions in the world. In modern day, a salesperson's personality is very different than an accountant's, or a policeman's. If everyone's personality was like a salesman's, all the bookkeepers would fail audits, and no one would know who their daddy was. Certain conditions would be a nightmare if everyone had the same clump of personality traits. It might make things predictable, but predictably lousy isn't evolution's thing.

This modern-day personality variety we enjoy (and are cursed by), appears likely to have been true even in the ancient past, well before our species appeared, because we see versions of a wide variety of personality traits in chimpanzees and other animals. Frequency selection is thought by most evolutionary psychologists to be how personality generally has evolved: we have a broad mix of traits, with all of them useful in some way. So that likely explains part of ideology.

But why are there these two common *clumps* of personality traits? There are 5 well-established sets of traits that define liberal and conservative personalities we'll be going over, involving a majority of Americans. Frequency selection alone doesn't seem to explain very well how we have these two groups of humans in which one is high or low in these traits, and the other is a kind of mirror-image opposite. The easy, normal reason why a species would converge on traits is called "stabilizing selection," which would be all of us ending up similar ideologically, the way one common, successful clump of personality traits might do. But that doesn't seem right; there are two sometimes-competing poles, containing two common, somewhat antagonistic groupings of specific traits. And it's probably not a coincidence that they are two very different *moral* tribes, meaning they have different ideas of good and evil. The trait differences seem fundamental, instead of just being kind of interesting.

A great deal of Darwin's work, and his most famous writings, dealt with an evolutionary method called "disruptive selection." Darwin found that some traits clumped into two in a population when "disruptive" situations came up repeatedly that benefited one specialty or the other. His famous case had to do with finches that had different-sized beaks on the Galapagos Islands. Small-beaked finches did well in the usual good weather, but suffered badly when droughts occurred, because the tender little seeds they depended on suddenly weren't available. Large-beaked finches survived in the usual weather, though their beaks weren't great for small seeds– but more survived during droughts, because they could eat the harder seeds that were all that could be found.

Those finches have a dual population pattern similar to the trait clumps to ideology in humanity, in that there were two poles of beaks, large and small, with variety in between. Is ideology, then, passed on through disruptive selection– are we specializing for practical reasons? No one is sure, but I think there's powerful circumstantial evidence that, in reflection of the two hemispheric world views and the personality advantages each has, that we've evolved a stable split population between the two. It could be related to specialties that are superior at different times, based on conditions, though it's also possible that there could be trait groupings that just are superior in different parts of our cultures, maybe through different kinds of employment, or other social situations. What those conditions might be, and even if this kind of selection is occurring, is a subject left to future scholars, though many hints can be swatted at.

There are theorists inside and outside evolutionary psychology that view conservatism as more useful in situations of high risk, and liberalism as evolved for doing well in low risk situations, a little like big beaks and small beaks, respectively. That's a popular line of thought, among both liberals and conservatives. The philosopher Ken Wilbur and others have integrated that idea as a lynchpin in Spiral Dynamics, a theory of evolutionary development of human psychology.

The folk wisdom behind this idea comes to the mind unbidden. If you need help, there's any version of the following parable– this is the conservative version– which makes its ways through the halls of churches, colleges, and loud bars, in many variations: 5,000 years ago, just after God created the earth, there was a village that enthusiastically encouraged trade with suspect, faraway villages, while gradually arguing away their once-princely military budget, in tribal meetings that involved singing Kumbaya way too much. These villagers end up getting overrun in a surprise attack from bad guys and they all died, because they were naive liberals, which you probably picked up on.

Conservative villages were just all-around better. They kept their military budgets high, using filibusters and threat-sensitivity, and scared all the bad guys away, because they were smart *and* wary, combined. And religious in a good way, too. The liberals bred like rabbits like many naïve, stupid people do, so even though they were killed off like deer every, I don't know, seven years, there were too many liberals anyway, because of polygamy, and morals, and stuff you don't even want to know about.

The liberal version of this story would make a better movie, (spoiler alert: violent sex scenes). People are naturally liberal, and singing Kumbaya almost always worked really, really well to keep money meant for equal opportunity and child care from being siphoned off to building the tribe's spear supply. And it'd be only liberals in the world except that the durned conservatives, who were greedy and paranoid, and insisted that everyone else was evil, *were* the surprise attackers (which they always hid about themselves in the history books they got to write, after they killed us). Then conservative men breed the way we know bad guys breed after they attack perfect villages; you've seen the movies. And that's why there's so many conservatives. It's, like, totally tragic.

In case you missed the sarcasm, there are quite good arguments against both these versions of the origins of ideology. One is that research has shown that, in one important way, we liberals are essentially just closet conservatives: we have some of the same values in low stress, but, under high stress, we quickly come to value security, strong leadership, insane amounts of "the rule of law," and the various forms of order, like simplicity, certainty, and strong boundaries.[4] Our opinions virtually converge with conservatives on what we think of as fair punishment, proper military strategy, and other risk-related endeavors. We take on their values.

Looking at liberals as closet conservatives doesn't explain liberal behavior in relatively low-stress situations, but it's not supposed to; that's when we're in the closet about our conservatism. We're on a break; we're doing our art, and Saturday morning yoga. That translation of liberals into conservatives under threat, as we saw when we all marched like lemmings together toward invading Iraq, is another reason why it may be too simplistic to talk about our relationship as soft versus hard, since liberals shift almost instantly under stress to the supposedly primitive viewpoint.

I bristle at the notion of conservatives as great at handling risk, merely because they talk so much about risk. I also think it's quite annoying to say that being concerned about safety and being threat-sensitive is the same thing. Liberals often clash with conservatives because we don't see threat-sensitivity as always good to have or act on, from a safety standpoint. Being threat-sensitive can often make situations more hazardous, not less– certainly in a nuclear age, and there's no reason to think it was much less true in the past.

Ideological divergences reveal themselves quite markedly all through society (business; church; the arts; child-rearing; job preferences), and they happen through powerful personality differences. Do we just ignore that? It's not reasonable to assume none of that has any evolutionary impact, that it can all be dumbed-down into who knew exactly how many jackasses there were over the hill, or who spent more time sharpening their spears.

Unfortunately for liberals, though, the case for an evolutionary justification for conservatives is even simpler than these arguments. Research shows that we are much more romantically attracted to people of our own ideology, because of personality. There are exceptions, of course, but it's a powerful effect, which a quick sample through match.com romance ads can show anyone in 10 minutes ("No conservative bozos"; "Don't even think of responding if you're liberal.") This is a clever way of seeing that the two ideology populations are *relatively stable*, through mate attraction. To say conservatism should just disappear, you have to make the case that mate attraction has nothing to do with practical advantages of any of their social, physical, or personality traits.

It's always possible that conservatism is heading down an evolutionary rathole, but I believe the more reasonable likelihood is that the specialized conservative perspective provides humanity practical usefulness right now, and probably not just a little; otherwise, they wouldn't be so common. After all, in America, roughly half again as many people call themselves conservative as call themselves liberal. The rest of this guide will bring up many possible reasons why they're still around, and why they like each other, and what on earth they do that's of any use. You can draw your own conclusions.

I take an odd comfort in their evolutionary success. It's not as if it means we *don't* belong here; there's billions of us liberals, after all, so the world probably needs us to do our thing, especially if there's so many conservatives messing certain things up. In the same way, they're not just hanging around to ruin our day and curdle everything they touch. I find it useful to ponder how they contribute differently than I might, because it helps me feel warmer toward them, and curious. It turns out that's not that hard. It's easy to appreciate many as individuals, which usually spills over to respecting some parts of their conservatism.

Recognizing an integral role for them in society also builds in a commonsensical humility we should all have about our world views– a humility that we either don't have, or that we leave under a pile of receipts in the basement, or that we flush down the toilet when we fish it out of our pocket accidentally. We can fight bad conservative decisions, or even murderous ones, while holding at bay an overall assessment of "evil decisions = useless people", which is false and counter-productive. It also helps hint to ourselves– gently now, gently– that we may have an ideological approach that isn't perfect for solving every problem of society, in every condition.

You can bury all that if you like; you can argue, as some do, that any useful conservative role was in the ancient, more violent past of our species. But you'd be arguing against good evolutionary psychology arguments, as well as neurological and personality evidence– and otherwise sounding like someone who likes to waste energy justifying their viewpoint.

But you men out there: if a conservative ever begs to mate with you because you're liberal, contact me personally. It may be the beginning of the great evolutionary disappearance of conservatives we all seek.

Personality Psychology .101

The word personality comes from the Greek word meaning mask. This is a lovely way of reminding us that we wear our personalities, in a way, over our real self. Something has to go over it, after all, since it's a mush of brains, or a soul, or somesuch. Below and behind what we see through personality is our true self, tangled mysteriously with what we value in life, only able to actually be in the world using the mask or cover of personality. It's a translator between the world and ourselves.

We are going to use the most popular and most accepted approach of personality scientists, the Big Five Theory of Personality, to discover what makes up a statistically average conservative personality; we'll do the same with the liberal personality. Occasionally, we'll clear away the furniture and watch these average joes fight; this will help immensely later, when we study biases and conversations.

The number five in "The Big Five Theory of Personality" refers to five sensible groupings of personality traits, with six to twelve traits in each grouping (depending on how detailed you count traits). Ideology statistically affects every one of the five major groupings, roughly as much as gender does. That should help us remember how pervasive and sneaky ideology can be, infiltrating into so much of our lives.

The problem with working with such broad clumps of traits, though, is the lack of useful detail; conclusions are mushy and vague. Luckily, each of these five groupings can be split into two,[5] so that the human personality is divided into ten pieces instead of just five. This ends up the perfect level of detail for our purposes, because each of these is easily understood, and doesn't involve either too detailed or too broad a level of coverage. Research has revealed five of the ten as critically different between liberals and conservatives, as well as the strange result that there are two other aspects that aren't much different between us, but that are looked at so differently by us that they somehow end up together on stage, duking it out as the stars of the show. So we'll be reviewing seven of the ten aspects of personality to get at ideology well.

All these personality traits can be described in positive and negative terms, because you can have too much or too little of any trait: we'll describe traits mostly in positive terms to start with, because we'll usually be focused on how our strengths reflect the world view that crouches behind the trait.

Conservatives score significantly higher in conscientiousness,[6] one of the Big Five, on personality tests than liberals, on average. Of the Big

Five, conscientiousness is the only one that researchers agree, hands down, is desirable for any employer to look for, in any employee– it has the highest value for predicting the successful future of an employee. Depending on the job, it may be good for someone to be strong in one or more of the other Big Five trait families, but it's *always* excellent to hire a conscientious employee.

Conscientiousness covers one-fifth of our personality, though, which is such a large amount that it's quite vague to work with. But conscientiousness has two "aspects," or groupings of traits, that split it in half: they're called industriousness and orderliness. Industriousness, or how hard-working, ambitious, and focused we are, isn't shown to be significantly different between liberals and conservatives. But– surprise!– conservatives have been consistently shown to be higher in orderliness than liberals. Tests that show overall conscientiousness higher in conservatives, then, are really showing higher orderliness.

Orderliness

We've seen that orderliness is at the heart of the left hemisphere's process-oriented perspective, so it shouldn't be a surprise that this is the single biggest statistical personality strength for conservatives. Of course, we liberals aren't at all used to thinking of orderliness in completely positive terms, especially if we're very liberal; there are scars most of us bear that we remember earning in battles with these exact values, personally and in politics. We'll get to the bad stuff soon enough, but I ask you to bear with the positive spirit of this section, and the lack of caveats about inflexibility or heartlessness or the like. It helps us learn about them better. Also, part-and-parcel of why it's hard to honor their strengths is because we tend to think of ourselves as superior beings in every way that counts, without realizing it. So take this section as an exercise in trying to blunt that notion in our unconscious mind a bit.

When negative feelings about traits that can be very positive come up, take the time and energy to examine the unconscious attitude which created that feeling. If you're lucky, you can connect that negative feeling with a personal experience, or a related strong opinion. If you can't do that– and most of us can't– then try to envision examples of where the trait may be very useful, to help your unconscious mind offset the negative prejudice with the information here.

The Values of Orderly People

Let's look at those fundamental values of conservatives again, but this time through the lens of personality. We'll be able to see how orderliness translates those values so that conservatives can express them.

An orderly person is usually either struggling to feel **certain,** or they're enjoying the certainty they've worked hard to create; that's the purpose of being ordered. Uncertainty wastes energy, eats up time, creates risk, and can be very expensive.

Consistency is certainty *over time,* with a routine that works well, a plan, and everything predictably in its place. This silent partner of certainty is why "flip-flopping" is considered a major character flaw by most conservatives: it's inconsistent.

Simplicity is order's way of molding the world into explainable parts, making it more certain. Unnecessary complication makes organization and consistency much harder, and requires coordination, flexibility, and alternate plans that can disrupt life at any time. An orderly person always leans hard into using simplicity to make the path to certainty shorter and easier.

Strong Boundaries must be created (demarcated) very well, to see and use them exactly how they should be; no squadrons of greyish guesses trying to replace black-and-white "facts." Orderly people create tight groups and clear divisions to feel certain. **Hierarchy** (or respect for authority, or conforming) is a primary form of boundaries; higher and lower, authority or conforming. Orderly people have an instinctive, deep appreciation for the rules, organizations, and people that create order in society; without those things, their world feels chaotic and risky.

Finally, **Tradition**, or everything we've learned and instituted as lessons from our ancestors, is an almost sacred map for orderly people to get where they want to go in life. Think of tradition the same way we treat precedents in law cases, which are carefully watched and followed; once made, they should be left unchanged. Tradition is the reference book, or book of order, used in a successful life.

These highlighted values above, all expressed mostly through orderliness, are all the conservative values that we talked about except security. I think the concept of order is so broad and fundamental to conservatism that the emphasis isn't captured completely in personality tests. We should remember, then, how orderliness is at the center of being conservative, and that it tends to take many different forms. If we don't see it onstage, we can be sure it's just behind the curtain.

Almost all of us are orderly in some ways. One liberal I know is addicted to his daily routine. In my consulting work, some jobs have required extraordinary consistency and detail-orientation, where a lack of orderliness on my team's part would've been deadly. One very liberal friend will tell me he wants to pick me up at 5:15; at about 4:55, he's standing at the door jiggling his keys, trying to think of new ways to make me feel guilty that I'm not ready to go.

But the orderliness of someone who's *very* orderly permeates more than a few pieces of life, so that it seeps further into their *philosophy of life*. When we say someone is high in a personality trait, we often find that they not only express that trait in more ways, and more deeply; it's also natural for them to use it as more of a reference point for their lives.

One very conservative nephew of mine exhausts me just watching him use incredibly energy to move from very useful hobby to very useful hobby, doing exacting home improvements, car repairs, and other practical tasks in his "time off." He manufactures happiness for his conservative wife all weekend long, yet he's relaxing through expressing his natural desire to order and structure his world. I can happily do that kind of thing at work, and I can enjoy it here and there on the weekend, but then I'm done with order until after I've whacked the snooze button on the alarm Monday morning. I don't prowl conservative bars trying to steal their women because they sense this weakness in me, right away. That's good, though: better to get my relative uselessness cleared up nice and early in the relationship.

Which of us, me or my nephew, is going to end up with order lodged firmly near the center of his life philosophy?

Bumpkins and Saints

All of those values combine powerfully, and they lead to **parochialism** in conservatives. Parochial is a nasty-sounding word to most of us liberals, but the word throws light on a problem we have with attitudes in ideology. The word's definition has been changing right under our feet. Merriam-Webster has it as "limited in range or scope (as to a narrow area or region)," which sounds straightforward enough, but other dictionaries make clear that it's an insult. Almost every modern use in books and on the internet is terribly negative, referring broadly to cramped outlooks, mean spirits, and other aspersions. The synonyms for the word are mostly quite hissy, as well. If we look carefully, we see that there's a nonsensical split between synonyms for parochial: there's the words that are closer to the pleasant meaning of parochial before the mid-1800's: rural, regional, homespun, bucolic, local and conservative; but the others are bigoted, biased, and petty. This word is going places, and they're not good places.

How or why is that happening? The root in the original Greek is pariokos, meaning stranger, and refers to the early Christians establishing colonies on their own, outposts where they could live and worship as they wished. When I hear the word now, I usually think of them huddled together on the coast of a windy, Greek island, courageously following their hearts. So the word parochial started out life as downright inspiring, then became broader, referring somewhat romantically to country life, with its many advantages. Then, as the modern world appeared, the word was wrenched over into its current usage, which is roughly a combination of stupid and stubborn.

I think the storied, symbolic meaning of parochial became stubborn dummies so quickly because of modern society's increasing orientation around city life. Simplicity has lost its appeal to the glitter of complexity; possibility rides as our constant companion now, with certainty set back in the rumble seat. Consistency has become so boring that variety has replaced it on the weekend dinner guest list. Despite my liberal leanings, this rushed abandon toward excitement and newness leaves me a little nervous, as I think it does many, liberal or conservative. The philosopher George Allan agrees with me, and is brilliant in advocating for a modern culture that balances respect for tradition with an enthusiastic embrace of novelty, which I see as a good expression of liberalism.[7] We should all stretch ourselves a bit, to ponder in our lives what the rush to stereotypical city attitudes might have us leaving behind.

Seeing parochialism as an expression of conservatism is to see why they tend to live in the country– why conservative is practically a synonym for rural life, from a statistical perspective. They appreciate simplicity in life, broadly– which is why it's much easier to find them in the country, or the suburbs. They love ritual, or tradition, especially in the form of close friends, family, recreation choices that are repetitive and pleasant, and local organizations that they can sink themselves into consistently for the long haul. Those strong boundaries they build aren't just for keeping people and things out: they put a protective wall around the people and places they're close to, and they stay deeply committed to what's within those boundaries.

Weekly organized religious activity is well over twice as common among conservatives than liberals;[8] it's one of the strongest basic demographic statistical distinctions between us. The biggest difference between the North and South in American towns is the church count, and especially the church size. Much of that difference is from higher orderliness. Respect for hierarchy is a big part of organized religion. Feelings of certainty are provided about the greatest of human mysteries (our purpose, and our uncertain future). The consistency of religious activity is also more their bailiwick, as is the social (group) reinforcement of their beliefs.

Religious dogma, or beliefs, is a pure set of traditions: ideas that help live a high-quality life, usually passed down from those we trust. The beliefs of organized religion almost always makes very little logical sense, but the supposedly rational parts of the picture are considered less important than the life results possible through following those beliefs. After all, it's also quite rational to be learning about being good to one another every week, to use even rough-hewn ways to keep a family strong, and to have a strong social net. Strong religious beliefs are an outgrowth of our left-brain interpreter, the meaning-maker in our head.

Every one of these characteristics of parochial life– side-stepping some facts through religion, avoiding novelty, the comfort and consistency of strong boundaries– can be poo-poo'd from one angle or another. I do that sometimes. The conservative version of balance between tradition and novelty isn't mine. But meditating a little on the word parochial can help us understand how we might be attacking values behind orderliness unfairly, with too broad a brush, just as it's unfair to call rural life stubborn stupidity.

The Advantages of Parochialism

In our liberal experience, depending on order so much can have toxic results, which can be so hard on us that it's often easy for us to miss the great advantages that these values bring conservatives. But there are so many. First is the fact that **conservatives are happier than liberals**, on average.[9] Order provides so much that makes us calm, and makes our life predictable, which helps with happiness. Many conservatives I interviewed across the country seemed to take their happiness for granted, as if it was a natural result of living a good life. Actually, they have their orderliness to thank for much of their happiness.

The left brain hemisphere tries to celebrate either the past or the present state of something, by focusing on healthy processes; unless it's an emergency situation, that emphasis means stability and purpose, which helps happiness– while the other hemisphere is focused on the future, on newness, and change that should happen. Remember how our contrasting perspectives tended to make the left hemisphere-dependent patients happy, and the right hemisphere-dependent patients miserable often; the real world is not the same as the world of split-brained psychology patients, but there's a valid connection.

Some don't want to accept this difference in our levels of happiness, and think they can grouse about happiness surveys being filled out by conservatives who are lying much more than liberals, for some reason. There are others who want to claim conservatives are happier because they're richer, or more white, though all those things and more have been controlled for in the statistical approaches to the surveys–and conservatives are still happier. I submit that, had you been around the United States as much as I have interviewing them, you'd agree easily that their advantage in personal happiness is real. And it's no mystery why. An orderly approach to life keeps things certain, consistent, and simple, all of which help keep people happy.

Naturally, then, conservatives **enjoy their jobs more**. This makes even more sense. If order, stepping through a checklist, and detail orientation is your thing, you're going to be happier at most work sites. That's a nice trait, simply because we spend so much time at work. It also means that conservatives can appreciate a different kind of work site, with less variation and more rules. **They work longer hours, and are wealthier** (after adjusting for ethnicity, background, education, etc.), which should also make sense; not because they're more ambitious or more focused, which we don't have evidence for, but because they express their orderliness easily there.

Every value driving orderliness is an orientation that is valuable in most businesses, especially in traditional fields. Their orderliness is at the heart of much of the attitudinal difference between the two ideologies about business. Liberals will often try to blame conservative economic success on inheritance and ethnic prejudice factors: those are involved, no doubt, but we often negate the importance of their personality advantages, that basic orientation. Their core orderliness gives them a justified, natural leg up in most work situations, as well as providing much of the scaffolding for their life outlook.

They're better educated, on average, after controlling for the usual complicating factors– not because of higher ambition, but probably because the *process* of our personal education can be put on a checklist and accomplished by orderly, consistent people better than by others. They finish more of what they start.

There are many other advantages to being orderly that have been shown in research, but that's a good enough sampling.

Talking the Walk– Industriousness

Most conservatives would believe themselves to be significantly higher in the personality aspect of industriousness, yet that isn't what's been found in two American studies. Conservatives often assume that "personal responsibility," which is a synonym for much of industriousness, is not a liberal value, because we don't talk about it nearly as much. This is one of two places in ideology personality where both ideologies walk the walk, but only one talks about it. It's a mysterious phenomenon, and it leads to misunderstandings on both sides.

I interviewed a conservative in Kansas during the early part of the research for this guide; he was a middle-aged man in an office job. When I asked him about his work, he assured me how hard he worked, and how necessary it was to put in the hours. He let me know how vital his job was, and how his hard work was necessary to get ahead; and that he was glad to do it, but it entailed sacrifice for his family. It was almost a core moral statement about life, one I'd heard many times before from his fellow conservatives, expressed in the same way, circled back to lightly, over and over, in a wide-ranging interview. This fellow was particularly adamant, though, so I asked him what his work hours were. He told me that he worked from eight to five, with an hour's lunch break, five days a week; he brought his fist down lightly on the desk as he said it. I was shocked that all that talk was about an average work week, and had to stifle a laugh. I'm not sure that anyone had ever heard me say that I had a great work ethic at that point, but I hadn't had a work week that short since I'd left school, and I rarely took a lunch break.

It's not that I'm too modest to tell people how hard I work: I can brag. I just tend to think a work ethic is beside the point for most parts of life. Once I knew to ask about work ethic, I found perspectives between liberals and conservatives were very different. That stepping over how hard we work, or how meaningful the work is to us, turns out to be common for liberals, and is partially supported by academic research.[10]

Industriousness just isn't as interesting to us. If we put it on a pedestal, it's a one-foot pedestal, not a three-foot one. I admire many people, for instance, who don't work hard at all, and many others whose work habits are unclear to me. One close, very liberal artist friend likes to lecture others about how evil and dehumanizing work is– any work– as if there's a reasonable case to be made in this world that we should all stop working. I have to interrupt him sometimes and point out how inane he sounds, and he laughs about it with me, good-naturedly; deep down, he knows it's a quite over-the-top position to take.

Yet this same friend can be found spending many physically demanding daily hours keeping a world-class garden in top readiness, with its intermittent and complex combination of variable needs; he's a whirling marvel of conscientiousness, both orderly and industrious, particularly in the spring as the garden awakens, and in the driest months of the year, while he has to be on high alert to keep the garden's darlings well-watered. He doesn't think of himself as industrious at all. He has other traits that make him blind to that strength.

Thinking in terms of being industrious is natural for someone who is inspired by that left hemisphere's love of keeping important processes going. That's their orderliness talking. It often helps conservatives to respect us if we can get over feeling awkward about mentioning our commitment to doing good work, or the hours we put in.

It's not an accident that when one visits people in the heartland of America, the question "What do you do for a living?" is usually asked within scant seconds, as a way to understand a core part of you better. After all, we spend a large portion of our waking life at work, and, though many of us hate to admit it, most of our life's contribution to humanity may well be best seen through what we do at work.

In Europe and even some urban and coastal American settings, our work is considered separate from who we are, and asking a question about it can seem rude. This reflects less respect for industriousness as a central core of ourselves. After living in Europe, I have to swallow my reticence to feel pigeonholed by that first-minute, American question about my job; still have to mentally remind myself that the questioner just wants to know me better in a healthy way.

In Europe, the question is interpreted as only a bit over from "How prestigious is your work?," or "How much money do you make?" This is a natural, healthy liberal attempt to make sure everyone understands that we're not defined by what we do for work— that our lives are much bigger than that. In my experience, though, conservatives are not concerned with our money or prestige when they ask. They're rarely that interested about the money-making part of work— they're interested in the processes that people take on and work. They want to know what kind of "engine" you are; they think *all* kinds of engines are interesting, and honorable, and important.

Revealing our relationship to our work is a way to help conservatives see us more accurately in their terms, by revealing a trait they think is integral to us, instead of hiding it or making it seem like we don't care about our work. If you work hard, or have an Americana-type job like blue-collar work, crow about it. It'll help you get accepted, and steer them away from potential resentments about us not pulling our weight in society.

Talking the Walk– the Conscientious Conservative

We've discovered that conservatives haven't been found to be stronger than liberals in industriousness, but there's a way that can be deceptive. Conservatives *can* be thought of as more industrious, in the sense that one's industriousness (focus, self-discipline, and ambition) can be more *effective* if one is orderly: it's like having a better toolkit with which to

43

accomplish one's ambition. For instance, industriousness *mostly* gets you through college, but it also helps to be detail-oriented, dutiful, and orderly when getting things done. At healthy levels, orderliness helps pull one's industriousness along to greater efficiency, thanks to an organized and detail-oriented approach. Industriousness and orderliness are a powerful one-two punch in business, as well as other socially demanding situations like volunteering, religion, the military, team sports, government work, and political campaigning. **Orderliness inspires conservatives to the possibilities of industriousness** to make them happy and productive, so that high conscientiousness (orderliness and industriousness combined) is seen as the essence of a successful life.

This way that orderliness has of opening one's eyes to the value of industriousness explains why conversing with conservatives about politics is often about the many virtues of being conscientious or industrious. "Personal responsibility" comes up over and over again, in a way that can sound like a meaningless broken record to us, until we get used to thinking more in those terms. Russell Kirk described either orderliness or industriousness as the central points for *every single one* of his "Ten Conservative Principles," available in the Appendix of that name. As we work to understand conservatives, this simplicity, the focus on one set of characteristics as the criteria that define one's life as a success, is a great advantage. It's a powerful inroad into strategies and techniques you can use to relate with them.

A great deal of self-help literature is essentially guidance on cultivating and encouraging our conscientiousness, whether it encourages a positive mental attitude (industriousness), faith in a higher purpose (industriousness), or the large number of ways to help satisfaction through goal-setting (orderliness and industriousness). When a person values conscientiousness, they see constant signals from the world that good things come to those who wait, and that our opportunities are surprisingly unlimited. Because of their orientation, and maybe because of their success in the workplace, conscientious people also tend to be confident about our market-based economy and the principles of capitalism, a system that is designed to reward work that isn't always varied, or interesting, or flexible enough for people who are low in orderliness.

Can a person be too conscientious? Yes and no. As with any of these 5 major families of traits, it can be a tad confusing to talk about being too conscientious, just as it is to say one is too emotionally stable, or too creative. However, I doubt I have to tell you that there's a rigidity and misplaced single-mindedness possible in orderliness, too: being inflexible or obsessive about your goals, say, or too disciplinary, or careless when it comes to exceptions. We see orderly people as missing the forest for the trees at times. **Rigidity is the problem liberals complain of most about conservatives**– an unwillingness to change when it seems past appropriate to do so. Most of my time as an activist is directly spent combating this rigidity, as creatively as I can. Conscientiousness that isn't given its marching orders using a good mix of other healthy personality traits can feel like a train that's lost its brakes. Much great evil in society has come about through misplaced orderliness, or an obsessive moralistic use of strong boundaries.

Understanding Conservatism and Fear

There's an underappreciated way in which an emphasis on conscientiousness is extremely useful: it helps people adjust their attitude and be happier in situations where others might be troubled. Conscientious people have better health and live longer:[11] one reason is likely that they have a can-do attitude, which has been linked in many studies to a stronger immune system. When a person feels a need to stay at a job that's repetitive, boring, or demeaning, they need a shift in attitude to stay happy: conscientious people can often do that successfully. Those with low levels of orderliness, like many liberals, have a harder time making that shift; repetitive and boring are two of our biggest cuss words. So the world rewards conscientious people, naturally and consistently, with both positive results from their work and goal-orientation, and higher chances of personal happiness because of their flexible attitude toward somewhat unpleasant situations.

This resilience has limits, though. Two large studies, one long-term,[12] have showed that very conscientious people who suffer long-term unemployment become far more troubled than the rest of us– they can become quite despondent and discouraged at failure. It seems that one reason they're focused on being conscientious is that the down side in life, when their orderliness doesn't do them much good, starts to take apart their whole world view, which is centered on being able to keep things certain, consistent, and hopefully pretty simple, like having a job and a paycheck. Their faith in the world hasn't panned out; their strong set of beliefs about the world rewarding them for being hard-working and orderly is starting to fray, or maybe disintegrate.

For very conscientious people, then, *the stakes in life are higher* than for the rest of us: people who value certainty and consistency have more to gain from things going fairly well (higher happiness), but also more to lose than the rest of us when failure or unpredictability happen. That combination of opportunity and vulnerability explains some of that intensity we may see about rule-following, keeping to a schedule, and trying to minimize uncertainty.

I have a similar belief about things working out if you plow ahead, but it's not as hard-edged; it's better stated as "work hard and everything may turn out alright; then again, you could get creamed." My life isn't dominated by beliefs about me needing or expecting control, so I can respond more directly to the crisis, instead of piling on stress related to my world view getting folded, spindled, and mutilated, right as I'm getting kicked hardest by life.

The many other studies showing conservatives to be more "threat-sensitive" than liberals, may be a version of this same awareness of higher risk to their world view. We certainly see this politically in attitudes about criminal justice and the military, but also in personal situations, with gun attitudes, protection of the family, and other ways. They're not playing the same game we are; more to gain, more to lose.

Their threat-sensitivity is usually misunderstood as having "fear-based" lives, which is a mistake we must rectify in our thinking. We can understand their threat-sensitivity best by asking a simple question: if they're so fear-based, why are they significantly happier than liberals in most situations? Or the related question: how on earth can somebody be can-do and yet worried about all kinds of things at the same time? It doesn't seem to make sense, at first blush. If people feel threatened, shouldn't they be wary and uptight? Shouldn't such sensitivity about security (or certainty) affect their overall happiness so that they're *less* happy?

This can be so confusing to the liberal. Happy? Can-do? They sure *look* miserable. Yes, they do, but one reason why, quite often, is that when those fears get pulled down from the shelf and dealt with, it's happening because we showed up. Statisticians would call that a *biased sample*, meaning you're not seeing them the way they usually are. Or we see their jackasses on TV, glowering and whining and threatening, and draw the same conclusion.

But the main reason why we get confused about fear and threat-sensitivity is that, if *we* had attitudes similar to conservatives about the importance of handling threats, the thinner boundaries we usually have in life *would make us dwell on those threats*. They'd be on our minds all the time. It'd drive us nuts. We project unhappiness and nervousness onto conservatives, because we know what threat-sensitivity does to *us*.

We're thinking about this like liberals, and need to imagine ourselves as more orderly. Those thick boundaries that orderliness creates in life, segregate life into pieces that are bite-sized, so that life can be handled logically, or systematically. A threat is important to them, but they address it as best they can, and then they set it aside. *Conservatives address threats, and then they put them on a shelf in a mental back room*, out of sight and out of mind, where things belong when they're taken care of. There are exceptions and complications to this, but we should bear in mind that orderliness is essentially designed to do just that kind of thing: to get concerns away from our awareness until the right time comes to bring them up again. It's part of keeping things simple and certain.

Let's take an example. For a conservative, a gun lets them put the question of security in that back room of their mind; the gun helps them sleep better. This is either a superhuman or alien attitude compared to mine, I'm not sure which. You couldn't pay me enough to keep a gun handy. I'd worry about kids getting to the gun. Don't they worry about that? Well, sure– so they do something about the worry, and then they stop worrying. They train the kids to use a gun, or teach them to be obedient enough to not play with it, and their sense of boundaries, combined with their strong certainty-seeking instinct (and, hopefully, their obedient kids), lets that concern get set aside.

I'd fret over the violence that would have to happen in a break-in; they'd concern themselves little with a burglar's health, because the boundary between their life and the burglar's is thick and clear. I'd have a hard time falling back asleep after strange sounds, thinking about maybe having to use the damn thing; the gun's presence would comfort them about their safety, and help them sleep easily. I'd have to train myself to load the gun quickly in the dark, because I could never leave a loaded gun around; they'd enjoy that training, with all those orderliness bones of theirs getting exercised. Or they might leave the gun loaded, with the safety on, and save the danger and risk of Marine-level gun loading skills in the dark, while half-asleep.

It's a kind of logical, removed perspective on things, which has some great advantages in certain situations. That separation or distance between people and things, those nice, clean boundaries, are *how* they're orderly. They believe in living a life where they take care of problems to the extent they should, and then they don't let the problems bother them, and they go live the rest of their life properly. That sounds reasonable, right? I like that idea. Work the problem, set it aside. Sounds great.

There is an exception to this argument of mine about happy conservatives with fears on a back shelf. It has to do with a minority of conservatives, typified by Donald Trump's most enthusiastic followers. The neuroscientist Joseph LeDoux characterizes them as anxious about the future in certain conditions. This is a little different than being fear-based, at least as we liberals would think of it; it operates differently in the brain. We'll talk later about how and when (and why) that anxiety gets goaded, and the effects that has on them and America.

We've been very positive about conservative orderliness, you and I, for pages and pages; we've been nice. But we need to pause the praises a moment to be clear about our struggle over orderliness. We can describe much of this a different way, and it doesn't sound nearly as good.

Here's the version many of us will recognize, particularly those of us who are activists: in their constant effort to be certain about taking care of threats, conservatives can oversimplify situations and not pay enough attention to detail, which can cause all kinds of problems.

That's the back side of being threat-sensitive, while still managing to be a happy camper: you could be dumbing problems down too much. Do you remember the "left-brain interpreter"? It's the fixation the left hemisphere has on solving problems and putting them to bed. Here it is in real life. Might get a burglar? Keep a loaded gun near the bed. Might get attacked by a terrorist? Start a "war on terror." Too many drug users? A war on drugs seems just the thing. Your 17-year-old daughter's pregnant? Find out who the father is, and have her marry the guy.

The happiness they derive through being orderly is a reference point they build their lives upon in a way we don't, that indicates to themselves that they have balance in their lives, that their world's been sorted correctly. That's the wonderful opportunity of the conservative mindset, and the great challenge for them as well.

A common liberal version of how higher happiness might have a kind of dark side goes something like, "hey, if I had to distance myself from the problems of the world to be happy, I'd rather be unhappy."[13] I like that about us liberals, because it means that we're willing to sacrifice our personal happiness for the common good; that might make a great difference in the world, at times. But if you look at that argument carefully, it's really more a way of saying "thin boundaries are morally better than thick boundaries." It might also be a way of saying "everything is interrelated, always, and to do good for those that suffer, we must suffer." That attitude feels a little heavy-handed, even if it's at least partially true.

I like the simpler, more direct, and modest retort of "orderliness can be taken too far sometimes." That sets us up to have a wonderful argument between us, even if it does sidestep rather slickly the issue of who gets to be happy, or correct, and who doesn't. This reconciles our two views usefully, using a straightforward finding long known by psychologists. Using a drive for simplicity, certainty, and consistency too eagerly, without discrimination– the way one can with strong unconscious drives– means we can use our strong boundaries to shove major concerns on a shelf *simplistically*. After all, a three-year-old child who takes a toy and won't return it to another child has set their concern for the other child on a shelf somewhere, because there's a simple value to fulfill, and an easy way to keep it fulfilled. An imperialistic war is a great way to be wreaking havoc with foreigners we don't identify with, due to misuse of strong boundaries in life, while we gain feelings of safety or economic success at great human cost far across the ocean, on a kind of autopilot.

We're fine with conservatives taking care of things by divvying up the world starkly based on their values, but we want to see care taken in advance with issues of complexity, or ones that matter. We'd like set-and-forget, and assumptions about certainty, to be used carefully. We watch conservatives use relatively simple tactics with issues that can be quite complicated, because an orderly approach allows and encourages that, almost by definition. The justification that the world is black and white rings hollow in our ears, because the "black" in that phrase secretly contains exceptions we care about, set aside cruelly in such calculus. The power of coarse distinctions is paid for at great expense, and usually by others who aren't benefitting from their higher personal happiness. We're often not sure what the ultimate cost will be.

If you look carefully, these largely unassailable general points are all just ways of questioning the indiscriminate use of strong boundaries, the way someone of my perspective naturally does. I could be doing a bad thing sometimes, thinking this way: I could be questioning the *proper* use of strong boundaries, because of my distrust of the strengths that orderliness provides. I can't be sure which I'm doing in a certain situation, but "there are roughly zones" of appropriate behavior, and we all have to find them. Not much of an answer, but it's the only one any of us has.

Strength and Weakness

The conservative strength in orderliness makes it easy for them to peg us as less detail-oriented, shakier on following rules, and not having a strong sense of healthy boundaries. They're entirely correct statistically. This is an example of the first basic principle in strengths and weaknesses of personality:

> 1. If we're strong in a trait, we can see other people's weakness in that trait.

Not perfectly, of course. And sometimes we can be wrong. But it's a simple, powerful point, and one of the main organizing principles of this guide. Think of one of your strengths, and then think of how many of your family and friends are weak in that trait . In a minute, you can probably think of a half-dozen people or more.

Of course, this principle is used incorrectly by people who have *too much* of a trait, because then everyone else looks like they need a verbal spanking at every turn, whether it be their lack of fashion sense, their poor car-washing habits, or how slow they are with their homework. We might argue this is happening with an extremely orderly conservative, and often, we'd be right. But be careful with that argument; try not to dismiss criticisms by those who are strong in a trait just because it sounds excessive. In particular, this dismissal happens often toward conservatives by saying "Oh, he's way too rigid,' without giving thought to the particulars of that person's point or approach. Try to keep in mind how straightforward it is in your case to see weaknesses from your position of strength, and to grant that capability of wisdom to others.

When we switch from conservative weaknesses and think about our own, we want that rule to go away. That's human, not ideological; we despise people thinking that they have us figured out, especially if they're conservative, and we question their judgment. Most conservatives are not too orderly; they may have problems in their outlook that come up because of their orderliness, just as with any personality trait, but that doesn't mean their orderliness strength is some kind of robotic, evil impulse. So, I try to meet them halfway. I'm incapable of always assuming they're right about points that seem driven by their orderliness, but I try my best to give them the benefit of the doubt, and think flexibly about what they're critiquing me over, or what's annoying me about them.

Think about your own attitude toward being respectful about rules and procedures, for instance, which is normally a conservative strength, and not something we liberals might see as a mindlessly straightforward, uniformly great thing. Now, there's absolutely no doubt that rule-following is wonderful and valuable in many, many circumstance; it's even essential for basic safety. But even so, we might feel suspicious about the basic notion of following rules; might easily imagine unfair rules, or situations where lives were ruined by bad laws being enforced unfairly. We often have ways of saying "think outside the box" that are more like "question authority ," or "rules are made to be broken." Think about how the word "orderly," or its close cousin, "dutiful," can sound creepy, or even scary, despite all the advantages we just went over. With a trait we're not strong in, that knee-jerk suspicion and doubt we feel about a positive trait, is an example of a kind of opposite, competing principle to the first:

> 2. When we are weak in a personality trait, we tend to value that trait much less, or misinterpret it, or not see the advantages of it.

Not that we necessarily are wrong in our critique of rule-following, under some conditions; it's just that, while you're putting that "question authority" bumper sticker on your car, it's difficult to appreciate at the same time how valuable it is to have a society where you're loyal to a president, you easily obey clear rules and guidelines, and kids conform and get straight A's. Because we're not perfectly flexible, we miss seeing some of the advantages of the trait. That's part of what it means to be relatively low in a trait.

Here's an example. Discounting orderliness, explaining it away consistently as evil, makes it difficult for many of my fellow liberal activists to identify with studying the detailed budgetary needs of a police force in a healthy, orderly way. We can ignore and vault over particular, fundamental concerns about officer shift coverage and hiring challenges, for instance. We might do it because we're not interested in that level of detail, or we may want to "starve the beast" (cut the police budget). Cutting the budget may be a great idea, but doing it without a well-placed dollop or two of orderliness is asking for a nightmare of political firestorms, misunderstanding, overworked (and abusive) cops, and crime.

These two principles— the advantage of the viewpoint of someone who's strong in a trait, and the disadvantage of those low in a trait— come up over and over with all personality traits, not just the ideological ones we'll cover. We've got the other fellow figured out completely, but for some reason he doesn't know a thing about us, because he's such a parochial dummy.

A brilliant, close friend who was profoundly weak in impulse control built an involved, compelling justification and morality around his tendency to go with what felt good: he died young through drug abuse, and I watched it happen, in slow-motion. He was a victim of the power of this second principle, of ignoring our blindness when it comes to our weaknesses. We have so many ways of denying how our personality weaknesses affect our lives adversely like this. If we think a bit, we all know people who are careless with detail, or impolite, or have difficulty with stress, who claim their weaknesses aren't the problem. If we think a little harder, we can come up with ways it's true of ourselves.

It can be tough to see whether we're being too judgmental or being accurate when evaluating others, but there are some good guidelines we can use with conservatives. We know the usual traits involved, on their side and ours. And liberals are actually quite lucky, because the first principle (that we have the other fellow figured out) is easy for us to verify, since there is a great deal of research information on the strengths and weaknesses of conservative psychological traits– much more than there is for liberals. The second principle– that we're terribly, horribly, no-good, very bad about seeing our own weaknesses– is more important for our purposes, even though it may seem as if it has nothing to do with conservatives.

As we think about our conservative friends, we should always be struggling with ourselves to better appreciate the traits that they're strong in– and our common weakness in those same traits makes that tough for us to do. We should be looking for the roles in society where those good traits can provide great benefit, and try to see where liberal personalities might not be as effective. Seeing such advantages is not only critical to understanding them, but is also a way to get used to thinking about human personality instead of ideology.

Conservatives have mirror-image weaknesses with the liberal personality, of course: our strengths are usually seen as disadvantages, or even moral flaws. It's time to turn to ourselves a bit, to see how we liberals tick, and watch how it tweaks them.

Chapter Three

PERSONALITY – LIBERALS

Progress might've been alright
once, but it's gone on too long.
-Ogden Nash

THE SINGLE, strongest statistical connection between personalities and ideology is found within the typical liberal personality, through the strangest and most controversial of the Big Five clusters of personality traits we'll cover. It was originally termed "intelligence," but that was quickly thought to be too narrow and deceptive a name; others wanted to call it "imagination." Now, most researchers call it "openness to experience," though many call it "openness/intellect." This is the only one of the Big Five that has a split or phrase in its common name, because these two aspects are too different to summarize well in one word. The intellect aspect finds conservatives and liberals roughly the same, but the openness half is where we leave conservatives in the dust.

With such a big difference between being open and our intellect, why didn't we just create a sixth grouping of traits– why shove openness and intellect together? Dr. Colin DeYoung, a personality neuroscientist, and his associates, have a compelling rationale why the aspects intellect and openness must be joined at the hip.[1]

The best way to see the connection is by making a list of the traits that make up openness/intellect, in an order that makes each of them closely related to the ones on each side of it. These detailed traits, on the left below, end up in the three rough categories, shown on the right:

Openness/Intellect Traits

Exercising pure intellect
Intellectual competence   **Intellect**
Need for cognition (think Sudoku)
Quickness/cleverness
Ingenuity
Introspection
Imagination   **Imagination**
Artistic pursuits
Being adventurous
Aesthetic sense
In touch with our feelings
Reflection
Fantasy   **Openness**
Suggestibility (easily hypnotized)
Conspiracy beliefs
Wild fantasies
Magical beliefs

Think of this list like the cereal aisle at the grocer. When you're buying cereal, the Choco-Bomb Delite-type of cereals are displayed next to each other on the aisle. As you move further down, you get to the sugary cereals that are pretending to not be sugary. After that come corn flakes and such, and then the cereals that are pretty healthy; finally you get to the end, where cereals contain 7 organic grains you've never heard of, harvested under a full moon. In the same way, looking at the above list of traits from top to bottom, each item is related to the ones near them, but as they get further apart, they start bearing little resemblance to each other. Move far enough away on the list and you can see that they're not related at all– they may even seem like opposites, like introspection and being adventurous, for instance. The middle of the list describes the gradual shift[2] between cold logic at the top (intellect) and wild, emotional fantasy at the bottom (openness). Imagination holds court as a kind of neutral ground, the peacemaker of the family: that center region has descriptions of people who are clearly enjoying the use of both their intellect and forms of openness– traits like a sense of adventure, or their urge to engage with the world, or with possibilities. As you go up the list from the middle, the traits show less interest in art, or travel, and more interest in thinking and logic. As you go down from the middle, you see less traits with interest in intellectual aspects of life, and more that are open to creativity, feelings, fantasy, and unique experience.

Those who are strong in openness/intellect usually draw from several places along this wide range. See if that's true for you. You may be both a lover of art and someone who enjoys discussing ideas or new inventions. You may be a witty conversationalist, and open to wild ideas; or desperate to travel to exotic locales, and in need of understanding the detailed, complex ins-and-outs of a field. Maybe all of these describe you. If you're liberal, several of the traits probably fit you to a T.

Creativity is Everything

Being exception-oriented like we are can be thought of as an interplay between elements on this list, particularly ones near pure intellect at the top, interacting with others in the middle or further down. The kind of intelligence that grows from experience (over time), called "crystallized intelligence," has been associated with using our intellect *along with* those traits in that middle and lower region, probably because we get stimulated so much. Strength with openness and imagination may actually help us by providing a sounding board of sorts for our intellect, giving it a chance to stretch us in a way that makes us *effectively* more intelligent. We may go back and forth between symbolic intellectual ideas and flights of fancy, to make progress on an art project; or use the intellect as a primary engine for brainstorming about new design ideas at work; or bounce along the list to several areas, making unintuitive connections to write something, or plan an adventure.

A revealing part of this list is the emotionally sensitive parts in the middle, where we pull in even broader parts of ourselves. We use openness and intellect together to sort out a conflict with our child, while paying attention to their emotions; to help a friend with a relationship problem; and to read a Henry James novel and appreciate it completely. Those effort uses compassion, creativity, and our intellect, all combined; they stretch us, and teach us how to integrate our intellect with the rest of our life. This is a key part of many liberal personalities, and an advantage; our close relationship with both *our own* emotional life, and the emotional lives *of others*.

Mixing our intellect and openness is how we liberals find and highlight the important exceptions that inspire us. Combining openness and intellect is essentially a technique for using our intellect well, or fully using it; researchers suspect that that may be why liberals do a little better on IQ tests on average than conservatives, after controlling (adjusting) for demographic effects like age and ethnicity: *we use our intelligence in more ways*. We also may simply spend more of our time using our intellect, because we like to use it so much in combination with the other creative, openness pursuits that interest us. When our focus is on being what Dr. Ramachandran called an "anomaly detector," we do many things that conservatives either avoid, or that they do in small amounts. We're on the lookout for victims of injustice; listening to odd facts about the world on National Public Radio; doing involved research in a new field of science; reading a self-help book, like this one; or going downtown to try out a new Afro-Cuban restaurant. We also use our intellect the same way that conservatives tend to do, to solve practical problems and do intellectual puzzles– but the average liberal is relatively more interested in using their intellect to speculate, explore (travel to exotic places, say), fantasize, or do art.

There are many imaginative or artistic individual conservatives, of course– every personality trait can be found in large quantities in particular liberal and conservative individuals. For instance, one far-right conservative I interviewed is a nationally renowned painter obsessed with variety, unhappy unless experimenting with technique, or medium, or subject matter. But even he'd tell you his politics are very unusual in the company of his contemporaries.

Walking the Talk– Openness/Intellect

Let's think back on the relationship between orderliness and industriousness a moment. Orderliness acts as a magic key of sorts, a way for conservatives to be *inspired* by industriousness, so that they let conscientiousness reign at the center of their life perspective. In a remarkably similar way, **liberals use our openness to "unlock" the intellect part of our personality, in a way that inspires us to place intellect at the center of our perspective**. Not that we're much more intelligent (nobody should care about a few IQ points): we're *inspired by intelligence* though our openness, so we tend to emphasize and rely greatly on it. We don't usually use our intellect side without looping in things like imagination, or art, or what's going on inside ourselves emotionally. Openness defines us as liberals, but, just as conservatives are inspired by industriousness, liberals are inspired by the life of the intellect, and they value being smart, or intellectual.

There are many ways this shows up in day-to-day life. One way is the odd fact that liberals are less likely to have bachelor's degrees than conservatives, but more likely to have doctorates. That's because bachelor's degrees have been traditionally a practical step, which conservatives emphasize and execute better– but liberals are more likely to fall in love with enlisting their intellect, in tandem with the love of novelty at the heart of their perspective. Many more of us, proportionally, go to school until our conservative aunt finally cuts off our financial support, because it's been 9 years and we're still trying to figure out what a certain genus of frog likes most in its ladies.

Conservatives might watch liberal graduate students, especially in social science fields, from the sidelines and shake their head (unless the liberal is an engineering or business student; that makes sense). Throw five of those liberal intellectuals together, and there might be one full, practical set of bones between them all. How many years can a liberal spend asking why is there air? (Ten. Twenty, if funding gets renewed.) They'd get lost on the way to school if their moms didn't still drive them.

And our highly related, often gravely impractical focus: in the battle between simple and complicated, we prefer complicated. Bad guys aren't bad guys: they're complicated mixes of genes, background, and chance. Capitalism: complicated mix of good and evil, must be watched. Relationships require genius, sensitivity, and a good therapist. Kids need space and flexibility, which requires a kind of intellectual, sensitive radar to sense where they are all the time emotionally. If you're liberal, you should probably get your Ph.D. in kid before having one.

Complication can be an addiction for us, and a default. The only reason for conservatives to get complicated would be to launch a rocket— something practical like that. Or designing a giant building, or a sugar-free version of choco-pops that sells like crazy. Something that makes money, or fixes a mysterious pool liner leak, or that can be restored to look like a million bucks driving down the road. For me, "practical" like that can sound like a waste of time— but that's where the conservative geniuses are all huddled.

When my kids were little, Sesame Street had a song with a verse that went, "Come on and zoomy, zoomy, zoomy with me!" Most of my kids flew around the living room singing with me awhile with the show, and that was it. One never floated back down to earth; 20 years later, with all that imagination tethered to intellect, he soars in occasionally on his way through the state, to breathlessly critique Ibsen or Dostoevsky with me for an hour, on his way past more rainbows, to yet another kingdom where showers and socks are rarities, and hippie girls love you anyway.

George W. Bush essentially campaigned twice trying to get across that he was about as smart as a fencepost, that all he needed was a solid grasp of basics because he was the sensei of commonsense and morals and delegation; he followed the Reagan "aw, shucks" approach to the notion of intellect. Conservatives ate it up and asked for more. John Kerry, in contrast, made a mountain out of somebody accusing him of having a lower IQ than Bush during the 2004 presidential campaign, treating it as an emergency, so that we liberals could understand clearly that he was a genius, the minimum liberal intellectual requirement for being a good President. (Their IQ's are roughly the same.)

Laugh It Up, Funny Boy

That imagination part of openness contains most of our artistic and creative traits, which are often speckled with emotional or empathic sensitivity. Humor is a good entry point into understanding our use of openness and intellect through imagination.

Ever wonder why there was never a successful conservative version of Jon Stewart? It's because humor is divided surprisingly firmly into liberal and conservative forms, depending on which hemisphere of the brain is titillated.

A great exemplar of conservative humor is Jeff Foxworthy, who is famous for saying things like "If you read the Auto Trader with a highlight pen…you might just be a redneck." This kind of humor plays over and over on small exaggerations of the familiar, and on gentle stereotypes.

You may have missed it, if you've been sleeping through your life, but conservatives adore stereotypes, and they use them instinctively, because stereotypes are both practical and fun, in their place. That's one reason why political correctness, which most people think of as avoiding all stereotypes, can be so annoying to them. For a mind that categorizes without thinking, stereotypes come naturally. Contrary to our common liberal prejudices, stereotyping (or generalizing) is both a strength and liability, depending on the situation and the stereotype.

It's possible to use small exaggerations and stereotypes with politics, but it's tough to continue for long in an interesting way, especially because we don't love the butt of political jokes as much as conservatives love rednecks. Conservative "versions" of Jon Stewart-like humor tend to be cruelly sarcastic instead of lightly superior; there's less joke to it and more point, a kind of direct anger that isn't particularly hidden– which just isn't as fun, unless you're very ideological. The one-sided stereotypes, accurate or not, and the harshness combine to make it seem too grindingly political to be funny in larger doses. Here, in contrast, is a Stewart joke, which even conservatives can find funny.

> President Bush delivered his first State of the Union address, riding high on an 82-percent approval rating, and with Attorney General John Ashcroft dispatching agents to interview the other 18 percent.

There's no reason why a conservative can't make up and tell a joke like that; in fact, there are examples of them doing similar jokes. They just *tend not to* because 1) it's not a simple joke, 2) it's not centered on anything particularly familiar, and 3) it's relatively emotionally complex (lightly sardonic). Also, outside of picking on rednecks, conservatives have a harder time poking much fun at "traditional values," where some of the easy pickin's are. And they're not as fond of being nasty— which makes a ton of material out of bounds (though quality angry/nasty conservative humor is a good niche).

It's always easier to make fun of traditional value as an outsider, too; fair or not, they're a sitting duck for modern sensibilities— Jon again:

"Divorce isn't caused because 50% of marriages end in gayness."

Complex humor is the province of bouncing back-and-forth between different pieces of openness and intellect: it involves both, almost by definition. It's not even accurate to talk about "both," because a given joke may involve linking one's intellect with several aspects of openness that have to do with emotional sensitivity, wild imagination, ingenuity, and a sense of art. Everyone can do it, in theory— it's just that conservatives don't do it nearly as much. Setting aside the comedians, though: as listeners, conservatives aren't as fond of broader forms of humor.

Not to say that conservative humor isn't funny— some of it is hilarious.[3] Personally, I love the gift many conservatives have with clever humor of the kind we're talking about, which I've experienced many times at get-togethers and parties. It can be incredibly witty. Some of the times I've laughed the hardest in life were at the hands of drunk rednecks, especially in the South, who employ their wit, usually on each other, with practiced, quick understatement, and a deep familiarity with their subject. I certainly can't keep up. The only people I find funnier are the Irish, in bars, at around midnight.

This isn't a competition about who's funnier; everybody gets a hilarious gold star. The conservative subject matter, tenor, and emotional range is a relatively narrow part of the overall scope of potential humor. The liberal dominance of humor, both on the supply and demand sides, provides a great insight into what our openness buys us, and why we're so dependent on our intellect.

Take country music— the fact that, as I tour around the less urban parts of the South and Southwest doing research, I'm forced to listen to either my own music or country music, since virtually nothing besides country is available on the radio, outside traditional Latino music and Rush Limbaugh types. Country music is a similar story to comedy: an art form that is twists on the familiar, with clear images and light skewering of people you recognize and appreciate. Perhaps one-eighth of music, approach-wise, if one is to be generous.

The art of writing a country song– deceptively difficult– is stringing clichés and hopefully-soon-to-be clichés together in a mildly surprising mix, always rhyming in a lulling, assuring way, so the listener gets an ultra-clear image of someone in a familiar situation (i.e., a well-known process). It's a linear story of some kind, with a little twist and a moral. Again, rhythmic, conservative-friendly language to say "Isn't simplicity, certainty, and consistency just AWESOME?! I love how our l'il ol' boundaries just seem to work out, don't you?" All very left-hemisphere, in celebration of a straight-ahead, beloved process or two, with many boundaries between good and evil, cheaters, patriotism (hierarchy/ authority), and comforting traditions thrown in. Contrast that with almost any other kind of music, other than perhaps teen pop. Other music isn't just in the business of providing a comforting validation of beloved, familiar, straightforward processes. And there's the one guitarist working in country music today; I can't remember his name, but he does the same, slick, incredibly fast guitar lick during the refrain of every song.

The neuroscientist and psychiatrist Iain McGilchrist considers music the preeminent domain of the right hemisphere, perhaps the best exemplification of what the hemisphere is about. We are inspired by the right hemisphere's contribution of a broader mix of emotion into the picture; seeing beyond and through normal boundaries; and the art of the possible. We write and listen to music that is relatively unpredictable, with mysterious, often nonsensical lyrics that we can't even understand often, with odd rhythms and pauses, and emotional colorings– the kind of thing that would get country listeners to change the station immediately, because many of them say the main reason they appreciate country music is "I love a good story." Again, conservatives like and write some great music outside of country (notably in rock and folk, as well as classical), but theirs is typically a relatively narrow portion of the art. We, on the other hand, are also fond of half-stories, confusing stories, various rants, steamy phrases, and things that sound intense but don't mean anything when you look at it on the page.

Our art differences parallel our relative appreciation of dogs and cats; we liberals like relatively unpredictable, incomprehensible things, while conservatives tend to want art that'll roll over and play dead, and lick their hand.

Poetry and painting have similar differences. Consider these examples

of poetry from a team of investigative neuroscientists.[4] This first one
activated the brain hemisphere that seeks out interesting exceptions:

Rain clouds are pregnant ghosts

The line connects two things that are quite separate ideas. One of
them, "pregnant ghosts," is quite odd. You have to think or feel a little,
or do both, before it sinks in, and then the line is meaningful and
interesting. In contrast, here's another example:

Babies are angels

This has some freshness to it, but not much; it's got about half a day
until its expiration date, and then the store will have to toss it. It's like a
line in a middling-quality country song, or a beginning poetry class
poem. It's loved and seen as poetry by the hemisphere that loves the
familiar, that likes word play sticking closely to existing beloved processes
like raising babies that are little angels, or having angels watching over
you, or marrying the angel of your life, or driving an eighteen-wheeler.
The right hemisphere wasn't impressed with that line, in the study; it
didn't do much to process the line, because there wasn't enough there to
treat as new, or mysterious, or unfamiliar– "Here," it said to the left
hemisphere as it passed it off, "your kind of thing." We liberals might
even say that the first example is *real* poetry, while the country song lyric
is something else, a slogan for Angel Baby Butt Cream. Some of us would
die a slow, certain death if poetry consisted of nothing but lines like
"because you're mine, I walk the line." Cute, meaningful, and quickly
boring.

Now, mind you, I've taught myself to enjoy country music– about a
quarter of the songs, anyway– and can sing along on road trips with
abandon. I want to reach down and grab my non-existent giant belt
buckle when I bawl out the choruses, and do that little humpy dance they
do while they sing along, with their pointy boots and the cheap beer and
all. Many of us liberals love some country music, though most that do
were raised around it. One reason I decided to learn to like it is that if we
took on even a tiny fraction of the good inspiration of country songs in
our lives, we'd probably be much happier and effective people. You're
allowed to scoff at that claim, but there's great meaning and wisdom in
many country songs; lots to ponder. You just have to be able to get over
that liberal feeling that you're getting dumber as the songs roll forth, that
your brains are leaking out of a hole somewhere, with the inexorable
similarity in tone and attitude and sappiness.

I like some country songs, but part of me longs for something else pretty soon. That part of me that needs more is mysteriously related to why a New Yorker is out on a Wednesday night until 3 AM, listening to a favorite ska band, even though they have to be at work at 9:30. We want a little bit of certainty, consistency, and simplicity, and a lot of uncertainty, variety, and complexity.

Is there a negative to our beloved one-two punch of openness and intellect? Absolutely. Though I'm a bad person to ask, since I'm deep inside the problem. But here's what I'm told: "You liberals think you're soo smart." Conservatives can't stand the sense of superiority that they see dripping from us constantly. **The liberal sense of intellectual superiority is the number one complaint of conservatives about us.** If you go back a page or two, you can see me arguably being mildly superior several times in just the way that annoys them.

Liberals misunderstand this critique to be a complaint about using our intellect too much. It's much more about two other things. First is the *way* we use our intellect: all that bouncing around between intellect, imagination, and openness. They get dizzy just watching us, and tend to get suspicious about the complexity of our approach.

Take the notion of spending on welfare: there are only a couple of principles involved from a conservative standpoint, and they drive the position from beginning to end, in the kind of first-principles focus that is their strength. For me, there are no first principles, or at least there are always potential important exceptions to those principles. Maybe we should reinvent the wheel a little. I think we have to look into all kinds of things to do welfare right, and I want to talk about them.

When I do that, from a conservative standpoint, I'm going on and on while seeming to ignore what matters: that welfare payments, if they're even appropriate at all, have to be for a limited period so that personal responsibility isn't tainted. To them, I'm bouncing around uselessly, sticking my "intellect" where it doesn't belong. Then I pop out randomly at some point with a goofy idea or three about new government programs– Free college for welfare moms! Subsidized jobs for welfare dads!– having adroitly skipped around the one, single point they see as pertinent, which I've avoided, because I like to skip the common sense part of the problem that is done looking at the problem within two seconds. I've got an intellect to work. Our exceptions need my creativity to come in and save the day. I smell the possibility of a great waiver on a (seeming) rule of life.

That's how they get exasperated. But how they get insulted relates to how exasperated and entitled we get when we get cut off 10% of the way into our arguments, with typically polite but unimaginative repetitions about our lack of common sense, their alpha and omega of policy. This seems so short-sighted and unintelligent to us that we start to misbehave, either being rude, or sarcastic, or making overt attacks on their character. The worst reaction, in a way, is just an entitled attitude that emphasizing basic principles equals simple, which equals stupid, which equals lower form of life, eminently ignorable and distasteful. Conservatives hear this as us saying, "if you weren't stupid, or at least less incredibly biased, you'd see how your one sentence answer is way too simple to capture reality effectively. Was your mother stupid, too— was that it? 'Cause then it wouldn't be your fault. You might still be able to get smart like me, maybe, if you try. But you're not going to try, because none of you ever do." They can get most of that just out of a look. And I don't blame them, because it's often all in there in our head, even if it's not being said.

In the final months of President Obama's tenure, Senate Majority Leader Mitch McConnell praised the Vice President, Joe Biden, by saying that the Vice President was a good negotiator, and that he didn't try to "lecture me, like the President likes to do to me and others, and sort of impress us with his intelligence...I think he could resist that, it's kind of grating on people; I hear that complaint from Democrats as well."[5] He praised Joe Biden as having "a personality type" that worked with Republicans, that wasn't insulting and off-putting. In an extended interview, he looped back to this personality-driven point several times. He viewed "the President's personality" as one of the main reasons why federal government wasn't working.

It may be easy for you to ignore that criticism, because of the source. I can't dismiss it easily; I've heard the same complaint, with practically the same wording, about dozens of liberals; I've heard the frustrated jeers of conservatives that "they think they're so smart," individually and collectively, hundreds of times. I still hear it about myself occasionally, though I'm better now at avoiding looking at conservative faces as a chance for a campaign stump speech for selling my intellect.

We can take these critiques two ways. We can use the first principle of personality strengths and weaknesses, and see it as conservatives using their strength in conscientiousness to critique the way we use our openness and intellect— which seems to be making us jerks. In accordance with the principle, that's almost certainly true. Or, we can use the second principle and see it as conservatives being weak in our openness trait, and complaining about something they don't understand well. We all know that's definitely happening sometimes, probably a great deal; maybe even with that welfare example.

So, if both those things are true, we should have a goal to use our intellect well– in shaping our beliefs, say, or understanding a complex situation– without letting *expression* of it make people feel inferior.

Mitch McConnell had what may sound to us like an odd compliment for Joe Biden as a negotiator, yet the way he said it made it seem like Mr. McConnell saw it as high praise: "He doesn't waste any time trying to convince me of things he can't convince me of."

Wait a sec: did he just say convincing isn't allowed? What the heck is negotiation, then? Isn't it all about persuasion? What about our brilliant insights, our inescapable logic, our inviolate moral vision: isn't it going to help change their mind, if they're truly honest?

No. No no no. Not for conservatives, nor humans– probably not even for dogs. Whatever negotiation is, it sure isn't suddenly, magically a place where basic respect of others' most heartfelt thoughts and feelings gets tossed out the window. It's not a place where the intellect is a Popeye muscle that can lift the thick lid on the bin of conservative ideas, so we can flop those ideas out on the deck and finally squish them excitedly together: "ohh...I under*STAND* now! Wow, climate change is such good science! I wish I was smart enough to get it before you splained it to me. Let me run home and correct everything I've taught my kids. Wait, though– before I go– gosh, what *else* can you teach me?"

At negotiations, the smart person helps put together the strategy for an expert like Joe Biden, who uses *other, more useful traits* in that setting. She helps with briefings and debriefings. She sits in a back seat against the wall, listening and taking notes. It's the kind of thing Mitch McConnell did as a junior Senator. Her biggest, hardest job is to keep her mouth shut. She has to do that job a lot.

Respect matters. Often, a much better strategy in negotiation is to spend time using your intellect to creatively *support* the feelings and some of the opinions of those you're in conflict with, or sympathize in detail with difficult situations your rival may be in. That may seem like a horrible idea, like giving away the cow you're bargaining for in advance. But a profound respect often ends up setting an emotional tone of forgiveness and generosity that can work emotional miracles in highly-charged situations, particularly in close personal relationships.

Creativity and Practicality– A Tale of Two Cities

Let's look at us from a conservative's point of view. A person strong in openness can seem quite unappealing to some conservatives, similar to how repetitive, dull work can feel vaguely immoral for liberals. I have had several interesting conversations with perfectly reasonable conservatives who nevertheless think that openness automatically means a lack of dependability, an unhealthy tendency to get distracted easily, a poor sense of risk, and a lack of respect for the tried-and-true.

Do you recognize those negatives? Those are things a conscientious person (especially one strong in orderliness) might find to be bad traits. Conservatives are essentially saying that our openness makes us less conscientious. The second principle we use to understand each other says that when we are weak at a trait, we underestimate how important it is: that's especially true when 1) conservatives think about openness, and 2) when liberals think about orderliness. In personality terms, that's a classic personality conflict. Our strengths are each other's biggest weaknesses.

Lining up some traits from openness and orderliness next to each other reveals the special problem these two personality poles might have:

Openness	Orderliness
Adventurousness	Cautiousness
Artistic interests	Dutifulness
Imagination	Orderliness
Fantasy	Perfectionism

Openness traits seem several worlds over from these normal orderliness traits, don't they? I completely understand why my conservative friends looks upon my emphasis on imagination with distaste and suspicion, or at least confusion: it seems to fly in the face of what is likely their highest (unconscious) value, orderliness.

Just by comparing these two columns of traits, we can see how conservatives high in conscientiousness might tend to be relatively low in openness—and that's statistically quite true.[6] The liberal and opposite version of this problem is also true: we all probably know artistic or adventurous liberals whose versions of cautiousness and organization were squishy, or see-through. Some of us know a plethora of such people, like the technicolor liberal I spawned.

These are useful, accurate stereotypes. They're also in keeping with the second principle above for understanding each other— that we tend to not take seriously traits that we don't have ourselves. Even the personality aspect names themselves, openness and orderliness, usually feel negative to those not strong in them. To many liberals, "dutiful" and "cautious" are almost scary terms— even when they're fairly dutiful or cautious themselves. The words sound as if they entail excluding or ignoring interesting things and following (dull) processes; or being slow; or not chasing excitement; or wasting time; or being exploited. Conservatives generally feel positive about those same words. Being open or imaginative usually sounds unquestionably great to a liberal– those are trait we're religiously committed to developing– but to conservatives, they can mean scattered, wasteful, or risky, an excellent way to show that you have poor common sense, or that you're not practical enough.

There's a spin we put on our language to emphasize the bad side of a trait in a prejudiced way. Diligent sounds better to liberals than dutiful; thorough can sound much better than perfectionist. Being careful about language, and being conscious about how negativity can creep into our assessment of people's traits, has been shown to dramatically improve personality tests, and job screening tests.[7] When we sense that we are reacting negatively to a trait, we should examine our feelings for unwarranted prejudice, because all personality traits are valuable.

Being prejudiced against dutiful, or cautious, or perfectionist behavior is common among liberals, and it can be quite short-sighted. That prejudice itself reveals that you probably aren't strong in the healthy version of that trait, so you don't understand it well enough to judge fairly those who are strong in it– you'll assume, maybe inappropriately, that the traits are being abused somehow, or that they're always a negative. The prejudice itself is a hint of the incomplete nature of your world view– maybe of your political one.

Oddly enough, when we understand a trait well, we are more sympathetic about those who use it more than they should, and we react to the problem more healthily. That may be because we understand a little better how reasonable it is to make the mistake they're making. We can also lead them out of the thicket they're walking into easier. It's as if we're nearer to them, psychically speaking, and can call out a warning they can hear and recognize, as someone who understands them.

Let's also remember, in the midst of wielding these judgments and stereotypes, that they're useful as general guidance, but need to be applied with care. A dramatized biographical movie has been made of Michael Weiss, a brilliant, very conservative activist lawyer who was disorganized, inconsistent and wildly imaginative.[8] One can also be a cautious, orderly liberal that doesn't care a whit about creative pursuits, like one good friend of mine, and many I've interviewed.

Getting Around Personality Conflict

Personality theory offers us a few wonderful opportunities to get out of these personality conflicts that ideology traps us in, and we'll need to stop the carousel a moment to get it right together. Let's look again at some traits that seem to clash between the stereotypical versions of ourselves we're sketching:

Openness	Orderliness
Attentive to Feelings	Rational
Creative	Orderly
Artistic	Deliberate

Those are not opposite traits, though they *feel* like they are. Some of the most interesting and successful people combine personality traits like this that are rare to see together. A successful mountain climber, for instance, should be strong in both adventurousness and cautiousness, juggling traits that aren't entirely well-fitted with one another. Some successful business executives I know are both very orderly and very open, and they find themselves well paid for their ability to balance those two orientations for a whole company.

Part-time Personalities

One strange, universal truth about personality is that almost all of us display flashes of many traits that seem to naturally conflict with one another. Personality is complicated in that wonderful way– miraculous, really. People who combine traits that are so different don't combine them every moment of the day: with some combinations, that's quite difficult, while with others (cautiousness/adventurous), it's impossible. In real life, we go back and forth to get them both done; we do them at different times, sometimes trading off after days or weeks, but other times in scant seconds. We get tired of being the smart guy, the wise guy, the supportive nurse, the cranky grocery clerk; roles also get old for our partners, friends, and children. Traits play off each other in patterns, like a call-and-response, or as an offset. This is how liberals can value variety so much, while being fond of our little rituals– can have complexity and simplicity both as values. That's true for conservatives as well. Many, for instance, have highly complex jobs or hobbies, which satisfy a part-time version of the impulses we've been describing as liberal.

At any moment, we can be quite unpredictable cusses. It's as if there's a container of every trait we have that's inside of us. As we "use" one, it's as if we empty part of the container, but it feels less fun or appropriate after a time; or maybe we use the whole container. We then go down the aisle, browsing our other traits, and find another one to use for awhile.[9] Later, when the first container has filled up again, through our mysterious connection to the fundamental values that drive us, we might go back and dip into it.

Depending how we're built, we may keep what looks like 500 gallons' worth of a trait to pour out on life, and tend to use it almost constantly, while we may have pints or thimblefuls of other traits that we use only briefly, or occasionally. Others of us have 5 gallons' worth of many different traits that seem a little opposed to one another, like paying attention to our feelings and emphasizing rationality; we may swing predictably back to each throughout the day, or switch in fear when our partner gives us the krinkly face. Some traits can be successfully used like spice in a meal: a tiny bit of extra cautiousness by a ski jumper in rough winds can change the arc of her life, by being used at just the right time.

This is one of the most beautiful things about human beings. Shakespeare took advantage of this in his tales; other than the parts where girls were unconvincingly convincing people they were guys, the complexity and unpredictability of his characters have mesmerized and inspired us for centuries, because complexity fleshes them out and makes them believable; they're more interesting because of their variation, and they feel more authentic.

Personality complexity is mostly changeability, or mutability (think mutating). *Personality is statistical*, and it has a random piece to it. We're not as predictable as we think. We only see personality across time in people, and when we describe them, we usually describe a kind of average of their reactions and actions, except when they're prone to dramatic, short periods of intense behavior that dominate our thinking about them.

An even weirder, more confusing part of personality's statistical side is that just because a person has a trait, doesn't mean they express that trait the same way as everyone else does. That's why we don't all show up at the same concerts or same churches; there's tremendous variety in what it means to be, for example, high in orderliness.

I might have narrow or broad expression of a trait. My version of openness might just mean that I like many types of fancypants literature, while I could care less about ballet, or other kinds of reading, or listening to NPR. You might be high in openness in a way that has you chasing all kinds of dance, other kinds of literature, and addicted to NPR in the morning. There's no such thing as pure openness. Our individual traits *combine* in ways that make sense out of the world for each of us alone.

Almost all of us veer greatly from what those who know us think of as our normal personalities, especially in certain conditions, or with particular people, or for short periods of time. Those exceptions can be crucial; they can also be surprisingly useful, random, harmless, or disastrous. That mountaineer spends nearly all of her time being cautious, ambitious, and orderly– planning and training– and then the odd weekend here and there being adventurousness, the risks greatly controlled by her long, careful preparations. Hitler took many baths a day in an attempt to stay clean, which is an obsession that overtakes very orderly people sometimes; but at the dinner table, he revealed a deep knowledge of art and architecture from ongoing studies, and made many wildly imaginative assertions of varying accuracy. The unusual breadth of his personality is certainly one factor behind his story.

A respected banker I worked with spent most of each day in long, disciplined hours of careful analysis, cross-checking data, coding, and plumbing the depths of financial statements— and then intermittently seemed to explode into someone else, employing his great gift for deal structuring, using his creativity and a salesman's gift for communicating with executives. Artist managers and agents are often rabid fans of wildly creative music or art, who are also good with people, and typically exceptional at the industriousness that characterizes most good businessmen.

This unpredictable, situation-based nature of personality can help us immensely. We can tap into those thimblefuls, or pints, or gallons of our own capability for healthy orderliness, industriousness, and the other traits we'll cover, to find a common ground— to truly understand the ins and outs of having their personality, from the inside. I've found it to be largely a matter of practice. Relating to conservative strong traits, even modestly or fitfully, provides an inoculation against some of the worst problems we are capable of causing when working with them. Avoiding the worst bits at sensitive moments is often enough to take advantage of your stronger traits, and get things clipping along rather well.

Beyond the mechanical learning of the ideological traits, this effort of gaining an *emotional understanding* of their perspective is a little stranger process than we might think. These traits of ours aren't exactly what they seem. Remember that personality is a mask: it's the bridge between our values and the world. So when people say we're expressing our personalities, that's deceptive: what we're actually doing is expressing our values through this rough-edged, flexible tool, our personality.

That difference is important, for a couple of reasons. Humans have many, many values that don't have to do with ideology, so at any given time, our personality is providing expressions of all kinds of things, often in a changing mixture, through the various amounts of personality traits we keep to express them.

We also mix personality traits in a thousand and one ways depending on the situation, so that impatience, emotional sensitivity, and a sense of humor combine to address a slow barista in a certain way. And we have the capability, at any given time, of being quite different than how we usually see ourselves. It's normal to go off-script, especially for liberals. We seldom acknowledge how inconsistent we are, and we almost never acknowledge a vital truth: **we should be inconsistent, so we can be our best selves**. Changeability is usually more of a strength than a weakness, unless you have an explosive anger problem, or anxiety attacks.

Instead of being controlled by a trait that crops up too often, or surprisingly, you can voluntarily develop capabilities that give you options to choose another response. Our personalities can change our whole lives, and only about half of it is explained through inheritance; that leaves room for possibility to leak in at the edges, especially if we remember that sometimes, we only need to change a little, for a little while, to make all the difference.

We all express the conservative values that we may not specialize in, even if we do it in small ways. Usually, when the traits do show up in us, we express them very differently than how we usually see them used by conservatives. There's some very good news that provides: **if we express those same, somewhat uncomfortable values, but in our own small or large way, it can provide us deep insights into conservatives**. I don't mean deep insights as in you could lecture about it for an hour; I mean deep in the sense of getting some kind of gut sense or feel of what having strong boundaries might be like for them, or a sense of dutifulness. You might not even be able to articulate what you learned through expressing those values, because such things are often inexpressible, but that doesn't make the realizations less real, or less valuable.

That's perfectly fuzzy, no doubt, so let's try an example. Because I am often upset about the conservative focus on certainty, consistency, and simplicity, and I know I'm low in certain aspects of orderliness, I have tried to think in those terms more. Maybe I only have pint-sized jars for the traits that take care of those values for me. I have other values– complexity, excitement, variability– that can conflict with those values, and they get a vat's worth of attention. We keep those lesser jars in the back of the room, and either ignore them or make fun of them. We might even go punch holes in those jars so they never fill up.

Instead, because I've learned that I'm relatively weak in the related personality traits within orderliness, I assume that I have ways of not caring about those values as much as I should, so that I distort and misunderstand them to some degree. This doesn't mean that I go vote Republican awhile: it means that *any* extra focus on those healthy values in my life makes me more well-rounded, and brings me a little bit closer to the conservative mindset, the same way that practicing my tennis serve, even a little, brings me that much closer to beating my friend Tyko. The English psychologist Daniel Nettle calls this effort going "against the spin," meaning you're working against your natural inclination. You want to do it enough to reduce the distortion, rationalization, and blindness caused by being relatively weak in a trait.

Driving Me Crazy

My kids and their friends use their safety belts without even thinking about it. But for me, it's been a huge hurdle to buckle up reliably. You're probably as good at it as they are– bully for you– but I had to get used to being inferior to a frank, rotating panel of 9-year-olds on the morning school run, often before the sun was up.

I can't tell you how much help that simple struggle with the dang safety belt has been toward understanding not just the value of certainty, consistency, and simplicity in my own life, but also, how lousy I am at chasing those values.

Buckling up seems to be the simplest thing in the world, and yet, even now, after years of this exercise– years of thinking about it multiple times a day– I only get the belt on before I drive away about half the time. Those failures help me understand how I'm fully capable of ignoring the basics in life to zoom off toward a goal in a big hurry; how I move through life wrapped up in details, and worries, and ideas, when I should be *certain* to do something *simple*, right in front of me, *consistently*– a thing as close to life-and-death fundamental as pops up in our day-to-day meanderings. I also hear myself talk about how important my health is to me, but I have to recognize, daily, that I ignore a four-second process that could rather instantly end any concerns about my health. Which makes me either an engine of irony, or two-faced, I'm not sure which.

There are a couple of useful results of consciously reminding ourselves about how weak we are in expressing some of our good values, the ones that are overshadowed by our favorites. For one thing, I have had thousands of safety-belt promptings to use those parts of my personality healthily in the last 5 years, which is having an effect. I'm probably halfway there, no matter what my kids say.

For another thing, when I have told this story to my conservative acquaintances, they get so, so happy. It makes them feel as if they've witnessed a great change in my life. This was mystifying at first, but now it's fun. They're looking at my face, but they're seeing a three-day-old conservative carrot sprout, with its first little green leaf appearing from under a dangling, dried seed shell. They look roughly as happy as if I had told them that I was voting Republican, because they're excited that I'm acknowledging one of their most important values, and that I'm working on it. It seems that simple for them. I think that, from their standpoint, watching me roll through life my normal way is like watching someone walk with two peg legs. They see instantly the connection between trying to develop an essential habit about personal safety and trying to do the right thing in a bigger way. They seem confident that I'm going to end up a much better person through the effort.

They don't even seem to care that much about the rest of the story, that I'm not much better at it after years of trying, or that my politics might be getting even worse, by their standard, not better. They know I'm liberal, and that I'll always take up space meant for useful people; they're just thrilled that I care enough to try to be more like them, even in that modest way.

This particular effort has taught me a thing or two about orderliness I didn't know, too. In the first few years, I noticed that I remembered the belt, and would tell myself "Good for me; I remembered! I'll put it on now, right after I finish with my next coffee sip." And then I'd forget about the belt instantly, because I was in the middle of fiddling with the radio or getting directions, or drinking coffee. I may as well have never remembered the belt, for all the problems I had getting it on. I had to create a complicated rule about how long I had, and how I couldn't think about anything else once I remembered it, and I couldn't ignore it unless I was a hundred yards or less from where I was going. Over a few years, I got pretty good at using that rule, until I rarely left it off after remembering it.

Which was all fine, except that it was engineered, complicated "orderliness", not like the easy version orderly people, liberal or conservative, do all day long. One day, it hit me: people being orderly about something don't put it off– ever– *and* they don't use any of the tricks I was using. That's– amazing. In at least some specific, skinny part of their life, they've actually *slaughtered procrastination* in their lives; murdered it. Just by pouring their vat of orderliness all over it. That felt miraculous to me; it still does.

About the fifth year, I discovered that the habit of putting the belt on after I remembered it was so strong that I had stopped having the tiny conversation I was used to having, something along the lines of, "Do I really have to?, ok, how about we get around the corner/get done with this song/finish my sandwich?, then I'll put the belt on." I'd beaten procrastination; not by being iron-willed, but by building a habit that allowed me to be as mindless as a conservative about the rule. No deep thinking happened anymore; remembering equaled mindless obedience, so that the two were combined immediately and unquestioningly into one thing in my mind. Like every other driver on the planet. I learned something crucial about what good orderliness is. I don't know what it is, exactly, except that I'm more healthily mindless than I was.

Since then, I've developed a better understanding of how powerful, and comforting, and lulling it can be to treat large portions of life "mindlessly" in this way. If one has that as a gift, I can see better how much persuasion might be necessary to shift off that kind of approach to life, because it has so many advantages. Not only do I sympathize more, but I also understand better how many political stances may just be a kind of weird back-end of not having a problem with procrastination.

The most lasting effect of this and other small habits for improving my weakness are emotional: I truly understand better, *as a feeling*, what valuing orderliness feels like, even though I'm crummy at most angles of it. That's not a lesson one can pick up by reading about it, but only through experience, the kind of lesson that comes through bits of time and attention piling up gradually. This silly, small effort has given me *much more patience* with people who I view as too orderly. They repeat to me over and over how vital the rules are, or how they followed procedure so it had to be ok, or they wipe the spotless counter down for the fifteenth time– and none of it bothers me nearly as much as it used to.

More generally, going against the spin lets me appreciate better how tricky it is to balance my strengths against my weaknesses correctly, when we are so bad at seeing our weaknesses. I'm less cocky about my version of that balance.

I have a few of these quite minor stretches into my weaker traits playing out in my life now. People should do this slight stretch against the spin about all kinds of weaknesses; mine I'm describing here are only different from general improvements that anyone makes in their lives because I use them on purpose to help me ponder the conservative values behind them. I take them as a momentary opportunity to meditate on what those foundations to their humanity feel like to conservatives (though one doesn't have to think of it in terms of our evil twin: after all, I'm just working on personality weaknesses I can't deny anymore). The appropriate efforts will be different for you, depending on your own personality sins.

I try to make my signature readable instead of brrrpping a random squiggle after the first letter or two: an effort at simplicity and consistency I find remarkably difficult. I try to work off a to-do list religiously, and fail; spend a little time every day on several family-related communications (instead of the ignore-then-spray method of interaction that's much more natural for me); religiously turn to look when changing lanes, instead of using the mirror, just as they teach in driving school; and eat a salad a day, in an effort to be more certain about hanging out for kids, grandkids, and the greatgrandies after that. None of these are earthshakingly difficult, and none of them seem, on their surface, to have a thing to do with being conservative. Yet stretching my life in small ways has helped me link more strongly to values I don't effortlessly frame my life around. They also help me whine about conservatives much less, since I know I'd make such a lousy one.

The point isn't for you to become conservative. That would cause me pain near my pancreas, and it'd ruin your chances with attractive liberals. The point is to work a little at understanding what the values behind orderliness mean; what a bite-sized part of orderliness means *just for you*. Like detail-orientation, or consistency, or a healthy boundary with a co-worker, or any orderliness trait you're weak in. These tiny forays into their territory end up much more useful when we're with conservatives than any idea you might've had about posing as a wielder of traditional values, or "framing" liberal ideas for conservatives, or bludgeoning their beliefs to death with facts. You'll have gained a small measure of what amounts to a common emotional language about their values, which helps everything along enormously.

You don't even have to change much; it's the thinking through the notion of, say, dutifulness, while you're doing your lame attempt at it, that makes the difference. That effort lets you **talk**, with real interest and real appreciation, about subjects that touch on dutifulness, whether or not you know much about the value, and whether or not you're any good at it. Talk of that kind is what makes up some of the best moments of a conservative life, day in and day out; words and detail and repetition about church, kids, the job, the Dallas Cowboys, and the mess-ups and whatnot of real life, all with the feel of a kind of hymn to those conservative values.

I'd go crazy if I had to think in that way all day like they do so easily. To a liberal, that can feel like being a traditional Mexican music bassist, smiling and bouncing between the same two notes; the song stops, and another begins, and there you are, knocking out C and G again, trying to smile in your suit. But we **like** to do it intermittently, for as long as our pint jar of being detail-minded, for instance, still has something in it.

This *is* a language we're discussing, by the way, like Swedish is a language: we use different concepts and words than normally when we use the language of conservatism, and we emphasize those words differently. Studies have shown that the same words get processed by completely different parts of the brain when we approach them so differently, so in some ways, it's even harder than learning a new language, because it sounds exactly like our language. At first, it's *supposed* to feel awkward to be translating; it's supposed to make your head hurt, and leave you feeling like you need a nap. That's what using a new language is like. Then you see the happy expression on their face when you croak out something that sounds a little like you're trying to be orderly, and it's all worth it.

It's true that the dramatic examples above of combining potentially clashing personality traits successfully are from the lives of exceptional people, like gifted leaders, or underwater divers, or self-made millionaires. But modest versions, like making headway with just this kind of ideological personality conflict, are done by almost every person on earth. I'm actually expanding my personality with these little exercises. Perhaps it doesn't make a big difference in my life, but I'm not sure. I don't think we *can* know if such changes make a difference, unless something dramatic happens, like I get in a wreck and stay alive because my kids are so wrong, because I really am putting on my belt more. But the struggle certainly makes me a more broad-minded person, with a slightly expanded set of values. Which turns out to be quite practical in the communication department.

We've found an oddly parallel structure in both ideological clumps of personality traits. Both ideologies test as roughly equivalent in industriousness, yet conservatives use high orderliness as a way to "supercharge" their industriousness, inspiring them to make industriousness, or conscientiousness in general, the driving force of their perspective (to keep important processes working well). Liberals do an almost opposite trick, using our high openness to use our intellect in so many different, inspiring ways that we place intellect at the center of our perspective (to find and focus on important exceptions to processes).[10] We've also learned how to use the two principles of personality strengths and weaknesses to better understand both conservative foundational values and our own personality weaknesses, by stretching ourselves to spend more of our time with our own orderliness, and by trying to listen to conservative complaints about us when they're likely to have at least partial insights.

We're ready now for the last three ideological aspects of personality. Just as we saw here, we'll be proud of ourselves sometimes, and squirm a bit in our chairs at other times, but we'll make a great start into the pitfalls and opportunities of working well with conservatives, as we begin to fold in how communication styles and our emotional lives affect this effort.

Chapter Four

PERSONALITY– FINISHING SCHOOL

*Knowing human nature for a mixture of
good and evil, the conservative does not
put his trust in mere benevolence.*

-Russell Kirk, 10 Conservative Principles

ORDERLINESS AND OPENNESS are maybe two-thirds of the
personality game in ideology, so congrats; that last chapter got you
most of the way to understanding our main personality differences. Most
of what's left is critical to understand for proper communication and
good relations– the social portions of our task. These will be found in the
Big Five personality factor *Agreeableness*.

In several early studies of ideology and personality, agreeableness was
shown to be the same for liberals and conservatives. Then, in 2010,
researchers discovered[1] that the two aspects that make up agreeableness,
compassion and **politeness**, were very different for us, and those
differences were canceling each other out under the covers.

The first finding was that liberals are significantly more
compassionate: we describe ourselves that way, but we're also scored as
more compassionate by people who know us, on statements like "He's
interested in other people's feelings." It's a strong, significant finding, as
personality effects go.[2] Nice news for the good guys, right? Not
unexpected, though.

Politeness

The bad news is that conservatives were found to be higher in
politeness. That one's hard to swallow. We get that we're more
compassionate than them; that's a no-brainer, since that fits right in with
our usual, mostly unconscious, stupid-evil-crazy theory of conservatism.

But, come awwwn! More polite than us? No freaking way.

And we've got a killer little set of arguments against that idea. Let's start with the obvious: look at the teeming parade of rude conservatives on Fox, whining and moaning and screaming and pouting. Then there's all the threat-sensitivity stuff we see from their emphasis on security— that the world is a dangerous place; it's a jungle out there; bad guys are just out of sight, stalking around, trying to find a kid to rape. You're trying to tell me, Scott, that these fans of crazy prison sentences, who keep loaded guns by their bed, are the polite ones? Did your statistics degree[3] come in a Cracker Jacks box? Was it wrapped around gum?

This odd conundrum around the wrinkle of politeness is surprisingly critical to understand and use; if you can shove this all the way down into your deep mushy parts, I'll give you a third of the points for your Conservative Wrangler certification.

Let's get the Fox News jackasses out of the way first. Studies show that TV pundits and politicians are *way* more ideological than we humans. It's also easy to forget that *they're in the business of entertaining us, to keep us there so we'll watch another commercial.* They're good at pretending like their news is important, when it's usually either gossip or making mountains out of molehills. They probably have a rude quota. How entertaining do you think it'd be— how many erectile dysfunction pills would they sell— if people heard this, as their squirrel brain switched channels:

> —...given the tensions involved?
> —Oh, I'm so glad you asked that question, Millicent. Let's look at those interlocking treaty agreements from the Scandinavian standpoint, which we just don't do enou-

They'd throw their shoe at the screen, yell at the platinum-blonde talking head, and buy somebody else's pills. I think we overestimate the inaccuracies of Fox News, but the emphasis and focus are quite unrelenting. "Look at Fox News!" is rarely good advice to analyze conservatives. They're rude on there because conservatives that watch Fox like watching rudeness, whether they're practitioners of rudeness or not (most aren't, but they like the spicy competitiveness).

Now: threat-sensitivity. This is the real meat of the issue. Do you remember what orderly people do when they're troubled by something? What do they have that we haven't got? Those astonishingly thick *boundaries.* They worry about how we're screwing up the world, and then— they don't worry about it. When they're not worrying about the world being a toilet flush away from death, it turns out that these supposedly agonized people are quite busy being polite, often spectacularly so.

My experience in a variety of mixed ideology settings strongly supports the research that the traits that make up politeness as defined in the Big Five– cooperation, pleasantness, compliance, straightforwardness, and modesty– are all, hands-down, more common in conservatives, no matter what you see among politicians or conservative commentators. The conservative parts of the Midwest and South are justifiably famous for being warm, friendly cultures. You can be mean, if you like, and say they are only that way among themselves, but even that doesn't dent the fact that they're quite warm and polite in their normal dealings in life– because they tend to hang out among themselves.

Politeness works hand-in-hand with conscientiousness in a clear, practical way, to support the traditional, hierarchical groups that conservatives are known for, socially and in business. It shouldn't be considered controversial that, on balance, politeness traits would be more important to them. It would be odd to be parochial, or rural and local-oriented, and yet less polite at the same time. As one New Zealand research team explained, politeness is an effort to *conform to cooperative efforts* of a group we're a part of.[4]

I lied earlier about their high politeness being bad news; it's actually fantastic news. Think about what it means to have a person you're trying to get along with who 1) is probably more polite than you, and 2) might use those big, thick boundaries of theirs to suck you into their in-crowd, or ingroup, *just by being warm and friendly with them.*

That's huge! It's as if someone left the back door ajar, and the guard dog's in the front yard. I'm not saying you should take advantage of people, but being nice, and having someone be nice back who might've been in a fight with you otherwise, isn't taking advantage of someone. *Go in the back door if you can.* You can always have a fight later over your differences, if you like. The point is that, because they're incredibly polite often, and, unbeknownst to many liberals, they're often quite naturally inclusive (that's also part of politeness), you can be part of the ingroup before they see your tattoo of a dog with Reagan's face. **And** you have a real shot at staying in the ingroup, even after your horrible politics get discovered, if you've behaved yourself. Remember: politics doesn't matter that much to most people, but also, even if they do matter, conservatives can be quite big-hearted, and overlook massive flaws, like your liberalness, in people that are already in their ingroup.

Another advantage I didn't appreciate is their example during conversations. I'm a fairly polite person, especially with conservatives, but I'm usually the less polite person in the conversation. I think this politeness advantage of theirs, which looks modest or medium statistically, is quite reliable and helpful. You know right away when it doesn't apply, too. When I get a little upset or inattentive, as typically happens more quickly for liberals, I can usually rely on them to be more even-keeled, and help me not capsize us with errors. There are big exceptions, of course: crotchety, mean-spirited, know-it-all conservatives aren't rare, but I've found their numbers to be exaggerated.

Politeness has a down side: it can be deceptive. Yes, conservatives can be nice *and* deceptive, like anyone who's polite, since part of being polite can be glossing over unpleasantness, even to the point of not being entirely truthful. That may be why some researchers think there's a natural tendency to be either very polite or very empathic, the way we see the ideologies statistically specializing in one or the other. Often, polite people won't let you know you're off-putting, because they aren't always direct or blunt that way. Don't assume that their warmth will save you if you mess up. With some, you can tell you've erred, though it may be a muted tightness; they don't stop smiling, they just smile less, and less enthusiastically. With others, though, there's almost no way to tell. Don't try risky topics, or get too informal, and then say to yourself "Wow, they're still smiling and friendly– they thought that was *cool!* They want more. If I was a kid, they'd adopt me!"

Politeness doesn't let you take chances with them, and it doesn't mean they'll love you. It means they're good in social settings, and they'll give you a chance. It doesn't mean you begin to think of them as your aunt and uncle right away, even though they're some of the warmest, nicest people you've ever met (though that may happen over time). Politeness is a great advantage when reaching out to them, but a certain reserve, respect, and care still needs to be used. People who are very empathic can translate politeness into closeness a little too easily.

Compassion

Compassion, as defined here, means having feelings of warmth, understanding, empathy, and tenderness. Conservatives tend to think of compassionate feelings as important, but as part of their moral toolbox rather than the end-all, be-all of morality; they'd tell you that feelings of compassion have to be balanced against other values to do the right thing. This attitude is tied to their orderly tendency to find and balance the elements of a situation; compassion goes in a bucket, like everything else, and gets used when they think best.

Thinking of compassion as only a logical sub-category of doing the right thing is maddening for us: it seems to be almost an opposite of what it means to care. Their conscientiousness influences them to be very careful with the idea of compassion, so that it's *effective*. They might tell you that they don't care how strongly you feel about an injustice, if you can't do anything useful about it. They weave compassion and effectiveness together much more instinctively than we do, through their strength in conscientiousness. This outlook is why many conversations about an injustice with conservatives have a "Yeah, but" quality to them: they might recognize that compassion is critical– but they also see how ignoring other aspects of what's going on can make that compassion impotent, or even counter-productive.

Our inspirational hemispheres play into this eternal argument. The right hemisphere, in the words of one researcher, "is dominant in the processing of emotional information."[5] This is one of the most well-studied differences in the hemispheres. The right hemisphere is dominant in interpreting emotional facial signals, maybe because of its close connection to visual processing, and the "picture," immediate method of grasping reality; conservatives have been shown to be weaker at understanding facial emotional cues.[6] The right hemisphere hears emotional information in voices better, and helps greatly with emotional parts of humor.

Because emotion signals are such an crucial part of the picture for the right hemisphere, as we liberals depend on that interpretation of reality, a strong emotional response can dominate the "picture" we experience. We *feel*. The other details of the situation can seem like fuzzy background, or even blacked out.

That's what happens to me, often; focusing on emotion through my empathy is one of the main ways I experience myself highlighting important exceptions in life. This is what happened to me when I watched the 29-minute video of Esa Wroth being held by deputies: his suffering was almost all I could see. Contrast that with my conservative acquaintance's viewpoint, who effectively said, "Yeah, but there are many other factors at play here," and he patiently went through the list of details he saw me ignoring. I don't doubt that he's roughly as compassionate in life as I am, give or take. But he tallies up the world into logical pieces, and then weighs them all together to understand what happened.

This is a good place to pause and ask the question: which of us sees the "big picture"? That turns out to be a loaded question. I don't think there's a useful answer to that question, or, at least, not one that will satisfy all situations. In this case, my own view seems quite narrowly focused, while the conservative is looking and weighing many more factors. From his perspective, I concentrated on a tree in the forest; from my perspective, the big picture involved seizing on what mattered in the "picture," rather than getting bogged down with aspects of the process that didn't matter, or weren't in play.

I think it's *preferable* to do what conservatives do, in theory; to weigh out all the factors carefully seems so sensible and balanced, and it appeals to my analytical side. It certainly doesn't make sense to me, at first blush, that one part of the story should automatically dominate, just because it's the emotional aspect. The problem I have with conservatives doing it their way, though, is that I often experience it as counting a few trees that have almost nothing to do with the "forest". What's funny is that conservatives will say the exact same thing, and it works at least as well, logically. After all, from their standpoint, I ignored the values of good law enforcement by focusing on the "tree" of the suffering of a drunk who broke the law and acted dangerously.

I don't want you to think that the difference is that conservatives have a detailed approach of building up a case, and that liberals wing it. Other examples, like health care or gun control, show liberals using a tremendous amount of logic and detail to build their case, and conservatives mostly sticking with a simpler, emotional argument. It's not a question of who talks the most, or even who uses more logic: it's about who is driven to highlight important exceptions, often through empathy, and who is driven by an attempt to balance factors that highlight or protect important processes (like insurance choice, the status quo, fiscal safety for the majority, and maintaining the nation's emphasis on personal responsibility). Both sides use logic and emotion to propel their arguments and thinking, but one is largely motivated by empathy (like health care for all), and the other balances a broader range of interests that usually includes empathy, but isn't dominated by it.

Which viewpoint is correct? Our actual, working lives provide an interesting solution. Let's move to a less overtly ideological example, where we've explained to our young daughter how her selfish behavior hurt her little brother, and she just burst into tears and ran to her room. One of us is energized and triggered by the intense, immediate, emotional information; that empathic part of us might want to hug her, or tell her it's alright. But the stay-at-home parent says, "Hold on– the fact that she's upset doesn't mean she's learned the lesson she needs to. We can't leap to that conclusion. Exhibit B is that she cried the last 4 times she did this today. And Exhibit C is that she's laughing in her room right now."

We do this kind of weighing out between dry facts and emotional information all day long. In our real life, there's a negotiation between emotional information and other information that can be very involved, because it's weighing out apples and oranges.

It's true that our ideology can often be apparent in how we weigh out evidence, like the example with a con artist daughter. But it's a weighing out nevertheless. The problem with the liberal, right hemisphere-inspired view when looking at things like police brutality is that it's a little like saying only the orange of empathy matters, while the conservative, left hemisphere method is like saying an orange is just one of the apples, so we can fold the orange into the spreadsheet easily, and figure out what to do. This conservative categorization approach would be perfect with the con-artist daughter, but it might be very wrong in a given police brutality situation, like some of the murders that occurred by police, almost all unrequited by justice, as victims died asking for their father, crying for their mother, or begging to be allowed to breathe. The liberal intense emphasis on emotional or empathic information would've been a problem with the con-artist daughter, but will be just right elsewhere.

If we were perfect human beings, we'd all count up the apples and oranges, and then deal with the discomfort of the fact that they have to be weighed against each other. But what does that even mean? Ultimately, this is a classic confrontation between the general and the scout, the left and right hemispheres, who have almost zero shared references for doing things. A couple of world views have to duke it out, often in a natural conflict between emotional and more factual information.

And yeah– the general wins way too much. Gotta *do* something about that, people. But neither hemisphere-inspired perspective is perfectly good enough alone to do life right. While the right hemisphere view of life is like a real-time, real-life image that tries to get at the gist of the exceptions that need highlighting, that doesn't mean that it necessarily captures truth in an absolute sense, the way people usually assume when they use the word "gestalt," or "holistic," as if one way of interpreting reality had a magic lock on sacred, complete insight. There are no rules in that world view; you make it up as you go along, based on what's happening, like the father tried to do with the con-artist daughter.

At the same time, modeling and categorizing accurately, so you can see the process properly and balance things, may leave you with a view of a situation that's piecemeal, lifeless, and inaccurate. Both viewpoints make errors in priority and accuracy, each in their own way. Both can, and do, create improper balance, strange ironies, and poor morals.

Ultimately, the limits of my own perspective are the reason why I chose to spend a great deal of time with my conservative acquaintance watching the brutality video multiple times, building up the detail of his outline of the way the process of prisoner containment and officer safety needed to happen. I only needed to watch any 10 seconds of the video to get my "gestalt," or overall grasp, of the main issue as being cruelty, but I wanted to hear his perspective, both to learn, and to find out if there was some hidden, fruitful conversation possible about some part of it, some part I couldn't see yet.

It dawned on me during the conversation that, if I was going to declare the deputy actions wrong, that I needed to be able to detail a reasonable alternative method of holding Mr. Wroth, and I couldn't do that, at first. Finding out that I didn't have a good grasp of that reasonable alternative was valuable, and not because it would help me to slam-dunk the argument. It was the middle ground in the case I was looking for; deputies could've managed a much safer and less cruel approach, that would've served both the police and the prisoner better. Being able to focus on that mechanical set of changes gave us something practical to focus on together, much closer to an alignment of our values. I had been closed off to a process-driven viewpoint: stepping through the problem with a conservative gave us both a useful step ahead, even though it wasn't where he'd wanted to go (his position was that there was nothing else that the deputies could've done).

As is often the case with conservatives, conversations we think should be about compassion, because we're talking about real victims and unnecessary suffering, can be turned into another way of stating that personal responsibility is very important. This cold-vs-hot, emotional-vs-not conflict comes up in parenting constantly, as we try to balance the competing values of justice and mercy, or independence and control.

But there's another reason conservatives also doubt our reliance on compassion: the weakness of many liberals with process and consistency. We are relatively strong in using our intellect, imagination, and empathy to assess a situation as needing improvement: those are the earliest tasks in any project. Are we as good at designing how to do what we want done– at doing the work that gets the goal done? What about the maintenance, once it's become something on a checklist, and all the newness is squeezed out of it? Not necessarily.

Let's detour over into efficiency a moment, because conservatives are all over us about it, when it comes to compassion; sometimes fairly, sometimes less so. It's a bit of a snarl, and we need to get it right.

Plenty of Blame for Everyone

Americans fail at achieving success with challenging projects for all kinds of personality-driven, cognitive and motivational reasons. There's a bias related to this failure: the planning fallacy. This bias has personal and group versions; in both cases, we consistently underestimate how hard it is to get things done.

In my work as a consultant effecting change in large corporations, I found clients typically badly underestimated the cost of projects, thinking it would cost half or less of what it ended up, and requiring about 50% more time, as well, unless they'd done a similar project before. Broader, replicated research supports this overconfidence amount as a good thumb rule. The error is so huge because of a universal combination of overconfidence, political/social pressures, bureaucracy, complexity's surprises, and the fact that life's unknowns lurk just outside the door, ready to unleash a 200-year flood, or terminal cancer, or a lousy programming team whose code was thought to be fine.

Most businesses try to pretend the project fallacy doesn't exist, and then they manufacture a big surprise and drama out of it acting as usual. Some fields don't get to think of the planning fallacy as an intellectual curiosity, though, or something they can afford to be surprised by: they simply must account for the planning fallacy due to risk of deaths. In nuclear engineering, they do an incredible amount of labor to get their design of, say, a containment wall thickness accurate– then, after all that detailed analysis, they stick a massive, mindless "safety factor" on top, that typically roughly doubles the wall thickness, purely to account for the planning fallacy. This sounds unscientific, especially after all that complicated math to get at the original thickness; yet they don't hesitate, because many generations of engineers learned the hard way that the planning fallacy extends deeply into every complex human endeavor. It would be unscientific to ignore the planning fallacy, even though it *seems* unscientific or irrational to an outsider.

The optimism of ignoring the planning fallacy regularly destroys whole companies. But this fallacy is even worse with political ideas, because political science may be the most interdisciplinary, hairdo-driven, and money-soaked of all fields, making it essentially designed for faulty planning. And, of course, there is no planning fallacy allowed in politics: how could there be? It's just a question of who's in charge. If the bad guys do it, it'll be a disaster; if we do it, it'll be done perfectly, by the day after tomorrow, latest. So vote for us.

Most of the complexity is *purposely* invisible in politics, too, for sales purposes. We like to substitute planning and expertise with moral thuggery and ringing pronouncements. We do this to reduce the feeling of uncertainty in voters, provide ourselves with a clear path temporarily, and to express our highest ideals.

The planning fallacy is Exhibit 1 for where focusing on morals or ideology misses the mark. Probably the main reason why wars are started, governments and charities fail, and individual accidents occur can be found swishing around in the guts of the planning fallacy:

someone got convinced that what they wanted was easy and safe to get, based on what turned out to be poor evidence.

Because of the planning fallacy, the hurdles between *feeling* compassionate and getting compassion *done well* are quite great. Of course, being conservative doesn't seem to improve your planning skills: being overly focused on order can help you argue yourself into an unnecessary war, and muck up the invasion and occupation, with the planning fallacy evident at every turn (many good books have been written that provide excruciating detail of the terrible mistakes of the Iraq occupation strategy, as the planning fallacy ground "10 or 20 billion dollars" steadily into over 2 trillion dollars of war expense.)

But the conservative weakness with the planning fallacy doesn't clear us of our own noteworthy potential weakness, one they should be able to provide input on. It's no argument to say, "They're just as bad as us!" If anything, their personality weaknesses with planning are the best evidence that ours exist.

One reason liberals might be weak at executing on plans is our strong interest in novelty itself. Our interest in important exceptions unfolds through our strong openness: combine that sensitivity or imagination with compassion or empathy, and it's relatively easy for us to feel strong emotion around suffering. We do it day in and day out as liberals. But **acting** on that charitable impulse requires traits in conscientiousness, traits that often don't come as natural to us.

Liberals don't even give to non-religious charity as much as conservatives that make the same income,[7] nor do we volunteer as much, despite our significantly higher compassionate feelings. I absolutely hate those statistics; you should, too. Somewhere between the feeling and the execution, we don't finish the job as often as our dutiful, list-bound compatriots. Our money isn't where our mouth is.

This is closely related to the second most mentioned lesson that conservatives all over America told me they wish they could get across to liberals: **they deeply resent being told they're not compassionate** . Actually, that's the short, sweet version of what I've been regaled with, in excruciating, sometimes hard-to-rebut detail.

There are a few things going on here. First is that they're actually relatively weak in compassion, which we can especially see when the situation in question is somewhere removed from their normal lives, like Africa, or, to be only a bit mean, any class of people or animal or geography that isn't in or near their lap. This has to do with orderliness, with categorizations, in that boundaries between their people and everyone else are thick, to keep things consistent and simple, and to follow natural hierarchies. There are circles that have thicker and thicker walls, going out from, first, around me, then around my family, then my neighborhood, my church, my county, my state, and my country.

This is part of being parochial, of being local in interests and motivations. Conservatives have a million ways of justifying this parochialism, most of which I completely buy off on. Much research shows human beings are far less compassionate with those we don't know, decreasing with the distance they are from our experience. This is another way that we're all just more or less conservative, in that the local, the near, the reachable have much greater resonance for human beings. Conservatives just carry this boundary-making further than we do.

Their main justification for not acting far from their parochial concerns is the human truth that we care more about what is closest to us because that's where we have the most control– no argument there. They then usually leap from that reasonable point all the way to, "therefore, we stick with our own," which is more order and boundaries than compassion talking. Some of the greatest needs, and the easiest to fill, can be far away from our own lives, and cheap, and easy, given good management; it's left to those who are relatively high in compassion, with thinner boundaries (less ordered) to chase those needs down, and do our best to fulfill them. We will often get little help from them on such fronts.

Their retort is that it's difficult to do charity effectively far from home, when you don't know what needs doing, you don't know how to do it, and you don't know if the natives even want it; plus, they point out, it's a liberal-inspired effort, so we'll screw it up, because that's what we do. This argument varies between either overwhelmingly insightful, or a mindless copout, depending on the situation. Sometimes, both seem true.

Thick boundaries don't explain lower feelings of compassion within their ingroup. Research isn't clear about ingroup compassion with conservatives, but another effect may be in play in their ingroup. Recent work[8] shows that conservatives sometimes reduce or even deliberately ignore their natural feelings of compassion when deciding how to respond, and it's not always a conscious effort. This is another way we see them balancing compassion with other values. I believe that's very common for them; that they may have a great deal of compassion for their children, for instance, but they deliberately blunt those feelings sometimes to try to do the right thing with them.

Conservatives want to be recognized as compassionate, because they're generally caring human beings. That's a reasonable wish; after all, they're only relatively low in compassion, and it's not as overwhelming a difference as is found between the two of us with openness. The hemispheric specialization they picked to inspire them has them a step removed from the emotional orientation of most liberals.

They recognize and feel the emotion, and get motivated by it, though, so they're quietly lining up to volunteer or contribute monthly to problems like disaster relief, or fostering children, or church services. It's that set-and-forget, matter-of-factness of their orderly approach which makes the race for effective compassion like watching the tortoise and the hare, at least in in local charity efforts. In case you missed it, we're the hare.

In contrast, we value and trust the early and loud expression of our compassion. For us, the whole process of analyzing logical points that need to be weighed, analyzed against who-knows-what, and factored in dispassionately can feel artificial, and too removed from the initial impetus to do good. But that doesn't change the hard truth that the conservative strength in orderliness means they might well use the lower compassion they have to kick our butts on the compassion playing field, *if* they choose to suit up and play.

Hard to hear? Yes. Overstated? Maybe– sometimes. Untrue? No, not at all. In keeping with the first principal of personality strengths and weaknesses, conservatives can easily recognize this weakness in us. Their strength in orderliness, and the way they value industriousness, allows them to see our weakness in executing on our compassion.

This hard truth is an intuitive result of the dynamics of personality. In chess terms, liberals are great at the opening game, and conservatives are weaker; and maybe we hold our own in the middle game, but there's strong evidence that our end game needs work, where traits of conscientiousness and politeness need to kick in. Conscientiousness should be paired as much as possible with empathy; it allows **effective compassion**, as opposed to the half, three-quarter, and one-eighth versions of it we liberals often dole out to our parched charities (particularly, ironically, the ones far removed from our own interests).

Hopefully, we can see how each of us struggle with compassion in our own way, and see the strengths and weaknesses of both versions.

Neuroticism

The final personality trait that impacts ideology a great deal is a tricky one, less straightforward than compassion and politeness. It's commonly called neuroticism, or, more politely, it's inverse, stability. To the modern person, neurotic means mild-to-medium crazy– not a very helpful term. But neuroticism is important and more precise: it's a measure of both how much we vary in mood, and how sensitive we are. Some mentally ill people are high in neuroticism, and some are low. Having emotional and personality variability is a *good* thing, and being a sensitive person is a *good* thing, even if we like to pretend that being even-steven always about everything is ideal. Being average in neuroticism is a good thing, because it means you can adapt to circumstances more flexibly, which helps you have a higher quality life. Like any other trait, though, one can go overboard both ways: we can be unemotional or insensitive to influence, or we can be moody, and emotional, letting the world get to us too much.

Liberals score higher than conservatives in neuroticism. Some researchers neglect this difference, because it's a smaller effect than the others we've discussed. But even tiny differences in personality can have a large effect in real life, and this one means something. For one thing, this difference in personality explains part of the difference in happiness between liberals and conservatives, because people low in neuroticism are less affected by problems, and have more consistent lives, less affected by the world; those with high neuroticism struggle to maintain their tranquility more under stress, so they're typically less happy.[9] For another thing, some researchers speculate that liberals are less likely to ignore injustice or other societal problems, because their social environment can have more of an impact on them.[10]

Neuroticism creates an intensity that can make us impolite or intense or miserable under pressure. If you want to see a sample of a high neuroticism crowd, drop by your average police brutality protest; check out some of the lyrics of the chants: "The whole damn system is guilty as hell!" These are not subtle requests my co-conspirators are making, typically with a phalanx of police glowering at them from nearby. They can get spitting mad and rather dramatic, but they're not consistently mean people. They're people who get worked up, who get intense. Many of my more neurotic activist friends are a delight to be around generally. Just try not to get them mad at you.

It's not all down side with excitability. On the contrary, they're the ones who show up for the rallies. They care, and they let it affect them– and they change the world because of it. It's beautiful, really. We owe much to high liberal neuroticism throughout history. Women are higher in neuroticism than men, and, while we complain and make jokes about it, their neuroticism helped out tremendously while they fought to get the vote, ignited the civil rights movement, and led the anti-war movement.

Meanwhile, over on the Dark Side, conservatives are lower in neuroticism, which makes it tougher for us to move them with emotional appeals, or any appeals, for that matter. Our usual solution to that problem, individually or in politics, is to make more emotional appeals, but louder, which quickly becomes a massive turnoff, and highly counter-productive. Our rallies confuse them. They ask me questions: why get so worked up? What is this accomplishing? How do these crazy people demonstrating actually survive in the real world– they can't have jobs.

Sometimes we have to do very emotional appeals in politics, but that's because we're trying to wake people up in the center, or a tiny bit to the right, so we can get people in power to pay attention. But it's almost never a good idea to try to persuade a conservative directly that way. There's no good way to influence a person low in neuroticism except with patient, logical, consistent pressure. With creative repetition, ideally.

Surprised? Disappointed? Well, this wasn't going to be a crystal stair.

Personality and Bias

Before we leave personality and start looking at biases, it's helpful to think about the biases that can come up for us based on our personality differences. Usually people talk about biases as if we all share the same ones as humans, but that's not true at all; we suffer from different biases based on personality differences, as well as cultural influences, where we work, or how we were raised. Keep in mind that these biases, like the personality differences themselves, are higher and more predictable for those of us who are more ideological, and variable or weaker with the rest of us.

When we see a personality weakness in others fairly clearly because of our strengths (the first principle), our biases can be triggered. But our biases are usually strongest in situations where the second principle is most important, when we don't see that our own weakness in a trait matters; when we undervalue the good aspects of a trait in others. That's why liberals can have high bias around issues where orderliness, or politeness, or stability (the opposite of neuroticism) play a key role. We might think, for instance, work that requires orderliness is easier than it is, or less vital than it is, or unpleasant, or unnecessary, or even evil. We can tend to take that kind of work on much less, even when it's called for– and feel perfectly justified in doing so.

Police or military service, which are traditional, hierarchical, and boundary-laden, are in the business of enforcing certainty and consistency: a strong majority of those workers are conservative in America, due to their emphasis on conscientiousness. They can be less respected by liberals, or more easily assumed to be doing either improper or unimportant work. Business management, for the same reasons, can also be naturally distrusted and discounted: their skills can be overlooked, or look suspicious.

Conservatives, on the other hand, probably have high bias around issues where openness should play in: they may be annoyed by any suggestions for changes to a system they're happy with, for instance– or so biased that they get used to fighting liberal recommendations, no matter what they are. They may be dismayed or even disgusted by artistic impulses a liberal might find inspiring or interesting. They can view adventurousness or creativity as risky, bothersome, or irresponsible.

To a lesser degree, liberals will have bias around issues where politeness plays a role, which can affect conversation in ways that are missed by liberals. Intensity can creep unintentionally into a conversation, and we can find ourselves justifying it out of anger about their opinions. Intensity can easily be interpreted by conservatives as rudeness, or disrespect, if only for a brief period– but it can deaden an otherwise healthy exchange, or quickly ruin it.

Conservatives typically have a perfect storm of both practical points to make and powerful biases to bring to bear on liberal attempts at charity, usually making our efforts out to be wasteful, or creating worse problems than we were trying to solve. This mixed bag of bias and good, practical sense also explains why conservatives feel so strongly that liberals are amiss relying so easily and completely on the government to provide services that conservatives feel could be done better through volunteer charity. The historically-recent conservative emphasis on the evils of government are strongly tied to their mistrust of our versions of charity. It's much less about government than it might seem, since they don't have a problem with large government that involves military and police. When a conservative says the word government now, they're referring to meddling, and compassion they see as riddled with abuses of order and industriousness.

How great a tempest stirs from seven little aspects of personality! We like to think our great political clashes are momentous, as either the shores upon which civilization falters, or from which our greatness will be launched. That may be. There is a simple alternate– the rather freeing notion that this tempest belongs more in a teapot, that it's a matter of people with different personalities who don't respect each other very well, or listen well to each other. Between these two theories, the dramatic and simple, is the unclear, distinctive path: that we evolved conjoined but separate, reflecting long-settled neural structural demands, to tend to disparate cares, with a raft of unshared skills.

How politics plays in the halls of congress or in the electoral arts is further afield of us at the moment. We're looking to be ambitious, too, but nearer at hand: we want to see how the weak servants of these opposing world views are meant to work together individually. By being attentive, the burden that our unconscious mind puts upon us will be lightened, and we'll see how our personalities and biases have distanced us from each other.

Chapter Five

THE GATEWAY BIASES

*Perhaps the greatest breach in nature is
the breach from one mind to another.*
            – William James

WE'RE READY for what might be the most practical part of this
approach to ideology: recognizing our deadliest biases, and
learning how to beat them back.

There's a phrase used by neuroscientists and cognitive scientists that
should be more common among the rank-and-file, because it sums up
well how we use our mind, and how biases can creep in. That term is
cognitive miser. It means that we're stingy about how much thinking
we do to get our lives done. Not just conscious thoughts, like what goes
through our mind as we respond to a question, but also all the
unconscious "thinking," or processing in the background, where most of
our choices are secretly made. Being a miser with how many cycles we
spend on any effort of the brain can help us understand why so much
goes wrong for us in the modern world, a place that isn't always best
handled by that ancient brain design. The thumb rule: if we need to
make a complicated decision, being a cognitive miser makes it unlikely
that we'll consider everything we should to make the right choice.

Probably the biggest way we're cognitive misers is that we love what's
called "motivated reasoning," which is a fancy way of saying that we
twist what we see, to turn it into an example of a familiar pattern. We do
this because seeing things the way we want to usually allows us to be ultra
super-duper misers with our thinking. If what happens is just like other
events we already saw and figured out, we don't have to change any our
ideas, and we don't have to ever have that uncomfortable feeling that we
don't know what's going on. Motivated reasoning affects where we find

91

things out, what parts of the evidence we actually consider (think token liberal on Fox News, being torn apart by trusted Fox regulars), and how we dismiss what seem to be strong evidence against our belief.[1]

This is a left brain hemisphere affair, as we discussed in the first chapter; that's the side of ourselves that's highly motivated to keep processes going faithfully, no matter what, to the point of making up fables and ignoring evidence. The "left-brain interpreter" puts evidence into patterns it already knows, even if the new information doesn't quite fit. This reflects a built-in design, and has to do with greatly valuing certainty, simplicity, consistency, and our authorities (sources). All those values combine to allow us to justify being cognitive misers, blundering through our lives, believing we know what's going on.

Most people change their outlooks on life in small ways over their lifetimes, but few of us change our outlooks much, and almost none of us change important opinions quickly, outside of a defining crisis. We develop and use a few related ideas over and over, usually ones we learned when young that stuck to our ribs, and we tend to apply them broadly to a loose family of subjects.[2] We then spend our mental energy and time over the rest of our lives building the thickest, highest mental battlements we can to defend those few ideas.

We're going to take a look at the foundations of those walls, the primary psychological defenders of our world view: our biases. For almost a century, psychology has been building detailed, undeniable evidence of the many biases we share, the ways we alter reality to interpret it our own special way. Biases might be the area of our life where we can make the biggest improvements. One of the reasons for psychotherapy, after all, is to identify and work on specific biases in individuals, to get ourselves working more directly and healthily with parts of reality we're distorting for unhealthy mental reasons. But the primary focus of *social* psychology is to identify these biases and understand how they affect our relations.

Some biases are an inevitable part of the human condition, of being alone in our own head, forever left to use only our own experience as a reference point. Anthropologists have made a strong case for many biases supporting social patterns in early man, or the physical safety of ourselves or our family. A good case can also be made that some of the biases just made it through the evolutionary filter as accidents, not because they aided us, but because humans could progress even with unhelpful biases. Evolution doesn't optimize so much as let decent versions of humanity keep going.[3] And some of the worst so-called biases are really thinking shortcuts, called "heuristics," that aren't necessarily flawed, and aren't a twist on reality the way a bias is– they're just a shortcut that might work well, if things are simple. In this work, to make things easy on ourselves, we use the term bias to mean motivated reasoning, biases and heuristics.

It's quite wrong to think biases are all bad. They're not. They serve some practical, positive purposes, and we'll look at a few. Later, we'll be learning to *use and rely* on certain biases to get along with conservatives. Now that our species is a kind of teenager in evolutionary terms, though, the negative sides of many of these biases and heuristics/tricks often outweigh their advantages. Their presence can make sensitive communication almost impossible.

Conservatives have a quite strong tendency to declare themselves unbiased, just like the solo left hemisphere does, which is a tough overlay to deal with on top of biases. Unfortunately– believe me– we have to get used to that two-tiered problem of high bias and "I'm not biased!" It can be a challenge, but it's best to think of their bias levels as we should about comparisons of intelligence, work ethic, and other things where differences in amounts are less pertinent than the absolute, overall levels. Recent evidence hints that we're not much less biased overall, so I wouldn't crow about our superiority, especially since both our bias levels are very high absolutely. In other words, even if they had *relatively* low cognitive bias levels, lower than ours, we'd all still have giant problems with them, because we'd both still have large *absolute* amounts of cognitive bias. This is an example of how each ideology loves to crow about its advantages, when it's like a one-legged guy bragging about how he can go run around the bases way faster than the other one-legged guy.

The Gateway Biases

In 2007, Dr. Emily Pronin had about a hundred Princeton students rank themselves on personal qualities in comparison with the average Princeton student– how considerate they were, their honesty, friendliness, and snobbishness. Before they started, Dr. Pronin let them all know that 75-85% of people tend to rate themselves as better than average relative to others in their group. **Every student but one reported themselves as better than average overall anyway**. Only one student in the whole experiment expressed any doubt about their own objectivity in the comments section provided, despite the clear advance warning about how special we all think we are. This lone nugget of Princetonian reserve? "Hmm. I wonder if I'm snobbier than I perceive."[4]

Similar results have appeared in other studies. I'm sure you can think of personal examples from your co-workers or family members that mirror these results. We simply think we're incredibly objective about ourselves, when we're absolutely not. This is the **Objectivity**

Assumption . It's the bias we need to start with, the first gateway bias, because almost all the others are allowed and given great strength when we assume we're objective.

It's easy to understand how this bias arises, and why it underlies the others. One popular name of this bias among researchers is the "Bias Blind Spot." The name was inspired by a small, hard-to-detect visual blind spot we all have that's caused by the physical structure of our retina– the optic nerve itself gets in the way, like somebody's hand reaching into the light at a movie house. In a similar way, this problem with objectivity is caused by a natural, inevitable blind spot. When we conscientiously look around inside the rooms of our mind to find biases, we can't see evidence of any, so we think of ourselves as objective.[5]

But there are ghosts in the palace; there are silent creatures in the walls. *Biases are usually completely unconscious.* The only rooms we have access to in our conscious minds *always* look clean and swept of anything that might distort our viewpoint. We can walk around and around our internal realm until we die and never see a single one– in fact, that's exactly what we all do.

Having biases is like being someone with mean friends who passed out at a party, and who's now wandering around with "IDIOT" written on their forehead. Biases can't be seen by us,[6] but they make us look silly.

We like to think we're objective because we're so careful and perceptive, as if it was an issue of how many megapixels we look at life with. Actually, objectivity has almost nothing to do with how well we perceive: *it has to do with what we* **choose to perceive**– *the things we work to point our "camera" of perception toward.* This is one of the most important lessons we can draw from this guide; learning it in our bones can be one of the greatest blessings we can give to ourselves and loved ones.

Negative biases will lead us to focus on negative aspects of others, or the situation, or ourselves; positive ones will do the opposite. The purpose of a bias is not to make blue look red, but to invisibly influence what we pay attention to in life: to choose subject matters and perspectives that color the observation just the way our unconscious mind wants, building up many layers of impressions, to convince us more and more deeply that the same limited set of beliefs are true.

Every once in a while, just to assure ourselves and everyone else that we're objective, we swing the camera around in a circle real quickly inside, pointing at all kinds of things. Never a single bias in sight. Congratulations! What a coincidence– you and I are those rarest of humans: we're incredibly objective.

Many researchers have told test subjects, before bias tests start, of the objectivity assumption, and what it will make them think, and it makes either little or no difference– they use it anyway. You can beat the objectivity assumption, but it's *hard*. We have to develop a habit of questioning our objectivity, which is difficult and unnatural. We have to do it while we're thinking, during conversations, and especially in situations where we have strong feelings.

That's tough– which should make sense, since we're talking about trying to beat some of the worst problems we have in our lives. I think of beating it as getting about halfway to perfect. Whether that's quite right or not isn't the point: it keeps me reminded how hard it is, and how it has to be a habitual struggle to even have a chance of beating it.

The objectivity assumption gets a big boost of power from the only philosophy the majority of mankind uses– it's called "**naïve realism**," our common, naïve belief that the world is made up of what we see, hear, feel, etc. It sounds straightforward– what else could the world be but what we pick up with our senses? Well, it could be plenty of things, because our senses tell us only tiny bits about the world. If our viewpoint is only made up of the things we either choose to see, or are forced to see, we should understand that we've constructed a very specialized way of looking at things. But we don't realize that, at all; instead, we use the objectivity assumption to cement our perceptions in our minds as the best, most complete way to view life.

We now know that this is a terribly deficient way of looking at life and other people, because the biases that reflect our underlying unconscious beliefs are lodged where we can't see them. Believing "what you see is what you get" in life is like saying that your camera is so high quality, so accurate, and so detailed, that nothing about reality gets past it.

But the camera can never see anything about the cameraman, and it can't see anything it isn't pointed at. How impartial we are is about what we choose to look at, moment by moment. The effort we make to get different perspectives; how curious we are about the possibilities; who we trust; the habit of careful inquiry; and what we do with the limited information that we do take in. Because we're assuming we're objective, naïve realism seals the deal, by helping us trust ourselves as great evidence gatherers. It lets us run along with distorting biases as if we have a great wind behind us. We think we're like careful, honorary scientists, because we have all these senses, picking stuff up like crazy. It's super easy to be accurate. Anyone can do it, as long as they're careful like me. Inaccurate people must be very lazy.

Many false eyewitness testimonies about events and perpetrators of crimes are caused by memory tricks and other minor biases: hundreds were proven wrong after DNA testing confirmed eyewitnesses were wrong. Experts estimate that many thousands more would've been overturned if DNA evidence had been kept from old trials. The objectivity assumption makes clear to an eyewitness that they don't have biases, but it's the witness's naïve realism that seals it for the unjustly convicted: the witnesses believe that what they see is the only version of reality possible. They *trust* what they thought they saw, getting the confidence boost they need to support that wrong impression, to swear an oath and say, "that's the guy– I *saw* him do it."

In 2000, when a U.S. Supreme Court decision sealed George W. Bush's election as President, the objectivity assumption and naïve realism together provided the assurance of objectivity to the 94% of Republicans who felt the actions were proper and balanced– and to the 84% of Democrats who strongly disagreed.

In competitive or stressful situations– politics, sports, the workplace, family arguments– the gateway biases allow many other biases to come into play, most of which can be seen by others who don't share them.

The only way we can usually get around these problems is by listening to others, who see our biases easily. But we don't welcome those corrections, do we? Especially if it's a political enemy. Anything others do in reaction to your biased behavior usually looks to you as if it came out of the blue, as if it's entirely uncalled for. You'll usually feel a need to respond to the injustice or inaccuracy of the correction. Both parties to a conversation usually have this problem, which naturally leads to an escalation of accusations, problems, and tit-for-tat behavior, with each side feeling morally justified to continue and escalate, because each feels objective and accurate.

It should already be dawning on you what a great swamp of misunderstanding we've stepped into in political conversation with just this one gateway problem. But we've only just warmed up. One of the first things our objectivity assumption and our simplistic view of reality allow is the most important mistake of all, the one that ruins lives, ruins most of our political conversations, and many of our personal ones. It annoys me greatly that we didn't learn it in grammar school.

The Fundamental Error

The biggest problems we have communicating come about because we never once get to look at anything through anyone else's eyes– not for a second. We can try to imagine another person's viewpoint, can struggle mightily to understand them– we can even spend all our time with them– but in the end, we're stuck with our own exclusive vision of the world, from that first upside-down spanking until we exit stage left.

I'm personally convinced that if each of us could just get into someone else's head for 10 seconds, like in Star Trek's Vulcan mind meld, the number of political arguments would go to a trickle of what they are now, and we'd work infinitely better as a team. Why, exactly, would that happen? For one thing, we'd be instantly well-informed about the background and situation that the person we're arguing with has brought to the table.

In Star Trek, when the mind meld ends, people unsquinch their faces, flop to the ground, moan a little, and then they fall together into a giant, teary hug spontaneously. They get gooey with one another, and they want to hang out with each other constantly. This fellow who was such a jerk becomes cool and interesting. I see now, says the black man to the white one, I finally see why affirmative action is so problematic. It was so hard on your family when your dad couldn't get that job that went to a black man[7]…and they'd say other understanding things like that. Except they don't have to, because they just picked it all up, in ten seconds. That's why they're crying like babies; it was intense. They sit together like close twins awhile, and bask in all that understanding.

The other thing they'd get out of the experience is even more important: they'd grasp the other person's personality, and learn how the other person thinks. How they make their decisions, what kinds of situations are difficult for them, all their little foibles, their secret strengths, their hopes, their fears— everything besides the history and circumstances that determines their lives.

What they'd get in a mind meld is everything we're missing to begin a perfect communication:

> 1. They'd understand the other person's situation and background (i.e., all their pertinent history, right up to now).

> 2. They'd understand the other person's personality (why that person responds to situations they way they do).

We are forever closed off from other people— that's the human condition. What can we do to make up for not knowing those two things when we want to communicate? Well, if we're good boys and girls, we try our best to put ourselves in their shoes, don't we? Mom taught us to listen carefully, and to try to imagine what it must be like to be that other person. We've never been anybody else, so it's hard to do that well: we've never had a different history than our own, so we might want to get whatever information we can about their background, so we can **imagine** what it might be like living their life.

If we can find out something about each other's background and personality, and neither of us is a jerk, or really crabby that day, we have a excellent chance at a great conversation, especially if we have something in common. Very commonsensical, right? Pay attention, get a little sense of people's background and personality, and go from there.

Now, let's assume we're going to have a *political* conversation instead. Both of us have political visions of the world that we consider universal—sacred rules we think can rarely even be bent, let alone broken. I believe that affirmative action is enlightened and critical for all of society, but you believe it is an unsightly scar upon the snowy breast of liberty. When we sit down to talk, do we care what each other's backgrounds are? Absolutely not. Why should we? We're talking universally applicable political Truth here. Tax the rich, universal health, mandatory abortion coverage; dismantle the EPA, tax relief, outlaw abortion. All the necessary laws for mankind's happiness can be dragged out and fondled in front of anybody, at any time, as long as the person is objective like me. In politics, where we get to embrace our half of the principles involved and ignore the rest, personal backgrounds make no difference. Right?

That notion, besides sounding stupid to a bright first-grader, is about 80 long years behind an insight that has become indisputable science, launching a whole academic field.

Kurt Lewin was a gifted, prolific German psychologist and philosopher, who emigrated to America after being wounded in World War I. He died too young, but did so much brilliant work at Cornell, MIT and elsewhere that he's considered the founder of social psychology, the study of human interaction. In 1931, he identified what eventually came to be recognized as the primary weakness in human communication: people made serious errors working with one another because they didn't understand the other person's situation or background well.[8] Ignorance of other people's backgrounds, and their specific challenges at the moment, can literally be a deadly problem in the business of getting along. This problem has been studied a great deal since then, and it is now considered one of the central problems of the relatively new field of social psychology. Hundreds of papers have been bent to the complexities behind one basic idea: our backgrounds should play as big a role as possible in our conversations.

We have a whole culture that's obsessed with pop psychology, but few pay attention to the way pure circumstance molds us. Notice that by ignoring people's backgrounds we rather neatly unlearn what mom taught us about putting ourselves in the other fellow's shoes to communicate well. That's the beauty of politics: both sides get around their mommy's lessons and all that pesky situational detail by claiming that their side's ideas are the best ideas in the world, and that the ideas work for everyone, all the time, no matter what. Lets us move right to the upset-at-each-other part we were going to get to anyway. Saves time.

That isn't the worst of it. If our political conversation turns difficult, and our history and circumstances aren't considered important factors, what *is* considered important? Well, everything we do is based on either our background or our personality, so...gee, someone's personality must be out of whack.[9] Fortunately, I know that I'm incredibly, remarkably objective– that's a miracle that seems to have happened at my birth. I'm looking around inside– nope– not my character that's the problem here: I'm dealing with the facts carefully this time, like pretty much always. So– that means *you must be the one with the personality flaws.*

Down through the years, I've been part of this whirlpool of toxic ideas about someone's personality hundreds of times, on the giving and receiving end. Of course, we can't always know those we speak with well; and there will always be limits to what we know about their situation and their disposition. But knowing these things are hard to find out is a wide world away from saying we shouldn't bother to try, because our principles are all that matter. By not trying, we make things way too simple: 1) Since my idea is right because I use logic so well, 2) your idea is wrong, and 3) since our backgrounds make no difference whatsoever in correct politics, 4) you have a personality or character flaw that makes you always bet on the wrong horse. 5) Gosh, I feel sorry for you and your crew. 6) Wait– I feel even more sorry for us principled people, because you guys are dragging the whole country down all the time. 7) You jerk.

This is **the fundamental error**. A person's political opinion is different than ours, and we tend to blame flaws in their personality or character for that difference, ignoring genetic and background differences as an explanation.[10] This is a narrow, good-enough version of the broader, more complex problem most commonly called the Fundamental Attribution Error, or FAE (it has other names as well, because a few different fields and pioneering researchers tripped over each other birthing it). The formal term has "attribution" in the name because when we make this error, or fall victim to it, we *attribute* problems to peoples' personality or character incorrectly.

Sometimes we use the fundamental error to blame a disagreement on a personality flaw, such as impatience, or closed-mindedness, or an inability to be logical. But often we skip right over personality weaknesses and use our very, very perceptive sense of realism to spear right into the core of the person's character: we nail them as evil. He's self-serving; dishonest; manipulative; selfish. Once we've got a *character flaw* figured out, communication is virtually done.

Technically, the fundamental error is a heuristic, or decision-making shortcut, not a bias, because we're not misinterpreting, so much as deciding we know enough to make a (bad) decision. But it's the deadliest heuristic there is, far worse than most biases:

–People **overreact, misunderstand, and withdraw** by not adequately taking into account reasons for incidents or viewpoints outside of possible personality flaws. This can be as simple as getting irritated when someone "carelessly" bumps us in the subway, or as complex as all the jealous fantasies a man might engage in when his partner comes home unexpectedly late. The invisibility of the other person's situation presents an unfocused, dark image where there might otherwise be a good, clear explanation– one we need but don't have. We don't like incoherence or uncertainty, or "cognitive dissonance," which is what that unfocused, dark image of the other person's situation gives us. So, we create in our minds a simpler story to makes sense of it all, by projecting personal problems on people. If we lack imagination or empathy, or if we have psychological problems, the fundamental error can force us to have powerful negative ideas about someone's personality– and there's little evidence the other person can use to counter that impression.

–Crimes like **battery** and **murder** occur because people see a bad personality flaw where there was actually a tough situation, or background causes. People are killed, hurt, or abandoned for dishonesty, infidelity, stupidity, or inadequate loyalty, or they're blamed for an act they didn't do, that maybe they couldn't possibly have done. Crimes become worse during the commitment because of this bias as well, because clarity deteriorates under stress (during an argument, say), and even more situational problems get blamed on personality flaws.

Nor are we done with examples of this error after the crime is completed. During **sentencing** and **parole determination**, the judge or board have the job to sort out situational reasons (mitigants) for the crime accurately, which is difficult. The people responsible to sort out mitigants commonly neglect making the effort to consider backgrounds properly because it's difficult to do, and because personality flaws usually seem "obviously" involved. Also, some **crimes based on intent** (for example, manslaughter) have enormous dependence on a judge or jury interpreting personality information that's hard to assess accurately, thanks to the fundamental error.

–Group crimes of **genocide** and **discrimination** are usually caused by the group version of the fundamental error.[11] Pol Pot of Cambodia examined the palms of people to determine whether they should live or die based on a background of manual labor: he killed them unless they had a superficial indication they were farmers. Several generations after the Belgians created and instituted two fictional races in Rwanda for imperialistic purposes— they divided people up by how dark they were, and assigned them a race, because they wanted whiter natives working in the government— waves of slaughter repeatedly occurred between the "races" due to projection of personality flaws (lazy, dishonest, sexually immoral, power-hungry) onto each "tribe" by the other.

The fundamental error is present to some degree in almost all of our important conversations when there is a difference of opinion between people. And it's not taken care of by understanding that you make the error, though paying attention to your own attitudes can help.[12]

Political conversations are a particularly pernicious host of the fundamental error, because we build in the worst version of it automatically by *deliberately* assuming situational information can't matter. Sometimes we generously assume their background caused what we see as personality or character flaws, but this amounts to the same thing— "This guy must've been raised rich— so out of touch." This tossing out or fabricating the other person's reasons for decisions is the secret fallout from having strict, universal political ideas that have no maybes or contingencies in sight. Other than stupidity, insanity or ignorance,[13] the other person's moral flaws seem to be the only possible reason they believe differently than me, thanks to my pretty perfect grasp of how the world needs to operate for everyone— my universal playbook.

Before we even start a political conversation, we are set up nearly perfectly for failure. That, my friends, is why our political conversations are so useless. Our assumed objectivity joins up with ignoring backgrounds to create the perfect storm of a normal political conversation, where:

- No one convinces anyone of anything.
- No follow-on research is agreed upon.
- No one learns anything useful.
- No one discovers any situation background for beliefs.
- The more abstract the idea (foreign aid vs. town square redesign), the more hidden biases come into play.
- Each person assigns false character flaws to the other.
- Each person made their world view even stronger.
- No one feels sympathy for the suffering of the other.

– No emotional connection is created.

The basic sign that you are a victim of the fundamental error (which travels hand-in-hand with the objectivity assumption and naïve realism) is that **you don't listen well** to the other person. Your mind wanders; you have no questions (except for the "What?! Are you trying to tell me..." type). While she's talking, you're thinking about what you're going to say next, or what's for dinner.

Interrupting frequently also means you're not listening well, especially when you're cutting off points before they're complete. Interrupting means you consider the other side's message not worth listening to, not just because you don't believe it, but because you don't trust that there's enough behind it to have a positive realization *of any kind*. It also sends a clear signal to the other person that their message is a generic one you recognize, not one that's real and heartfelt by them. That you think you've heard it all before. That it's not anywhere near as important as your upcoming retort.

When you hear a conversation with a certain kind of chiding or entitled tone, you're hearing the objectivity assumption and the fundamental error in action, almost always with both people– differences of opinion are being attributed completely to personality flaws, and it all becomes drivel:

> "...that's exactly what Russell Kirk was saying about being prudent."
> "You want to talk about being a prude?– you really want to go there?"
> "Wow. News flash: prudence has nothing to do with being a prude."
> "Well hey, you should probably alert your party of that fact..."

Or my favorite conversation style for identifying biases, which, unfortunately, loses its delicate nuances when set down on the page:

> "You should be-"
> "-in the REAL world-"
> "-should be read-"
> "-the REAL world we-"
> "-your MIRANDA rights."
> "have to DEAL wi– oh, my Miranda rights, oh yeah, let me guess,–"
> ...

Here, then, are common impressions people have about the other person's personality or character flaws, that show they are active users of the fundamental error:

- The other person seem illogical, like screws are loose.
- They seem stupid. They keep saying the same, not-bright things. Mommy must've had a to-do to drop him on his head once a week.
- They believe that way because it's in their own interest.
- They won't believe anything that requires them to change.
- They won't believe anything that requires them to think.
- They're lazy, dishonest, two-faced, shallow, or like quick fixes.
- They're not driven by principles; they can't handle the truth.

We may very well be right about these perceptions, but that's what's so silly about our political conversations: persuasion is a lousy goal to have with political conversations, and we're only worried about all that character stuff because it affects whether we can persuade them or not. If we keep a relatively open mind and are looking for ideas that make sense, or finding out how ideas make sense for others, the other person's character flaws are almost completely beside the point. If you have nice, broad goals for the conversation, you're not too worried about how lazy the fellow is, or how often he calls his mother.

The Point of Political Conversations

Sometimes, when we debate politics or watch others do it, we're mildly interested in learning something, like a minor twist on the opponent's point, but we rarely involve ourselves to learn something truly practical, or to make an important decision. We enter these situations with our objectivity assumption and the fundamental error in play, so we can feel objective while employing any bias we want about the opponent's personality, to any end we want– like thinking he's an idiot, or dishonest, or that he's been warped into Voldemort by his insane ideology. The whole process is designed to prop up our world view. Political debate lets our biases make us feel good, and gives us confidence that our viewpoint is accurate.

You might think that you would have to win a political debate to get your feel-good payoff. Nope: it's much easier than that. **These gateway biases allow everyone to win debates, especially when it's important to do so.** You can "objectively" see that you soared, and that the other guy was a ding-dong, or evil, or a mental cripple in some way. Polls on debates show vast differences in opinion between parties as to which candidate did best, even when the average result gives it clearly to one candidate or the other. If it wasn't for the everybody-wins aspect of using our biases, we would avoid political debate, because it would call our beliefs into question too often, which would make us uncomfortable. And we don't do uncomfortable— we only do correct.[14]

We usually think of our biases as minor parasites we flick off easily when we pay attention. Not only is this wrong, but it's a quite unhealthy perspective; it's evidence of naïve realism working within us, of believing we perceive everything about reality, with a little effort. It's much more accurate to think of our biases as some of the central ways we define ourselves and *create* our reality.[15,16]

There are many short-term "advantages" that biased thinking provides us. Here are some that should help you understand why they thrive, even in today's society.

— In uncertain situations, we can convince ourselves of certainty and get out of doing things we'd otherwise have to do. Much of our unconscious mind's work is to eliminate uncertainty using various tricks.

— We can make short-term decisions due to self-interest or some other hidden purpose, which speeds things along nicely. This allows us to make moral compromises without being aware of them, instead of having to work toward a better, long-term solution, which the cognitive miser in us would prefer to avoid.

— When change is required, we can convince ourselves it's not needed in the short-term, and ignore the requirement for awhile.

— We can save time and research requirements for decisions by reducing the number of parts of a problem we have to consider. These heuristics, or cognitive shortcuts, are sometimes truly useful. Unfortunately, we tend to also use them when they're inappropriate, like when the situation is complex, as in politics.

— Biases allow us to use only a few simple models of how the world works. We can form-fit almost any situation into a recognizable type of problem with workable solutions, by overlooking countering evidence.

— Our biases allow us to think we are at least partially right when we're wrong, so that we can feel valuable or useful.

Being of Two Minds

Our unconscious mind is much, much older than our conscious part, and much better at its job. Actually, there isn't a sharp line between conscious and unconscious, and the line between varies, depending on what's going on. Primitive parts of our conscious mind have existed for a very long time, and can be seen in many animals now, but rapid expansion of our conscious capabilities are evolutionarily recent.[17] The forehead of mankind sloped straight back in the earlier species of mankind: during over 99% of our development, there has been very little frontal brain matter, the part of our brains that enables complex language, self-awareness, complex abstract thoughts, and deep reasoning.

This conscious mind, what we usually incorrectly think of as ourselves, is thought by most evolutionary psychologists to have evolved to help the unconscious mind do a better job of getting the food, safety, and other goals it wants, because it helped us use *time* to our advantage; it helped us *plan*. It also lets us consider more aspects of a problem. But these skills are just tools; "we" still use those tools for the same reason, to take care of our unconscious selves. Most of the conscious mind that wields them has only just arrived on the scene, in evolutionary terms; it hasn't been promoted above this support role yet. In other words, who I think of as me isn't really me. It's just a particularly useful part of me that resides mostly in the upper, frontal, left side of my brain.

Thinking your conscious thoughts are all of yourself is a great way of defining naïve realism; I find it a helpful way to remember how hard a problem it is to beat naïve realism, because it's a good reminder, at any moment one cares to remember, that our real life is much broader than everything we're aware of consciously. We tend, instead, to think that the unconscious mind just takes care of breathing and blood pumping, that what we see and interpret consciously is all we need to understand reality, and all we are.

Most of our unconscious motivations, probably the vast majority, are perfectly healthy. Our unconscious mind learns sometimes, and it can balance some complicated situations out. Love and our other feelings are mostly unconscious in origin and in effect, so our unconscious selves can be positively saintly, and even complete and careful at times.

On the other hand, we like to ignore, along with conservatives, that *unconscious means, by definition, that we don't know what the heck is going on in there, or why it's happening.* Terrible stuff can feel wonderful to us in the moment. I've always admired Ralph Waldo Emerson, for instance, but in his time, ethnic prejudices were common, and so he "felt" perfectly moral holding some of the nastiest opinions about the worth of some ethnic groups one can imagine. Because we're steeped so completely in our time and culture, we can only guess whether an idea is healthy or not, based on clues available to our conscious mind, like past results, or what mama thinks. And we're not very good at that kind of guessing. Some ideas that feel great are shoved into the conscious mind by powerful, inappropriate unconscious urges, with a big push from biases and heuristics. These are exactly the kinds of things that are happening when we smoke, lie for shallow reasons, eat too many cookies, ignore the kids improperly, keep too disorganized an office, argue about politics, bite our fingernails, have affairs, make decisions too quickly, ignore reasonable requests, or act in ways we regret immediately.

Our willpower, the correction engine of our conscious mind, is supposed to save us from these problems. And it does, to a certain extent. But our will is more like a sprinter's short-term, hard effort, not the computer-like, eternal endurance the unconscious mind has when we want something. As efforts of the will lose out over time for us, the short-term benefits of unconscious behavior chug right along, and stay the popular norm for us at home, work, and play, especially under stress. We eventually almost always see the workings of that machine-like consistency undermine our conscious intentions. It's easy to see in our friends and acquaintances, and it's happening to us in the same way. We should realize that we chase short-term desires incorrectly all the time *by design*, we'll continue to, and other people will keep systematically grinding away to achieve their short-term desires as well, at our expense.

Fortunately, we're starting to get a handle on ways that our conscious mind is built on this circuitry that knocks and veers us around as it did our ancestors 100,000 years ago. If we want a chance to be free of the more predictable, unnecessarily limiting aspects of our machinery, we have to understand the dumb-dumb moves we all make as a result of human nature and inherited weaknesses.

Many of our most devastating mistakes and moral errors– even the crimes we talked about earlier– are far more unconscious than conscious. One of the interesting aspects of social psychology research is how individual, unconscious actions lead, in a cascading effect, to large-scale societal injustices like vicious discrimination, corruption, and even genocide. We "sin" against each other without fully realizing our error consciously. Social psychology can help us avoid some of those behaviors as a culture.[18] Simply knowing more about our internal architecture may let us greatly improve our whole species' behavior and quality of life.

The links between our two minds are so slick and automatic that our conscious mind only rarely has to admit to itself that there's a secret, unconscious engine hard at work behind virtually everything we do, feeding us the seed of most of the thoughts and feelings that drive our behavior. Those rare times when our naïve realism breaks down and we get a glimpse of the power of our unconscious self are usually face plant days; days of tears, or apologies, or misery, of "What was I thinking?!" Our basic unconscious needs explode onto the scene, while our conscious mind stands back and waits out the tornado that's unexpectedly touched down near the middle of our life. Or, depending on your personality and the situation, our conscious selves might be waiting while unconscious impulses actually help out, like Jesus clearing the temple of money-changers, or expressing ourselves tenderly with someone we love.

Much of that volatility in our relationship with our unconscious mind has to do with our history. Our modern reality is much more abstract and much less physically dangerous than the one we were designed for. For instance, it's not healthy for fight-or-flight set of responses to come up when our boss upsets us with comments about incorrect formatting on a report: we don't need the rush of adrenalin and blood flow to our head and extremities. Today isn't the day to grab a stapler and kill him with it, to protect Pebbles and Bam-Bam back in the cave. But for certain situations, fight-or-flight is all some of us get, the only circuit available in our current design. We are largely driven by systems that aren't optimal, and aren't very controllable by our conscious mind.

A simple metaphor for the conscious mind is as the visible portion of an iceberg, with the business end, the nonconscious mind, underwater. Just as it's foolish for a ship's captain to think of an iceberg as only what's visible, so it's foolish for us to think of ourselves and others as our conscious minds only. Most of the problems we get into in life are not related to the part of the iceberg we can see, but the hidden danger beneath. Now, you can peer into the water hard, and you might be able to see some of the iceberg underwater, and that can be important. But for most purposes, almost all of ourselves is hidden. In our society, at this stage of our development, we still like to ignore that about ourselves.

There are two other metaphors that can help us think of ourselves in new terms, to enter more fully into the strange world of biases and the nonconscious aspects of political life. One is the metaphor of the elephant and its rider,[19] used helpfully by Dr. Jonathan Haidt in the study of morality and discipline. The rider can be thought of as the conscious mind, and the elephant as the nonconscious mind. This metaphor allows us to see how lumbering, powerful and potentially dangerous the nonconscious mind is, and how reliant the rider is on skill, practice, and communication skills to work effectively with the elephant.

The rider learns to use the elephant for what it does best, providing the guidance needed for the elephant to be most useful and safe. Another cool lesson from this metaphor: naïve realism has us living our lives pretending as if there is *no elephant*; life is just a matter of the conscious mind just doing whatever makes sense

Like any metaphor, the elephant and the rider is in the business of describing a certain situation. It's easy to think it's describing the whole relationship between the conscious and unconscious mind, but that's not its purpose. The focus is on the relationship between the two parts of us when an emergency happens, like a moral situation. It also shows that one must train the elephant well to have a successful life— but that even a brilliant trainer still has an unruly elephant sometimes.

There's another important lesson about the unconscious we need now. Do you remember when Obi-Wan Kenobi was trying to sneak past a road block in Star Wars, and he said to the storm trooper, "These are not the droids you're looking for"? The storm trooper went on mindless auto-pilot, allowing the good guys to move on, undetected. Just like that storm trooper, our own conscious mind, under our normal naïve realism, is like the puppet of a ventriloquist show, appearing to be acting independently, but really acting as a slave to a deep-hewn set of nonconscious values that have it in thrall. In other words, the elephant's not just the unpredictable surprise boss when things are stressful: the elephant is the boss, period. And the boss doesn't look like an elephant, either. In fact, it's largely invisible.

Here's a parable, then, on the way to a final metaphor.

The Boss and Her Secretary

In a land near you and me, there's a boss and her personal assistant, or secretary. The boss, like the unconscious mind, has a huge job; she's in charge of physical safety, and basics like the urge to reproduce, be loved, and protecting her world view. Sits in her office, and rarely comes out. Think Howard Hughes, the rich recluse: refuses all interviews, and communicates via her secretary, through one of those speakerphone, intercom thingies.

Some of her instructions are mandatory and specific, blasting orders and actions. Sometimes the boss herself might intervene, if it's an emergency; the secretary just holds the little button on the speakerphone down, cringes, and looks away while the boss screams at someone, or takes away their birthday. Usually, though, orders are mumbled to her secretary in the language they share, and there's more flexibility and less urgency, so that the secretary can get what the boss wants done however he sees fit.

This secretary can be a poser sometimes. He likes to burst into the waiting room and pretend as if all the orders he has to give out are his own deep thoughts, carefully considered. He acts as if he can do what he wants— and he can, from a certain angle. But his version of freedom usually looks like doing exactly what his boss wants, layering on his sense of style, and adding to the color scheme a little.

Other assistants aren't so cocky; they know their place, and are happy to be loyal, consistent, and unquestioning. Have you ever known administrative or personal assistants in real companies that seem born to disappear into the role of being the perfect extension of their boss?

Then the boss, removed from the real world as she is, starts making mistakes. Boyfriends are coming and going, boss; boss, your hair smells like stale tobacco, and your skin looks bad; mom's mad at us, boss. The boss seems to just want what she wants, and continues with mistakes. Maybe the secretary just keeps going along, collecting his paycheck; he tells himself it's none of his business. Or maybe he takes a little pride in the business, and tries to convince a removed, self-centric, safety-oriented boss to change for good.

Look at yourself, for a clear-eyed moment; look at me. We're secretaries for our unconscious minds, the two of us, communicating here through wispy, newer parts of our brains. That's not pessimistic; it's biology, and evolutionary psychology. It doesn't reduce us, to realize this: it explains us. One of the reasons that life is so beautiful, and agonizing, and mysterious is because we can't know ourselves fully. This is the great lesson of Jung and other pioneering psychologists of the last century: we aren't who we seem, and the adventure is to delve further and further into who we are, with no end to the game.

There is some brand new evidence that consciousness, or awareness of such things, is expanding very rapidly, along with the little-known rapid social evolution we've been undergoing the last 10,000 years or so.[20] Many things we did unconsciously earlier in our evolution are now quite conscious. There isn't a clear, magic wall between the conscious and unconscious parts of ourselves we're talking about; that twilight area between seems to be expanding, shedding more and more light on our behavior and the motivations behind our efforts.

So there's some hope for the future. But there's a tyranny to being caught in a specific epoch with the rest of our species, like insects in amber. Pretending it's different will only hurt us badly. It's too late for that. Our species is only an unruly teenager in our development, and yet we've got fusion bombs, and high-stakes interdependencies with countries whose names we can't even pronounce. Dozens of murderous dictators ensure the misery of billions; Henry Kissinger still wanders free.[21] Should we secretaries still be keeping our mouths shut, grabbing our paychecks, and watching bad TV all night, while our bosses pull their antics?

We don't have to be so enabling of a strong unconscious mind as the secretaries in the story, but most of us are. It's difficult to stand up to that boss, to even try to be persuasive. We don't want to be "mindless," cheerleader secretaries, letting our unconscious selves off the hook every chance we get. She may be the boss, but that doesn't mean we have to fawn, and let our conscience go dark while we do her bidding unwittingly. We want to be more like Secretaries of State, using our limited independence, observation powers, and our potential influence to be persuasive with the boss, while having the humility and wisdom to remember that we may not be influential.

For many of us– those of us who are trying to be Secretaries of State– there's negotiation going on between our conscious and unconscious selves all the time, even if we're not aware of it. The conscious mind is able to influence our overall, combined life, but, as we have seen, there are all kinds of tricks the unconscious mind has put in place to keep that relationship one-sided; to stay the boss. So, for "me" to learn something politically means that "we," the conscious *and* unconscious sides, must learn it. This two-stage nature of learning is one of the essential points of this guide. True learning involves both parts of us, and it has almost nothing to do with facts. That's one of the reasons why it's so hard to define what wisdom is, and why it's so easy to tell the difference between wisdom and spouting facts.

The question of what a secretary like us should do to be more like a Secretary of State, and less like a temp from the secretarial pool, is mostly a matter outside the scope of this guide; it probably involves a spiritual practice, reading great literature, and being nicer to your mom. We owe it to the world, and ourselves, to try to understand what it means to be honest to ourselves, so our personal problems don't bleed out unnecessarily onto those we love, those who depend on us, and into the world.

Persuading our unconscious mind to change anything involves 1) the strength of our conscious initiative, 2) good timing and 3) either inspiration or disaster. Obviously, you need initiative to want yourself to change first; strong desires are good, though tiny, easy, partial steps, taken consistently, can be even more powerful.

Timing is a requirement, too; sometimes, we're just not ready to change. We'll die with all kinds of weaknesses we were never ready to fix. Our unconscious mind is ancient– we probably inherited its basic structure. It's the most mysterious thing in the universe. Parts of us are going to go out of this life about the same as they came in. We'll always have to pick our battles.

Inspiration is the third, overlooked factor of personal change. As we flail around in this post-postmodern life of ours, always slouching toward easy, quick solutions, it's easy to forget that **inspiration is the only voluntary catalyst for transformation**. If the boss gives an order that isn't healthy, the secretary must make a powerful emotional or inspirational argument to change her mind, or the boss won't listen.

Inspiration shouldn't be a vague idea, or magical, or rare. It should be a common occurrence, and we should look for it close at hand, not on mountaintops in Tibet. Often, inspiration is just education, especially when we're young; it makes sense to avoid a bunch of heartache, so we lean away from it, like a parent or teacher shows us. No big deal. Inspiration that helps us with our unconscious mind is also found in good books, good people, going to church, volunteering, short breaks during work– in all kinds of crannies of our lives, if we look.

The chance to be inspired is why heuristics like the fundamental error and others we'll discuss offer an enormous opportunity to mankind. Heuristics are errors in thinking, not biases emanating from deep within ourselves; we teach ourselves to use those errors. They are personal and cultural *habits*, which is why every culture relies on them differently. We're susceptible to good training about them– inspirational education.

That's why I'm so annoyed that social psychology has known about the fundamental error for going on a century, and knowledge of that error hasn't gotten out of upper-division college classes. Good moms invented an easy, partial version of a fix many thousands of years ago: they've been telling their kids to put themselves in the other person's shoes. Scientists and parents have the potential now to translate that lesson very clearly to children, to make the case powerfully and completely, in a way mom couldn't. Instead, academics still have a half-dozen names for the problem, all of them with ten syllables or so, and they squabble about details with each other.

You don't need to wait for them to enlighten you, fortunately. But when we're older, our "boss" has soaked herself in the fundamental error and other heuristics so long that they're very difficult habits to break; many of us can, but it doesn't seem common for people to try very hard. It seems very dependent on how inspiring the education or call to change is, and how much pain the habit is costing. So, much of the answer for beating heuristics has to be early education from parents, churches, community groups, and schools. Over the next century, I believe we'll see a great deal of that.

There's only one way I've found that our adult unconscious mind can consistently be inspired to shed these heuristics and biases and learn something challenging from someone else. It's actually miraculously easy, often: *we experience a positive emotional connection together.*

Inspiration only happens through emotion, which is the currency of our inner life. A positive emotion about a person, such as respect, or admiration, or empathy, or sympathy, can open a door you didn't see was there. Of course, it's great to have the feeling be powerful, but that's not necessary to begin to loosen our unconscious mind's rigid stance toward both them and their ideas.

That one emotional experience, even in mild form, kickstarts yet another bit of great news. A wonderful principle of communication, especially with most conservatives, is that *when someone feels heard they naturally open up, and they can hear you better.* This is part of how we have evolved rapidly over the last 5,000 generations or so, as we became incredibly complex social animals almost instantly, in evolutionary terms. It's so advantageous to the species that people who were good at subtle emotional communication survived, and people who weren't didn't. One person's empathy tends to "transfer" over to the other, involuntarily. *Emotions arise almost completely from our unconscious mind,* and they're communicated between people in a raw, powerful, mysterious way, mostly nonverbally. In that sense, our unconscious minds communicate directly with each other when a breakthrough of this kind comes, when one of us cuts through to a good understanding of the other person's perspective.

This is a huge advantage for us, because conservatives are feeling-driven, despite our stereotype of the crabby, spiteful, far-right meany: the notion of leading with feelings, of having feelings change the timbre of a dialogue, is a natural one for them because of their more trusting attitude toward their unconscious mind, and their very social version of reality. Some of my greatest joys have been when I have had this emotional connection or understanding arise in me during a conversation, and had my conservative guest reciprocate an increased respect for me or my ideas almost immediately. It doesn't at all mean they'll love all your ideas; that depends on the idea, and lots of other details about you and them. It does mean they'll be *much more open* to hearing your version of those ideas.

Liberals and conservatives seem to have very different ways of dealing with the unconscious mind. Nonconscious communication often gets *ignored* by us liberals, especially intellectuals. Liberals are especially prone to assume that we're two conscious minds interacting, when that isn't at all what's happening. Even if we're not intellectual, we tend to think we're "reasoning" our way through life accurately in our conversations. If we're intellectual, we emphasize data transfer between ourselves too much, and think of "myself" in terms of our logical and experiencing self, the tiny conscious part sitting in the front room, in front of the real boss's lair. It seems like an extension of our emphasis on the intellect as the seat of our personality. That emphasis is only one step over from thinking that we're very rational, and scientific, and purely conscious. That's often our version of naïve realism. We're like the secretary in the story who likes to pretend that he's really the boss.

Implicit Bias

I discovered in a test that I'm prejudiced against African–American people at roughly an average level for a Caucasian American. You can do the same test at www.implicit.harvard.edu.

Maybe my result sounds awful to you, or maybe you're just not used to people telling you their prejudice levels. Should you even respect someone with "average" prejudice levels? What a backwards guy.

We're not used to admitting prejudice at *any* level, but we must get used to acknowledging and accepting our own high levels of stupid-seeming, common prejudices about ethnic groups, age, sex, and many other goofy things. It doesn't define us, but it *is* human.

One interesting angle on my results is that my prejudice level was also about the same as roughly a third of African-Americans' prejudice against *their own ethnicity*.[22] In reality, our "boss" has mysterious, deep-seated ideas, and those prejudices are not our personal fault: they're mostly cultural and genetic. We build a world view of others based on our genetics, experiences, education, and who influences us.

The notion of "implicit" bias is confusing. Scholars aren't very helpful as of this writing about it, but our approach here should help. All bias is subconscious; what we've been talking about is "implicit bias", even though we say bias: implicit is another word for hidden, which describes all unconscious bias, by definition. But as that bias becomes conscious– as the secretary starts to get more involved, by helping out the boss's prejudice with justifications, enthusiasm, and other support– it becomes more and more appropriate to talk about racism, sexism, or ageism.

Unfortunately, we can't ever draw a clear-cut line between being prejudiced and being racist or sexist, because our conscious minds are *always* in the service of the boss. For instance, I could be trying carefully to be fair to an African-American applicant best qualified for a job, but my biases might cause me to refuse him a job anyway. That sounds racist, in an important way– after all, it didn't matter to that candidate whether I was trying to be fair, or muttering about black people to my co-workers before the interview. The whole point of trying to be aware of bias is to realize that our secretary is *always* capable of expressing our hidden prejudice in the world in a terrible way, so we try to allow consciously for it.

The reason why the picture is confusing relates to the secretary's role in all this. As the secretary's support of the boss gets more and more enthusiastic— when we prohibit all black families from moving into our real estate development on purpose, for instance— the secretary has crossed right through the gray area we all must live in, where our internal machinery might cause problems, into working explicitly for a deeply prejudiced boss. That's a secretary that isn't acting as a Secretary of State; they're directly channeling a powerful unconscious impulse.

We can reduce the effect of our (implicit) bias by being careful, and taking time with a decision; by hanging out with people we're prejudiced against (which might actually reduce our bias); and by paying attention to our thoughts and feelings. If we don't do those things, our biases will have more of a chance to surface in our actions.

While we should challenge ourselves to be careful, we should always remember that very few people are immune to bias. It's important to forgive yourself and others for having this very human tendency, but to also have our conscious mind do good shuttle diplomacy between the world and our unconscious mind, to prevent ourselves from causing problems with our prejudices.

The relationship between the boss and the secretary isn't any one thing: it's mysterious, complicated, and it varies by person and situation. But there are strong ideological patterns. I've mentioned that it's common for conservatives to deny their biases, or to minimize the size or importance of them. Another way of putting this is that their secretary is very loyal to the boss, and won't believe a bad thing about her. Conservatives often get annoyed and suspicious about "liberal" science that alleges that there's all this hidden *whatever* that the secretary is ignoring; it sounds like the usual left-wing manipulations to them, something about overlooked problems (exceptions, in the sense we discussed) that are designed to stop them from doing real work, and send them down some random liberal rathole. Their secretary isn't going to do anything without the boss's say-so. Worrying about bias sounds like claptrap to someone steeped in the objectivity assumption, naïve realism, and the fundamental error. The risk for conservatives, then, is that denial of bias can lead to problems, because their bias is unexamined.

Liberals have a kind of opposite problem: we *might* admit to bias, in theory, but we tend to pretend it doesn't affect "us", because our secretary is so independent and so intellectual and logical that we've got it covered. We say all the right things; we're friends with black people.

We're just so sensitive and kind that we've overcome it.

That liberal tendency to act as if we have our prejudices under control, while complaining about conservative prejudice, makes conservatives livid, because they know at some level that if the prejudices exist, that we liberals have them, too. And they're right; our implicit biases still cause problems in the world, even when we mouth that we have them.

More broadly, conservatives are uncomfortable with the liberal more narrow form of a "rational" perspective. They *like* not having rational explanations for all their motivations. They trust the boss; they believe in her, and are comfortable relying on her. You can even see it in conservative manifestos; they're quite familiar with their unconscious, and they trust it. It's where their sense of certainty comes from. It's where all that "trust your gut" talk emanates from.

In some ways, that's a great way to live, and examples of how and where it makes sense to be instinctive and intuitive are pouring rapidly out of psychology labs nowadays. But it's worse in other ways. The compliant secretary does what he's told. He's the kind there's no talking to. Hard to butter up. Can't work an angle on him, ever. Loyal *to a fault*. They more directly channel that left-brain interpreter from chapter one, the meaning-making part of our unconscious mind that makes up rationales, using whatever mix of fact and fiction is within reach.

Political Correctness

The liberal pretension of seeing ourselves as mostly conscious, rational, and in control can appear as political correctness. We're not going to address political correctness completely, because it's surprisingly involved, but a bit about it is important for understanding conservatives.

If people say things that might reveal prejudice– if their secretary isn't particularly careful with his outside messaging– many liberals can get very offended, and react intensely against what they've heard. But it's quite likely that the offended liberal shares those same prejudices, or others like them, maybe even at a higher level, so it's an odd situation. We don't want insults flying around unnecessarily in society; we should all try to live in a pleasant, accommodating world. But on the other hand, we should all be very tolerant of some intolerance (prejudice), because we ourselves are no better than anyone else. So being properly careful– being "correct" in a healthy way– is an effort to strike a balance between being tolerant to the errant person, and being kind to potential victims.

An important part of what's happening is that the liberal's secretary is being careful to limit the *outer evidence* of their boss's prejudice, while the conservative's isn't bothering to do that as much. A mousey secretary can view such limits as being dishonest, because they trust the boss, work hard for her, and reflect the boss's will and attitudes as best they can. An independent-feeling secretary, though, might think they've magically beaten prejudice just by being able to *say* the right thing.

If we remember that, we can usually acknowledge that the unkind word or act usually isn't revealing anything outrageous, or even unusual. I've been deeply inspired by liberal activists who can be kind while being clear to someone about an inappropriate or crude thing that was said; who can let it go, and make it very clear that the other person is acceptable, an equal, whether the person takes their advice or not. That kind of activist is able to get across kindly that we're all in this together, and we're all still learning. The world of our bosses is a messy, weirdly timeless, imperfect place, and each of us is inextricably linked in this way: we all screw up the same kinds of things. When we react very strongly to revealed prejudice, we are usually trying to pretend that real life is about the secretary, and that similar prejudices don't exist within ourselves. That sense of an entitlement to pounce on a misdeed or inappropriate word is also part of what conservatives mean when they say we think we're soo smart: we're pretending we don't have the same prejudices, and seem to delight in watching closely and catching people in understandable errors, as if we secretaries are supposed to be trying to win a game of who looks the most correct at the end of the day.

Political correctness also involves situations where real, painful discrimination can cause genuine, important societal problems. The difference between that need for authentic activism and the struggle described above is something that activists have to determine themselves. Those of us not on the front lines of important causes should be very careful about our judgment, though, and remember that other, less healthy psychic forces might be behind our actions when we're not being tolerant.

The conservative trust of the boss can help us see what being true to themselves means to them. Pretending the secretary is the boss, that the secretary's opinion and wording matters enormously, and that everything is pretty squared off and polished inside our liberal brain, are all highly annoying to them.

It was very confusing to liberals when Donald Trump's followers said in surveys that one of his greatest assets was his honesty, when there was so much clear evidence that The Donald was, by far, the most untruthful candidate nominated by a major party in modern times. But their opinion makes sense when we realize that one important notion of honesty is letting the unconscious mind's *feelings* be reflected more directly in our words and actions, so that the conscious mind isn't *masking* the real self. In that sense, his fans saw him as honest– as true to himself.

This difference also partially explains why our candidates can go on and on with facts, to try to sell their ideas, while our opponents might counter, as George W. Bush did once in his 2000 election to rousing cheers, with nothing more than a forceful "I'm against it." It's why they get away with outlandish statements, and the media doesn't even bother to correct them, while lies or errors on the liberal side are often watched closely, picked at, and puffed up into scandals. We liberals are not as good at understanding the urgent necessity of direct, unconscious-driven emotion to communicate in politics well.

Finally, organized religion is much more common for conservatives, because it's a forum where odd dogma is accepted by the conscious mind, in order to get into a position to learn simple, useful, powerful lessons in a form that feels helpful to the unconscious mind. The unconscious mind could care less how logical the dogma is we use as scaffolding for our lives– and some of us secretaries can back that bet up unquestioningly. We whose secretaries instinctively sniff out and avoid goofy dogma can more easily talk our way out of taking in straight-forward, healthy lessons, playing hooky from church to be more logical elsewhere on a Sunday morning, maybe with a mimosa in hand. This isn't necessarily a great advantage in life, no matter how many atheists repeat how religious dogma is the great bugaboo of the human endeavor.

I recently attended a four-day conference where we did many goofy, even stupid things, every day. The entire set of data that was passed to me during the whole conference can be easily summed up in less than two minutes– but we were there to be *inspired enough to take in that data, in both parts of ourselves*. That ambitious goal took four days. Truly taking in anything important is a matter of recruiting emotion, inspiration, and the intellect all at once, so that those lessons can actually lodge within the boss. Conservatives usually get that idea (much) more easily than we do.

Any relationships more involved than the one with our dry cleaning lady are more about our unconscious minds than our conscious ones. That's one reason why positive emotional experiences with a person wipe away whole swaths of biases like magic, especially for conservatives. We'll discuss more about how to get to those positive emotional moments in the conversation section.

Simply knowing about our own biases also provides a great leg up when working with conservatives, because we can begin to better address the unconscious needs we both have. To restate the heart of this whole effort: **most of the progress toward understanding and working with conservatives is made through understanding ourselves**

better. By understanding and respecting our own biases, and seeing our own example, we see conservatives more accurately. We don't get as upset when their biases come up, or when they react opposite to us. We expect the biases and work explicitly to minimize them, without getting all worked up over the fact that there's a largely involuntary engine driving most of what a person says and feels. By eliminating cognitive road blocks to understanding, your relationship will improve without any more effort on anyone's part.

Once you've dampened your biases, you can pay attention to your own feelings here and there while conservatives speak, as if you have a third person popping in on your mind to check on things

Say you're speaking with a conservative co-worker you're not close to, and you notice how upset you're getting while she's telling you about a date she had with her husband that didn't go well. She seems way too subservient to him. What do you do with that feeling? Does it crowd out other parts of her story for you? Does it turn into anger at her, or her husband? Does it make you feel impatient, or sorrowful? None of these are inappropriate feelings, per se– but how examined are your feelings? Are you just stewing in them while she speaks, and then forgetting them?

You shouldn't just let the feelings pass through– you should pay attention to them– if not at the moment, then later, when you have time to think. Does the intensity of your feeling seem appropriate? Part of her attitude is almost certainly genetic, and part has been layered on since birth, through her childhood, her teen years, and maybe through her husband's influence. Do you have a sense of those influences? Are you making assumptions that bleed into judgments about her or her husband, or their church, or their politics? Is it wrong for a conservative woman, raised in a conservative home, to be so deferential? What are the consequences for her, given her personality, and her husband's? Does she have an alternative? Does she want one?

These are the kind of questions that come up for me constantly when I speak with conservatives. Some are prejudiced, or silly, or unanswerable; some are balanced, while others are immature, because all that's inside me. That's what struggling to make empathy appear looks like, especially across ideological lines. Asking ourselves these kinds of questions allows a bit of a miracle to occur almost effortlessly: our nonconscious minds become less frightened and more pliable. The fundamental error becomes less instinctive. We wonder more about their background influences. They become more complex before our eyes, and easier to relate to. Healthy attitudes seep in slowly, too, like tolerance, patience, and respect. We get less trigger-happy about our impressions. Our strong ideology-based feelings moderate.

There often comes a time in these conversations when something she says feels as mean, or rude, or stupid, or thoughtless as getting a paperweight dropped on your toe. A flash of "I don't like her," a general, negative emotion, might suddenly well up from far below, because our personality differences are usually quite fundamental. The basic solution is again related to understanding the roles of **our** bias and **our** mindfulness in relationship success. It won't make the feeling go away, but it'll make it possible to draw a contour around it, to name it, and watch where our opinion goes from there. Our immediate, intense response doesn't have to be an absolute comment on their quality as a person. We can negotiate with that gut response, and we should.

Great communication with conservatives is so ambitious that I focus my efforts much more on goals related to myself than goals about them. I try to be the best listener I can, and I try to convey the pertinent parts about myself– how interested and curious I am– as accurately as I can. I relax about the other person. After all, I don't have control of the situation. There's a couple of secretaries and two bosses in this meeting, and "I" am just one of the secretaries. I think of the objectivity assumption and the fundamental error. If I get background information down well, I can better steer myself clear of my know-it-all tendencies. I understand better that the big players, our two unconscious minds, are not listening to my clever speeches, or appreciating my brilliant points and counterpoints; they're just putting up with it, waiting it out.

The beginning of having an influence is shutting down the power of my objectivity assumption, trying to not use naïve realism (trusting my perceptions too heavily), and doing what I can to minimize the fundamental error in my judgments. The title of this book is not "Tricks for Liberals to Kick Serious Right-wing Butt"; the notion of "winning" an argument is illusory, slippery, and counter-productive. Assume you have about as much to learn from them as they do from you, give or take, no matter how silly their ideas seem. In a critical way, their ideas have nothing to do with it; you're trying to get at the person behind the ideas, trying to see why they picked the facts and tools they did, and how they use them, which is more important than the ideas themselves.

You've taken the first step already toward that goal, by understanding how our naïve realism, objectivity assumption and the fundamental error poison the effort to understand one another. We use these gateway biases to allow many other biases to creep in. In the next chapter, we'll go through the most pertinent biases in ideology that these gateway biases let in. We'll make sure these follow-on biases don't get by you, and review some conversational examples. Pretty soon, you'll be barking out biases while you watch TV, like a blackjack dealer calling out cards.

Chapter Six

THE WORKING BIASES

*The first principle is that you must not
fool yourself; and you are the easiest
person to fool.*

— *Richard Feynman*

NOW THAT WE have reviewed the way our gateway biases work, we're ready to understand our working biases, the ones we erect on top of them, using them as foundations. We are going to shift from talking about ourselves a moment, and take a closer look at conservatives, who often have a different relationship with their biases and the decision-making shortcuts (heuristics) that we all use to quickly get a handle on things.

John Wayne, who was famously conservative, said "If everything isn't black and white, I say why the hell not?" What's your impression of that attitude— does it make you nervous? Like most liberals, I find that attitude a little scary. All of us dislike unknowns and dissonance, and all of us are quite biased, but conservatives often *more explicitly value* biases and heuristics, because they greatly value the certainty and clarity that such shortcuts offer.

This is what they're doing when they say "I go with my gut," a sentence that still makes me shudder, even after years of interviews. They're wired to be addicted to closure (certainty), to enjoy its great advantages we've been talking about, things like happiness, consistency, strong social connections, and so forth. Statistically speaking, we don't see the one without the other. My "gut," like everyone else's, is a machine-like place where both good and bad ideas form, because my unconscious mind does wonderful and goofy and dangerous things.

This seems odd to grasp for intuitive people, because they've trusted gut feelings their whole lives as good, instead of thinking of them as coming from somewhere unfathomable and maybe good. But we shouldn't pretend that a great, all-knowing God, or magically absolute sense of right is shoveling your conscious mind great truths on demand.

Almost all of us go with our feelings, in the end; that has to be alright. It's not black-and-white thinking to ponder something greatly, and then go with feelings, even if it conflicts with some evidence. That's sorting out greys carefully and making a decision. Black-and-white thinking is going with simple logic or feelings *quickly*.

The thumb rule for when it's good to embrace black-and-white thinking is that shortcuts are good for simple decisions, but they're bad for non-experts to do anything but simple tasks. No matter what your gut whispers to you.

That seems straightforward, but it's not. One's gut has a tendency to happily grow an opinion on both simple and complex things– to clamber up and around anything you throw at it on its way to feeling certain. And then there's the best end-around of all: that many biases help us think something complicated is simple, so that we happily use shortcuts for decision-making when we shouldn't. That's the planning fallacy's job, remember? That's our tendency to think a task will be easy to do: "C'mawwn, just sign the contract. Stop being a whiner. You think too much. We're gonna be rich."

Most bias instruction goes through explaining a whole string of them breathlessly, as if cramming two sentences about each of them into our conscious mind is all we need to do: "Ah! I get it now– won't ever do that again." Big mistake. There's a longer list of biases in the Cognitive Bias Appendix, and I've tried to give you brief, clear definitions there– you can get through that in about ten minutes, and it's both helpful and humbling. But since real learning with deep lessons like these must involve teaching *both* our minds, and has almost nothing to do with the facts, the best way to cover biases is to go into depth about just a few. They tend to operate similarly. If you know a little about these already, it'll help, but it's not necessary. If you figure out a few detailed patterns, and your gut listens along, you'll get a great leg up on many kinds.

Watching and staying focused on how your innards handle the situation is helped by thinking situations through in more detail; it'll be more likely you'll recognize the pattern when you experience it, and be able to do something about it. A slo-mo look at the mechanics of common biases teaches us to not get sucked into the battle, and helps us keep our eye on the prize of strong communication and relationship-building. The goal is opening up unconscious minds to others– our own first. We'll concentrate on six particularly common political biases, which will help us with ten times that many.

Everyone But You Gets This, Jeez

Our first political bias is a rough one for beginners to the game of political conversation: it may be one you remember falling for. Young liberals are often anxious to talk politics or religion, excited about changing the world with their impeccable logic. They get disappointed, frustrated, and confused when the first conservative they tell their ideas doesn't buy them, at all. This is **the transparency assumption**, the notion that our idea is simple and intuitive when it's not. Assuming transparency comes about because we think we're so objective and logical that we can convey our insight in a way that no one can possibly refute. Like other biases tied in to the objectivity assumption, it results from the human condition, the fact that we're never able to see things from other people's perspective. In politics, this bias happens because we are blind to how ideological concepts are embedded in the very words we use, so the persuasion task we're trying to do is actually impossible, give or take.[1]

Conservatives and liberals use this bias in a similar way: an idea gets reinforced as simple and intuitive when we use our ingroup shorthand. Assumed transparency that's developed within a group of like-minded people can usually be recognized by how short and sweeping it is, and how few facts are required to support it. It sounded like this among our conservative friends, just over a month into President Obama's tenure:

> "This is now the Obama bear market."
> (Lou Dobbs, 3/9/09, The Lou Dobbs Show)

To conservatives, that required no support or explanation. Between liberals, the same kind of shorthand sounded like this:

> "The conservative propaganda machine began perpetuating the 'Obama bear market' myth long before the 44th President even took the oath of office."
> (John Perr, 3/16/12, crooksandliars.com)

Both phrases, "Obama bear market" and "conservative propaganda machine," are assumed to be transparent within our respective in-crowds. Imagine yourself as an arm-waving pundit, sitting there with Lou Dobbs that day: you'd say 'Hold on, Lou: whatever gave you the idea this bear market was Obama's fault?' And you'd be correct to do so. In the same way, the liberal contention by John Perr is highly controversial, and yet part of us processes it as logical and reasonable, or maybe a near certainty. Our prejudice against conservatives allows us to easily accept an image of an organized horde of conservative spin doctors, bent on manipulating the truth, murmuring together in dark rooms, planning how they would pin the recession on a candidate long before they were elected.

Our friends help us understand that an idea is transparently obvious through these kinds of shortcuts, and they reinforce that impression. This is a reminder of how incredibly social our unconscious mind is. That tunnel vision effect is the reason for some of the stranger political movements, fundraising activities and legislative proposals, as a few like-minded people get together and decide that something they agree on is a great idea. There was a city council 3-2 decision in Oroville, California about 30 years ago that *required* people to carry a visible weapon in the downtown area, as an example to the rest of America of freedom and order. The "Stop Online Piracy Act" brouhaha of early 2012 is a bit of a case study of this groupthink version of assumed transparency, as a small group of legislators were able to get the act considered and brought to the floor of the House, only to be surprised by a massive outpouring of bipartisan political power against the act because of its simplistic, far-right design.

If you're anxious to talk with someone ideologically different about a political idea, it's likely you're assuming your idea is transparent, or you're anticipating knock-'em-dead persuasion. You don't see any ideology-laden or biased parts to your point, and see it as universally true, therefore universally obvious.

As we get older, we usually control this bias better, not because we overcome it, but because acting on the bias is so nasty that we stop trying. We pre-blame their character for the problems they would have understanding our point, and don't even bother. Our friends, good and smart people all, get the idea right away; evil dummies never get our kind of thing.

You see this bias in arguments when someone asks what they think is a "simple question." Here's liberal commentator Rachel Maddow interviewing Art Robinson, a Republican candidate for congress from Oregon, in 2010, just after their initial greetings. Before the interview, Ms. Maddow has described a legal, anonymous donation that funded an ad campaign for Mr. Robinson: he pops on, she greets him, and plows right in.

MADDOW: It would be illegal for somebody to try to give you [a direct] $150,000 campaign contribution, to write you that kind of a check. Isn't this essentially an in-kind donation of that size?

ROBINSON: What's legal is the donations I've received from 3,500 people to support my campaign. I'm happy to have this help...

This beginning breaks the first rule of political conversation, as almost all talk shows do. The initial requirement of any effective political conversation is to minimize the objectivity assumption and the fundamental error. One needs at least a short introduction of each other; an outline of views; and something– anything!– that will humanize the two for each other. Talking about family a little, or shared experience, or reasons their overall ideology stirs them; some chance at that one positive emotional experience; a sense that the candidate is safe there, that we'll be at least tolerant of his world view. Think about unconscious minds when you look at people in potential conflict; don't think about facts. The host shouldn't have just prepared the candidate to be less defensive; she also needed to provide her own unconscious mind some context for the disagreeable views that were coming.

Ms. Maddow delves right in instead. We can be almost certain, even as the conversation starts, that there will be a predictable set of the two gateway biases (the objectivity assumption and fundamental error), on both sides, that render the argument worthless for anything except for the usual strengthening of everyone's biases and opinions.

Ms. Maddow has asked a "simple, transparent" question, and she gets the kind of redirect to a positive, related point that is a common technique for candidates. She gets this redirect because Mr. Robinson doesn't hear it as a simple question: he senses it as an attack. It *is* a leading question, since she's implying that the money might be tainted, which seems disconcerting enough for Mr. Robinson to begin defending himself without answering it directly. They've already started speaking past each other less than 10 seconds after their greetings. Speaking past each other, or trying to redirect each other, is always the fundamental error at work– we think we're having to get around a character flaw, to the truth, by leading the other person by the nose. Like frequent interruptions, redirects happen because of our belief in our universal truth and their personality weaknesses.

Here is Ms. Maddow's next question:

MADDOW: ...if you get elected in part because of this funding and you find out it's from criminals or foreign interests or communists or something, wouldn't that bother you?

ROBINSON: Doesn't it bother you that Mr. DeFazio [Mr.

Robinson's Democratic opponent] gets $500,000 for his campaign from special interests that he's done favors for in Washington?

MADDOW: Well, we're not– but what about the -

ROBINSON: The American people don't know where his money comes from. And your representation that this money could come from criminals is simply a way of trying to smear them and smear me by association.

MADDOW: Well, who are they though?

ROBINSON: This campaign d–

MADDOW: Who are they? Who are they?

Assumed transparency is often the first bias to barrel through the doors when assumed objectivity and the fundamental error hold sway. Ms. Morrow explained in advance of the interview how excited she was to have this interview: a bad sign. Sure enough, she jumps in immediately with a point she assumes to be powerful and clear, practically saying that the candidate has a moral obligation to ascertain the money's source. Right from the start, Ms. Morrow is **escalating**, even though it seems unconscious on her part. The image of her question in her conscious mind may have been much more neutral, getting clear early in the conversation the obvious fact that anonymous money could've been contributed by anyone. She may have wanted this simple, logical underpinning to make an attack on Mr. Robinson's ethics. That certainly seems to be Mr. Robinson's take on the situation, anyway, and he's having none of it.

The conversation might've still been handled differently by Mr. Robinson, right after the "wouldn't that bother you?" question, if he wanted to try to redirect the conversation into a more positive direction. He could've said, for instance, "Yes, it's obviously possible that the money was from a dirty source, but unfortunately, I have no control over the law that allows anonymous donations– and this terrible incumbent is taking far more money, money that we *know* is buying influence. I think your viewers should be much more concerned about him working directly on lobbyist's behalf, than about a donation from people who have kept their motivations confidential. I have faith that these are good people donating to my cause, who want improvements in government, just like my other 3500 smaller donors."

That's the kind of redirect that Ronald Reagan and Bill Clinton achieved consistently, and it's possible when we don't get too defensive. You can use that technique in your own charged conversations, when things start to go a little bad; find a way to generously acknowledge the point, and turn it to the good. We'll talk about that later.

But Mr. Robinson went on the defensive instead, in the absence of any introductory warmth, background, or common ground. The fundamental error was triggered for both of them, so that each of them looked across Rachel's table and saw a manipulative idiot. He didn't *trust* her because he thought she escalated unfairly, right as the rodeo chute opened: the suggestion that he may be ignoring a moral obligation by accepting the money was filtered through Mr. Robinson's biases, and became in his mind a direct attack on his integrity, which it wasn't (not yet, anyway). Thus began a loop of subconscious-driven, tit-for-tat behavior and escalations by each. Mr. Robinson stated that she was smearing the reputation of both him and the American people with her question. This was Mr. Robinson's own escalation, justified through bias, and the tit-for-tat continued throughout the interview.

He never answered the question. Nothing worthwhile was shared between them, on this or any other subject. All that was left now to accomplish was the reinforcement of each other's biases, the mutual validation that nearly always ends these exercises, as they validate each other's opinions that they are both morally questionable, dense, and insulting. Ms. Morrow's technique was more subtle and passive-aggressive, and she claimed the higher moral ground as she played to a sympathetic Democratic audience, while Mr. Robinson was more direct ("calling a spade a spade"), to defend himself with the swing audience he was trying to reach, as he tried to take back the moral high ground.

Later, at several points, Mr. Robinson also assumed transparency in a way himself, but this time as a persuasive technique: "everyone knows exactly what you're trying to do" (this is technically called the false consensus bias; many of the biases bleed into each other, like these two). That's a common attempt in group or public settings to claim consensus for our case among viewers, and it can be a powerful technique to rally those that agree with our point, or who are on the fence: here, Mr. Robinson may have used it in hopes that a large portion of viewers might feel that Rachel was being unfair.

Probably the most common use of the assumed transparency bias in the media are the various versions of "The American people want…," which is an attempt to recruit people to our ingroup's idea by making our idea seem popular and reasonable, as obvious to everyone else but them.

Even in this simple, seconds-long argument, assumed transparency leads quickly to several personality and bias issues that add to the conflict intensity. Ms. Morrow was unable to get any other Republican candidates to agree to be on the show for over two years after this incident. She strikes me as well-meaning, hard-working, and sincere, but can you blame them for staying away?

Starting off Right with Conservatives

My first intense political conversation with a conservative was a short, searing introduction to the art. My new bride's Aunt Mata was a John Birch (hard right) Republican, happy that Reagan had been elected, but sad that he wasn't conservative enough to do what really needed to be done to save America. At the time, I agreed at least somewhat with some of her beliefs, because I was raised conservative, and I looked forward to talking to her.

We started talking politics less than 3 minutes after she came over. Oops. Her first point was that people should take personal responsibility for their actions– a lynchpin of conservative thinking, maybe the most common point they make in conversation. I smiled, leaned forward, and said "Really?" in what I thought was a conspiratorial, playful way. I guess it wasn't. I believe she felt that my tone was disrespectful, because of our age difference– maybe the over-familiarity, or a sense I might be challenging her. I'll never know what it was, but her whole demeanor instantly changed. She colored, stammered a bit, and went on to explain with a bit of emotion what she meant. I knew I'd blown it, that the playfulness hadn't at all registered the way I'd wanted, but I wasn't sure what to do about it, so I stayed silent some minutes to let her elucidate her viewpoint. I then told her how happy I was to hear her say what she said. But by the time I agreed as heartily as I could, I had lost her. She turned sullen, and refused to talk anymore. I tried to backpedal as furiously as my verbal legs would let me, but the visit petered out quickly. They left abruptly. Later that week, she called to ask my wife to come visit, but told her, "please don't bring your husband."

By introducing what seemed to be a questioning of her opinion, the kind she had had to deal with a great deal in California, I had unwittingly recruited several biases against me. She lived a few miles away, but I never spoke to her again. She passed away a decade later.

I had unwittingly played into a heuristic, or shortcut in decision-making, called **anchoring**, in which Aunt Mata relied too much on an early piece of information to make a judgment. Our early impression tends to stick even if we get other better information later. In legal circles, this is called the "belief perseverance bias," and it's addressed in volumes of legal research, and when strategizing a litigation approach, because it's so powerful. We anchor on people's physical and personality traits; characteristics such as "good person," "stupid," "haughty," etc. get glued on their forehead, and don't get easily changed once we put them there. We also do it with political ideas: usually, the first opinion we hear about a subject that agrees with our ideology is the one we will die believing.

While anchoring exists for everyone, it is particularly conservative to anchor hard; they have more clearly defined in-groups and outgroups, and use many biases, like this one, to define you as they try to make their environment more certain. A key part of black-and-white thinking, of going with your gut, is dropping a giant anchor overboard, quickly. That's not to say they're negative or suspicious at first: they're usually quite polite when meeting. But if you came into a room to make friends with Aunt Mata in a holey T-shirt, 3 day's beard, hipster posture, and the greeting of "Waddup?," she'd have you packed out to Idiotland for good before you got close enough for the high five. You're not such a simple case obviously, but try to imagine the (many) reasons why a conservative you're meeting may take offense or be less than ecstatic at meeting you.

Efficiency in decision-making is higher priority to our unconscious mind than accuracy, which may relate to our ancient lifestyle and our early thinking abilities. That priority order is ignored by us all in our mental lives. We can decide that's mentally lazy, if we like, but there is a more useful way of thinking about it. Our unconscious mind is tasked with an incredible array of duties, and its desire for efficiency when figuring out the lay of the land grew out of having to find the tradeoff between accuracy and speed that allowed us to survive. Even now, our mental shortcuts (heuristics) are mostly accurate and helpful, but we do complex things occasionally in modern life, and we often mess those up when we use heuristics like anchoring.

Personality and Preparation

There are times, especially with the far right, when personality clashes happen because you just can't relate to each other. So be it. No matter how many pearls you scrawl in the margins of this book, sometimes someone else is a bridge too far for you to reach. Often, it's because one or both of you are too impolite, but it's not just that. Openness, orderliness, and stability are not easy lands to traverse if they're unfamiliar countries for you. My own experience is that, wherever we are in the political spectrum, we can only reach about half its distance in any direction with any reliability in personal relationships. This means that someone who's far left can read this guide all day, and meditate, and get their chakras aligned by a professional, but their odds decrease greatly when they try to relate to anyone more conservative than someone in the middle. Center-left can reach center-right; far-right can reach centrists. There are many, many exceptions, but that's a good thumb rule.

For anyone that's a stretch for you ideologically or personality-wise, we have to make the grownup choice to somehow balance "being ourselves" and taking simple, powerful steps to make sure the conversation goes well. Rather than trying to be insincere, or scheme, we should be trying to focus on great courtesy, interest, and respect, while getting our physical, viewable side in order. The idea is not to be a different person, but to prevent distortions from happening because you forget the importance of bias. You can become a kind of temporary, honorary conservative that way, when it counts– at the beginning. If that initial connection is strong, you will get more leeway with your nutball ideas or your unruly kids later, because you successfully leveraged anchoring; instead of anchoring hurting you, it helped.

This is our first example of where a bias or heuristic can help you. Yes: a distortion of reality in your favor. We've been emphasizing the way biases ruin everything, but that's only half the story. A great introduction might slot you into the good-guy bucket, where you have the tendency to stay, and be defended like one of the gang.

Having an excellent beginning, developing a genuine interest and appreciation, and spending quality time with conservatives are the best tools you have to beat the **outgroup bias**, our negative stereotyping bias against people we don't normally come across. Big people, slow people, conservative people, women, Mexicans: if our unconscious minds could talk, they might give a little lecture on all kinds of things about each of those groups, because researchers have discovered that almost all of us have illogical unconscious opinions about these groups. Our brains are driven by efficiency, and our unconscious mind has welded people and situations together in clumps to make sense of the world, instead of seeing everyone as their own unique selves. It takes work– slowing down and paying attention– to treat people like themselves. You have to seem worth it, which is a surprisingly big hurdle for us cognitive misers.

While conservatives can have a strong outgroup bias, the great news is that they are often happy to find out enough detail about you, to create an exception and let you into the ingroup. Contrary to our beliefs, it's more common among them to default to including you in the ingroup than to assume you're part of the outgroup. You can at least get a kind of temporary, honorary-membership status, because that's the kind of thing they do as polite, positive people.

There's a wide range of where people put you, in their mind: depending on how much they value politeness, or politics, or something else about you, you could be put in their ingroup, their outgroup, or somewhere in the wide middle, as they decide about you. In sensitive situations, like ideology, there's often more than one factor involved.[2]

Being in the ingroup, even temporarily, is a little miraculous with conservatives. Not that they think your political ideas are acceptable, but if they've noticed that you're a good person, that usually weighs in more heavily. Many take pride in being able to get along well with a liberal. You wouldn't know that from listening to conservative talk radio, but it's much more a part of their ethos than we allow them. Many like to be flexible about differences between people; most think that's part of being an American. They value individual freedoms highly, and I've seen them be astoundingly tolerant of all kinds of strange, unlikable characters out of loyalty. Just like liberals, a conservative crowd is full of all kinds, and they usually use the notions of personal liberty and tolerance to accept each other and group together strongly despite their differences. If you can get into the ingroup, you will be given much the same leeway.

Once your relationship is sound, it still doesn't mean it's necessarily advisable to talk politics. If they avoid the subject, I certainly would. You can always ask about topics that are secretly cousins to political subjects through personality. Parenting; volunteering; job situations; organizing and scheduling; all of these are sidelong ways to absorb what it means to be conservative, and topics like these are a great way for you to begin to appreciate in your bones some of the good, bias-busting elements of their life.

Within yourself, anchoring and the outgroup bias can be reduced a great deal by being conscious of them, and trying to beat them. If things take a less than stellar turn, take conscious care to not anchor your negative impressions of people: tell yourself that you are not seeing the whole story. Take the same approach with political points: get in the habit of consciously fighting anchoring by working to find different perspectives, especially when you notice you've adopted a very particular opinion from one source quickly. You'll avoid wielding your cognitive miser samurai sword at the wrong time.

Being careless with anchoring is like letting your kid play with matches. Our unconscious mind runs *instantly* with an initial impression usually picked up in a few seconds or less, and rapidly sends our conscious mind off to justify the boss's guess. In a study, people who are asked to estimate probabilities of an event happening guess a *much lower* chance of it occurring if a researcher just asks if the odds of it happening are low;[3] hearing the word "low" at the beginning sped their mind skittering around in mental neighborhoods where the word low might be comfortable, and voila, the estimate comes out low. The instant someone says anything while we're thinking about the problem, we "mindlessly" anchor on it, even though there's no logical reason to.[4] Unfortunately, negative words like "no" or "poor," or even "sorry" may accidentally cause anchoring if used in the first few seconds, so we should be clear, positive and cheerful at beginnings.

We can't avoid this kind of initial bias completely, but unless we use conscious care, we'll distort our acquaintance's reality needlessly. The simplest things, like good initial eye contact and a firm handshake, or a bit of preparation, or careful attention, can play a deceptively large role in making or breaking a relationship or conversation.

In contrast to my aunt Mata's intense rejection, a confrontation or unpleasant visit often means much less to a conservative than to you, even if they display disgust, or get angry or impolite. I'd say that's much more common than my aunt Mata's reaction, though both happen (she was very far right, where anchoring tends to be intense). Many move on almost as if the emotional unpleasantness never happened, because they take the notion of tolerance seriously. We can leave the experience with a much worse feeling than the conservative does; more emotionally affected.

That sounds like an opposite of anchoring to liberals, but it's just admitting that even a strong anchor is often still negotiable, if we're pleasantly stubborn about it. Poor anchoring can be addressed, and usually should be. Conservatives can have their stereotypes about liberal rudeness reinforced by the way we end a conversation, or by our unwillingness to come back to the table and engage on a personal basis after a conflict has occurred. Our effort will be both appreciated and rewarded by the majority of conservatives.

Consistent effort and a thick skin are needed, particularly with difficult people, or those with whom we've had a conflict. I regret that I never tried again with Aunt Mata; I may have been able to break through. When things are challenging with a person, try to remember that you're built to be internally tortured more by these difficulties than conservatives are. Their more natural acceptance of conflict, and their thick boundaries, can sometimes make reconciliation or useful compromise very possible, or even easy, when it seems to you as if the two of you are thousands of miles apart. I've gotten used to ignoring my own fear or frustration after a clash. There is a mini-form of anchoring that can take place every new day, because newer impressions can also have a big impact from being so vivid (a version of anchoring called the availability heuristic, because the new experience is more "available" to the mind, more vivid). You may find that a new day, especially after a long break, may allow the two of you to re-anchor on a better footing. Re-anchoring, called anchoring adjustment, can happen using information presented in a better light, or in more detail.

What Do I Know, Ask the Boss

Recent work in evolutionary psychology has shown that the most dramatic evolution of our species lately have been in our social skills, especially our ability to learn from each other, and follow each other in complicated hierarchies.[5] Our ability to lead and follow one another in complex ways is the primary way we developed culture. This respect can be taken too far, of course; if it is, it's called the **authority bias**. This bias lets us use information given to us by a source we respect, like our supervisor, and not do the verification we should before acting on the information.

The authority bias exists because it allows us to be cognitive misers, and duck a tremendous amount of complexity. If we hear something on our usual news source, do we need to hear it from a second reliable source to believe it, or from someone with a different opinion? Yes, we probably should. But how often do we do that extra research before we start spouting off about it?

Let's add a little complexity. Some authorities, like a cello teacher, probably don't need to be questioned much, even through you're depending on the information: they obviously know much more than you, and they have mastery over a relatively narrow set of information—like how to play an instrument well. Other experts, like your English teacher, may need to be double-checked occasionally, because there's opinion mixed in with the expertise, and because the field is relatively complicated. Still others, like your mechanic or doctor, probably need to be verified with a second opinion in many cases, unless you've known them a long time, because their work is risky and difficult. And a spiritual leader should always be validated against others if it's controversial advice, because of the potential cost of failure.

Our dependence on authority should vary, depending on the situation, so it can be a little tough to see whether we're using the authority bias, or if we're wasting our time doing unnecessary research. We can even be guilty of the authority bias by being too inspired by song lyrics, or misusing something we read and were inspired by. There aren't any obvious rules. We should remember, though, that the authority bias is tough to avoid, especially when we're taking advice from strong personalities, or celebrated experts.

Now— politics. If you get information from a pundit you trust, you may be getting it in exaggerated form. You might be getting only half the story, so that it leads to a wrong idea even if it's mostly true. That's the most common version of the authority bias in action. The research required to beat the bias wasn't necessarily to check a fact. The pundit may not have been lying, but did you get all the facts you needed to see the situation accurately? Maybe; maybe not.

This bias can be attractive because we're joining a crowd, an ingroup that we like, as we adopt the authority's opinion. Also, the interpretation you want is often exactly the pundit's ("I LOVE this guy!") Research may make you disagree a little here or there on some things, but the difference isn't enough to warrant all the time it would take to look it up– after all, saving all that time is why you have that great pundit in the first place. Right?

No, not right. It doesn't matter that you generally agree with the authority. If we're serious enough about an idea, we should be in the habit of finding an alternative viewpoint on it. You'll be surprised how useful that habit will quickly end up, even if your "authority" was 90% right, an inhuman level of accuracy; that will still end up making you wrong or harmfully partial way too much.

Right-wing radio is so incredibly popular in America because conservatives are very susceptible to the authority bias. Almost all the orderliness-related conservative values we addressed– consistency, certainty, simplicity, hierarchy– lean them toward people like Hannity, Limbaugh, Anderson, Ingraham, Jones and Levin. That's one reason why we should be much less hopeful about changing their ideas about facts. Right-wing news is more accurate than many people give it credit for; where the real problem usually can be found is the lack of any background for a fact; the missing context; the facts left unsaid. It ties back to our original point about naïve realism, our usual philosophy of life: the problem isn't whether we're accurate or not, but what we're spending out time looking at. The audience is often being fed things that are true, or mostly true, which makes them feel confident; it's just not enough things that are true to provide a helpful, balanced picture.

There aren't any wonderful secrets to dealing with the authority bias well that I know of, other than trying to be careful about our own use of sources. It's a big problem for the right, and will continue to be. We anchor on ideas the same way we anchor on people. It's never a good idea to think you're going to persuade a dedicated conservative radio fan on any standard liberal-conservative conflict point, because Rush has covered that same point adequately roughly twice a week for the last decade; you don't have anything to add, except lies.

Ah Hah! Just as I Thought.

Allow me to make an introduction: authority bias, meet the **confirmation bias**. The confirmation bias lets us use evidence just to confirm our beliefs, so we can feel good about them. The confirmation bias also encourages us to ignore or misinterpret evidence that challenges our beliefs. We use the authority bias to rely carelessly on whoever we like for political points, because we're just going to use the confirmation bias to reinforce our beliefs anyway. The two together are tough to beat for narrowing our perspective and making the whole business enjoyable, like reading a well-written, predictable novel. They help us create a black-and-white world; there's bad guys, good guys, and a bunch of simple ideas about what the bad guys do, and what the good guys need to do.

Conservatives tend to suffer both these biases relatively strongly. If they're ideological and well-informed, trying to convince them of most political ideas, or of what you consider facts, is a waste of your time (though if you have a good relationship, you both can chink at the corners of your world view and be successful intermittently).

Lately, the confirmation bias has ballooned into a little field of its own among psychologists, because it's become clear how much we do this. We treat our favorite ideas like movie stars treat their handheld poodles, constantly petting and loving and smooching them, instead of doing whatever else we should be doing with our brains. That's the kind of thing we're doing while we're busy being cognitive misers, avoiding the more useful information trying to get through our cranium to where it might do some good. Psychologists call the field of studies **motivated reasoning**, because it has tentacles that reach into the many biases that happen because we're so *motivated* to think a certain way. The field is getting incredibly complicated, and we don't need to be experts. But in particular, they study the complicated wrangling of reality we use to:

- make our ideas look good,
- make bad guy ideas look bad,
- ignore what makes our ideas look bad, and
- ignore what makes bad guy ideas look good.

We might think that conservatives use motivated reasoning more than liberals, since they use the authority bias, anchoring and other distortions so avidly. But the evidence on motivated reasoning is still mixed. There is one group of people that we have good evidence use it more than others, though: on average, if you're 1) good at figuring things out, and 2) you're ideological, then you use the confirmation bias much more enthusiastically than most people.[6]

That may sound strange, but it makes sense. It has to do with how many reasons a bright or careful person can conjure up to make a case. I hang around many smart people, and it's amazing what pillars of funk they can build with all that intelligence, and how fast and earnestly they can do it. My most dramatic experiences along these lines are with academics, some of whom are the most ignorantly ideological people you could meet, as well as the most brittle thinkers. Among conservatives, this is a very well-known tendency of academics, and they think of it a little unfairly as a basic liberal pattern of stupidity, in the "they think they're soo smart" category.

I was once with a close friend, a physics genius– a nuclear physics genius, mind you– who tried to convince me patiently for about ten minutes, with graphs and equations, that if you ran to your car in the rain, you'd get exactly as wet as you would if you walked to it. Because you're out there in the rain more time when you walk, sure, but if you run, you're going to smash into a boatload of unnecessary raindrops. Raindrops you could've avoided smashing into if you would've just walked sensibly through the downpour, like a physics genius.

I remember thinking while he was patiently drawing one of the graphs that I'd be telling the story of the physics genius in the rain my whole life, and I have been.

Arguing Our Way to the Truth

The findings about the bad biases of problem-solving ideologues align perfectly with what's known as the Argumentation Theory of Reasoning, developed by cognitive anthropologists. This theory makes a persuasive case that early mankind originally just had intuitive and simpler thinking, like chimpanzees. Reasoning is a big improvement, chaining a few ideas together to get something done. Instead of "I'm hungry, let's go kill a deer," you might think "I'm going to get hungry, so I'll make a stabby pointy thing I can throw, so I don't have to jog for two days to run the next deer down."

It seems like a no-brainer that we started reasoning so we could be more successful at hunting, and perform all the other whatnot of hunter-gatherer life better. But one problem has nagged at researchers for decades: if reasoning well makes such a difference, why are we so terrible at most kinds? They realized that reasoning started for *social* reasons: so that we could *argue* more complicated points, as an alternative to physical violence, threats, or other terrible solutions to conflict. This concerns a period in our species' history when roughly 15% of humans died from murder; even terrible arguments were huge improvements over the alternatives.

Here's what makes this theory strange, wonderful, and probably right. If reasoning began to justify people's ideas, that means that reason is a servant of our intuitions– in other words, that our conscious mind is the servant of our unconscious mind. Reason would act as a translator of sorts of what the unconscious mind wants. And that's exactly what anthropologists and evolutionary psychologists see in experiments.

If reasoning was designed from scratch for problem-solving the way we usually assume– if our unconscious mind had just decided one day, "you know, I need a genius, computer-like guy around here, so I'm happier and more productive"– we'd be independent thinkers, wandering through life making dispassionate points that lead to the truth. Politics would be incredibly boring, since we'd deal with useful facts and risks, probably with accountants doing it all, instead of all the tall, male lawyers with great hair that do it now. Biases that cause much of our violence might have disappeared. We wouldn't have been able to rip apart the primitive, inflexible logic of that conversation between Ms. Morrow and Mr. Anderson so easily.

What seems to have happened instead is *our unconscious mind wanted to do exactly what it was doing, but better*: "I'm going to get killed if I can't show them I'm worth keeping alive"; or "I want to convince my way into leading the tribe, instead of risking getting killed"; or "The last time I raped Thog's daughter, Thog almost killed me; how can I attract a woman tonight?" Reasoning, which was really just making arguments, wasn't verbal when it started, but non-verbal, as we see in chimps: primitive, pre-vocal "reasoning" for the unconscious mind's desires.

Motivated reasoning, or the confirmation bias, fits right under the wing of the Argumentation Theory of Reasoning. The more you like working on problems, the more tools you have to make more arguments– and the evidence is that you're more likely to make them, true or not. This should make the brighter of us much more humble and careful, because that reasoning power we pride ourselves having wasn't built for what we assume it was. There's even good evidence that part of the purpose of reasoning is to *fool ourselves* into believing things, in a natural extension of our unconscious mind's gifts that way. That may sound strange or horrible, but it makes sense if the conscious mind is mostly the good servant of the unconscious mind.

This is a little-known, deep criticism of the power and usefulness of reasoning. It's helpful to remember reason's origins, to keep ourselves humble. Reason can help in some ways, no question, but we also use reason just to persuade, and enthusiastically remake the world into our unconscious mind's image of it. We assume we're using logic to get at truth, when we may be just building a more elegant-looking path back to our unconscious mind's opinion. Other personality characteristics besides intelligence, like compassion or conscientiousness, can be much more useful when trying to be accurate in life.

You use motivated reasoning a great deal, and so do your friends. We almost never try to take the other fellow's side, or try hard to see a broader or contrasting perspective from the one provided by our favorite source of news or opinion, the way a good reasoner would. In my experience, we liberals are only rarely even able to acknowledge maturely a very good counterpoint to our opinion.

As long as most of our political conversations with friends consist of various complaints about conservatives, the pile of distortions we drag into the situation stack upon one another; our half-right ideas zing around the whole time, like bullets in a spaghetti western.

Sealing the Deal

Before we leave biases, let's cover two tricks we use on ourselves when we're in strong conflict, so that our biases can keep working. We have a great deal of mental energy getting spent behind the scenes to keep that unwieldy stack of biases working, and protect our beliefs. It's a serious investment– which creates an odd problem. We put so much of ourselves into keeping our ideas *feeling* certain that, if they start looking wrong, we usually become *even more* committed to them, to keep feeling safe in our cocoon of beliefs.

This is **escalation of commitment**, another heuristic. It's our way of fighting for what we believe in, of being loyal to our world view, our friends and our heroes, as the pressure increases. This is our personal version of America's late escalation of the Vietnam War, our final push in the face of known failure, directed by Richard Nixon and Henry Kissinger. It caused the majority of Vietnamese and American deaths in the war, and all the Cambodian deaths. In business, we see this heuristic used to pour good money after bad into a poor investment, even though one of the first things covered in business school is the need to ignore "sunk costs" as water under the bridge when making decisions about the future. That's tough to do. It means accepting we might be wrong, exactly when we're trying to reason ourselves and everyone around us into seeing that we're still completely right.

Escalation of commitment happens during strong disagreements, often on both sides, especially when someone has made a potentially good point that we're not prepared to defend against. We run and grab this heuristic when we aren't getting to use our confirmation bias the way we're used to; things are being said on the other side that are too reasonable, making us uncomfortable. Isn't that just the *worst?*

Escalation injects an especially irrational turn to conversation, marking the end of the line for reasonable discussion, and the beginning of circular arguments, ad hominem attacks, desperate leaps of logic, and odd emotional bleats. It's easy for each of us, in these situations, to see the irrationality of the other person, but we're blind to the excesses we're using in response. This happened at the latter end of the conversation between Ms. Maddow and Mr. Robinson, as they started to speak furiously over each other and appeal emotionally to the audience.

Our other trick under stress is much more common. If you can get a handle on fixing it, your life may take a big turn for the better. It's the humble tit-for-tat situation we get into with people. You know– she did that, so I did this, and now we're even–? It seems straightforward to us, like a blue-collar version of the Golden Rule: be nice to me, and I'll be nice back; do me wrong, and I'll do *you* wrong. Simple. Seems healthy. If the world would just pay attention to tit-for-tat, you'd think people would just self-correct, and start behaving, since it's so sucky for us if we're rude or mean.

The problem is that, if we think someone did us wrong, we don't pay back what people dished out to us: we dish out, on average, **forty percent more pain back.** This was the finding of a group of scientists[7] who told pairs of test subjects to push each other exactly as much as the other pushed. *Every single person involved* consistently overestimated how hard the push they received was, and not by a little. At one point, both people in one pair came up separately to the researchers and asked them if the other person had secretly gotten instructions to use more power every time: "Was this some kind of psychology experiment?"

Oddly, enough, this brutal tendency of ours is related to why we can't tickle ourselves. Our minds have a way of tuning down our sense of what we ourselves do, because of a complicated prediction our brains have to make whenever we do things, when accurate feedback would cause problems in our reactions at normal levels, kind of like being able to tickle ourselves. When we feel another person push us, it seems to be a much stronger signal to our brains than the one we felt when we pushed them, because it *is* a much stronger signal– it's not dialed way down by being predictable, like it is when we try to tickle ourselves.

Social science hasn't copied this study with people arguing about politics– that's tough to do. But a similar intense escalation seems to naturally occur with each other when we do tit-for-tat with someone who's upset us in an argument, or hurt our feelings, because the same biological systems are involved in the sensing of the wrong. Gang rivalries are a particularly cruel and stark example, where small insults quickly ramp up into drive-by executions. But if we pay attention, we can watch it occur between children, sensitive partners, co-workers, and celebrities who play the drama out publicly. Somehow, we can't sense the damage we're doing to another as it goes out— but we sure can when it comes back our way.

There's an incredibly valuable lesson available to us, which can change our life's course dramatically if we take it seriously: know that we have this awful bias that makes tit-for-tat thinking surprisingly inaccurate, even dangerous, and always, always work hard to give other people the benefit of the doubt about how intense or mean they meant to be. Ignore problems, or talk to them about it, but don't start trying to *imitate* how much damage they caused you, or take the attitude that they need punishment like what they dished out. You will almost certainly be unfairly escalating, because of a biological problem with the senses.

This can give you a fresh perspective on some ancient biblical advice: "If someone strikes you on one cheek, turn to him the other, also...do to others as you would have them do to you." That's the Golden Rule, which is *designed* to allow for our distortions about other people's intentions. Use the Golden Rule itself, instead of the blue-collar version.

A useful twist on this was given as advice to Supreme Court Justice Ruth Ginsburg by her mother-in-law: in every good marriage, it helps sometimes to be a little deaf. We seem to be built neurologically to take things way too seriously, so we should get used to giving others a much wider latitude than we might think fair.

We like to think of our biases as these unfortunate distorters that stand between our mind and reality, keeping us from understanding the truth as easily as we'd like. We have to accept that *both our biases and our conscious mind are the faithful servants of a "reality" created and maintained by our unconscious mind.* Most of those biases are doing exactly what they were built to do. Without realizing it, especially under stress, we contort, or pick-and-choose reality to align with our beliefs, to what our unconscious mind wants to see.

Here's our simple, naïve sense of what's going on:

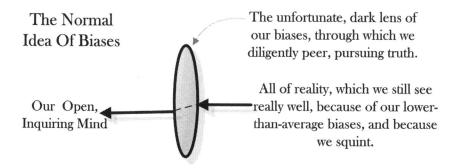

The Normal
Idea Of Biases

The unfortunate, dark lens of
our biases, through which we
diligently peer, pursuing truth.

All of reality, which we still see
really well, because of our lower-
than-average biases, and because
we squint.

Our Open,
Inquiring Mind

This is people's idea of biases; it implies a slight distortion, if one isn't careful. But that isn't it at all: biases are a key tool of our unconscious mind to keep us chasing its goals, and bend reality to its bidding, for both healthy and unhealthy reasons. It looks more like this:

How We Really Use Biases

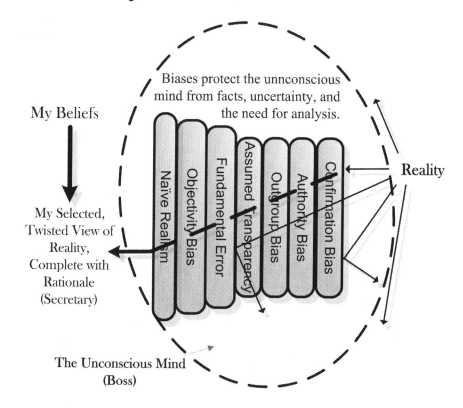

Biases protect the unnconscious
mind from facts, uncertainty, and
the need for analysis.

My Beliefs

My Selected,
Twisted View of
Reality,
Complete with
Rationale
(Secretary)

Naïve Realism

Objectivity Bias

Fundamental Error

Assumed Transparency

Outgroup Bias

Authority Bias

Confirmation Bias

Reality

The Unconscious Mind
(Boss)

These two versions of what's going on couldn't be more different. Instead of interpreting reality pretty well to live, we use partial, distorted portions of reality to reinforce our beliefs. Some pieces of reality are never seen, of course, but then other pieces are missed because the confirmation bias killed them, or they were twisted or destroyed by any number of the other biases along the gauntlet. In the naïve realist version of life, we get through a little distortion and see reality well enough to do a good job. In actuality, we manipulate reality with bias and heuristics, to bend it to our unconscious idea of how things are. Then, we act based on that internal, created version of reality. In the optimistic version, reality dictates our actions; but in our real lives, our beliefs are used, not reality. The only way reality that doesn't agree with our world view intrudes on our lives is when the signal is so strong and clear that our biases are unable to filter it out.[8]

Conservatives bring the same, sad layers of biases to the party as we do, but they're not likely to be particularly delicate or nuanced about employing them, because of how biases help with feelings of certainty. The more political of them are usually familiar with the liberal arguments about their strong biases, and there's a common pushback from them that either takes the form of minimizing their bias, or saying that bias is a big problem for everyone. So, with an attitudinal problem to boot, there may be a dozen more biases and heuristics atop these we've covered involved when working with them. You can read about those bonuses in the Cognitive Bias Appendix.

We've talked about the neurological origins of ideology, the personality factors, and the landscape of both gateway and common biases. Now, keeping those factors in mind, we'll look at the way that the real world forms us into ideological creatures. We can understand conservatives individually pretty well just knowing what we've already reviewed, but to see why they act as a group the way they do about climate change, or prison reform, or tax policy, we have to understand how they're affected by one another, and how the world affects their focus.

Getting past the worst results of our biases and understanding the ways we make decisions poorly allows us to stand at the edge of each other's lives, peering in through the murk, finally asking some of the right questions.

Chapter Seven

A WORD ABOUT POLITICS

*...we're going to end up like a lot of
the other places, and we're not going
to have a country left.*
— Donald Trump

L ET'S STEP BACK from the snapshots of individuals that we've
been taking from all these angles, and look at how conservatives *group*
themselves, and how those groups come to believe things, with all those
brains and personalities and biases interacting together. We need to
know them politically, or *socially*. It's good to know what conservatives
believe, to understand and work with them well, but it's essential to see
why they believe what they do, and how they get to those beliefs.

Making general pronouncements about conservatives everywhere and
always is dicey. But we have great statistical evidence that, in modern
America, there are two types of conservatives.[1] As we cover those types,
we'll talk about the "bad boys" of each type, subgroups that are giant
headaches for other conservatives and for us. Finally, we'll look at how all
those different people work together, and the strong influences they have
on each other. That will help us understand what we see them doing in
politics today, and aid in our conversations with them.

Social Conservatives

About two-thirds of conservatives are **social conservatives**, which
means that their natural fondness for order makes them try to live lives in
keeping with quite specific moral and behavioral ideas. They want
individual behavior in society to conform with their moral ideals, so that
America is successful. This is the type that most follows tradition, often in
the form of religion. That can be as simple and healthy as encouraging

marriage rather than living together, or trying to keep a family close, or encouraging volunteering in the local community or church.

Guiding society's behavior can also have a darker side, though. In South Africa, during apartheid, social conservatives dominated the government, and prohibited TV in the country until 1976 to maintain control over what people were exposed to. In India, social conservatives fight to establish India as purely Hindu, and to suppress other religions.

Well over half of our social conservatives are traditionally religious, but whether they are or not, they usually want to see laws that preserve traditional values. In America, besides wanting us to obey versions of Christian principles, social conservatives tend to be hawkish on national security, as a natural extension of their orderliness and desire for control.

Authoritarians

Social conservatives are often high in **authoritarianism**,[2] a confusing term that academics have used in different ways for generations. A good way of thinking about authoritarians is that they want *conformity* to their ideals, and they like *strong authority*. Scientists don't have a test that shows whether we're "authoritarians" or not; they can only test us as high or low in authoritarianism, so we should be quite careful labeling specific people authoritarian.

Think of being high in authoritarianism as being very focused on the success of our own group, less focused on individual freedoms, and comfortable using authority to have people outside the group obey societal rules. While these things are true about all social conservatives, authoritarians ramp it up a great deal.

To our ears, that sounds disquieting. We like conforming, at least some, and we're ok with obeying societal rules, but that bit about being less focused on individual freedoms is a little creepy. And "using authority" to get what we want sounds manipulative.

Until recently, the most popular academic term for the statistical concept behind authoritarianism was "right-wing authoritarianism," or RWA; it's origins were from just after World War Two, when a measure was designed of how fascist people were. Most social conservatives measure high in both the modern version of authoritarianism and RWA, so both terms drive them crazy, especially now that the terms are becoming more common. Since the average conservative measures about 65% as high as the maximum possible score in one common measure of authoritarianism, and "high" is anything above 50%, it sounds like (liberal) academics are calling most conservatives goose-stepping Nazis.

They have a point. After all, liberals can be controlling and intolerant, too, yet the concept has still mostly been called right-wing authoritarianism anyway. The measure is specialized to only pick up the conservative version, and almost all the research available on authoritarianism is exclusively about the conservative version. Yet the two greatest genocidal tragedies of the modern era, caused by Stalin and Mao Tse-Tung, were examples of left-wing authoritarianism.

One researcher calls this liberal version "postmodern authoritarianism," because it can't be measured in the same way as "normal" authoritarianism, but the results can be just as frightening, and maybe even worse.[3] The great socialist thinker, essayist, and novelist George Orwell spent much of his life fighting right-wing authoritarianism, but made it clear that he feared the left-wing version more. He endured intense fights with American fans of Stalin for many years, and wasn't shy about connecting Stalin's approach to the intolerance and disrespect for freedom he saw among the West's activists.

American colleges are famously populated nowadays with many intolerant liberals who want to force a certain kind of conformity in thought and action, who are comfortable shouting down guest speakers and administrators, or firing people for political incorrectness, in violation of the spirit of free speech.

Modern left-wing authoritarianism isn't just a college problem, either. In my work as an activist, I've had to address our own form of authoritarianism in various activist communities a great deal; it can be surprisingly vicious and counter-productive. The broader liberal community has many authoritarians buried within it, as well. In 2013, an anonymous women who told a confusing, biased-sounding joke about AIDS to her 170 followers on Twitter almost instantly became the most popular person on Twitter for a day, lost her job because of intense, direct public pressure on her employer, and endured death threats; the cruel, violent, and vindictive responses were virtually all liberals.

There are also two conflicting points that both sides should be able to agree on, that should help liberals and conservatives both be careful to not be quick-draw McGraws about how horrible authoritarianism is. A large part of authoritarianism as normally defined has to do with wanting strong military and police forces. First, threat-sensitive people might pick up on a threat faster and better than those low in authoritarianism would, and help avert a crisis. We can and should recognize that as a possibility; there are historical examples of just that kind of early-warning benefit from being authoritarian. Churchill's seven years of warnings about Hitler, as he was bitterly opposed the whole time by liberals, is the most infamous example in the last century, but there are others.

At the same time, there's also the possibility that threats can be *made worse* through an aggressive attack on a perceived threat, or that threats can be *created out of thin air.* There are also many historical examples of that, such as most of the wars America initiated in the twentieth century.

Because most social conservatives register as high or very high in authoritarianism as it's defined, researchers have recently been trying to rename and reframe the concept so that it can be seen as more useful and less simplistic than as just an attack on conservatives. One conservative researcher called a similar construct "directiveness," which captures something of the focus of their perspective. One of the leading authoritarian researchers said she would've preferred to call it "difference-ism," emphasizing how they see the world as about managing differences between people. Another is trying to popularize "social conformity-autonomy," which I think is a pretty good description, because it makes clear that the measure is trying to figure out whether conforming or being independent is more important to you.

The most popular test for authoritarianism currently is incredibly simple, and seems quite innocent. Here are the four questions academics usually ask to decide how high in (conservative) authoritarianism you are. If you prefer the second choice for all four questions, or for three of the four, you're high in authoritarianism.

> Please tell me which one you think is
> more important for a child to have:
>
> Independence or respect for elders?
> Self-reliance or obedience?
> To be considerate or to be well-behaved?
> Curiosity or good manners?

Now, what's wrong with those second answers? Personally, I wouldn't choose three or four of those second choices, like most social conservatives do– but I wouldn't say, off the top of my head, that it's terribly unreasonable to, either. On its own, each question could go either way. For me, it depends on the kid I might be thinking of. You could argue alongside conservatives that being high in authoritarianism is actually *more healthy* in some ways– and you would most certainly be right. After all, if you pick the second answer every time, you're almost certainly a very orderly, polite person– that's not all bad. As we've said, there are advantages that go with the disadvantages of being high in any of the five ideological personality tendencies we've covered.

So if those responses can be healthy, why bother to measure authoritarianism, anyway? Why make conservatives angry with all this in the first place? What's useful about the concept of the balance between conforming and independence? It turns out there's a simple answer to those questions: being high in authoritarianism is strongly associated statistically with all kinds of things most of us liberals think of as strong negatives, and other things that just *are* strong negatives. If you're high in authoritarianism, you're *much more likely* to be racist, and comfortable with discrimination, restricting personal freedoms (privacy, sexual, religious), very heavy punishment of criminals and enemies, and an aggressive military. This is the brutal, undeniable, statistical back side of some of the healthy traits we've praised in earlier chapters, the orderliness and low neuroticism that buy them stronger nuclear families, higher average education levels, higher average levels of happiness, higher earnings, and so forth. All that great stuff has a cost elsewhere in society, at least when high orderliness is involved: authoritarianism reflects much of that cost.

It's amazing that such a simple, seemingly innocent set of questions about child-rearing can reveal so much, but it does. Statistical work shows that conservatives only tend toward those negative things to the extent that they are high in authoritarianism. In other words, there's a tendency that many conservatives share that makes them more likely to become racist, or aggressive militarily, but it's not being conservative that makes them susceptible to that kind of thinking; it's authoritarianism. The two things are most assuredly different.

It's worth digging into those questions a little, to understand why so many bad indicators can be associated with such innocent questions.

If you value independent thinking in a child more than you value them conforming, like me, you're going to be low in authoritarianism. But I had to think about the answers, because people should be balanced, and it's hard to guess what proper balance is with a child. If everyone raised kids like I ordered up when I answered those questions, you might well end up with too many interesting, curious, independent, disobedient, ill-mannered adults.

The personality traits orderliness and openness tend to be traded off genetically, because they're opposing skills, to a certain extent; as humans, we tend to specialize in one or the other. That specialization also gets at this same notion of conforming versus independence.

Here's four answers from someone who's low in authoritarianism (me), on the left, next to a person's answers who's very high in it.

Independent	Respects their elders
Self-reliant	Obedient
Considerate	Well-behaved
Curiosity	Good manners

These are two completely different kinds of kids we've ordered up, aren't they? Being very high in authoritarianism means that, at *every single* chance you got, you voted to make the kid conform. You weren't balanced. Hidden in such a single-minded pattern is an assumption that they knew what's best for *any kid, anytime*; that all kids need what amounts to orderliness training, first and foremost, and then they can worry about their hobbies, whether they're happy on their own here or there, or what color they'll ask to paint their nails. If they were good today.

The kid on the left is kind, independent, and curious, which, at least to liberals, seems at least somewhat well-rounded. The other kid? She's an obedience specialist, with good manners thrown in, in case all that obedience didn't please daddy enough.

If we met her, we'd almost certainly think, "She's a good kid." But if we paid attention to her, we might see that those other individualizing urges may be missing. That's the problem. She might end up a wonderful human being, having been raised well, with love and care– a nice, orderly human being, with normal variation and plenty of independent thinking. But she'll *tend* not to, often. Statistically speaking, she has a tendency to want to force people to live her way, and she grows up trusting of the kind of strong authority that might've molded her. Someone could convince her– again, statistically speaking– to believe false things relatively easily; or she can be manipulated into doing questionable activities through misplaced, overly enthusiastic obedience or loyalty.

What the data is telling us through these four simple questions is that **emphasizing order so much is a problem for society**. That's the lesson of authoritarianism. It's too much of a good thing. A living, breathing "good kid" can't be built by just emphasizing that they need to conform; we also have to encourage their own ideas, their own motivations, and their interests. The kid on the right has about a third of the picture right, and now needs to go grow a personality, like the kid on the left, or like more moderately orderly kids, like these below, built using two answers from each side:

Balanced Kid 1	Balanced Kid 2	Balanced Kid 3
Independent	Considerate	Self-reliant
Obedient	Respects their elders	Well-behaved
Self-reliant	Curious	Curious
Well-behaved	Good manners	Obedient

These three, it turns out, are about as robotically well-behaved as we should order up children, statistically speaking; if more than two of our four answers are about behaving well, we're getting into authoritarianism territory, with all the potential downsides, the same way that, statistically, two glasses of wine a day on average is great, and three is clearly a problem. Not an automatic disaster– but pushing it.

There are always some social conservatives around who want to "make America great again" in odd ways, or make America less sinful, or make America more white. They're in the minority, and they used to be spread evenly between Democrats and Republicans. Once the southern Democrats were done migrating to the Republican party in the 1990s, though, they became a much more potent voting bloc together.

The real problem occurs when conditions arise that make people feel threatened. All of a sudden, many of the people running around with high authoritarianism get "triggered": a much stronger urge to force others to conform to their view kicks in, so that we pass laws meant to force society to conform much more. This is what happened when American politicians overwhelmingly approved the Patriot Act right after 9/11, in a flurry of emotion. Suddenly, the FBI could wiretap without a judge's approval, foreigners could be held indefinitely without trial, and secret searches of private property became lawful. Democratic Senator Russ Feingold was the only member of the Senate who voted against it; later, Democrats fell all over themselves trying to repeal it unsuccessfully.

It's this triggering that's the problem. We all tend to overreact under certainty; authoritarianism is only a stronger *tendency toward anxiety* about the future if they're goaded into it. If those high in authoritarianism don't feel threatened, there's strong evidence they're no different than anyone else.[4] When conditions are seen to be threatening, though, or people are persuaded by someone they admire that there's a threat, they react with a strong push to limit freedom, discriminate, or, if they have a strong military like we do, to go to war.

The Republican party figured out in the 1980s, once they gained most of the southern white Democrats, that most of the party members were high in authoritarianism, and that they could help the party cohere and improve voting participation by triggering authoritarianism. Now, the attempt to stir anxiety is a normal part of their platform; it's hard for those high in authoritarianism to ever *not* feel triggered. This is the value of the endless anxieties conjured based on the phrases "war on terror," "war on crime," and "war on drugs"; they create a permanent emergency situation for authoritarians.

It's even worse than that. These excessive people often become leaders in politics, maybe because they feel so strongly about their viewpoint, and they get intense, loyal followers. As we saw with the Patriot Act vote, people who wouldn't have been seen as high in authoritarianism– other conservatives and liberals– are easily influenced by these highly threat-sensitive, passionate people, and can eventually join them to force conformity and cruelty to happen. That's another way that liberals should think of themselves as "little conservatives." With a little time and anxious, repetitive persuasion, we can come right along with unhealthy authoritarian ideas. We're all social creatures; over time, our political enemies can have enormous influence over us, particularly around issues of personal or national security.

Starting about 1981, as the nation took that conservative turn, and as Ronald Reagan began aggressively employing the "war on xxx" language of authoritarianism, we ratcheted up our incarceration rates dramatically, especially for drug crimes. 1984's Federal Sentencing Reform Act imposed horrific minimum sentences on federal prisoners that even today are still an option in many state cases, where, depending on whether they're tried under federal or state law, criminals may be forced to serve up to ten times as long for a crime. Then, in 1986, possessing crack cocaine was punished with ten times the sentence imposed for cocaine possession. Authoritarianism was a disease that took over a nation obsessed with "solving" the crime problem by putting away bad guys. All kinds of "directiveness," "difference-ism," and "social conformity" started happening all at once.

By 1994, despite increasing prison populations by over 300% in just the 14 years since Ronald Reagan was elected, a fever for even harsher punishments took hold of the nation. Americans bought into a new, incredibly punitive crime bill, sponsored in its earlier form by social conservatives high in authoritarianism, but eventually popular with over 90% of Democrats as well. That law eventually locked away about a fifth of black men younger than thirty, many of them permanently through three strikes laws and horrible mandatory minimums. The individual stories of devastation are heart-wrenching. As a member of Families Against Mandatory Minimums, I saw thousands of horrible injustices, like Mandy Martinson, who got a mandatory 15 years for living with a drug dealer and having a gun in the home, or Edward Young, who got a mandatory 15 years for being a convicted felon and having 7 shotgun shells (and no gun) in his home; lives crushed by us, acting as their distant avenging angels.

Crack cocaine use finally peaked in 2006, twenty years after Reagan's draconian sentence increases, with no evident effect from the law. In 2008, as the insane cost structure of our prison systems started to become obvious, those high in authoritarianism started to be more anxious about government expense than crime; politicians began to shed some of the worst excesses of the 1994 crime bill. Scholars mostly agree now that the bill was a terrible mistake, except for the benefits to inner cities of increased police forces. Almost all Democrats that voted for the 1994 crime bill now say they regret it; that it was a kind of collective insanity. It was normal to react to the crime wave we had; it was just terrible to react the way we did, in lockstep with vengeful, know-it-all, callous authoritarians, obsessed with obedience and punishment.

Collective insanity is a good way to understand authoritarianism, when it gets going. The vote to attack Iraq in 2002 cost over a quarter-million Iraqi lives, and well over two trillion dollars. That's over $60,000 for every man, woman and child in Iraq, over $300,000 per family— not including the debt costs our grandchildren will pay (the war was fully financed by debt). The enthusiasm on the conservative side, and the eventual enthusiasm by a large minority of liberals, was textbook: authoritarianism coming to the fore, followed by liberals getting slowly convinced by those high in authoritarianism to not oppose the invasion. Sometimes, most of doing the wrong thing is doing nothing.

It's common now for people to blame President Bush for fooling everyone into voting for the war. But he did less fact-mongering than we think; mostly, he led a movement toward authoritarian behavior by stirring up moral outrage and revenge fantasies. As president, he was uniquely qualified to be the strong leader that authoritarians always desire, and he played that role well. Only a few of us were in the streets protesting that particular collective insanity. "Weapons of mass destruction," and the deadly gasses and nuclear piping the CIA supposedly had intelligence on were no reason whatsoever to attack one of many poor, dysfunctional Middle Eastern countries with a loudmouth, cruel dictator who hated America, whether such weapons existed or not.

That insight never occurred to our leaders or populace, liberal or conservative. Instead, most of us convinced ourselves there was a bad guy we could attack, which would settle the score for the attack on the Twin Towers, and somehow fix terrorism. The supposed facts about weapons and terrorism were a good excuse to act on a desire, nothing more.

That's authoritarian behavior. Bad ideas that make way too much sense to overly orderly people. If conditions are right, authoritarianism can rise to power in the government quickly.

Personality-wise, those high in authoritarianism are a little different than average conservatives: they're more orderly, less polite, less compassionate, and lower in openness/intellect. The strongest single indicator of an authoritarian is how much education they have; as you get past high school and further on in education, your likelihood of being authoritarian goes way down. In other words, on average, they're the meaner, less intelligent, less educated, and more inflexible conservatives. These are the people who foamed at the mouth to invade Iraq, imprison massive numbers of black youth over drugs, and who then lured us in enough to get it all done.

Donald Trump is high in authoritarianism, and so were most of his fans, who have the classic personality profile, on average, with a little bit of a salesman's outgoing nature (extraversion) thrown in.[5] In fact, according to one researcher, the four-question measure of authoritarianism was the best predictor of voting for Trump that could be found.[6]

Trump's popularity with those high in authoritarianism was a near-perfect example of how authoritarian behavior depends on how threatened they feel, and how they believe that strong leadership can save them. One way to explain Trump is to see him as the strong leader authoritarians had been waiting for. He was able to froth up a feeling of unease and anxiety among them, which triggered them to begin talking and behaving like authoritarians. At the same time, his soothing, confident presence comforted them into thinking that someone had finally come around who could cut through all the nonsense that kept Americans from succeeding like they did before. During the 2016 Republican National Convention, there was a moment during Trump's acceptance speech as he stood, in a classic posture of disdain and hauteur, pausing as his adoring fans chanted:

> Yes, you will!
> Yes, you will!
> Yes, you will!
> Yes, you will!

His promise immediately after– "I am your voice"– was quite off-putting to most Americans, but it was the perfect thing to say to his fans, to sooth their concerns and ensure he would lead them out of the wilderness to the promised land.

A powerful leader is almost always involved in strongly authoritarian movements, and sometimes they're demagogues, or a kind of savior. Some speech patterns common to Donald Trump, Joe McCarthy, and George Wallace solidify authoritarian commitment while making reasonable responses by others difficult. There are rhetorical devices, known for centuries,[7] that thrill their fans and provide messages the fans understand perfectly, but that are hard to confront effectively by outsiders. Here are examples, on the next page. The quotes are Donald Trump's, from his presidential run.

Ad hominem– personal attack ("Can you imagine that, the face of our next president?" [about a female candidate])

Ad populi– Voice of the people ("I am your voice"; "No one likes her")

Ad baculum– threats of force ("Tell him I will remember those statements"; "Like to punch him in the face")

Exaggeration– ("Our military is a disaster.")

Repetition– ("It's bad; It's *baad*"; "It's unbelievable, unbelievable"; "She's a liar…the most crooked…lying …dishonest.")

Paralipsis– saying things one can disavow ("I was just kidding"; "I retweeted somebody that was supposedly an expert, and it was also a radio show…am I gonna check every statistic?"; "All I was doing was referring to a picture that was reported"; "I didn't say that [when he did].")

There are always fights going on between triggered authoritarians and non-authoritarians within the conservative ranks. With Trump, that quarrel spilled out onto the street so we could see it. As everyone was scurrying around and shouting each other down, some of Trump's most bitter, powerful enemies were other social conservatives.

The authoritarians among them loved his fight against immigration, his protectionism, his stance on torture and surveillance, and his tough-guy stance on defense. He was also the very picture of a strong leader, which authoritarians find irresistible.

The social conservatives more concerned with traditional values of honesty, sexual morality, freedom, modesty and integrity were disgusted by him, and so were many who liked being tough on immigration, foreign affairs, or protectionism, but who thought he went way too far. The less intelligent and less educated were charmed or inspired by his constant exaggerations, lies, and risky errors. His fans were very pleased to have a candidate who was "true to himself," not hiding his concerns even though they were politically incorrect. There were also many caught in the middle, attracted to the certainty he seemed to offer, and his seeming candor, but repelled or frightened by some things he said. So, social conservatives loved, hated, or talked themselves into backing him, even though they're all the same "type" of conservative.

Hopefully we can keep in mind that the nicer, smarter, and more educated social conservatives side with us against authoritarianism, and we can all work together to keep cool heads when authoritarians are losing theirs, so that their influence isn't as strong. We should remember the example of Barbara Lee, the only congressperson to vote against the vague, unlimited "war on terror" authorization in 2001 right after 9/11. She seemed like an un-American nut to people at the time, and received death threats and thousands of angry letters. On the floor of the house before the vote, she pleaded with her fellow representatives: "Let us not become the evil that we deplore." That might be the best response we can make to ourselves as authoritarian thoughts come to us, when others encourage us to find shortcuts that quell our own uncertainty.

Economic conservatives are the second type of conservative. They focus on making sure individuals or ingroups can succeed in society, particularly through money. They want low taxes, low business regulation, and a stable, strong economic system. Economic conservative personalities have more variety than other conservatives. As a group, they emphasize the competitive aspects of social life. This makes them less polite and less compassionate than the average social conservative; on average, they're also less orderly, and higher in openness/intellect.

Though people usually think of economic conservatives as all about the free market, that's actually only the view of libertarians, about a quarter of economic conservatives. Many economic conservatives *like* government controls that protect and subsidize industry, or that allow other forms of economic or political domination by the powerful, like monopolies, tariffs on foreign trade, and money in politics.

Most have a domineering, nationalistic sense of how to handle immigration, foreign relations, and national defense, as an extension of their naturally competitive attitude about life.

It's hard to say much more about pure economic conservatives as a group. That may seem like a problem, but because they often have higher openness than is usual for conservatives, and it's uncommon for them to be as high in orderliness, we can usually relate to their personality better. They also often overlap with some of your politics, since they're often not in agreement with social conservatives. Getting along with roughly half of them is a breeze; the others range from challenging to impossible.

The Strong Prey on the Weak

Just like the social conservatives, economic conservatives have a core group of excessive club members who bring tendencies to the game that we find unhealthy. These economic conservatives have **Social Domination Orientation**, or SDO, which means they believe that the strong (or rich) should dominate the weak (or poor) to benefit society overall, or for the good of their favorite ingroup, or for their own good. They see life as a battle; they think that might makes right, and large economic inequality is healthy. Although their urge to dominate is mostly about money, it doesn't stop there, and they have many of the same prejudices that triggered authoritarians have. Social Dominance Orientation has been shown statistically to lead to prejudice against minorities, lower economic or social classes, countries, feminists, the homeless, the unemployed, and imagined threats to economic success, like immigrants.[8]

Unlike all that subtlety around "social conformity-autonomy" and authoritarianism, the SDO test is straightforward: not to put too fine a point on it, but to me, the questions measure how much of a jerk you are. Here's a sample (you're supposed to say how much you agree or disagree):

Some people are just more worthy than others.

Donald Trump's kind of exam. Trump's an authoritarian, but even more, he's an economic conservative with SDO. That double-down is why he seemed like such an orange-haired alien to us liberals. Many of his fans were also high in both. Research has shown that these two impulses of authoritarianism and SDO– to conform to your ingroup, and to have your ingroup dominate through strength– tends to roughly double the problems we see with prejudice, racism, and seeing threats where they may not be. A large proportion of Republican politicians are high in both, which causes us tremendous problems. Fortunately, that's much rarer among real people, among the populace.

Another problem SDO shares with authoritarians is that SDO can make politicians comfortable with quick, massive, risky change in a way that other conservatives and liberals find frightening. In Trump's campaign for presidency, he often indicated a willingness to make drastic changes in policy, which made many conservatives nervous, but pleased those with SDO.

SDO has a different personality profile than for most economic conservatives. People with SDO tend to be wealthier, better educated, higher in openness/intellect, lower in orderliness, less polite, and much less compassionate. Those with SDO were enthusiastic followers of Donald Trump, probably even more so than those high in authoritarianism, and it made for a odd mix of fans. The average income of Trump followers was much higher than that of the average American, even though his authoritarian base had a low average income,[9] probably because of his strong SDO following.

SDO is something we have to deal with in America twenty-four hours a day, seven days a week: there's no triggering, and no frothing up by politicians necessary. There are always relatively mean, relatively wealthy conservatives who like to throw their weight around– and they have a whole crew of other SDO people who support them, believing that America will be stronger and more successful if they're allowed to dominate society. That's a powerful push toward inequality, no matter what the rest of the nation does, in or out of politics. Money talks.

While we can usually get along with other pure economic conservatives pretty well, conservatives with SDO don't fit the mold, unless you are powerful or useful enough for them to take you seriously. That's why Donald Trump seemed to think the words "loser" and "weak" explained a great deal, why he used them over and over in situations when no liberal would; his version of black-and-white thinking is weak versus strong, or loser versus winner, because of self-orientation and low compassion.

I realize that's pretty discouraging, but it's reality. Think of SDO as a kind of junior version of having the personality of a psychotic. Not to be alarmist, or paranoid: psychopathy takes the game much further along, of course, to a complete lack of compassion, often combined with clinical narcissism, but SDO types are like the cub scout version. I believe I've worked with four psychopathic executives in business[10]– they're somewhat rare, about one to two percent of business management, according to two studies. But I've worked with many general and marketing executives– a sizable minority– who had SDO.

As you can imagine from that test question sample, even everyday conversation with them is often power brokerage of one form or another. Unlike other conservatives, if you appeal to their compassion or politeness with a request, unless they're fond of you, your request is taken as a signal that you're weak, which, to them, is often the ultimate insult.

I recall one executive who was fond of pontificating about how one should avoid at all costs hanging out with "hoochie men," which it turned out meant to avoid spending any time with people who weren't brilliant, aggressive, and lucky. The rest of mankind were contagious.

A world divvied up simplistically between the strong and the weak can be tough for liberals to relate to. The challenge when dealing with them is to be confident, capable, and have the appearance of strength. If that doesn't apply to you, it's likely you don't belong in the room. The exception is the work-hard, play-hard type, who you may be able to relate healthily to while parasailing, climbing Everest, or very occasionally, in a charity-related project.

Conservative Groupishness in Action

You should have a sense now of how much of an effect the "bad boys" of authoritarianism and SDO have on conservative politics. The educated versions of these extremists are typically more politically active than most conservatives, which is why so many are politicians. They're constantly motivated and energized to drive conservatives away from moderate positions on human rights, national security, traditional values, and inequality.

Rather than looking at conservatives as either economic or social conservatives, we can also consider whether they have either SDO or triggered authoritarianism, or not; whether they are status quo conservatives or not. The first way that division helps has to do with our old friend, order. If we don't have enough order in our lives, we can be careless in deciding what to do, or not consider everything we should, or not prioritize well, which can lead to being careless, and making bad or risky decisions. Some liberals can have that problem, and so can conservatives with SDO, because we're both relatively low in orderliness.

But if we have too much order in our lives, we have a surprisingly similar problem: we can't weigh different parts of the problem out properly. We don't prioritize well. We're like a father who gets upset at a child for making a dramatic-looking, harmless mess while the kid makes a great birthday gift for their mom. Our values get hard edges; we don't combine them well; we only emphasize some of the things we should, because part of being orderly is a desire to simplify things. Even if we see all the principles involved, we weigh them out poorly, because our orderliness is driving us more than the other parts of our personality that might help us balance our values more healthily. Conservatives can struggle with this problem— but authoritarians can be *relied on* to make those kinds of mistakes.

When President Bush ordered torture at CIA black sites and Guantanamo Bay because of the "war on terror," he assumed that the only real issue was whether torture would be effective to get confessions: his orderliness simplified his decision making too much, so that his certainty-seeking nature got the best of him. He saw the goal of minimizing the risk of terrorism as so high-stakes that violating the Geneva convention, ignoring a United Nations condemnation, and rejecting the traditional American respect for fundamental human rights were all unquestionably worth doing, to get any information that might lead to capture of other terrorists.

That decision turned out to be an error, not only because interrogators famously got only lies instead of confessions, as tortured prisoners tried desperately to please their captors; but also because the publicized abuses and deaths from the poor management of torture had a negative impact on international relations. Publicity of the torture and abuses also served as a recruiting tool for radical Islamic groups, and it offended liberty-oriented Americans.

A more balanced weighing out of values– a lower, balanced use of orderliness– would have resulted in a different decision about torture. The same could be said of the Citizens United decision to allow corporations unlimited financial influence on the political process, in the name of free speech; the 1986 crack cocaine and 1984 federal drug sentencing guidelines, in the name of morality; and protecting abusive police officers from prosecution aggressively, far beyond what reason might dictate, in the name of security.

So either too much orderliness (authoritarianism), or too little orderliness (SDO) can have people fighting for changes that are risky, because they don't weigh out everything they should fairly. Either they think the risk is worth it, or they don't see the risk.

Another reason why it's useful to think about relatively moderate, status quo conservatives separately from those high in authoritarianism and SDO is that it helps us see more clearly the difference between being healthily conservative and being excessive about order. This can be pretty tough to see in politics, because it sometimes seems as if triggered authoritarians and SDO types have a vice grip on all Republican policy and PR. But among individuals, you will find that people who aren't "bad boys" are much easier to talk with and work with, even if they're far right in their thinking, because they're more polite, more compassionate, and moderate in their use of order in their lives.

A final reason why it's helpful to remember these moderates and potential extremists are thrown together in the Republican party, is to remember that those battles between them are purposely hidden by their leaders and newsmen, who desperately want to give an appearance of unity. We should never forget that reasonable conservatives may be able to listen to ideas that aren't authoritarian or SDO arguments. Good logic can have a powerful effect, especially over time, even when it seems as if it doesn't.

Status quo conservatives can be strong allies in our battle against authoritarianism or inequality, maybe our most influential ones. I believe that they're often more important for liberal causes than liberals are, because they have more influence with the bad boys. We aren't privy to the many times they have saved the nation from excesses pushed by their leaders and peers in back rooms. During Donald Trump's run for the presidency, many healing, enlightening conversations happened between liberals and status quo conservatives as shared concerns were found about his dishonesty, carelessness, and hopes for wrenching change.

The Great Unifier

One topic tends to unite American conservatives, and that's a hawkish approach to personal and national security issues. Lately, thankfully, a string of cripplingly expensive, stupid wars have made many of them more isolationist– but they still vote for aggressive increases in military budgets, due to their hawkish approach to threat.

This can be confusing and scary to us liberals, even though we're used to it from the right; we see more easily that pushing around one's weight, on the streets or internationally, can actually make the world less safe. Conservatives often complain about us not being threat-sensitive enough, but liberals think that if we're *effectively* threat-sensitive, we'll focus on de-escalating much more, and do much more peace-keeping.

One reason why conservatives tend to be aggressive militarily is the influence of the strong minority of them high in SDO and authoritarianism; these two groups assume easily that forcing others into doing what we want can only lead to good, and they have great influence.

But status quo conservatives don't need much inspiration from their bad-boy crews to be hawkish. Roughly 80% all conservatives want a strong, aggressive military (except for most of the libertarians, and the 10% of conservatives I call the confused, who are actually politically liberal).[11] That aggression seems to be a natural result of the appreciation of hierarchy and strong authority that their orderliness provides them. Their attitude might be different if we were a weaker country; orderliness might get a person to be *less* aggressive, then. It's as if being relatively high in orderliness turns "peace through strength," an idea that many liberals can identify with, into something more aggressive.

There's also the problem that, when conditions are good, "peace through strength" means a giant horde of military doing nothing but drilling. My own experience as naval officer convinced me that a "standing force" doesn't easily stand around, especially when our leaders and populace hold them in such high regard. Politicians consciously and unconsciously think of them as a resource that we should *use*, especially when seemingly short-term opportunities come up (Iraq, Libya) to use our military strength toward authoritarian and SDO ends.

That shared connection between conservatives on aggressive security policy is a strong binding force. Naturally, it's used aggressively by leaders to keep the team together. In the 1980's, a one-two punch of, "If you're with us about a strong military, you need to be with us about xxx" began to be used, to get conservatives to accept the specific economic and social policies, the platform they thought could make for the strongest united front possible against liberals. Even though conservatives are naturally quite split on many economic and social issues, linking their enthusiasm for the military to a *particular* set of unrelated issues was a very successful technique, leading to strong unity. Large swaths of them feel quite differently about social issues like abortion, and economic questions like whether there should be high tariffs or not— and yet those wide differences of opinion aren't seen to play out in the media, or politically. They get ironed out in back rooms. Suddenly, social conservatives might care deeply about deficits, which they hadn't considered important before; economic conservatives might actively fight against gay marriage.

How does that happen? Recent research is showing how remarkably flexible people's policy beliefs are. It turns out that we have a vital unconscious goal that policy flexibility can buy us: a *social identity*. We build our social identity as a member of our desired group by deciding unconsciously what to believe, or persuading ourselves that certain policies make sense to us. American University's Elizabeth Suhay has shown with Social-Emotional Influence Theory that, if we're very social beings like many conservatives, we might choose the policies that categorize us as *faithful, predictable* conservatives, not the ones we might choose using logic, or even that we're attracted to through our personality. We decide our views through a kind of groupthink.

It's a specialized form of groupthink, though. Very social people decide their beliefs at least partially by 1) *conforming to what their ingroup believes*, to feel pride and belonging, and 2) *fighting the beliefs of the outgroup*— running away from the baddies' beliefs— to avoid feeling shame. Both of these steps are seen in politics, especially among conservatives. In experiments, even if participants didn't necessarily believe everything their ingroup believed, they were careful to *not believe* what their outgroup believed.[12]

This first part— that we conform easily to beliefs, quite apart from reasoning individually— is a painful truth about the "social construction" of our beliefs. But the second part— that we also work hard to not be like the outgroup– explains a great deal of the conservative-driven polarization we see in modern politics.

Republican leaders have long known that they need both of these steps to best rally their socially-sensitive crowd, and they usually do it in a kind of reverse order from what one might think: first, convince the troops to hate the bad guys; second, get them to love the good guys and imitate them. They know that the best way to have the rank-and-file avoid their enemy's opinion is to make them disgusted by their enemy, so that they'll feel shame if they agree with liberals; then, the troops don't have anywhere else to go but toward the specific platform, where their conforming instincts naturally lead them.

That's one reason why Republican Senate Minority leader Mitch McConnell seemed to publicly insult President Barack Obama as often as he could for eight long years: the job wasn't just to make strong allies; the first job was to make the enemy disgusting. While Democrats do much the same thing, our competitive sensibilities aren't as strong, because of lower conscientiousness; the one-two punch of hate-your-enemy, love-your-family doesn't come as instinctively to us. Authoritarian and SDO types, who are always well represented in Republican political leadership now, naturally lean into this kind of leadership approach, though the deep polarization that results is a terrible downside.

Social-Emotional Influence Theory is a powerful, complex set of social causes and responses, with a healthy body of research behind it, and interlinked theories from several fields.[13] This impact of our social nature on our beliefs and actions should be a little disturbing; it's one of the ways that the metaphor of us as a secretary working for a boss is powerfully accurate.

When individuals conform to group beliefs, they do it in several ways. We might be going through the motions, purely for appearance's sake. We might be *trying* to follow the policies or the leaders, in a form of brainwashing that's tied to the authority bias. We might actually like most of the policies, so that conforming is pretty easy and natural for us. Finally, we could also be completely bought off on the need for the world to use the ideas. Those of us who are political climb part or all of the way up that conforming ladder to find a home for ourselves in our ingroup.

One important reason why so many people avoid politics is that creating social identity like all this is hard work mentally; the cognitive miser in us doesn't like it. We might've found other, easier social identities that we're happy with, so that adding another one, even for a good cause, sounds like– work.

It may be quite common for us to have a belief just to have a social identity as a group member, and to not even realize that's why we have the belief. That doesn't make us little Satans. Our social identity is held by a tether to our overall personal identity, but they're not the same thing; people who aren't very political might have a very weak connection between the two. Those of us who are very political may have a strong social connection to our ideology, so that our social and personal identities are integrally connected. We talk logic, but we are working hard to keep ourselves within a specific social net.

The personality psychologist Jordan Peterson is fond of telling a story of how monkeys can watch a nearly motionless snake for hours; he's pointing out how fundamental it is for us primates to be fascinated by our enemies. I think of that whenever I see one of the endless parade of books with titles like:

> Help! Mom! There Are Liberals Under My Bed! (a children's book)

> Losing Our Religion: Why the Liberal Media Want to Tell You What to Think, Where to Pray, and How to Live

> Makers and Takers

These books sell, and they just go on and on and on, in a way the liberal versions rarely do.[14] Being evil and disgusting makes us fascinating to our relatively orderly, competitive, threat-sensitive "enemy." The layered, repetitive effort of categorizing us as disgusting, watching us be disgusting, and explaining to each other why we we're disgusting, all helps them feel more orderly and more correct. It's soothing. That's also a primary explanation of the popularity of all the stories and rants on talk radio. They murmur about the enemy for tens of millions of conservatives while they work, providing a kind of low-level reference point, a gossipy, National Enquirer-version of the great battle between evil and good, told by their heroes.

One very cool, bright side of this way of looking at all this polarization energy is that it's more about conservatives solidifying their ingroup than it is about attacking liberals. The language and attitude of polarization is more about trying to be loyal to their group than anything else. In many conversations with loyal conservatives, I can't help but take this perspective. At a certain point in many of the conversations, it becomes clear that either their social identity is quite flexible, or they easily make an exception of me. All that polarization talk suddenly seems in those moments to be for reasons that have nothing to do with real people like me, who look them in the eye and have particulars to their lives. It seems to be a helpful version of the *availability heuristic*, the tendency to anchor on what's vivid, "available" to our cognitive miser self to select a reality.

For those of us who are just trying to get along or work with an individual conservative, that's very good news, indeed. It means that reality can be split into a couple of pieces, for practical purposes. Right then, they don't need to make sure that I stay far away, over with my dirty, venal, evil, smelly, banal friends. Lucky me; Lucky us.

Zooming out internationally for a moment, conservatism all over the world reflects how fundamental personality is to ideology, and how little the actual political topics might matter. The issues vary tremendously by geography, and over time, because conservatives as a group tend to become fans of whatever has gradually evolved as normal in their area, even if it's not great. If their state and town are bigoted, they are; if everyone wants high taxes or low taxes, so do they. They want changes, usually along the lines of economic or social conservative wishes, but they want those changes controlled and slow. Slow for them, anyway; they don't care nearly as much if the changes impact outgroups dramatically.

The former Soviet Union had many citizens who were conservatives. This might shock people, but we just have to pause a moment and think about it. It's not as if Lenin magically shocked people in the U.S.S.R. out of their conservative natures by proclaiming it a communist country; it was no different than it would be here if our government suddenly became very socialist; there'd still be just as many conservatives around.

Ideology might best be defined by personality, as modern political psychologists tend to do, not by issues.[15] This should help us understand how socially constructed our ideology is. For instance: how did those old U.S.S.R. conservatives react when the Berlin wall fell, when communism ended? Did they whoop and holler and start planning free market miracles? Nope. East Germany's conservatives were *very annoyed* when communism collapsed there in 1989. Many of them are *still* annoyed.

That kind of response by conservatives has happened in many different kinds of conditions. "What!?," you might say– "How can conservatives be communists?" Well, it's easy. Politics is about personality and culture, and if our personality says it's huge to keep things the way we have it, more or less, then that's much of what we want. They'd lived in a communist country a long time; they were used to it. Guaranteed incomes, predictability, known bad guys, tiny overhead, no money; no problem.[16]

This is another version of the same point we just covered, that our social and cultural lives can be completely dominant in our political position and we might have no idea, because us secretaries aren't privy to the boss's thinking; we assume the secretary carefully thought through everything and arrived at an ideology, when our unconscious mind, with a powerful set of evolved social instincts, set in a particular culture and time, steered itself to a certain social status without informing "us." Recent work shows a very strong connection between the party of our President when we're children and our own politics many years later, even though we would probably all consciously say that, for instance, President George H.W. Bush has nothing to do with our politics.[17]

Some of the world's leading scholars on ideology are not at all sure that economic and social types of conservatives are a permanent, universal classification of the world's conservatives, even with the strong international evidence they have. Social effects are so powerful that the two types could be a shifting, meandering accident of history.

All we can depend on is personality, our basic dispositions: conservatives are *amazingly flexible* policy-wise, but not personality-wise.[18] Their main characteristic isn't anything about markets or freedom or abortions or anything else they talk about: the majority are mostly about order, which, among other things, is about keeping things the way they are for the ingroup– as academics say, they're in the business of "system justification," or rationalizing how things are good as they are for their ingroup, or good enough. Even when conservatives seem to asking for change or improvement, their preferences can be seen to usually be system justification at heart, such as foisting their own moral code on the rest of America, or changing voting laws to reduce the power of minorities, or tariffs that protect their economic status. The platform position of American conservatism might well be an accident of geography, history and genetics sitting on top of a rumbling, steady engine of system justification.

The flexibility of human beliefs and attitudes should help us never forget how powerful a tool self-categorization is for Republican leaders, to help herd their followers into one particular, cobbled-together set of beliefs. It should help us see the battle for the soul of the electorate more accurately as much more about understanding and reaching the unconscious mind. At the same time, we should realize that we can have our own, personal social impact on a conservative in conversation, and alter or soften beliefs unconsciously just by being "available" and real, not a symbolic evil, used for political and social purposes.

You're in Charge Now

Let's put ourselves at the top of the heap of American conservatives for a moment, and assume that we've got to get them all together, so we can beat the ultra bad guys, the liberals. Let's also assume that we don't care about polarization. And that we're perhaps a tad Machiavellian, like many real conservative politicians. How would we win?

Here's what I'd do: first, I'd emphasize a strong military and police force. That's fundamental: conservatives that were given our strong military and our financing ability would likely be aggressive militarily even if they were communists, or the Swedish version of conservative. I'd especially incite the SDO (dominating) and authoritarian (conforming) extremists, who would rattle their cages about national security for me.

Then, I'd do daily press releases and press conferences that were long lists of things that reveal all liberals, and especially their leaders, as dirty, liars, wrong, disorganized, stupid, and callow, each and every day of their pathetic little lives (Bet you think I'm exaggerating. You might need to take a dip into some conservative talk radio, or check out one of Ann Coulter's books– I don't know which to recommend– *Treason*, or *Slander*, or *Guilty*, or maybe one of the meaner ones). They'll need that hate-the-bad-guys message like mother's milk. This will have them scurrying away from Clintons, illegals, and all those science lies, with their gag reflexes triggered by the time I'm done with them. Yesss; come, little babies; come to papa. It's safe over here, among friends.

Then, once I had their little souls cupped in my palm, I'd *mix all my messages across social and economic lines*, so that they would all get the message that a prototypical, standard conservative believes all of it, social/moral and economic, based on the clump of concerns that will help me get the most money and backing, to keep the whole affair running at top speed. I'd make sure everyone understood that being pro-life is the twin brother of low taxes, and that low regulation is the brilliant cousin of traditional marriage. A happy family, pulling together.

For the social conservatives who don't care about economic issues, it's easy for them to shrug and say "sure" to low taxes and the like; and they do. The economic conservatives are a bit more complicated, because they're quite varied, but roughly half or so are totally fine with lining up alongside fighting for traditional family values and other social conformities that might seem random to them, as long as their hot buttons are supported.

For most of our lives, leading with the far right, centralizing power, and smoothing over differences has worked great for conservatives. It's such a no-brainer to do what I'd do that it's incredibly difficult to find a conservative politician (other than the rare libertarian) that doesn't proudly and loudly sell themselves as a member of both conservative types, social and economic. And why not? Why would any conservative politician, or any conservative, for that matter, take issue with what other conservatives believe strongly, when he hasn't got a strong opinion on it?

That would only risk losing a partner in battles that they all want to win. So they don't cross that line— with the result that the politicians who fight for both types have had excellent control over the Republican party for generations.

But the world is changing. Our neat plan isn't working nearly as well as it used to. We're going to go through two examples of how the two status-quo conservative types, SDO types, and authoritarians have started working with and against each other, upending the time-tested plan above, ruining all of their beautiful wickedness.

The Party Crashers

In 2009, this system of stringing everybody together as a team behind the extremists hit a major pothole, as the Tea Party burst on the scene.

We have good data showing that when society feels more threatened, we grow many more authoritarians, and we can do it almost instantly. After the 2008 election went to the Democrats, dedicated conservatives became very discouraged about America's leadership. Losing respect for leadership makes people feel threatened; it's been shown to be the most predictable way for authoritarianism to grow.

At the same time, the extreme enthusiasts of letting the dominant in society succeed, the SDO types, were also becoming extremely frustrated with the economic situation, because they sensed a society that was trying to emphasize equality through the Affordable Care Act, and they were frightened by all the money being spent to pull the nation out of the recession. Their fight against large government and business regulation merged with the forces of authoritarianism to fight for a combined platform. Politicians started cropping up, with great popular appeal, who didn't represent the moderate, status quo conservatives, with that neat, uniform platform. These new folks thought that the party platform wasn't prix fixe; they thought it was a deli meal, that they could have their hot buttons at last. Unlike most conservatives, these extremists didn't concern themselves with order and stability. After threatening for years, their representatives in the legislature were able to gather enough support from SDO and authoritarianism to shut down the government to make the point that our national debt was getting too high.

The majority of Americans were against the government shutdown from the beginning, but that kind of unpopularity isn't going to stop extremists. After America's credit rating went down, which triggered a worldwide selloff of stocks, and after stories of government workers not being paid got out, America turned strongly against the Tea Party organizers of the shutdown. The Republican party got some budget changes they wanted, but they lost a quarter of their approval rating among Americans in a month. The popularity problems quickly allowed the less extremist conservatives to take power back from the Tea Party, to again work together as a more united party. A more stable, less SDO-driven Republican party slowly climbed out of the hole it had dug itself into. The deli shut down; Republicans were again being handed their meals by leadership.

So: status quo conservatives and Republican party leaders resisted Tea Party ideas, but many more social and economic conservatives had quickly become triggered authoritarians as a result of liberal victories that made them feel threatened, and creative incitement of polarization.[19] The extremists worked together without strong opposition from the more moderate social and economic conservatives, because so many authoritarians and SDO types showed up so quickly that it became politically risky to fight the extremists. Both extremist groups decided to focus more on SDO's hot-button economic issues, to be practical. Then, the damage and the uncertainty caused by the shutdown made both SDO and authoritarianism less popular again. Conservatives started to feel less threatened by liberals, as other problems, like looking dastardly and dangerous, suddenly distracted them. Status quo conservatives were able to take back the domination of the government they'd had before, though not easily, and not completely.

The plan you and I conjured for conservative world domination, herding our sheep the way Ronald Reagan used to, isn't looking quite so winsome. A couple of the stool legs are wobbly. Triggering authoritarians and supporting the SDO crowd is riskier than it used to be. They beat back the extremists and won the battle, but extremists can't be controlled as easily anymore, and they might try something else.

The Donald

To understand conservatives during the 2016 presidential race in the same way, we'll need to think about the same chess pieces: the two conservative types, SDO, authoritarianism, and the conditions conservatives perceived, or conceived, as threatening. But there was a new chess piece now: a strong leader to rally around.

The same frustrations that were present in American conservatism during the Tea Party's heyday were still around. Trump, who, according to one of his wives, took occasional inspiration from Hitler's speeches, was an explosive catalyst of authoritarianism, but in a way that confused everyone. His intimate knowledge of the way he could rally those high in SDO and authoritarianism, through his vast experience in business and the media, allowed him to froth up their concerns, and inspire them to believe he would be their voice. Because messaging that appeals to triggered authoritarians and those high in SDO is shocking to normal, status quo conservatives, many who weren't his target audience dismissed him as a crackpot, ignored the concerns of his followers, and enjoyed the gossipy news sound bites he spun for us every day. Like monkeys watching a snake.

As he climbed the polls, seeming to surprised status quo conservatives to defy gravity, they found themselves in an eerily similar situation to the Tea Party uprising in Obama's first term, with that same mixed feeling of kinda-sorta getting what they want, but losing grip on power. Their plan was exactly the same as it'd been before the Tea Party showed up, the same plan the Republican party has had my whole life: emphasize security like crazy, whip up disgust of the nasty liberals, and make up a somewhat random pile of social and economic platform items to rally around. But Trump was going another way, unlike all sixteen other candidates for the presidency. He emphasized security, too, but with an inspiring, isolationist SDO twist (let's make all them no-account countries pay for our security help; let's shake up who we work with). He emphasized disgust of *both party elites*, inspiring extremists and enough status quo conservatives to believe that a "pure" outsider would work miracles. Mostly, though, knowing his real base, he pushed a narrow, perfectly authoritarian and SDO agenda of feel-good, populist whatnot. As the extremists did with the Tea Party surge, they helped whip up enough excitement among the undecided status quo conservatives and libertarians to bring them along as Trump supporters.

Over a period of seven months, Republican Speaker of the House Paul Ryan was forced to act several uncomfortable times, while he was unable to outwait the extremists, and unable to lure his followers back to the fold. During this period, a slow but steady trickle of status quo conservatives pointedly left the party or rejected Trump's nomination.

But Speaker Ryan didn't feel that he had a choice, as he tried to balance party unity with not giving power to the extremists. Over those months, he inched inexorably all the way from "this is not conservatism," in an early, courageous rejection of a horrible part of Trump's platform, through a long, unprecedented period of not endorsing Trump while condemning his main ideas, all the way to endorsement. "I feel confident [Trump] would help us turn the ideas in this agenda into laws to help improve people's lives," he eventually said, "that's why I'll be voting for him this fall."

The 2016 Presidential election wasn't just about authoritarianism and SDO, but the extremist role was clearly a leadership one, enabled by a strong leader. Hillary Clinton's slip about Trump's core followers being "a basket of deplorables" revealed the error of her campaign that almost every expert made, assuming that regular, good people, including many Democrats, would not be swayed by simplistic authoritarian and SDO slogans, threats, and exaggerations.

Speaker Ryan and the other status quo leaders were left to try to exhume their old three-pronged strategy– hate the bad liberals, love the good conservatives, love the mandatory menu– while they struggle to again address the front created by extremists, this time with a President at their head to represent them. If the status-quo conservatives keep playing with fire by deliberating triggering authoritarians with the-sky-is-falling messaging, rallying aggressively around national security– and if the left treats the embattled white working class as an enemy– populism will continue to occur that we can't beat back with the collective wisdom of moderates.

For a while, it seemed to be everyone's hobby to pick on Democrats in excruciating detail for not predicting Trump's upset. Many of those critiques are perfectly valid– indeed, they power much of this guide, and fixing them is our shared goal. You're working hard to understand conservatives yourself by reviewing this book, and the Democratic party will continue to try to remake itself for broader representation. But amidst all the navel-gazing and self-improvement, let's not lose track of the main driver of authoritarianism: the power of a strong leader to trigger uncritical, threat-sensitive authoritarians; inspire SDO conservatives; and lead a frustrated populace into vague, hopeful revolution.

Let's circle back to working with individual conservatives a moment. We can adjust our way of working with someone as it becomes clear that they're an economic conservative, or a social conservative, or high in either authoritarianism or SDO. It doesn't have to be complicated; it's mainly a matter of how orderly they are, and how mean they are. With some practice, you can adjust your approach almost automatically. I don't want to leave you with the impression that the basic guidelines on conservative personality can't be successfully followed: they usually can. But with extreme examples, and in situations where politics is directly involved, divvying up conservatives in more detail can be useful.

The Republican party figures into conservatism as both a leader and a sideshow. Knowing the mechanics of how the types of conservatives relate to each other, and how they both deal with authoritarianism and SDO, will help you relate better to their task of finding their way, in a world where all that drama is being stirred up by extremists, politicians, and the media.

Another takeaway: it might be easier than you think to talk about politics, if you're speaking with a conservative who has her "social identity" as a conservative, but doesn't identify strongly with specific conservative ideas. I've had many conversations with conservatives where I seem to have convinced them of an idea considered liberal. In my experience, this happens easily with about 15% of people who tell you they're conservative.

While this sounds like a liberal winning the lotto to some people, I believe that almost everyone who's influenced by political ideas can usually be convinced of the exact opposite the next day, and they usually float back to a prior belief, as if they never talked to you. In other words, one of the reasons why I don't get excited about political conversations is that most people whose minds seem changed aren't really affected; political points can't hold a place near their heart. They don't care about the ideas, or they don't reason that well politically. Those of you who are activists, trying to get voters to support you– it can actually be easy and maybe effective to get a significant minority of people behind you for a week or two, on a grand, last-minute push for votes. But on a personal basis, in terms of changing lives and minds– no.

If they're in it *entirely* for social reasons, though, you can usually tell because they're going through the motions enthusiastically, but they hate talking about it. This is extremely common; it seems to be practically an epidemic among conservative wives, who are often naturally conforming and apolitical, but are up to their neck in a conservative social set because of an enthusiastic or dominant partner. Bringing up politics with such people, even at a political rally or as an ally, creates a deer-in-the-headlights look within a sentence or two, as soon as it becomes clear that you want more than an enthusiastic nod in response. They'd rather be anywhere else, with anyone else right then. Their body language is "I'm not here to *talk* about politics." If you look for it, you'll recognize the type instantly. Many seem unaware of any of this – they have come to see their scant social connection to the cause as what it means to be political. Now you come along and insist that they're supposed to actually be interested, or have an opinion, about all this that they only believe for social lubrication purposes. Maybe you could go away soon–? That'd be nice.

Remembering that we instinctively conform to our groups for social reasons can help us relax our bad habit of explaining or denying liberal and conservative ideology in logical and rational terms, or thinking of conversation in winning and losing terms. Logic may be involved, but we should keep in mind how socially-constructed our belief sets usually are, and how different we would all be politically if we weren't programmed so intensely to clump into such chance-driven social sets.

Because a pairing of an individual conservative and a liberal is so different than this blob of general ideological myths and habits and social bric-a-brac that we've all constructed, we can often find a secret passageway to a whole new little ingroup with them, on the fly. Rules that seem sacred get shed easily, or at least held less tightly.

This flexibility was made apparent to me during a long series of polite but pointed conversations with an extremely bigoted conservative. He had a highly-developed theory that liberals needed to be wiped off the face of the earth; he was also intelligent and well-meaning, in his own peculiar, xenophobic way. If he had his way, he said he wasn't clear if he would allow people like me to live; certainly I'd be forbidden to own property and vote, and I'd have to forfeit my job upon demand by a conservative; beyond that, he'd be flexible about my life, depending on how most conservatives felt. After all, liberals could be sterilized and allowed to die out naturally, as a humane gesture.

Once a few initial skirmishes were over, our exchanges were a little surreal for me; I'd never interacted with someone who wanted me dead. But he treated me respectfully, and considered all my points fairly. I eventually recognized that he had neatly divided me from all other liberals in his mind. I'm convinced that he didn't do that just because I was nice or logical or special somehow, but because I was a tangible human; I didn't fit with the more theoretical "liberals" he lugged around like a bag of ghosts in his head. We were able to start from scratch.

Many of us do a similar reset with people. If we have the time to get to know someone, we don't treat them as if they were just their worst possible characteristics, or define them by how wealthy they are, or their race, or their looks. We can be surprised at how and where an ingroup can be formed with a conservative, how good we are at "socially constructing" a relationship on the fly.

The social part of being conservative is a mixed bag of goods and bads in terms of how it affects us when working with individual conservatives. The bad sides can seem so important. There's polarization– both the social separation, and the way ideas are unfairly demonized. The conservative coalition-building takes full advantage of our primitive nature and the way we secretly express our social nature through politics. There are authoritarians waiting to get triggered, and SDO types sawing away constantly at our principles and programs. It's not clear how long moderates will be able to beat back their ideas, because liberals all around the world aren't responding well to populist concerns about economic stability.

We should also be able to recognize the good side, too. Much energy around polarization isn't designed to push us away as individuals, but is serving social purposes, to buy a social identity. The social aspects of ideology afford us many opportunities to make personal connections that we might otherwise think would be very difficult. Remembering the social construction of belief should also help us stop trying to pretend we wander around "reasoning" our way to beliefs, like computers that should all come up with the same next chess move.

Conservatives that aren't extremists can be very strong allies of ours on the political stage, too. I was quite heartened by the courage and wisdom of individual conservatives who rejected their party's choice for president in 2016, who had stirring reasons for why they did it. That was a tough thing to do for such social, loyal people, dedicated to beating us.

We've now gone through four of the five sciences of this guide: neurology; personality; biases; and social conformity. We're ready to trace our way back to where we started, when we asked together how we handle the *moral* portion of our relationship– how we juggle the conflicting goals of working together and stopping conservatives from wreaking havoc on the world.

Chapter Eight

MORALITY, ANGER, AND DISGUST

> *Whether one seeks to be an angel or a devil, there would appear to be power in moral deeds.*
>
> *— Kurt Gray*

THERE ARE A MILLION ways to derail a relationship with a conservative. That's true about relationships with anybody, though, so it's no reason to freeze up in advance, or to approach getting along with one as any particular miracle. Little mistakes can't be helped, because we have so many ways we can err; any conversation that succeeds is full of stumbles, and pauses to clean our eyeglasses. But the big mistakes are easy to avoid. The first rule is:

1. Don't get mad.

Easy, huh? See, I told you.

OK. As a tiny descendant informed me recently, I'm being tricksy. First of all, in some conditions, it's perfectly reasonable to get mad at a conservative: it might be the right thing to do. We're not talking about those times. We want to focus on those times when you get home and you think, "What the heck did I just do?"

The usual reason we get mad at them is because they say or do something that feels **immoral**.[1] So far, our focus has been on neurological foundations and personality to understand our differences, but when it comes to tough situations, we have to pay attention to how morals climb into the wagon.

It's little known in our culture that morals, the values we use to decide what's right and what's wrong, are tied in closely with our ideology— so closely that it can be tough to determine where ideology ends and morality begins. This notion of ideology deciding morality, or the other way around, seems wrong. Maybe it is. But understanding how it happens can step us through the storms we might encounter with conservatives in conversations, meetings, negotiations, and personal conflicts.

What is morality, anyway? We said that it's *feeling strongly* about how we treat each other, but what does that really mean? Our moral impulses are experienced in tandem with our *emotions*– lots of them. Let's look at these feelings of ours a moment; it'll help us figure out how morality wedges itself into our life, whether we want it to or not.

We use emotions much more often in our lives than we think, because many of them aren't dramatic; they help motivate our thoughts, our movements, and how our relationships go. Yet emotions all appear to be processed very similarly by our brain, in just a few basic ways, even though we have ten thousand details and nuances and intensities in our emotional life, gradients of the different emotions being felt.

This similarity in our heads was quite unexpected when it was discovered; almost everyone thought that the variety of our feelings needed many kinds of complex circuits in the brain, but they don't. In fact, emotion processing shares a small number of common circuits with other kinds of non-emotional thinking; they don't look fundamental in there, even if they feel arm-waving big, and unique, and complicated. Their complexity and variety arise from more basic processes, like our other thoughts. Yet again, we see that we're very efficient creatures– cognitive misers– varying as little as we can, to get as much done as we can.

The tremendous variety of emotions that appear are *constructed* out of more basic forces, just as a piece of paper can be creatively used to create thousands of different origami. Theorists think that emotions are a way we express and motivate ourselves, based on a combination of what we think about the situation ("it's hot today," or "wow, she's a cutie"), and what we might think of as our mood (good/bad, and how strong), what psychologists call our "core affect." We use these basics to wheel our way into and through emotional experiences that fit with the time and place we're in, to get our life done well.

The great psychologist William James once said that there are as many kinds of emotions as there are shapes of rocks on a New England farm; he felt that we needed all that variety to be flexible and powerful enough in life in all the situations. If we were sensitive enough– some people are– we could describe many different kinds of anger or fear we're feeling, and each of them is getting made up as we go along, based on who we are, and the unique situation. Cognitive scientists, neuroscientists, and psychologists call our on-the-fly way of making emotions **constructionism**.

Constructionism buys humans the ability to engage flexibly and powerfully with an incredible variety of complex challenges. It's as if all our familiar emotions, and the tiny variations and mixes of them, are like farmer's market booths, crammed together in the same parking lot; they're not like skyscrapers, spread out all across the state– it's not "WELCOME TO THE FEAR CENTER" in there. Emotions like jealousy and feeling smug, or livid anger and resentment, are next-door neighbors, so to speak, and we're picky buyers, flitting around, buying a little of this, a little of that, and different vendors are selling almost the exact same thing. Neuroscientists watching a living brain can't recognize even what seem like quite separate emotions very well, like your GPS might not be sensitive enough to figure out which booth you're visiting at the farmer's market. There are also several common brain circuits that create various versions of anger, joy, and our other emotions.

This close and variable relationship between our emotions may be why we can use our creativity, a positive attitude, or even a simple change in our location to shift our perspective and our feelings in a useful way; to calm down, say, or make other emotional changes that might be healthy. Of course, we can go the other way, too; anger or grief can ramp up similarly, as if they were fifteen feet over from feeling a little melancholy. There's great evidence that meditation, inspiring experiences, and even changing locations have a way of helping us shuttle over to other booths, when we might buy into a more useful emotional approach to a tough situation.

We wander between the market booths, too, "changing our minds" about what we're feeling, usually without even noticing. That's how we work with what we think of as different emotions when we have a complex problem, when a child hasn't reported in at midnight as promised, say, and we feel angry, frightened, and impatient all at once. Each emotion is used along with other kinds of thinking and desires, like part of a team. The brain isn't juggling ferociously if we feel frustrated, hopeful, and a little sad at the same time: in a way we don't understand well, those labels of the feelings are helpful, but they're not hard little balls of reality; they shift and mix based on what's going on inside and outside of us. People experience the mixes of emotion, but few of us can define each of them out in pieces, because it's strangely simple and natural to feel them in this mixed, changing way, together.

The power of all that neurological simplicity and tremendous flexibility has a cost, though. When we experience harm, we have a whole, wide possible range of negative feelings (frustration, anger, fear, annoyance, panic, disgust, etc.), depending on the situation. But no matter what emotions we feel, and what the harm is about, a moral judgment usually floats into the scene at the same time, without us even thinking about it, as another one of those thinking processes that are so similar and intermixed with our emotions. **Our minds then fuse together those feelings of harm and our moral impulse directly**.

There's little or no difference to us between something being morally wrong, and what we think of as harmful.[2] This seems obvious, in a way; it's something we might agree sleepily about, in the morning line at a coffee place. But it's actually a meaningful, profound point.

Let's say you have to pick up some medicine at the pharmacy before work, but it's past opening time, and they're still not open; it's made you late for work. Maybe you're worried your boss is going to give you a hard time about being late, which you don't need; or maybe you'll be late to a meeting you're running. You were already rattled by your daughter changing her clothes for kindergarten four times. Negative emotions are pouring in: we'll call them worry, frustration, and eventually irritation, maybe anger. Somewhere between one and five minutes late, as soon as it all piles up enough, we start feeling seriously harmed– and we start to feel morally wronged.

We probably welded together this shortcut between the emotions related to harm and morality as a species long ago, maybe because our minds have no way of knowing absolute right and wrong; we might've started to use our feeling level to decide what was moral. But when morality and harm are welded together, if something feels immoral, like not going to church, we also feel as if we've done harm to somebody. In other words, we don't just turn harm into morality; we turn morality into harm, too.

If we think it's morally wrong to eat dog meat, it *feels* as if someone or something is being harmed when we eat it, and when we see someone else eat it. Which is a little crazy, since we might eat pieces of chickens or pigs until the cows come home. Who's being harmed– the person eating it? Society? The dog? Some mysterious mix of all of them? When we ask people what the harm is in a situation they think is moral, they can't always explain it, and some of the explanations are a little goofy; but they have feelings happening that they associate with harm anyway.

There are lots of problems created by this fluidity between morality and harm, but one of them is important in ideology. Morality is about doing good or bad to other people. That means that we can't have a moral problem– can't have an evil act– without a victim, and somebody who did it. This is what's called by moral psychologists "dyadic morality," because it means that morality has to involve a dyad, or two different parties.

That's yet another statement that we all can see as obvious, before we've had our coffee in the morning. But look at what that means: if we're actually linking harm and morality, *any* significant harm we see, or experience, or even think can happen, is morphed easily into a moral problem—which means that the harm created 1) a victim, 2) an evil act, and 3) a evil perpetrator.

That's a huge leap! We just grabbed a guy off the street, put him in a black coat, and threw him onstage.

Let's look at how that might work. Back in the pharmacy parking lot, we have a growing sense of a moral violation while we wait for the pharmacy to open, because we're suffering a swirling, negative, growing mix of emotions; that's the first odd perceptual fact. No one is truly trying to harm us personally, but as we get more and more inconvenienced, we start gradually thinking morally. We know there's a victim, because it's us; that first part of a moral situation is easy. We're getting wronged by this unexpected delay, which is the "evil act," the second part; that's also easy. Finally, the real magic trick: we *create a perpetrator* with bad intentions. She's not here yet; she's busy elsewhere, somewhere she doesn't belong, doing us wrong. Or it could be her boss. Who cares, though? The whole lot of them deserve our searing, disgusted expression when she opens the door. We might even be bold enough to do the right thing, and tell her off like she deserves.

See what we did there? We've gone from being inconvenienced, to being harmed, which then got flipped right over into morality. We got to imagine up and hate on a perpetrator that *has* to be there, hidden deep inside the building.

This key way that morality works is very similar to the fundamental error we covered, where we assume the situation has no bearing, and we blame any problems we're having on the person's character. Our solution is also similar: we have to tell ourselves in that situation what we're doing– that we're not being fair just jumping to morality with our problem. The lady who's supposed to be opening the store might have had a heart attack; she might be driving her mom to the hospital; she might be sitting in her car crying, unable to get it started. There will be plenty of time later to get moral about it, if we need to; in the meantime, there's no need to get mad at her in advance, to save time; no need to put a deposit down on she's-a-jackass.

It really does work, by the way, talking to yourself like that. Lots of very kind people do it all the time. The point, though, is to realize that most of us don't; for most of us, harm = morality = find the jackass.

Because morality and harm are joined at the hip this way, we also do a kind of opposite trick: we create victims, usually ourselves. It's an enormous waste of energy, in ideology and elsewhere. We take a moral position, go roust up some harm to blame on the bad guy we had in mind, and get people excited about being the victim. Think the gun lobby, who you and I are harming by– thinking bad thoughts about their guns, and hiring politicians who will come in the night and take their guns. Or think attacking Iraq; Iraqis were going to suddenly harm us like crazy, because they were nutso Muslims with secret gas.

Ideology has one additional wrinkle to add to this strange affair, which we might think about while we stand there, late for work, waiting for the pharmacy to open. Fine, we might think, the person opening the door late obviously isn't trying to harm us directly. But they, or the manager, or some dingdong is harming us *indirectly,* by not doing their job. We don't actually care if they are directly trying to harm us personally; for all we know, it could be someone who was careless about setting their alarm. But whatever the problem was, it was at least an indirect carelessness, or an undisciplined employee– someone done us wrong. Maybe the supply company was late, or the manager didn't train the store opener well. Doesn't matter: there's no excuse for evil; dig deep enough and it's there.

This morality-making we can do is such great news for the ideology business. If our heads are in the business of turning even mild levels of harm into moral wrongs, *we're going to be in the business of finding evil perpetrators,* both direct and indirect versions; bit players and stars. And the great thing about ideology is that we can find them quickly, if we're clever and paying attention. I can, anyway. Rich people, careless people, religious people, whiny and lazy and greedy and biased people. All offstage; all messing with the lights and sound and props, leaving their lipstick stains on costumes. They're probably giggling about it together, too, right now. Evil people do that.

Creating bad guys may seem unfair of us, or like careless thinking, and it usually is. But we need to have a little more respect for how and why our minds switch back and forth between hurt and evil so easily. The link is very old, and was built for a mostly-good purpose. Indirect harm, like this late pharmacy opening, can seem innocent, but it can be a deadly serious problem. What if someone at the pharmacy had promised you the night before that you'd have your medicine by 9 AM, and you went into anaphylactic shock while you waited until 10:30 to receive it? Morality is most assuredly involved, even if it was caused by a late delivery, or a long line at the pharmacy.

Indirect causes of harm may kill or harm more often than more direct immoral actions like rape or murder. This is the story with each little piece of the long chains of small corruptions in Africa, where soap or antibiotics commonly disappear from hospitals "for no reason," killing just as surely as a bullet or a machete. Dozens of involved people took bribes, but none of them can be directly blamed for the soap shortage. Just because someone getting hurt only ties back to sleeping through an alarm, or not testing a rocket's seals in every possible operating condition, or de-icing a plane wing incorrectly, doesn't mean we shouldn't take the error very, very seriously. All we're saying when we promote something from a problem into a moral wrong is that what happened was very, very bad for someone, and unnecessary. Well, very, very bad can be caused by a small bribe, a missed checklist item, or an engineer who makes an incorrect testing decision.

The most maddening aspect of life in many areas of sub-Saharan Africa is that generations of corruption have trained many people there to *dis*connect harm from morality. Sounds great, in a way– very mature and kind– until the soap disappears at the hospital, and everyone just shrugs and slogs on with dirty hands, killing patients without comment. That's an example of where you want emotions like anger and outrage to take over, and switch that harm directly into morality.

So there can be excellent reasons for our minds to create a morality play out of harm sometimes. That doesn't mean we should moralize all harm– but most of us seem to anyway, because *sometimes* we should. We're wired simple that way. As usual, our cognitive miser self comes through for us.

The psychologist and neuroscientist Lisa Feldman Barrett likens good problem-solving to how the Avengers work together. All kinds of thought types work together to figure out how to solve problems. There should be somebody who can do science well, logical and focused, while moving quickly; an "empath," with their eyes closed in the corner, trying to get in someone's head; and Captain America should drop in "with a touch of morality." A strong man with mechanical skills might be good, and an emotional stretchy guy that can also help with the planning. Good decision-making involves many variable parts, and it's not clear that any of those superheros should always take charge, because life isn't always best managed by our science side, or our strong man self, or any other specialist part of ourselves. And, unlike what many dead philosophers preached, emotions *have to* play a role in our decisions. Usually, when emotions don't seem to figure in, they're hidden, being folded in unconsciously, behind some fake attempt at logic. Emotions play an important part of any accurate moral response, in a balance with other factors; they shouldn't necessarily dominate, but they deserve a vote.

We don't have a special moral brain circuit, either; the only difference between moral decision-making and the rest of our choices is that we really really FEEL our moral situation. So we have to be careful to not be completely driven by our emotional, harm-driven impulse, as if it was a special signal from God, or some inner core of eternal knowledge. Our thinking about moral problems should follow this same Avenger, team-based approach as the rest of our life.

The psychologist Joshua Greene likes to use a rule of thumb about good moral decisions: if we can't seriously entertain ideas that counter our "gut" wishes, we're probably not making good decisions. We're just acting like a mousey secretary. We should be putting up a fight occasionally, not just going along.

Morals for Groups, Morals for People

Let's look at the kinds of harm that we turn into morality. A group of moral psychologists, led by Dr. Jon Haidt (pronounced 'height') have put together some useful categories, or "foundations," of our moral values, using extensive international research. Their approach is called Moral Foundations Theory. Some of these foundations have a direct relationship to real harm; others are more indirect. Here are the more direct moral values, expressed as positives, or avoiding harm:

> Care of others (avoiding cruelty– the most common "foundation")
> Fairness, or justice
> Freedom

In moral foundation terms, these are "individualizing moral foundations," focused on protecting individuals that can be harmed. There are others we could consider as well, like honesty and self-discipline,[3] but the first two are clearly the most common of our moral concerns universally. Liberals tend to value them more than conservatives, and we tend to think of morality in terms of caring for others and fairness.

There are also moral values that can be thought of as protecting *society* from harm, rather than individuals; these are termed the "binding moral foundations," because of how they're designed to bind people into healthy groups. We share these values with conservatives, but they tend to value them more strongly, and talk in terms of them more:

> Respect for authority, or for good sources of guidance
> Loyalty to people and groups we care about

A respect for sacredness, or purity

These binding moral foundations can be thought of as less direct and less obvious, at least for liberals. Think back on waiting in the parking lot for the pharmacy to open: if the worker was lazy, and just took too long a smoke break to open up on time, that's more of a violation of the loyalty foundation, and maybe authority. He didn't come out and machete you down, but if he did, that would be direct harm.

A clever study showed that most people think of the great majority of their day-to-day morality choices and experiences as about caring or not caring for others, or being fair, or other individualizing foundations.[4] So the binding foundations *seem* to enter in much less in daily life.

That's deceptive. If you asked someone waiting for the store to open, they'd say they were being directly harmed by a jackass, when it would probably be more appropriate to call it a binding foundation violation. Remember how morality is also designed to help us take care of the more indirect problems, like corruption, where there's probably not direct cruelty. In the end, even indirect harm, from not enough loyalty, say, will eventually cause people to suffer directly. Binding foundations tend to be indirect because they help us see *what* was unfair, *how* someone was cruel, *when* we should try to be fair, or *who* we help or hurt. They should be looked at as underlying or inspiring the difficult job of being kind and fair. Many people go to church to get weekly reminders about these binding foundations or values, so they're more moral in their lives– so they do less direct and indirect harm.

Dr. Haidt and his team have done great work championing these binding foundations; he makes the point that all of society would do well valuing binding moral foundations more, because they help us build and keep strong social ties, which makes us happier and more helpful to one another.[5] Our modern life is splintering and separating us too much, resulting in weaker families, less cohesive churches, removed government, and the slow erosion of community groups, charities, and other institutions that help us support and inspire one another. These more tribe-oriented moral values have their roots in our pre-historical period, and they are mostly healthy adaptations.

All of this is fine by most of us liberals. I've taught these ideas to many of us, and it makes sense to us, but doesn't resonate greatly. There's nothing to argue with, but it doesn't inspire us, especially when we talk about the more social of the moral foundations. Not that we liberals don't value such things: research shows that liberals underestimate how important these binding moral foundations actually are for our fellow liberals as a whole,[6] similar to how we don't think of ourselves as industrious when we are. We seem to assume these social moral values in our lives, but we don't think in terms of them. For us, it's easier to think about morality in terms of caring for one another and being fair. Golden Rule stuff; no big deal. Avoiding direct harm and injustice. Loyalty? Sure, if it helps you be nice.

Then I teach conservatives about it, and the reaction is completely different: a strong, immediate enthusiasm. They dance jigs; they proclaim themselves finally seen by science for the first time. For some, it's as if I've given them a Rosetta stone to morality. The cranky ones respond with an attitude of, "sounds right. About time an academic came up with something useful." Whenever that reaction happens, it reminds me of the animal psychic I saw interviewed, who says she goes to ranches to talk to misbehaving horses, and the horses always start out the psychic conversation with "finally; one of you idiots can talk."

The secret to that difference in reactions between liberals and conservatives has to do with the binding foundations. In keeping with their emphasis on orderliness, conservatives want some clear rationale for *how* and *when* to be caring, or for exactly *what* to be fair about. They know they can't care for everyone all the time, so they want social rules about *who* to help, and *why*. They like to look to their authority figures, and those they're loyal to, and what's sacred enough to inspire them, to guide their moral lives. They think of the binding foundations as a family of ancient, very successful adaptations, lynchpins to our initial success as a species.

Let's look again at that set of conservative values we obtained from evidence, to see why conservatives are so much more excited about the binding foundations than we are:

Safety
Hierarchy (conforming, obedience)
Tradition
Order
Certainty
Consistency
Simplicity
Boundaries

We liberals can be quite confused about why any of that, outside of safety, has much to do with morality. But a careful look shows them all to be just a half-step over from **strong social ties and stability for the group**, which is what the binding foundations are all about. Being safety-oriented means to work as hard as possible for the security of those most dear to us, not just ourselves. Valuing hierarchy greatly means finding our place within a network of others, accepting authority over us, and thinking about ourselves much less as individuals. Tradition ties us to one another strongly, the way institutions and groups build in interdependence. The other values can be seen as tactical varieties of orderliness, the strongest conservative personality trait, in which we use strong boundaries to define our role and our "working group," because we can't care for everyone, and we can't be fair to the whole world. Every one of those conservative values point them in the direction of focusing on the binding foundations, to provide direction to their moral lives. That's why they do the little jig when they find Moral Foundation Theory.

That's them— but let's talk about us. The binding foundations, or the more social moral values, can sometimes have what feels to us like a love/hate relationship with the individualizing foundations. Let's address the love or complementary side of that relationship first.

We liberals use our sense of loyalty, respect for good guidance, and reverence for the sacred to complement and build our support for the more direct moral values of kindness and fairness that we liberals resonate with. Those binding foundations improve and focus us, so we're as morally good as we can be.

That's a great way to think about work to support community or political groups, or going to church, or reading self-help books. After all, morality is sometimes about being kind to ourselves, but it's mostly about our social or group life. We build up these social values in our lives, so that our overall moral approach is improved. By focusing on being loyal to who and what we respect the most in our lives— our partner, our work, our friends— we can remember or be prodded to do things that care for them well. Respect for authorities such as teachers or family leaders, or being inspired by sources of sacred wisdom such as great art, or nature, or literature, also serve to propel us to do what's right.

Because of their "groupishness," conservatives relate better to this *process* of building and maintaining our moral structure through emphasizing the binding foundations— but we do it right alongside them, even if we don't see it. We don't build giant churches to do it, like they do in the south; we do it our own way. The binding foundations are how everyone *develops and maintains a strong moral framework*— to be more caring and fair, and more oriented around the Golden Rule.

The other day, I was short with my mother over something I thought she should know. Immediately afterwards, my respect for her (my loyalty, and my respect for her guidance) stopped me in my tracks, and forced me to think about why I'd spoken the way I did. Working through it, I realized that she had no responsibility to know what I thought she should, and I felt guilty; I'd presumed in the moment to be justified in my attitude, and created morality where there wasn't any; there was only a mild bit of harm, because I unexpectedly had to take time to go find out something she'd once known.

For a few minutes, the notions of respect for authority, loyalty, and sense of reverence for her worked within me. I tend to experience them together like that, often, in a kind of a mush; I think most of us do. I took the time to think about how patient she is with me; how selfish it was to expect her to stay updated on something that had little to do with her; and how the world turns quickly, so that I may not have her in my life soon. I developed a different perspective than I'd had before. Swirling around these less direct, binding moral concepts in my mind helped me come around to understanding how I can be more caring.

The lesson doesn't end there. Over the coming weeks or months, I'll need to check in with myself to make sure that I've actually learned the lesson, that I carry with me more naturally a sense of loyalty and respect for her. This is similar to the idea of going to church to stay on top of things morally, deepening our commitment to the binding foundations. I'll try to use my sense of them to keep course correcting until politeness and respect comes so naturally and completely that even in situations where I'm hurt by something mom did, directly or indirectly, I won't flip from inconvenience, to harm, and then to morality so carelessly.

So: the binding foundations provide me a natural, almost systematic way to develop and maintain my moral approach, by using the binding, social moral foundations for inspiration and clarification.

There's another, less comfortable side to the binding foundations, though. Sometimes, they have to be used to modify or even cancel out a more natural direct, caring response, for a greater moral purpose.

Direct compassion and the individualizing foundations can naturally take a back seat to a vision of life as centered around our station in life, such as in the workplace, or in a poor family, or as a citizen during wartime. That may not be obvious immediately, but some of our greatest moral dilemmas involve clashes between social and individual values. Valuing loyalty, authority, and sanctity the way we should has to affect large swaths of our lives, and bleed over into situations that aren't so straightforward as not being rude to your mom.

Let's look at some sensitive situations, and think together about whether the binding foundations conflict with or complement the individualizing ones, and what we should do about it.

"I won't take a job that forces me to move my family away

from extended family."

This might not even seem like a moral decision, but it often is for some. Should I use my loyalty, and my respect for the sacredness of family ties, to sacrifice money, career, and what's fair to my family's future opportunities, to stay near relatives in this hick town? Who's harmed if we leave, and how? In this case, individual desires for freedom and fairness can be seen as conflicting with loyalty, maybe authority.

> "You've lost phone privileges for disrespecting your mother."

Un-oh. Little Bella's smart mouth is going to cost her, big time; no endless Facetime calls for hours on end for a week, while she gets to learn how respect for authority is necessary. Superficial or short-term kindness toward Bella takes a back seat to meaningful kindness, of the sort that better prepares her to thrive and survive in the world outside of the immediate family.

> "The scriptures teach us to be faithful to our wives."

Over and over, weekend after weekend, cheap little hotel rooms go unused, as individual freedom loses out to loyalty and respecting the sacred in our lives.

> "A good Ranger won't hesitate to jump on a grenade to save their comrades."

If you're the company commander, you expect your men to do this in a crisis; you're trading the ultimate cruelty, in a sense, for respect for authority, loyalty, and what's sacred to him. In this case, the binding foundations that conflict with care are there to help us remember a cause that's even bigger than our own life; so important that a wife may become a widow, and a son may become fatherless, to save a mission from failing, or to save the life of comrades. The willingness to do this is why we have such high regard for our military.

> "Keep your eyes wide open before marriage, and half shut after."

This is usually told as a joke, but it's actually a deadly serious point that comes up constantly socially. It's saying that truth itself, and doing what's right, can completely change once one has committed oneself to being loyal to another. All rocky relationships cause harm for one or both of the partners, but valuing loyalty helps couples eventually build a happy marriage despite being yelled at, or ignored, or misunderstood, or being lied to. Marriages that fail are a failure of loyalty to indirectly win out over the more direct cruelties that can overwhelm us in the moment, or drain away our attachment over time. If loyalty didn't override an understandable, strong reaction to our partner being cruel, we wouldn't stick around; we'd walk. This buttressing of weaknesses in care and fairness helps all of us, anywhere we share life with others, anywhere morality plays out: in the work place, in our homes, and in our friendships. And learning to turn the binding foundations to our advantage this way is the best tool we have to become more moral people.

Notice how these are examples of *competing values in tension*. Wading through situations where individual and social values conflict isn't always straightforward morally; even if it is straightforward, like jumping on a grenade, it may not be easy. That's because conflicting moral impulses are involved, and how to mesh the two properly is a matter of judgment.

I don't know any liberals that can't see the logic of that. But thinking about what's going on as "loyalty should be more important than care and fairness" sets off alarm bells for us. Not that we don't do offsets and tradeoffs like that; we just don't think in those terms so simply and starkly, because we're not as orderly. Another way to look at it: we're not so quick to think in terms of tradeoffs because of our respect for important exceptions in life. We're not as interested in guidance, or rules for our morality, nor in paying quite as much attention to our authority figures to decide our moral response. And for good reason. Loyalty can be misused, or overemphasized; being obedient to authority can be an excuse to allow cruelty; treating things as inappropriately sacred can overwhelm and distort our morality.

For me and others, a very direct version of caring or compassion rules our roost; I'm automatically wary about considering ways to offset that impulse. Even talking about offsets, or rules like who to be kind to when, make me nervous. When compassion seems to be draining from whatever calculus that's being used for a moral decision, I smell a rat. The Golden Rule, after all, seems like pretty simple math. How does one draw the line? Where do we let care or justice be "offset" by authority, or the sacred?

"Due to mandatory minimum sentencing, I'm forced to sentence you to no less than 20 years for possessing over two ounces of crack cocaine."

Authority (the law, the criminal justice system) has dictated what to do, because society has decided that the war on drugs is sacred. How moral is that cancelling of fairness by authority?

"Say one more word and you get the belt."

That's a facile, common trade of cruelty to buy respect for authority. I've been in a home where dad had his own silverware, and children knew to avoid his drawer: what is that emphasis on respect for authority teaching those children? And is screaming or belittling the coin we should use to buy respect and obedience?

"It was well within procedure to taze him repeatedly"

"She wouldn't have been raped if she wasn't out partying in that outfit."

"He was 10 minutes late a second time, so I fired him."

"God hates faggots."

"Operation Iraqi Freedom has begun."

Those are all examples where a sense of loyalty, or obedience to authority, or a notion of what's sacred, is allowed to weigh more than straight-ahead compassion, which can allow inappropriate cruelty or injustice. These kinds of problems are what make liberals much less anxious to sing the praises of the binding foundations: throughout history, some of the greatest enemies of proper compassion have been abuses of binding foundations. That doesn't mean we shouldn't appreciate loyalty, authority, and sanctity; it just means that we don't cheerlead about them blindly.

Compassion isn't one of those of eight, order-centric conservative values we listed. It's also absent from their manifestos of conservative principles. A conservative might explain that with, "Come on– our compassion is exercised through *all* our values." And that's true. As we saw in chapter three, they are compassionate, just not as compassionate on average as us, the way compassion is normally defined (by feeling level). They have a different feeling experience, and they express their compassion differently (more practically).

But in all of Russell Kirk's Ten Conservative Principles, the closest he gets to mentioning compassion directly is on the back end of the ninth principle: "Knowing human nature for a mixture of good and evil, the conservative does not put his trust in mere benevolence."

That's almost sarcastic, isn't it? It's no wonder we liberals miss seeing their compassion in moral decisions– it feels buried, muted, hidden from view. Compassion is sometimes mocked as simplistic like that on the right. At other times, it's woven in with other ideas, or "balanced" against other social values, in ways that can seem like rationalizations for ignoring it. Liberal manifestos of belief are like reading synonyms of the words compassion and fairness: for us, trying to be moral in the moment, with who we're with right then, is the primary guide for our morality, inspired by that right hemispheric orientation around immediate, specific, "living" situations as guidance for action. Stopping to think about other factors can be seen as a way to avoid proper behavior. We experience just that sort of excuse-making all the time in our lives, as cruelty happens. For me, that's a great example of why I work so hard on police brutality issues: cruelty is stepped over on the way to some other value that appears moral to somebody, somewhere, but that I see as immoral in that moment, with that victim.

In contrast to our near-obsession with compassion, conservatives have a built-in need to tread carefully with the notion of helping people. To them, humans are tricky and contrary, a grab bag of motivations– "a mixture of good and evil." Many conservatives purposefully avoid talking about compassion. If you twist their arm, they'll admit that they view love as the centerpiece of a good life. You might have to break the arm before they say it, though, or do a little waterboarding. It seems to hurt many of them somewhere near the kidneys to say things like that, unless they're wearing a suit and have a hymnal in their hand.

Remember how an emotional response to suffering by a liberal is often responded to with "yeah, but…" by conservatives, especially if it's pain that the conservative feels unable to directly, personally address? That's them trying to fold in the binding foundations to adjust, in some way they see healthy, our impulse to be compassionate. That attempt can feel quite annoying for us; it can feel immoral. It smells like self-involvement to us, or selfishness. Sometimes it is, and sometimes it's not; that's what makes the binding foundation emphasis a two-edged sword.

In 2016, when North Carolina made it illegal for transgender people to use a bathroom that wasn't for their "biological sex,"[7] most liberals saw this as an issue of fairness, or justice– that it harms transgender people when we force them to use a bathroom that makes them uncomfortable. The conservative view was that the sanctity[8] or privacy of society was much more valuable than fairness for the transgendered; that much more harm would be caused to those who use those bathrooms presently to have transgendered people use it, too.

This is another example of liberal focus on an important exception to the current process, in the form of transgendered people's concerns, and conservatives asserting that the existing process doesn't need an update with such exceptions. Here, then, is the heart of our liberal reticence with the binding moral foundations: when conservatives speak of using binding foundations, they're often also saying they concern themselves with care and fairness toward their ingroup, those they feel most loyal to and most reverent toward, who are those closest to them (family, church, town, country, etc.). In many situations, that seems fine to us. But in other cases, we liberals can see the binding foundations as reducing or eliminating compassion inappropriately to protect some (from change, discomfort, confusion), while causing harm to others not in the ingroup. It becomes a question of who we act caring toward, and who we're cruel toward, with middle ground hard to find.

This kind of disagreement gets quickly thought of in pure, strong moral terms. Maybe it should be. With our history, maybe it shouldn't be easy to resolve deeply-held beliefs from the past that seem so straightforward to both sides, around things like gender, religion, and freedom. We're addressing strong values on both sides, that exist because of human nature, history, social life, or a combination.

History and the tide of modernism may make it seem that liberals are on the right side of these arguments we make for our important exceptions. But it's only a small hop over from there to assuming we know exactly *how* the changes should happen, and *when*, and *why*. In the arguments about North Carolina, I noticed a common liberal attitude of "get over your hangups about bodies; no one's getting harmed with inclusion." But we should be careful with those assumptions, because it dumbs down an emotional, complicated subject into "I'm right, and you're wrong," which should always make a warning buzzer go off in us somewhere. A moral stance may be inevitable in this case, even necessary, but a moral *fixation* is always a bad idea. We don't know what's inside the minds of people very different than us, and we can't know exactly what needs doing, and how, or the kinds of problems that might crop up. If your mind is going often to "that's stupid" in these situations, you're probably not asking the right questions.

I don't want to pretend I know how to handle such conflicts; you see I'm not providing any bushy-tailed solutions. But knowing what *not* to do, and avoiding attitudes that are unproductive, can be a powerful aid in an eventual solution. Even in intense activist situations, where more than polite discourse is needed, we shouldn't be anxious to run with moral justifications, because part of the cost is a near-guarantee to substitute potential solutions with anger and disgust. Sometimes necessary, yes, but not at all preferred. If we can, we should always avoid moral claims, because they automatically polarize, and move most discussion points off the table.

Many of our political conflicts, like North Carolina's transgender law, are a battle between the values of the individualizing and binding foundations. The indirect effects of the binding moral foundations aren't always noticed in our day-to-day lives, especially by liberals. The police brutality case of Esa Wroth from chapter one was a similar clash between valuing binding or individualizing foundations, as I advocated for seeing the primary moral driver as direct cruelty, while my conservative acquaintance saw it as the harm caused by a lack of respect for authority and the law, and a lack of loyalty to the peace officers who did their jobs per procedure.

I'm quite sympathetic to arguments that we should be a more "hive-minded" people,[9] even though I usually don't balance my social moral values the way conservatives do. The point isn't to do what conservatives do, but to appreciate the universal need for a tension between individual and social moral values, and to remember how emphasis on the binding foundations can help us be more caring and fair. Just thinking and talking in terms of this relationship between social and individual values is helpful, because it helps us get over the instinct to be annoyed when a conservative starts talking about something besides pure compassion in a conversation about a moral situation. It can help us be a little more sympathetic to the other factors they may see as playing in, because we'll be used to seeing how we do the same thing. We'll assume that such things are part of the conversation, instead of a signal of selfishness.

We should use the notion of finding balance between moral values to guide many of our conversations with conservatives, because they think in those terms; many of them find it a fascinating tension to meditate on, and it leads to many interesting discussions. It's one of my favorite ways to break the ice in political conversations. You can teach it in about two minutes, and they resonate with it in seconds. Building a greater respect for spiritual or community organizations and other groups; paying attention to principles other than just direct compassion to guide our lives: and having a broader sense of how to use our intellect– discussions around these ideas can enrich both our lives, and lead us to ways to work better together.

As researchers have worked with the moral foundations, they've discovered that in many situations, there's no need to get complicated about them, because they tend to work together in these two clumps of individualizing and binding foundations, which complement, modify, and conflict with one another in different situations (in statistical terms, the binding foundations are highly correlated; they tend to get used together).[10] The foundations used aren't a sacred list, per se, but what researchers have been able to see through observation. They can be thought of in different terms, and there are candidate foundations being considered. We don't need to remember anything complicated or tick off specifics of the theory to use it fully in our lives. Once we get used to thinking in individual-versus-group terms, we see it everywhere, and are less easily goaded into excitability around our moral positions.

Budgets Versus Feelings

Constructive opportunities to think about offsetting social moral values come up naturally and often. One prominent forum is addressing budgets. Many bipartisan projects, such as Living Room Conversations, and the National Coalition for Dialogue and Deliberation, get liberals and conservatives together, and many discuss budgets. You can usually find local groups easily with a web search. Budgets have been found to be a powerful way to get everyone pulling to reach a shared goal, and it teaches inherent tensions between good values.

In 2013, there was an excellent investigation by National Public Radio that exposed how our disability pension system was being abused through bad incentives, in the name of compassion; that lobbying and easy qualification combine to make the system unusually expensive, incenting people not to work even if they can, costing America billions. It was inspiring at the time to see NPR cross the invisible line that seems to discourage liberals from focusing on balancing their direct attempts to limit harm with concerns that are more associated with binding foundation concerns, and to see the wonderful variety of healthy responses from a mostly liberal audience.

Liberals tend to avoid the subject of government budgeting, while it's relatively common for me to see individual conservatives obsessing over it. That's what happens for orderly people whose feelings of compassion throb less in their mind: they naturally turn to think about the practicalities involved.

I subscribe to a conservative organization's newsletter that tends to focus on government expenditure, called the National Center for Policy Analysis Daily Digest. It's eye-opening how much focus rank-and-file conservatives can place on government expenditures. Just reviewing the titles of the stories helps me remember that government money use is an excellent example of a more indirect form of trying to avoid cruelty—one I have no right to ignore merely because it's not about direct compassion. As with most conservative lobbying efforts, I find that high bias levels make most of the stories feel deceptive, incomplete, or even false. But the point of reading the newsletter isn't to grade conservatives on how biased they are: it's to find the occasional good point that broadens my view, so I can walk the talk of my social moral foundations, and remember to broaden myself, to care about more of my values than the ones my friends and I keep naturally just in front of my face.

It's not in the least anti-liberal to balance the fiscal health of the nation with compassion for individuals, or to care about how bad incentives can destroy our sense of personal responsibility. It's common sense that liberals need to care about such things. The fact that we draw different conclusions than conservatives about where that balance is shouldn't prevent us from acknowledging that balance between competing good values is how the real world must do morality.

Conflicts about moral balance create the most deeply felt rifts between us. But knowing how the chasms open up can help inoculate against the worst effects, by allowing us to acknowledge maturely the legitimate moral values in conflict with our own, rather than rejecting conservative views as simply immoral.

Getting Outraged

In a very good study, liberals were shown to consistently underestimate how compassionate conservatives feel. As said, this is the second biggest complaint conservatives have about liberals: we think they're not compassionate. We've reviewed how that perception is a bit of a master key to solve the puzzle of why we can get so, so upset with them. We may or may not be interpreting their compassion level correctly (although we should remember our earlier point about *effective* compassion, and about how comparatively generous conservatives are to even non-religious charities). But even the idea of talking about balancing things against our compassion can sometimes anger us, or create **moral outrage**.

We know that there's a balancing act to do between values when it comes to doing good. What bothers us is usually an unexpressed *feeling*: that *talking* so much about balancing things out sounds like excuses for lacking compassion— the "yeah, but" way of talking about care for others. Talk about doing more harm than good, or the dangers of not sticking close to home with our help, or cutting social programs: these seem to us to have all been commonly used to justify apathy, neglect, and even cruelty in real life. We *know* this to be true in some situations.

But then we make a big mistake with this knowledge: we assume that's what conservatives are always doing, when they are often doing no such thing, or the situation might be very different than how we frame it. We let ourselves get angry over it. We feel justified in moral outrage.

Let's take a modest, beginner example, remembering the general lesson about balancing individualizing and binding moral foundations. You're at a conservative's home after work, barbecuing. Your friend's 13-year-old son comes on the porch and enthusiastically insists the largest steak is his, and you laugh. He's charming and funny, at the age when they eat 10% of their body weight a day. Your host excuses herself calmly and motions her son into the kitchen. They are out of earshot a minute. She returns, apologizing for his behavior: you smile and say, "They inhale food at that age, don't they?" and talk about your own appetite at that age. Your host changes the subject. It becomes clear later that her son has been sent to his room for the night without supper, because he'd been rude to a guest.

You're not mad about her behavior, are you? I wouldn't be, but I'd be uncomfortable, like I'd stepped into a time machine and inadvertently spun the date back to the fifties. I had a similar incident happen once, and all evening, I wondered how their young man was doing: how hungry he was; if his mother was addressing a long-standing impulse control problem; whether that sort of thing happened often; and if such harshness ended up making the boy feel as if he never measured up. The kinds of thoughts a liberal with tenuous boundaries in life has. I was a flagon of internal splutter all night.

Does she have compassion for her son? Almost certainly. But it's buried, isn't it? At least to a liberal (A conservative reviewer read that part and wrote, "It's not buried!! IT'S RIGHT THERE.") It's hidden by the actions of a more involved moral response, and a different set of values. Compassion was there, even though we might not see her regret his suffering, and she might not voice any concern about him.

Does *effective* compassion require that she mentally hand-wring like a liberal might all night, about a tough decision? She weighed out a group-oriented moral value: in this case, the teenager's respect for a guest of the family. Like a lot of these cases, her concern was a kind of mush of the binding foundations: a little about authority (respect for parents/older guest), a little about loyalty (putting others ahead of oneself), and a little about keeping social norms sacred. She balanced his development as a young man against caring about his suffering, and he came out the short-term loser (and, hopefully, the long-term winner). Since one of her orderliness skills is to minimize uncertainty about her decisions, it can actually be part of her moral approach that she should enjoy the evening despite his discomfort, to have empathy working only in the background. She might be dismissive and straightforward about the situation if it came up: "Oh, he's a wonderful kid. Just needs a basic lesson here and there." Simple. Easy, if you're not a liberal weenie like me.

The moral approach is complicated and a little contradictory, if you map it out: there's respect, love, loyalty, care, and the way that his politeness quotient was seen as requiring more self-discipline. But the scenario itself isn't complicated at all, not from his mom's standpoint, anyway: he's out of line— oops— out he goes. Black-and-white, like John Wayne ordered up. Giant boundaries invisible to you and me suddenly show themselves to be there, like one of those force-field walls on Star Trek. She's loving him through teaching politeness and respect.

This balance, or "tough love," is the central part of effective compassion for conservatives.[11] We do the exact same thing, just not as much or as naturally as they do, so we don't think in those terms so naturally. They can have a near-obsession with even the concept of balance, when it comes to morals. My kind of compassion— the kind where I laugh off adolescent excess, where I let the kid have the biggest steak after a blustery mock fight over it, because I know he's got hunger pangs that rival a pregnant woman's— is probably suspect to a lady like this. Not funny, at all. Partial, immature, misplaced; maybe dangerous. She might think I had a bad upbringing.

That's a mild example. The son is older— the main downside, if any error did happen, wasn't in potential psychological fallout— just in making a growing kid hungry. Maybe she goes in there later after you leave with a tough love version of bread-and-water, to fine-tune and drive the point home.

But there may be other conservative child-rearing situations that are not so nuanced and may not be executed with finesse. I've been in the same house with a good, conservative family and experienced spanking in anger; frequent yelling; harsh punishments; very high criticism-to-praise ratios: paying far less attention to a child than seemed appropriate when in pain, or after completing a difficult task well, or just when they wanted attention.

These are not the anything-goes, permissive-parenting problems that our liberal friends often have; they're a kind of opposite. They can create strong disgust within us, even physical feelings of sickness, because these approaches seem so morally wrong.

Maybe you're not angry yet with these scenarios— still just disoriented, or alienated? I hope so. We're still on gentle scenarios, but you're reaching a little outside of your normal moral foundations to try to understand someone with a broader set of them. Not always a better set, mind, but broader.

One angle on the problem we should get used to is that we have different roles in society that we fulfill, based on our personalities: in the case of child-rearing, these are conservatives raising future likely conservatives; people raising similar people. The parents have to use their personalities as best they can: a budding conservative may well require a certain kind of training to end up morally strong, in both individual and group-oriented senses. What do I know? Part of the argument is that there's a parallel universe involved, due to genetics and circumstances. An odd idea, yes, but their playing field and rules differ radically from the ones we should use with our batch of future liberals. If that wasn't at least partially true, there'd be a good case to be made to take the whole business over, to shuttle all those conservative kids off to the centralized optimizing collective, where they'd get that simple, pure compassion of ours in big, clean doses, and be happy ever after. Above the entrance gate would be our motto: "Every Child Gets the Biggest Steak"…no? Why not? If your answer is because it'd be too expensive, you've missed my point somewhere. Off to your room, then, with no supper.

Another angle that can be comforting is thinking in terms of tradeoffs. I wouldn't have done what my friend did with her son, but I don't believe his pain was wasted or damaging; he probably learned *something* useful about politeness and caring for others, and he didn't die of starvation. At worst, he suffered a poor tradeoff.

Of course, we know they make mistakes as parents. But we usually can't be totally sure they made a mistake in a specific situation, even if we can talk for 15 minutes about why we think they did. But even if they do make a mistake, *we can almost never know how big a mistake it was*, no matter how awful the act seemed from our moral perspective. Different playing field, different rules, entirely different personalities. Getting angry in most of those situations is acting on feelings of entitlement, because our moral sense is violated, and because we assume we know what's going on in some absolute moral sense. We're treating *our* morals as the only absolute good.

It can be challenging to think through ways to suspend our moral judgment like this, but the effort is worth it.

The way conservatives say that liberals get mad too easily is they say we are *intolerant*. They're right. We are prone to consider conservatives intolerant, yet are way too likely to let ourselves off the hook about our own intolerance. The comedian Lenny Bruce made a wise statement that would be funny to me, if the truth of it wasn't responsible for so much pain and misunderstanding: "The liberals can

understand everything but people who don't understand them." What we
don't understand are people who seem eager to balance other goals
against compassion, and who are convinced that there is one general,
good approach to living correctly. People who seem light on compassion,
who lack flexibility, who violate the rule of "different strokes for different
folks," can make us angry enough to assume the moral high ground, be
rude, end friendships, and create feuds or permanent divisions in our
workplace, our neighborhoods, and in local politics.

If we're average liberals, with mild weaknesses in politeness, high
compassion, and higher-than-average neuroticism (reactivity), we are
surprisingly susceptible to a disgust that leads to what we've seen on
college campuses since 2014. That year, liberal students began heavier
use of the group version of the transparency assumption, our trick of only
listening to our ingroup, of developing wrinkly, goofy ideas inside an
echo chamber. It quickly became more common on campuses to be
intolerant toward people liberals think of as intolerant or cruel. Don't
make that mistake. In truth, nothing about the conservative moral
perspective magically alters our responsibility to reach out maturely and
clearly to conservatives, and to be good examples of tolerance ourselves.

Now, the more difficult scenarios. These are more dramatic examples,
where we're probably seeing ignorance or intolerance, and can't help but
have an internal reaction. In the following, try to imagine how you would
feel. What if a conservative is acting on their world view in a way that
feels narrow, uninformed, hurtful, insulting, or downright immoral?
Which of these scenarios are morally wrong? Would you raise the issue
with them? How?

> – Your cousin won't bring his beautiful children to the
> extended family reunion, so the rest of the family has never
> met them– because the family adults curse, and teenagers
> may sneak off and smoke pot, or drink.

> – Your uncle still won't speak to his son, who got a DUI two
> years ago.

> – Your brother listens to you talk at length about starvation
> in North Africa, and then says spiritedly, trying to close off
> discussion, that "we shouldn't have anything to do with
> that– it's none our business, especially now, with our own
> problems."

> – Your conservative supervisor fires an otherwise skilled and

well-behaved friend for raising her voice in a private
meeting with the supervisor.

– Your friend at the community garden blurts out matter-
of-factly that the EPA should be abolished.

– An acquaintance passes on, in great detail, his theory
about how homosexuals always have many partners, are
always unhappy, can change their ways, etc.

– Your co-worker complains loudly about a different liberal
sin or two every day, as if everyone within earshot agrees
with her.

– Your stepfather tries to lecture you on various detailed
traits of "wetbacks."

Here's what I'd like to suggest may be possible: that these scenarios
are not worth your anger; that they are not worth a relationship: that the
people behind these statements and beliefs may be more valuable than
any potential lesson our anger might offer, over any one thing they can
say or believe. That they, as people, might be worth either ignoring their
statements, or working with carefully to address how the statements made
you feel.

To be tolerant means precisely to put up with intolerance, and to do it with
patience and discipline. After all, being tolerant of different races, ages,
sexes, and incomes isn't much of a problem for us; we usually think those
"exceptions" are interesting and important. Our intolerance comes up
because we choose to pretend that intolerance isn't allowed to exist; that
we have the right to decide that it ends, now. That's succumbing to the
same intolerance we condemn them for.

Teachable moments are important to look for, and take advantage of.
I have been in similar situations where it made sense to convey that their
words upset me, and why; sometimes, it ended well. But deciding you
might do good by talking about it, and having an involuntary anger
response and talking about it, are two different things. This is the
difference that both liberals and conservatives need to understand better
about political correctness. Being politically correct should mean that
we're being *good people*; it's that simple. It shouldn't mean that everyone
needs to be exactly like us, or that they're making a huge mistake when
they have intolerant attitudes, or ignorantly use unhelpful terms.

We can convey our concerns about people's intolerance or ignorance without being judgmental about them as people. We can be kind while we do it, and matter-of-fact about our feelings, or about what we know. Among young people on campus, there has been a maturing of the notion of political correctness that has also sprung up, right along with the intolerance, that can be inspiring to witness. Young people who insist they have the right to live their own way, but who don't condemn those who are intolerant. Who patiently and unapologetically teach when it feels productive, or necessary. Who understand that the world needs to change, and to learn, but that everyone isn't coming along at the same speed, and that's ok.

Each of us is made up of a lot more than our limitations, no matter how bad they may be. We've all wandered on a detour or two through life, and picked up bad ideas and habits along the way that afflict others. One good way to remind oneself to be tolerant is to remember our own odd weaknesses, and recognize how deeply we want to be accepted despite having them. Moving past others' foibles, even their intolerance, can be seen as a way to recognize, and accept, our own weaknesses. And don't think your tolerance won't be noticed; it makes a big difference for conservatives to be accepted as they are, especially when they know that their beliefs are alarming to you.

That was the first principle of avoiding problems with conservatives—*don't get mad*. Here's the second.

2. Try not to get disgusted.

Yep—keeping it simple, keeping it real. Less to memorize, less to tell your shrink.

Have you ever been so offended morally that you felt physically sick? That's a modern version of disgust. Disgust almost certainly evolved as an effective way to keep us safe from poisons and dangerous microbes. Babies are disgusted by certain tastes or textures. We develop disgust for smells from waste or rotten food. As we get older, our culture helps us— trains us— to each develop an involved set of things that disgust us, and we avoid them as much as we can. As modern adults, we can be disgusted by many things that are not dangerous at all: our disgust has moved well beyond food and smells into things or situations that violate our moral values, and things that remind us of our animal nature, or of death. Things that *feel* harmful.

Research of disgust is a broad, deep field, but we still aren't clear on it in some ways. It's an odd-man-out, for an emotion: there's getting mad at Jake hitting you, getting sad when Jane leaves, getting glad when Joe shuts up— and then there's the emotion you feel when you open the

197

yogurt and it's green.

Sometimes, we're just disgusted, but usually, disgust gets mixed up with other emotions, as we get mad about Jane leaving the yogurt way in the back where you couldn't see it, and frustrated because we wanted to eat it right then.

If we have a strong reaction when seeing child-rearing techniques that we don't agree with, we might feel disgust along with other emotions, too, as we turn a sense of harm into a moral event. We might feel sacredness is being violated. This is an example of the rather vague nature of sacredness for many liberals. Conservatives have a clearer set of values that generate a sense of the sacred: they can often clarify quite well what they consider sacred and what disgusts them. Liberals have compassion as their most sacred value, and not many other values to discriminate quite as carefully about. Violations of any moral values can create disgust– it's another one of those emotions we swirl in and out of in life, without as much distinction as we usually think.

That's Disgusting

Interviews reveal that conservatives understand liberal motivations better than we understand theirs.[12] It's a fairly large effect: it's also quite obvious to me anecdotally, as I speak with conservatives and liberals about each other. With our emphasis on the intellect, and our higher empathy for others, how can we be so weak at understanding conservatives? It seems like we should ace understanding conservatives. Unraveling that mystery is very helpful in helping us get less mad and disgusted with them.

Many studies have shown that conservatives have higher average levels of disgust when it comes to contaminates, or purity considerations. This seems to be the reason why older conservatives react much more strongly to homosexuality: they see it unconsciously as a kind of contamination. Conservative more active sense of disgust is so reliable and marked that it predicts conservative voting fairly well, in America and elsewhere without knowing anything else about someone.[13]

But what gets ignored in this focus on conservative disgust is the great strength of liberal disgust when it is triggered, and its powerful effect on our relations with conservatives. I believe our disgust response is high enough to distort our view of conservatives because a combination of our strengths are violated. Yes, we're compassionate, and we may default to emotional information to evaluate what's going on, to advocate for the exceptions we care about. But there's also a group of openness traits that are easy to miss that play a part.

There, in the middle of that long list of openness traits, are the ways that we enjoy and interpret *emotion*. Art of all kinds enlightens and inspires to emotion as perhaps its greatest role, with a special emphasis on empathy, since nearly any human drama being played out in painting, music, dance, or elsewhere asks us to project ourselves into others, and live through them. Our gifts with broader imagination channel us naturally into other people's experience as well, as we place ourselves elsewhere in our minds. Finally, our higher inclination to look within ourselves, to be interested in our own feelings, provides us a better reference point about others, especially a better understanding of what it means to be in a state of needless suffering. And all of this, as appears to happen with all our openness traits, is fused mysteriously to our intellect, perhaps the seat of our self-identification as liberals.

We're high in compassion, yes, but we're also holding down another part-time job: we experience our life by feeling our way through the ins and outs of the emotional world.

In other words, just as conservatives have a hidden strength and focus on orderliness, foisted and fostered by their other characteristics, so we have a hidden strength and emphasis on our *emotional life*, propelled through compassion, openness, and the intellect. And the crown jewel of that emotional life is the powerful emotion of empathy.

Based on many interviews and witnessed experiences of liberal disgust, I think this full-scale emphasis on the emotional life causes us to be horrified by anyone who blunts their emotional or empathic response in an effort to understand the situation, the way we just described conservatives doing. Their logical approach, combined often with personal reserve, conflicts deeply with our need to interpret the world and make sense of it through our emotions.

That's where our misunderstanding of them comes from. When disgust, one of our most powerful emotions, enters the picture, it overwhelms us, and it distorts our view of their motivations heavily. In interviews, liberals will often just say that conservatives have no compassion; that they operate out of a desire for power. Of course, conservatives who disgust us may very well be evil. But the statistical evidence is quite clear that we misinterpret them more than they misunderstand us, so we must weigh the evidence quite carefully before yammering on with harsh judgments.

Not only do we see them as evil in those moments we can't see their compassion working, but they appear to be trying to hide that evil by talking about random details, or anything they can, except the only thing that we care about. It seems to us to be an attempt to manipulate or distract us from what's happening. A few doses of this experience, and a lesson has been ground into our bones about the absence of conservative compassion. That can make it a habit to react with disgust in similar situations. Even the ***mention*** of certain other factors outside suffering in an incident can begin to trigger disgust in us.

For liberals, then, disgust is relatively rare, but it tends to come to us in a rush with those who we feel lack compassion. This particular pattern reflects an ironic fact: we may be appreciative of complexity, but when situations appear to need compassion, we suddenly become quite simple creatures. We typically get visibly angry or upset, can feel physically sick, and treat people who seem to lack compassion badly.

I phrased the rule about disgust as "Try not to get disgusted" because it's very hard to avoid disgust in the moment. It can help if you prepare yourself, if you know you'll be in a situation where you can expect to be disgusted, usually over what you see as conservative cruelty. But most of the trying is learning these principles of morality and personality that can help us avoid disgust, or at least take it down a peg, by having a better sense of what's going on from their standpoint. If you can humanize the conservative through relating better to them, your chance of a strong disgust response go down greatly.

My experience with conservative disgust is as a kind of opposite to our reaction, in keeping with research that shows wide cultural differences in how and when we experience emotions, how we express them, and the emotions we use in the same situations.[14] Conservatives are *nuanced* with their disgust. They have shades of it; gradations. They use it like you might use the sense of smell in some situations. It's a tool of judgment and discrimination, and seems tied into carefully setting boundaries in life.

Liberals can feel disgust very strongly, but research has shown that conservatives get disgusted *easier and more often* than liberals do. As with other ideological differences, one of us has very strong occasional disgust (liberals), while the other has higher overall (average) levels. For them, feeling disgust and avoiding negative things is akin to how Michelangelo peeled and chipped away at marble to find the human form below: they use relatively nuanced versions of disgust to guide them away from situations and behaviors that aren't what they want, to focus on what they do want.

On the surface of it, one would think that being led by the moral foundation sanctity in life would mean that they approach or enjoy what's sacred in their lives– which may be true for conservatives. What's overlooked is that *sacredness is also experienced by sensing and avoiding what disgusts us.* Disgust sensitivity is probably one reason why conservatives polarize so readily, and why so many can fall so obsessively for demonizing liberals endlessly on talk radio. It may also explain why they conform so well socially, per Social-Emotional Influence Theory, by not only choosing a platform of beliefs, but also avoiding the beliefs of the bad guys, the liberals, through disgust.

I think conservative disgust ties in with the strange, strong evidence of conservative strength in the sense of smell, where the disgust response long ago originated in humans. They seem to have a way of "sniffing out" situations, and then use appropriate, mild levels of disgust to set a boundary that doesn't just max out all at once, like liberal disgust. The emotional reaction is muted. Some research has shown conservatives with broadly higher levels of specific types of brain activity than liberals when disgusted, yet reporting the same perceived level of disgust: this may mean that they're used to interpreting and dealing with greater impacts from disgusting events without being as emotionally affected.[15] It feels to me as if mild levels of disgust are so common for them that they learn to live with it, so that it doesn't overwhelm them unless there's a strong reason to be disgusted.

When I'm around liberals who are disgusted, it's hard to miss. With conservatives, in situations like business or casual social situations, it can be hard to detect, yet the effects can be dramatic, at least over time. Their politeness often takes the form of being reserved, after all, so what they're thinking and feeling doesn't spill out as readily or clearly, even if they're experiencing disgust.

The gradations of disgust seem to be part of their threat-detection instinct. I think instinct is the right word: it's built-in, it's active, and it doesn't appear fully conscious. I first noticed this in the business world, when meetings would fail over something that I either didn't notice, or that was so subtle that I barely noticed it; it seemed to be problems they sensed with my approach– things we'll talk about later, having to do with ideology-related conversation style and unconscious signals. Later, I watched it clearly occur with liberal co-workers occasionally, when they were having problems with conservative supervisors; twice, I was able to verify with the conservatives involved that a kind of controllable disgust response was in play. I've also been able to have conversations with some relatively open conservatives who have admitted to this kind of controlled, cool version of disgust. I've experienced or watched it many times since; it has shut down interviews, ended conversations, and ended relationships, but usually, it's not that dramatic.

What I'm calling a disgust response can be explained away as simply setting strong boundaries, or thought of as distaste or simply dislike. To me, these are distinctions without a difference, in that they are a pattern I don't witness with liberals. It's the behavior during and after an incident that's important. There's usually almost no lashing out. They exercise great self-control, and don't appear emotional, but nevertheless a door shuts in a dispassionate, sudden exclusion. It's a strong boundary-setting, which doesn't become perfectly clear until attempts to reconnect are unsuccessful. It's a little like the classic Southern Californians who say "let's do lunch," and then fall off the face of the earth.

Constructionism shows that emotions like disgust, anger, and dislike don't have the same distinctions we think they do.[16] They can share the mind, especially over time, without as much distinction as we once thought. They mix in ways that make facial expressions or other ways of detecting what's going on difficult, especially if there are large personality differences involved. Conservatives can experience some of their emotions in different ways than we do– and, of course, they're often processing them with a quite different personality. Things are going on that we can't understand well. This should be taken as a lesson that we should be careful about thinking we know what's going on inside the minds of people who are not only different than us, but who would express themselves differently even if they did feel the same.

The good side of the conservative disgust response, then, is that it's not usually done with overt anger, and it's rarely strong (except for the consistently rude minority). The bad news is that it happens relatively commonly for them, and mostly unconsciously, so you can cross their "lines in the sand" easily without knowing it. You might be thinking "that didn't go great, but it'll be fine," when it didn't, and it won't.

The third rule of avoiding conflict with conservatives, then, is:

3. Don't be so disgustingly liberal.

Let's take a simple example. If our conservative mother of the hungry teen was committed and sure about her decision to send her son to his room, how might she react if you make clear somehow that you think the punishment might be too harsh? She might suddenly see you differently. A failed version of her son, maybe, decades hence– still impolite, still clueless about the basics. You might be pretty disgusting in that moment, the way we're using the word here.

Or, maybe she'd be fine with the question, and patiently explain her rationale. But what if you had violated sacredness over and over all night, even though each one was a small mistake? What if you had used a mild swear word in front of her teenage children after:

– Making an unclear joke about ideological differences;
– Bringing up negative subject matter to talk about;

- Slouching in your chair a great deal;
- Gossiping about a mutual friend;
- Talking with little eye contact;
- Drinking a little too much.

Little things add up for everyone. It's doubtful those things would trouble most liberals that much. For conservatives used to a different set of assumptions about life, though, a slightly careless approach on our part may stack little feelings of disgust against us that we're not even aware of. And of course, something that seems small to us can be medium-sized or jumbo to them. In her case, maybe cursing with her children around would be a large, if not jumbo-sized error, at least one strike in a three-strike game. Throw 'damn' into the mix 2 hours before, and asking about a parenting decision could move us from a simple, potentially strengthening conversation to dealing with disgust, maybe even a potential end of the relationship.

The rule isn't "Don't be disgusting." You're a liberal interacting with a conservative: you're going to be mildly disgusting, here and there. The point is to not be disgusting *often*, or to enough of a degree to warrant rejecting you. We violate this rule when we don't honor their presence with the proper amount of attention and respect.

Because conservatives can be both blunt and reserved, you may either get clear signals where you have erred, or no signal at all, or something in between. Best to avoid finding out which it will be.

4. Be careful with sarcasm and negativity.

Sarcasm and whining aren't wrong to do, on occasion: conservatives can be extremely sarcastic, and enjoy it in others, though it's more rare for them than it is for bright liberal types. Some can also be endlessly negative. I'm suggesting, through long experience with conservatives in many settings, that these innocent-sounding tools of social interaction can gradually degrade the quality of a relationship, or weaken its foundation when important personality difference is involved, just as they can with anyone. Sarcasm and negativity are always best used with those closest to us, and in careful, controlled doses. There are whole cultures that avoid them like the plague. In a few seconds, or in stressful situations, these innocent American habits can unexpectedly spin a conversation or situation out of control.

5. Curb the habit of saying how complicated things are, or that everything is about shades of grey.

Expressing things insistently in terms of grays is a liberal instinct for some of us, like me: we don't feel comfortable only hearing half the story, especially when it's the half (or the quarter, or the eighth) of the story we think doesn't matter. Questioning how simple things are, or making things complicated can be quite annoying, because the usual conservative preference is to keep things clear-cut. You could annoy them this way getting an ice cream cone, by talking about the ingredients: it doesn't have to be a sensitive subject to be annoying, just a grinding tendency on your part to sound like a special report on National Public Radio about some tiny part of life. You shouldn't have to suddenly change your personality to black-and-white thinking: you just need to have the grace and sensitivity to not be annoyingly, throbbingly liberal, by not erupting your every thought out of your mouth.

The problem with spraying your perspective around in living color, everywhere you go, is how it can grind good people's patience to powder, or even unpredictably alienate them.

You can share anger about a terrorism act with your conservative friend, and bond over it. But if you must continue– if you have to murmur something about needing to improve international relations so there are less terrorists in the first place– you may have earned a misplaced sense of integrity at the cost of conveying that you're not loyal to your nation, or that you're clueless about protecting yourself from murderers. This kind of "yeah, but" instinct of ours, which is part of being ideological, is part of this same "dude, everything's, like, waay more complicated than that" attitude. It can pop out of us when discussing anything that touches on conservative values you don't share as enthusiastically, or moral values you don't see the same way.

6. Short and sweet is best.

This rule is actually more of a commonsense guideline, a recognition that we shouldn't set ourselves up for failure with misplaced optimism. A fishing trip together to a riverbank before an all-day one in a boat. A double date before a shared family outing. Coffee before lunch; lunch before dinner; dinner before skiing; skiing before camping. The power of time to mess things up is consistently undervalued, especially after a good experience together. You can be a less-than-perfect pairing and have a great experience together during a one-night stand, but if it's a long period, you're suddenly demanding a much better, more natural pairing, and that is a much higher standard to achieve, particularly across ideological and moral gulfs.

This respect for time is essential in sensitive conversations. Set a time limit in your mind, try to get to the point, cover it, and stop talking. The later drivel on the topic can loop you both into disagreement as your attention wanes, discipline falters, and you remember that it's waaay more complicated that what she's saying.

Remember the simile of vats and jugs and gallons and pints of personality traits that we must rummage among and grasp from our inner rooms: if you run out of patience a half-hour into a 12-hour fishing trip on a canoe, with a talkative fellow who's mental tackle box is full of dastardly opinions, the thimblefuls of traits that you were counting on from your back rooms won't get either of you home safely.

There's a tremendous amount of exciting research going on to help people with the ideological divide, because many related fields–anthropology, a dozen different branches of psychology, neurology, cognitive sciences, and others–are learning to speak with each other to triangulate their way to useful help. The bad news is that we're not using the information we already have well; researchers are deep in the wild, machetes humming, and their mamas are sending in sandwiches, but the jungle grows up behind them, while the folks back home watch talking heads. The field of morality is the best example of that mismatch: all kinds of great work, all kinds of abuse of the basics of morality by us regular folk, with great anti-lessons from the pundits.

It'll probably be a few more years until we figure out how to do Jedi mind tricks with conservatives, to bend them to our will. Liberal researchers may be in various dark rooms as we speak, working out the hand movements and voice tricks, funded by forward-thinking billionaires who invested early in Facebook and Paypal. While we wait for their secrets,

1. Don't get mad.
2. Try not to get disgusted.
3. Don't be so disgusting.
4. Be careful with sarcasm and negativity.
5. Curb the habit of talking about how complicated things are.
6. Short and sweet is best.

Chapter Nine

CONVERSATIONS – THE BASICS

The Dude: It's like what Lenin said... you look
for the person who will benefit, and, uh, uh–
Donny: I am the walrus.
The Dude: You know what I'm trying to say–
Donny: I am the walrus.
– The Big Lebowski

IN PREPARING TO relate to conservatives, let's set aside that the
effort is usefully dumbed-down to any one thing– words like difficult,
scary, easy, formal, delicate, risky are all too general. Bad stereotypes,
you see. We have spoken in generalities so far about each other to get a
handhold here and there, to make sure we don't violate what are best
thought of as basic rules.

Now, we're at the level of detail we've been crawling and dodging and
scrambling toward– we've got ourselves a specific human being, where
many of those rules and tendencies may not hold. Or they hold like
crazy. With each person, statistics are both powerful and dangerous, but
the risk is manageable. The difference between prejudice and
preparation is like the difference between an ignorant entrepreneur and
one poised for success. The ignorant run with simplistic ideas: the well-
prepared do their homework, *and* pay attention as they go along. We
can't wiggle around bullets like Keanu Reeves in "The Matrix," but we
can wiggle our way around many of the common traps with
conservatives, because we've covered the basics.

We won't be going over everything that makes for great conversations
with people. We'll stick with a few principles and a few skills, what I've
found to be most useful– some from theory, most from messing up with
southerners.

206

Preparation

A great conversation follows principles, beginning with that of good preparation. Communicating well with those who are ideologically different is rarely a random event, borne on the wings of luck.

The best preparation for good conversation is being a good person: generous in spirit, disciplined, modest, optimistic, and thoughtful. On behalf of reality, I apologize for the inconvenience. It amazes and frightens me when people assume there are secret, magic keys to relating to others that are well removed from whether or not we're good people. There are a thousand books out there about making good impressions on the way to getting yourself a hot wife, or a billion dollars; most sound as if successes of that kind are a customized, psychological version of dodge ball and whack-a-mole.

I don't want to say that techniques aren't useful, but we like to gloss over being good people because it feels vague, and because it's hard to do anything about. But we should never ignore the ongoing American effort to have technique win out over substance. Salesmen can be divided up between those healthily focused on serving the customer, and those focused on the best way to get your money from your wallet to theirs. None of us want to buy from the latter.

It's good to fidget less, or shake hands well: those are useful tactics in a conversation, but they're not aspects of being good. Just remember the basics: if you're hot-headed, willful, too proud, overly sensitive, inflexible, or not a good listener, any advice you follow here is only going to be partially successful.

This is not a trivial point, or parenthetical: it is the end and the beginning to me, defining exactly how far you can go with conservatives, just as it provides an exact limit on my own personal relationships, and all facets of my life. The section on biases should also remind us that it's not enough to do a quick audit of the inside of your skull and say to ourselves, "Yeah, I'm wicked good today; lemme at 'em." Sadly, we can feel good-willed, but not *be* good-willed when it comes time to act, especially if we're tired or in a bad mood. Crummy life decisions and weak-minded habits haunt us, and come steaming out from our unconscious mind to control us.

Now that I've known these ideas and practiced them for years, I make many less technical errors that I used to, so most of my issues with conservatives are usually because of my personal problems. I upend conversations with impatience, for instance, or distraction, or because my upcoming clever idea makes me inattentive, unwilling to stay with their point. It's normal to ignore our weaknesses by using our biases to blame problems on others, or on their ideas: it's normal, but it ain't right.

It's also easy to just take the attitude, with a shrug, that "oh, well; this is who I am; take it or leave it." That my problems are just my inborn genetic personality weakness. From a certain angle, they might be– but that's way too easy. Sometimes, a personality weakness like impatience becomes a moral problem; it gets promoted from annoying to harmful. Something to work hard to fix. **Morality plays itself out through personality**, like the rest of what we do, which most of us would prefer to ignore. I'm more patient now in conversation because I've suffered enough from the problem to change, and tried to pay attention to my embarrassing errors enough to do better.

Use the binding moral foundations in your life to be inspired by good ideas, good people, the world, and those we love, to goad yourself into working on yourself, the way spiritual teachers have urged since the light went on for our species. Don't mistake all this talk of personality trait strengths and weaknesses as an excuse to duck the importance of being the best person you can be. If you're a jackass, getting you through good conversations with conservatives would take a much thicker book, and it'd still have to come with three coaches and your mama taking turns at your solar plexus. And no– being smart doesn't give your jackass side an advantage– it just makes you a smart jackass, which is much worse.

Being a good enough person to have a useful conversation is like showing up healthy to play. Using the research on biases and our personality differences is akin to learning the rules of the sport, and buying the basic gear. It's quite remarkable how many mistakes you'll make violating the rules, even though you know them now: but breaking the rules doesn't end the game, it just means some kind of penalty or setback. No big deal, usually.

Theory doesn't translate well to reality until we've used it awhile. If you're a Southern or Midwestern liberal, you're an old hand, in some ways; if you haven't done much of it, you'll likely have a rough go of it early on, because you're like a beginner at hockey trying to skate, fiddle with a puck, and avoid getting slammed all at once. Maybe you've got the gift: for me, it wasn't pretty.

We also bring other traits that don't have to do with ideology to the party, that are either going to help or hinder the conversation. One in particular– how extraverted we are– can have tremendous impact. It's the main driver of how we engage with each other socially. If you're extraverted, you're in luck, mostly, just like you usually are in social situations. But keep in mind how that strength can make taking a modest and restrained approach difficult, which might be sorely needed with a person.

Introverts usually have it harder in social situations, though modesty and restraint will be easier. Introverts should go "against the spin" of their personality at times, and they usually can, if they prepare and practice, and can learn to trust themselves. There are several wonderful guides to handling introversion well, such as Susan Cain's *Quiet*. The short version: don't be simplistic about what it is to be introverted– that approach to life has unappreciated power and insight; short bursts of being outgoing and warm are quite possible; preparation helps; confidence, goodwill, and calm are more useful than being super friendly and bouncy. These are all particularly helpful points when working with conservatives.

We should learn everything we can about the particular person we'll be with. Those general personality traits we've reviewed won't all be followed by either you or your conservative friend. Also, each of you will bring particular versions of them, with our own versions of being open, or being orderly. They'll also be extraverted or introverted in their own way, which will play a role.

With people we already know, try to think of them anew in advance, to find fresh approaches and things to avoid. Remember to include thinking about yourself, your own traits, in the preparation. If you don't know the person well, others you trust may be able to help with insight about them. Find out whatever background information you can. Hopefully, the conversation itself will mostly be gathering background on them, but it's good to know about them before you start. If it makes sense in that situation, letting them know that you were interested enough to find out about them can be powerful.

If it's an important conversation– about your position at work, say, or to address a conflict with a relative– we should use the techniques of premier athletes. Take some time to yourself in advance, to prepare your mind. You should be able to get yourself in a positive frame of mind, and reduce any unwarranted nervousness by calming yourself. During this pause, visualization is especially helpful.

Visualization

Visualization is best thought of as imagining, as clearly as you can, specific ways the conversation might go. You don't need a class in visualization, and you needn't worry that it's whacko: it's a simple idea, backed by great science. In an odd way, it gets you used to the situation, and helps you relax, as if you've already done it once. You almost always see top skiers weaving gently, with their eyes closed, before their run:

they are working their way through in their imagination beforehand, as vividly as they can, because solid research has shown it to be incredibly effective in changing how we approach decision points, hard spots, and confusing moments– even when we don't know much about what's going to happen, or we're wrong. We can, for instance, visualize an extraverted female interviewer, and still do better with an introverted male. Unexpected resistance can't knock us out of the saddle as easily– and almost all these conversations have surprises and resistance. In an unintuitive way explained by research, visualization allows us to experience disappointments, successes, and even surprises before they happen, in a kind of pre-reality the brain takes seriously.

Visualization can also help you adjust your attitude, and be less frightened. You may also improve your basic preparation as you do the dry run, by remembering a useful fact you'd overlooked, or deciding to bring something pertinent. That's happened to me many times, as I walked through the meeting in my mind and noticed something missing.

You should use your gift of openness and imagination to do as detailed a guess as you can at how the conversation will actually go. The technique is called visualization because visual and other sensory images create the powerful template our mind can use to experience the meet in advance. Try to see the person's face; feel her hand as you shake it; imagine the actual conversation. You should be able to sense emotions that might come up.

Skipping visualization is a common error. It takes energy, and we cognitive misers hate that; it can feel a little foolish; it's associated with new age humbuggery. Get over it. It can be fast: for most people, 3-5 minutes is plenty to get most of the benefits. If the conversation is going to be of great import, such as with a relative you've had a problem with, preparation is incomplete without it. If it's a key interview, or an important sales call, you should visualize longer, and answer questions you think likely, out loud, in a mirror. It's amazing how helpful it is to have answered a question already through visualization. When we do a good visualization, we get a boost of confidence that's warranted.

Let's do this! We know we'll have some problems, because we're not perfect, but we've read this guide; we've got some basics down. We know as much as we can about the person and the situation, and we've prepared with visualization. We're ready.

The First Ten Seconds

What are those first ten seconds going to look like?

There are more than ten biases and heuristics that can crop up in those first ten seconds within the mind of conservatives. Think of it as one getting triggered every second from when you first see them. Beginnings may not be everything, but they're a big slug of it. This cognitive miser business has two sides to it: most of the time we don't pay attention to much, but at beginnings, the cognitive miser in us is busy and alert, whirring away.

The best way for me to respect how miserly we are with our thinking is to remember the study that showed even saying things in a different order when describing a person creates a different attitude about the person; our minds are already trying to eliminate uncertainty by anchoring before we even hear the second item. That's just during normal conversation; during the heightened awareness we usually experience during beginnings, we anchor even more enthusiastically.

If you're around conservatives longer than about 20 minutes, you have a great chance of hearing about how much they trust their gut. Not to be mean, but what that should mean to you is that they like their biases. So your job is to make sure they build only positive biases, which are just as easy to get rolling as the bad ones, and just as long-lasting.

A quick word to those of us who have to repair problems with conservatives we've had in the past. There's not just one beginning to a relationship. Every experience we have with people can be a partial redefinition of how you work together, especially the first two or three opportunities after a problem. We can chip away at an inaccurate impression by trying again and again to show them the truth about us. Anchoring is powerful, but it doesn't have to be the end of the story. We can take advantage of the availability heuristic, when a vivid or more recent example of ourselves can *adjust* a poor anchoring from before.

Different conservatives will give you fewer or more chances to begin again this way using the availability heuristic– and it depends, of course, whether you didn't say thank you once, or you shot their kid. But they often appreciate more than we think that we make a cheerful or contrite attempt to come back again, to try to relate effectively: it appeals to their notions of fairness, and the value of determination and effort. Particularly competitive ones often treat disagreements quite casually, even forgetting what might have seemed to be important. You never know.

This ability to forgive and move on is how the radio superstar Rush

Limbaugh was able to stay in business after his oxycontin addiction problems, and the related lies, hypocrisy (people with drug problems "should be sent up"), coverup, and legal problems. It's how ministers keep their jobs after sexual scandals like Jimmy Swaggart's. You may think of forgiving such people as accepting hypocrisy, but it's more accurate to think of it as the conservative gift for allowing their ingroup to move on, to accept that people make mistakes, just as Christian scriptures instruct.

The crabby ones won't move on– not with you, anyway. I'd put them at about 10% of conservatives. Be careful, though; I think roughly twice as many *seem* as if they won't come around, but that's part of how they roll– putting up a tough-love front, pretending like you blew it forever. If in doubt, I'd give it a shot; lots of them are softer than they appear.

Whether it's the first ten seconds, or a second version of the first ten seconds, it shouldn't be planned. Visualizing it is great, but don't choreograph. It's stiff and insincere. A better way to frame the task of the first ten seconds is to eliminate any chance the other person has to misinterpret your goodwill, politeness, and other good traits. Practice a version if you're serious, maybe in the mirror: pay attention to your posture, your voice, and especially your true attitude toward them. I've filmed myself practicing for business introductions, to better see the signals I send at beginnings; all you need is a phone camera, a pillow to prop it up with, and thirty seconds. Preparation of this sort should never be thought of as artificial, or staged. You're about to make an effort to communicate in a language that's not entirely your own, and you don't want to mess up the basics.

The below are ideas, not a checklist. Everyone decides in life how much they can adjust their behaviors before they feel they're acting, or being insincere. Some of the suggestions are out of place on a farm, in a bar, or with certain types of people: on the other hand, if you're an informal person, say, the suggestions that sound the worst might be the best for you, because it's quite easy to be unnecessarily off-putting. So– here's a loose set of considerations, within our framework of personality.

Scattershot Guidelines

There are few more universal rules of good interaction than an initial firm handshake– man or woman, large or small. While you shake their hand, look them in the eye, and smile warmly and sincerely. This is an especially telling signal to conservatives. A sincere smile is about a feeling you have inside you about them, which means that you should have deliberately thought positively about them in advance.

212

If you think you may be lower status due to age, work position, or any other reason, use slight bows; sir or ma'am; Mr., Ms., or Mrs.; a deferential attitude, if appropriate. This is the single most important thing you can do with law enforcement, a group with whom one should use these stereotypes aggressively, to avoid potential problems. Among conservatives, order means boundaries, which mean hierarchy, which means you're one of the little people sometimes. Part of the language.

Good eye contact is the clearest, simplest way to convey good will and confidence. Avoiding eye contact is associated with dishonesty and insecurity by most people, especially when we don't know the person; I think this is especially true of many conservatives. Some of us, like me, have to look at odd places sometimes, to form a thought, and that's fine: form the thought, and get back to eye contact. But when they're speaking to you, *always* use eye contact, as in 100% of the time; that's the most important half of the conversation for building rapport.

"Good energy" is a nebulous term, but we recognize it when we see it. It's our good nature naturally leaking out. We convey good energy with enthusiasm (congratulations, extroverts), sincere interest, sitting a little forward, active involvement (head nods, smiles, mirroring, listening carefully to what they say) and a steady focus on the person you're talking to. Having good energy also means we're telegraphing interest, even though people don't think of good energy that way.

It's a mistake to think that being sincere means doing what comes naturally. Part of good energy is conveying sincerity with body language and attention. It's natural for me to stare out a window while people talk, but that's almost a perfect lesson that I don't care about them, no matter what my intentions are. Being natural is a nightmare if it means people misinterpret us.

High orderliness can mean they place an emphasis on how you look, as well as neatness and organization. Modest, high quality clothing, appropriate by their standard, including appropriate shoes. Good grooming: quality haircut, clean and trimmed fingernails, shaved.

Good posture, standing and sitting. This is a closely-watched signal; for many of us, particularly in business and politics, posture is used much more than it should be as a cue about traits that conservatives value greatly, such as optimism, competence, poise, forthrightness, and initiative. Rounded shoulders, weight on elbows, swayed back, slumping, or even leaning back in a chair– all these commonly send false, immediate signals about your personality that are anchored on immediately by the unconscious mind, and their input cannot easily be erased or offset, even with impressive results. Americans have mediocre posture in general, but it seems to me that liberals are winning the race to the bottom, even if we're better about overall health.

The mind-body connection is expressed through posture; working on it has many mental benefits. Working on it by throwing one's shoulders back a minute before an interview isn't going to cut it; by five minutes in, you'll be slumping and leaning, as usual. Changing posture can change attitudes, and how you react to the world.

Lots of what people mean when they say "she had good energy," or "he was alert," comes down to posture. Look in two mirrors to get this right, so you can see yourself from the side: if you haven't done this before, it'll probably be eye-opening. Research in biomechanics has shown that there are wide variations in posture between cultures, and through history. Our current, popular forms of sagging, curving, leaning, and tentative postures in America aren't the top-of-the-line models. The heavy unconscious emphasis on posture ties back to the instinctive importance posture has of showing how we "stand" in the world, how we position ourselves when we pay attention, and whether the world scares or stimulates us. To find out more, and to pay the attention you should to posture, look up videos of the Gokhale method, or buy the KENTRO guide to stance; both are fast and effective. It's not about looking like an ex-Marine; it's about feeling and conveying health and energy.

If in doubt about what to wear or how to act, default to a more conservative style (surprise!). This can mean polishing shoes carefully, a choice about jewelry, a hairstyle, or the choice between two shirts. They don't penalize you much for being overdressed, for example, whereas underdressing is a death-dealing blow in some situations (even with relatives). Some versions of being in style are too rad, even if you'd pass with flying colors as stylish elsewhere. In liberal cultures, being overdressed is a distinct risk; among conservatives it's much less so.

These points impact much more than the first ten seconds, but beginnings are where most of the effort pays off. A hidden benefit of paying closer attention to the start is the opportunity given you to fine-tune your overall attitude and approach.

The Rule of Yes

In improvisational theater, the actors have what I think is the hardest job in the world: take a random idea thrown out by one of them– not necessarily a good one– and instantly run with it to make it funny. They have one main rule I adopt to conversation whenever I can: the rule of yes. Improv calls it the rule of agreement, but that seems tame and low-calorie; we're going with yes. I'll use an exclamation point to help you get the point: the rule of yes! Oh heck, let's go all the way– let's capitalize it– the Rule of Yes!

In her book *Bossypants*, Tina Fey shared the idea:

> If we're improvising and I say, "Freeze, I have a gun," and you say, "That's not a gun. It's your finger. You're pointing your finger at me," our improvised scene has ground to a halt. But if I say, "Freeze, I have a gun!" and you say, "The gun I gave you for Christmas! You bastard!" then we have started a scene because we have AGREED that my finger is in fact a Christmas gun…I always find it jarring when I meet someone in real life whose first answer is no. "No, we can't do that." "No, that's not in the budget." "No, I will not hold your hand for a dollar." What kind of way is that to live?[1]

The great thing about the Rule of Yes! is that it's such a *tangible*, specific technique. You just don't disagree. Period. The show must go on. The point is to avoid even milder versions of "No, my friend, you're mistaken." So, no "Not really," no "I see it differently," and definitely not "Maybe, but…," or "Yeah, but…" (which usually sounds like "I can tell it's going to be tough dealing with you.")

If you're the tech repair person at the office, and a cranky guy at work says, "You guys screwed up my computer last time, and it hasn't worked since," you say "I'm sorry. What's the problem?" Or you say, "Oh gosh,, these things are freaking complicated." Or, "Really? Let me help." And this last really needs to be like, "Oh, darn." Not like, "Oh, you think so, huh?"

Here's a tougher one. You're with a neighbor you don't know well, and he hates the nearby amazing park that your kids live in all summer; says it's full of creeps and thieves. You can say, "Yeah, I've seen a suspicious looking teen or two in there," and wind your way around to something you like about the park slowly, so you avoid a "Yeah, but" vibe. Or try "Teenagers look so scary nowadays, with the hair and the clothes." You don't say, "Oh, those kids are all fine," or, "I've never had that problem." These are versions of the Rule of No!

Why don't you just go on from there, then, if you're all about the truth? Why not just tell them "You don't know what you're talking about." It'd be so *honest*. You don't say it because it's rude, and because it's counter-productive. The **goal** of a conversation drives everything; it decides the truth we serve up. This is something that many extroverted people understand in their bones, as they worm their way into people's hearts, that way some of them have of going full deli mode with the truth. When people say, "I'm just being honest," they usually mean they see a chance to be rude, so they're taking it. It'd be honest to open the phone book and read it out loud, too. And more productive. It might be true that your insecure daughter is overweight, but you don't wake her up every morning by saying, "Good morning, dear, you're fat." There are truths we avoid like the plague when we're good people.

"The truth" is a whole, wide universe of things, swirling in and around what he said– but you picked up one easy lump of it and ran with it, straight to No-ville. Your neighbor may have had a bad experience with a scary-looking teen, or been creeped out legitimately once there; or maybe he has some odd issue with teens that you don't need to lose relationship points over. What do you care? Your kids are going to show him gently that he's wrong all next summer; that should be enough of a no for you.

This guideline holds even for fundamental disagreements, because there isn't just one story behind every facet of reality; there's usually two to ten, once you get used to thinking in these terms. If your neighbor is off-putting and blunt about your daughter making noise in the back yard, you can sincerely apologize about it without making your daughter a bad person, or setting a precedent that she'll always be silent. It's no fun that you upset them, right? Is it always the point to run right up onto your throbbing Real Truth of the moment, that– I don't know, pick one– they shouldn't be so freaking noise-sensitive, or they should telecommute on the other side of their house, or only bad people dislike the happy shrieks and squeals of five-year-olds?

Once you acknowledge their basic, hear-the-words-I'm-saying point with the Rule of Yes!, you can go all kinds of places to find commonality about when to make noise, or how much, or where in the yard. Or they might calm down surprisingly, as has happened to me many times in equivalent situations, and apologize right back immediately, because they realize that they're in a crummy mood, or because your cheerful attitude makes them feel guilty. If the problem goes on and on because your neighbor turns out to be a jerk, there's plenty of time down the road to change from the Rule of Yes! to the rule of what a friggin' numbskull, let's throw the garden slugs in his yard. But at the beginning, there's an opportunity to build a relationship, and a lady with a noise upsetting her; there isn't a problem with emergency insults of your daughter.

The Rule of Yes! is one of a few ways of practicing aikido in conversation– and wow, do we need aikido with conservatives. In that defensive martial art, the classic interpretation of what one does is to take the energy of the attacker, who is typically lunging in some way, and *twist the intention* through using inertia and balance into something that benefits you. You might grab her stabbing spear and yank on it, so she loses her balance. Then you do something else– I have no idea what– but that's when you win, is the point; big time. She has a knot on her head, or an inconvenient hole in her, and is very sorry about poking her spear at you.

Yours is a more friendly situation than getting the castle stormed, but it's similar because a conservative might say something challenging, and you'll end up agreeing with part of it– like yanking on the spear– so that it's a bonding experience rather than a divisive one. People try to pick fights almost without meaning to, especially if you're talking about politics, and the Rule of Yes! will be your salvation, because they'll realize how nice you were about what they said.

Another technique of this family is to praise an insight that you find partial, or even dangerous as an overall solution, but a perfectly acceptable idea in isolation. This is very difficult at first, but you get used to it. It feels dishonest sometimes, even though it isn't– it shouldn't be, anyway. When someone defends their punitive approach toward their children that you find harsh, I might say "that must be tough on you sometimes," to turn the focus to their own feelings in the situation. Or I might say "that might've been worth considering a couple of times with my teens," which I can say, because my kids got more slack from me than was good for them occasionally. Going extrovert-on-overdrive would be "Oh, totally. I beat the crap out of my kids; good for you." Instead, I pick my truth, like we always must. At some point, maybe somewhere around "I should've done that more," it becomes a lie for me– but I don't worry about that. With practice, your creativity will prevent you from shoveling bullshit on their head to bond, because honesty– authenticity– is the lion's share of relating. After a while, you won't be thinking in terms of "balancing" truth-telling against bonding; you'll just do both. If you practice, and remember that *everyone always has to pick which truth to run with*, you'll be fine. Tell the truth, *and* be clear about what you mean. It's our naïve realism that encourages us to believe that there's only one response to a situation.

I often disagree with people in some sense, but still find something to acknowledge, to turn it into agreement, usually by pointing out valid principles in tension: "I couldn't do that, but I can sure see some advantages to parenting that way sometimes." There will be plenty of time later to get as nuanced as you pleased about how horrified you'd be with a strict approach, but the world of details, and principles in tension, and exceptions, allow us to extend the Rule of Yes! into situations where we can build rapport without having to back straitjacketing children. All we have to do is admit to something with a possible, or limited, reasonable rationale.

Our approach comes more naturally for women, on average, as Deborah Tannen explains wonderfully in her masterful *You Just Don't Understand: Women and Men in Conversation*. Sorry, ladies: hopefully, we're not boring you terribly. Believe it or not, we're going a bit fast for most of us men. Our speed in this section relates to hormones. We have a special hormone.

Women tend to think of conversation as an effort to establish rapport, while men tend to think it's a way to exchange information. Many men also think it's a chance for some competition, a sideline business in conquering, which they don't get enough of through weekend softball and work. An information exchange approach makes arguments and disagreements and "one-up" efforts (trying to be dominant) more natural, while building rapport makes all that rather horrible. Rapport building is agreeing with each other, over and over. Judging by some womens' conversations, it may be best done while talking simultaneously.

Agreeing with someone on a point, and following up on it enthusiastically, doesn't mean that you agree with every aspect of what they said. *They know that.* You're not agreeing that it's the main point: you're not even agreeing that it's a particularly useful point. Nor are you lying when your favorite point conflicts with their idea somewhat: conflicting ideas are often both true, in a world where values like freedom and protection, privacy and openness requirements, and many other offsetting principles must be balanced, where real-world situations make any single-minded, antiseptically clean solution unacceptable. Now is the time to take advantage of your strength in openness, your creativity, and flexibility, with the improviser's Rule of Yes!

You're choosing to agree, when you could easily disagree, because you want them to feel that you respect their opinion, and you value the relationship. Honor the true things they say, all the way down until it's so skinny a truth that you can almost see through it. Part of the reason why we should bend over backwards to agree is because things that seem true-but-weird, or true-but-so-what, often lead to weird, unrelated points you learn from. That's how I usually learn from conservatives: it starts out with "you've got a [tiny] point," moves through "did you mean…," to me thinking about religion a little differently, or admiring something their mom did, or learning something about politeness.

Everyone has their own idea of honest. I respect that, but I'm in deep with Tina Fey on this one: roll with it. Being too stiff to see the good in people's opinions is no way to live. The world is full of useless, inappropriate, rude, random, and hurtful truths. It's especially full of misplaced truths. There's a wide world of truths to choose from in every instant; part of the measure of a good life is which ones we pick to run with, and which ones we share with others. That's another way of saying we should bust out of the constraints of naïve realism. When the goal is rapport, we use the Rule of Yes! to pick truths that establish rapport.

In conversations, we say "That's a good point," or something like that. We say that a lot, and we mean it when we say it. That's also the Rule of Yes! in action, because it's high-fiving them about their thoughts. We also say "I don't know" if we don't know an answer, and "I should research that more," and "I never thought about it that way." Even if we're men, we say these things.

Rarely, someone will say something I just can't slather with a useful truth, like certain "you liberals are…" insults, or "God *commands* us to use the rod on our children." You can take the attitude that it's time to run with your heart palpitations and take them on. It's your choice, but I almost never do. Why, exactly, would I do that? I try to be practical, and it usually isn't. I sleep fine at night, whether or not I happened to meet one of the scumbags or fanatics or people in a bad mood that the world is filled with that day. I'm not prowling the streets looking for people to argue with, so why would I decide I had to carve a message on this particular fellow's forehead right then?

There are people who are *effectively evil*. If you like to sound scientific as much as I do, you can call them empirically evil. They probably aren't really evil, but they have such terrible ideas, and can do such bad things, that they may as well be. With them, I use what I call the null set, inspired by my confusion in math classes. There may be things to say in theory, but you're up there on the improv stage, and you're thinking, aand – there will be a tiny silence now, because you can't build on that. So you start something else, pointedly and happily. You go full random. Your kid's science fair volcano; how much you love the stripes on the tie you picked today; how fun rocks are sometimes.

I learned this from a Jewish friend, years ago, who had to endure cruel, uneducated statements at work about his heritage. There are people in the world, remember, who have had to wrestle much greater challenges than these we're discussing, for whom getting along with the average conservative is child's play. He didn't get upset, because it was impractical at that place of work. He never assumed it was his yolk in life at any moment to magically transform the stupidity of a random *goyim* by raining down wrath on him. He'd just look up and cheerfully say, "Hey, did you paint that?," pointing at a picture on the office wall.

There would be a period of cognitive dissonance, as the person slowly understood that he wasn't going to be able to continue that particular line of inquiry. He was let down slowly, though; there were key seconds during which he was thunderingly confused about whatever my friend said, while it dawned on him at the same time that the conversation was done. That's a lot to process and still stay mean. Being both cheerful and random– picking his truth creatively– somehow got across rather miraculously that what was just said was wrong, wrong, wrong, without creating a scene; I think it got across a good chunk of what a fistfight over it might have. Or own version of going random doesn't have to win awards, and can be much more subtle, but it will get across a version of the same thing: we're going to scoot around that subject, you and I.

Usually, though, we're capable of agreeing on an opinion; if so, we're almost guaranteed to hear a good point or two. It may not be the whole truth, or it may be a widely-abused truth, but if she's stated a good chunk of truth, call her on it.

If the conversation is easy, The Rule of Yes! doesn't matter that much; you'll probably succeed because your personalities or interests mesh, or the planets are all aligned. But **The Rule of Yes! is the single most important tool for *difficult* conversations with conservatives.**

When it's a challenging or risky situation, the Rule of Yes! will also be tough. It's the hardest part of improvisational theater, after all. You have to find something good about what they're saying, even though it would be much more natural to go with one of the many rejection ideas that have come into your head while they were talking. Those are exactly the times when you need to be creative, remember the goal of the conversation, and pick the truths to point out that make it work for both of you.

To use the Rule of Yes! well, you'll need to practice on many innocent victims. Teenagers are great to try with; they're usually painful enough. Little kids are good, too, because you can flub it, and they're so creative they might like what you said better. With most, if you don't know how to agree with what they say, you can cross your eyes and make a buh-buh-buh sound, which would be better than what you were going to say, anyway.

After conversations, review the number of times you sincerely said "I didn't know that," "That's a good point," or "I never thought about it that way." See how well you avoid the "Yeah, but…" way of saying "No, no, no, wrong again."

The Rule of Yes! will change your life. You'll start picking the right truths to blurt. The appropriate gender will swoon. You'll achieve nirvana. Conservatives will like you.

A Good Soldier

The master of a certain kind of conversation was Dale Carnegie, who insisted we start with enthusiasm (a code word for extraversion), and with faith. In his book, *How to Win Friends and Influence People*, he distilled lessons from a quarter-century of teaching over 100,000 people about selling themselves. It's targeted at business people, so guess which ideology's personality traits are most lauded and emphasized.

His overall approach uses the Golden Rule, and encourages us to be optimistic. Treating others as we would like to be treated is so simple and powerful; we mouth the Golden Rule, yet we rarely *formally* think in those terms, in the sense that the science demands of us. We should.

How many of the traits required by Mr. Carnegie's book are liberal traits? Hmmm. Let me count…cough, cough…actually, he does talk about openness and empathy a little, like many entrepreneur types. But his book is an insider's guide to getting along with conservatives, by acting more like a good conservative. It's not for everyone. When some liberals read his books, which are essentially a call to conscientiousness, politeness, and a salesman's extraversion, he can sound manipulative, shallow, or artificial to us, despite his assertions that sincerity is essential. We don't like the titles, like *How to Win Friends and Influence People*: too peppy, too direct. It oozes cheese. Part of us can't trust it: that positivity and directness is fishy.

An uneasy feeling can also come from the book's emphasis that attitude is everything; if you want to make a friend, get busy liking them; if you want to respect someone, well, get on with it. This is a hurrah for conscientiousness, especially industriousness. A liberal can take that attitude as trying to brainwash ourselves, or as letting the other person brainwash us.

If Mr. Carnegie's entreaty sounds unrealistic or insincere, I ask you to meet me halfway to him: to notice that what a conservative thinks is polite is a kind of unconditional interest and respect on your part– a clear faith they she'll be worth it. If you don't clearly show respect and interest up front, you may be accidentally getting across that she has to earn your respect. You might seem tentative about them, not particularly warm, or not sure that things are going to work out. So, consciously give them the gift of your interest and respect up front; be generous with your clear attention, without asking for anything in return.

I have seen this problem with attitude play out many times in my role as a corporate consultant, particularly with senior executives. Most business cultures should be considered conservative despite the no-tie, relatively informal versions of most businesses today; even in much of high tech and young companies, where many conservative attitudes hide behind a libertarian frontispiece.

Liberals walk in with the Tree of Liberty tattooed on their foreheads and walk out thinking it went great. They went in to get across that they're smart, independent, and take-charge: but they unwittingly conveyed that they were smarty-pants, lacking in common sense, and not a team player. This leads to the first of the three "nots" in conversations with conservatives:

1. You ain't there to be smart.

As we discussed, the way we liberals value our intellect is rarely appreciated by conservatives: they don't mind us being bright at all, but they're not bought off on using intellect the way we do, hard and fast. In conversation, we often "project" how much we value intellect onto the conservative, meaning we assume unconsciously that they appreciate and use intellect our way. In our effort to please and relate to them, we'll sometimes go overboard with clever ideas or concepts, which can either lead to our thought landing with a thud at their feet, or, worse, an impression that you're too clever for your own good, and for theirs.

Issues are especially common in situations where there's a status difference between you: brilliance and creativity have their place in conservative life, but it's not supposed to shine during initial conversation. Other traits should take precedence, remember. We can be anxious to display cleverness, unconsciously trying to curry favor with our strong suit. The best we should hope for at the end of a conversation with most conservatives should be something on the order of "what a good egg," or, at work, "she's a good soldier." If you can keep in mind the difference to a conservative between "she's sounds like a flaky genius type" and "she's a good soldier" in initial meetings, you should be fine.

That's so important that the second major no is a subset of this need to initially keep your smarts to yourself:

2. Don't show your cards all at once.

Liberals may like people who are understated, modest, and talented, but conservatives adore them. Their internal church bells start pealing all at once. It speaks to several of their highest values: competency, modesty, and respect. You focused on them, even though you could've shown off impressive strengths: that speaks to you being an excellent team player, with a sense of hierarchy and decorum. "Gosh. So much there, but doesn't have to telegraph it."

3. Don't talk too much.

There's some statistical evidence that liberal openness and compassion are often coupled with extraversion, another one of the 5 major trait families. It's not a strong effect statistically, and there's some controversy about it. But if extraversion is a strength of yours, use it to get across warmth and enthusiasm, not information.

Shutting up can be tough for us, because, again, our strengths determine our morals and approaches: our skids are greased to get across warmth and interest the way our personality dictates. The Conversation Café, an attempt to bring people together on diverse topics, has brevity as the last of their 6 rules; Cicero's ancient Rules of Good Conversation include the same point as a rule.

I was in Los Angeles once, that bastion of liberal openness; a colleague and I stopped at a bistro for lunch. It was the kind of southern California eatery that can't figure out whether its motif is shabby chic or polished hippie, so it was casual and warm. Our waitress was the most extraverted person I'd ever met. Within 90 seconds of her initial greeting, before I'd even gotten my water, I knew that she was an aspiring actress of middling talent (her opinion), and she was in the midst of a messy divorce, though she didn't blame him; she had two kids, was heartbroken, but only for the kids ("no, it was good, really..."), but came to work anyway because, well, what's a girl gonna do?...and, then, with a little shake of her head and a smile, "So what can I get you two to drink?"

Personally, I love her kind of gonzo-level, effusive openness: if you don't experience people like her in Southern California, you're missing the area's best cultural experience. But her flash flood of emotion, body language, and waay-too-much-information might've left two conservative ladies clutching their purses and looking for an emergency exit. Similar to the spirit of the Rule of Yes!, we choose which truths we reveal, to keep the focus on building good rapport.

Poker is a good metaphor for how to avoid these three no-no's. Think of a friendly, penny-ante game of poker. We're mainly there to enjoy each other. It may be warm, and it may be informal, but we still don't let people know how good we are, and we only reveal what's best for the task at hand. The best way to proceed well is with our own version of quiet competency. There will be plenty of time later, when you're done pulling in your fair share of pots, to tell them war stories about separating fools from their money. But you don't bet all your money at once, you don't bluff aggressively, and you don't make comments about how you're in the business of raking in pots. Show, don't tell.

The poker metaphor forces us to realize consciously that, at the beginning of relationships with conservatives, there should be a component of reserve, or distance, or boundary, or role-setting– whatever descriptor clicks best for you. Talking too much (even if *they're* talkative), an emphasis on revealing our strengths, and having an impressive intellect, all get in the way quickly.

This distance-setting might make sense to the mind, but be lost on the heart. Most conservatives understand the point that "good fences make good neighbors" *instinctively*, particularly at work and in common social situations, but for those of us high in empathy and emotional sensitivity, thinking about relating and reserve at the same time can feel like walking with a shoe heel missing. Thick boundaries can feel unnatural to us; we think crummy fences make good neighbors. I've watched many liberals blow this in interviews, thinking that the task is to be instant best friends and confidential buddies. The worst part is that the average liberal will never know they just biffed it, because their conservative colleague is being polite and smiling the whole time. The only clue you usually get is a mild lessening of warmth.

The rules Dale Carnegie uses may not necessarily play to the strengths of liberals, but the whole approach's emphasis on the Golden Rule certainly does. We have the interest and ability to use our empathy: we can put ourselves in their shoes. We should be aware that good conversation is based on that strength, not the raw amount of our contribution: if we use our sensitivity well, and keep in mind the no-no's, we can do a great job of understanding the other person and responding to them well, through Mr. Carnegie's suggestions to:

- Develop a genuine interest in them.
- Pay attention to their background and personality.
- Sincerely help them feel useful, or valuable.
- Highlight the positive instead of the negative.
- Be respectful and polite.
- Let them finish all their points; never interrupt.

The simple, positive, feel-good advice from Mr. Carnegie is most of what a person needs, assuming one can read it without feeling manipulated or jaded by the worship of conscientiousness, politeness, and extraversion that's called for on every page. The fact that it feels like you're being lectured to by a bouncy, ramrod-straight ex-Marine, should be taken as a chance to practice treating challenging sessions with conservatives as if you were learning a foreign language, so you roll with the oddities graciously. That's what I tell myself, anyway, as I cringe at the old-school twinges throughout the book. A fine alternative is a wonderfully readable update of sorts that incorporates modern psychology, Leil Lowndes' *How to Talk to Anyone*.

Topics

If you're preparing to talk to your boss's boss, you may not have control over the topics of conversation. For the rest of us, talking to acquaintances, family, or co-workers, we have a little more choice. Actually, topics are easy, because there's only two rules:

1) Ask them questions about themselves or their interests.
2) Let them decide what topics to cover.

The Golden Rule is your guide. Empathy leads the way. You focus as much as you can on them and their interests because that's the best way to relate to them.

Studies have shown that when you ask people about themselves, they think you're nicer, and they like you more. This is such a powerful effect that I've felt guilty using it sometimes. Interviewers usually love talking about themselves– without realizing it, they're thinking, "Gosh, this guy is so interested in me that he must be brilliant, insightful, and good at work." I once won a contract through a long interview where I was asked two questions, and I asked about ten– and one of those questions was about when we could start.

The same basic idea works wonderfully in personal conversations. Of course, when they want to talk about other things, go with it. The other person generally determines the topic because you are trying to relate to them: wherever they lead determines the path. You're there to learn about them and their interests.

At some point, often amazingly far down the road, they'll ask about you. We all like to talk about ourselves, especially if we've been listening a great deal. It's easy to zoom off about your own life, and reflect after the conversation that you ended up doing most of the talking. I hope you make that error much less than I have. We men are particularly prone to this problem, since we like to treat challenging conversations as a verbal version of our résumé (information exchange); or, sometimes, we want the chance to dominate.

When I am with conservative friends and colleagues, and I'm not engaged in something practical, I think of myself as a junior cultural anthropologist, in the business of listening, of paying attention. In the social sciences world, the cultural anthropologists are the ones thinking about all the ways that mankind interact with each other. They're always trying to figure out the tools and approaches of various cultures. It's a terrifically broad discipline, with few big theories, only little ideas that work here and there. If it has anything to do with the messy life of humans, though, cultural anthropologists seem to have to stick their flag on top of it, arguing with the other scientists who got there first, often quite correctly. They know they don't know much, that there's endless amounts of mystery involved with mankind, and that they'll die not knowing much. So they soak it all in carefully and happily.

If we take a similar attitude, we can't help but grow a natural respect for people like conservatives, who live a complex, successful existence so different than ours, even though they're just down the block. The faults that loom so large at first start to fade into the background with them individually, replaced by idiosyncrasies, particulars, patterns, and surprises.

Chapter Ten

ON LISTENING

*Listening is an art, and many people
do not have the capacity for it.*
-Thich Naht Hanh

LISTENING IS A SNARL of a subject, much messier than we give it credit for. Brutally multi-disciplinary, actually– with elements housed in linguistics, psychology, communications, neurology, cognitive science, philosophy, and cultural anthropology. There are specific listening skills required for challenges with different types of subjects (technical; abstract subjects, such as politics or religion; or relational listening, as with family or a lover) and different listening situations (with strangers, in classes, speeches, with lovers, at work, etc.). Listening skills also vary with bias, intelligence, and culture (depending on where we're from, we tend to listen quite differently in similar situations).

Scholars at the International Listening Association have a long list of subjects they want researchers to make even basic progress on; they complain about the current lack of credible theoretical foundation for how listening happens. Even when students study listening explicitly in a classroom setting– which happens about 1% as much as they study public speaking– most of what's taught is not grounded in theory, but is the result of caring people passing on their lame, politically-correct opinions, mostly centered on repeating how important listening is. All this while employers consistently rate listening skills as one of the top three desired characteristics of any new hire. In short, we either treat listening like a magic skill that we either have or don't, or we pretend we just have to want to listen well, and the skill part shows up at the door the next morning, like a mail package.

When Thich Nath Hahn, a Buddhist monk, teaches that some people can't listen, he's referring to the fact that some people are "in too much pain" to listen properly. This is a Buddhist way of saying that their life experiences have warped them too much. We're going to assume you're capable of listening, but the useful lesson behind his point is that our nature and our circumstances always severely limit how well we can listen.

We need a look at a specific form of listening: we're trying to understand people we want to be friends with, who we disagree with about many fundamental things. That narrows things down drastically, and allows us to focus on the problems this kind of listening unearths within us. Some types of listening have not been shown to benefit from training, but this kind of listening can be improved greatly through practice and study.

This isn't conversation training yet. This is strictly a one-way affair. Everyone should give a good gallop at virtually unlimited listening of the kind I'm suggesting you do. You'll be uncomfortable at first with just how much listening in a conversation entails, especially when it gets emotional for you, when you disagree with things being said. The fact that it's essentially not possible to do it well shouldn't throw you off the horse— that's like saying it's not possible to be the Great Communicator in a relationship, so we should give up communicating.

Some marriage therapists suggest that we each try to give 100% during difficult times in a relationship, rather than thinking in terms of 50-50, as we usually do: by giving 100%, and doing so freely, we develop the ability to give without expecting in return— and they watch us do it, and respect us for the effort, discipline, and politeness it takes. Giving 50% means you might be able to high-five your partner at the midfield line every once in a while, at best— and that's assuming both parties make that kind of full effort.

George Gilder, a conservative thinker, had a way of characterizing capitalism as all about **faith**; that entrepreneurs give gifts to people to get the ball rolling— free samples, or time and energy, and throwing money into a dark hole in the ground as they start a business— in a gesture of faith, so that good people and good products will find each other. The gift of listening is similar to that "gift" of capitalism, in that somebody has to start the ball rolling, and that start is your faith in the person, the belief that something good will happen from it.

What a horrible word to use on you, when I know you're so godless and intellectual. But there's an unassailable cognitive reason for faith. If you want to talk about listening well as some kind of statistical bet that the person might say something useful, that's fine, but it's a little bloodless to me. Get into the affair, dang it: you're going to find out cool stuff. *Believe*, brothers and sisters. They're going to be unexpectedly interesting, and have traits you'll admire. Have faith. Settle in and listen.

Listening shows second by second, in as clear a way as possible among social animals, that they're valuable to you, enough to spend both your greatest assets, your time and energy, to understand them. It practically forces the other person to know that you genuinely believe something good and useful will come from speaking with them. I have come out of the trance of a solid half-hour or more of the kind of communication difficulties that are possible with conservatives, and had them shock me with a hug, or express strong emotion at having felt a connection on their most sacred beliefs. It is not a common thing to be heard well, especially out in the political badlands.

The great psychology theorist Carl Rogers took the position that communication fails simply because people cannot listen, and built a whole movement of therapy around listening skills, which he developed into a high art. His first principle of true listening was developing what he called "unconditional positive regard", the attitude that you accept this person you're talking to completely, as is, as long as they're not causing direct, immediate harm with their actions. He felt that this broad openness was essential to healthy personal development.

Dr. Rogers sounded sometimes as if a person could just decide they were going to accept someone completely, and bang, that's that; done. That's not true. There's a discipline to it, and practice involved, along with a whole lot of living right required, to get past normal, moment-to-moment prejudices and mindlessness.

Dr. Scott Peck taught a *temporary* version of unconditional positive regard that he calls bracketing, which is "enlarging and extending" yourself to include the other person by shedding "one's own prejudices, frames of reference and desires so as to experience as far as possible the speaker's world from the inside." Dr. Peck suggests bracketing away these internal aspects that can hide parts of the other person from us. He said unless you can successfully wall off this internal noise, "each present moment is just a repetition of something already seen or experienced," because we will have colored every experience using the same tired, internal machinery.[1]

Maybe bracketing is possible, but, again, it's not something you just wake up and start doing, even if it's a temporary effort, a kind of sprint. But the notion of doing something "just for a little while" can be unexpectedly powerful. It's a good diet technique, a good way to be nice to jackasses, or to endure a crummy job– "I'm just going to not eat any sweets until the afternoon today"; "I only have to be nice to him until 4 PM."; I'm going to listen really well for ten minutes." Something about having an achievable, finite goal makes it possible to listen a little better with a prompting that we'll do it "just for a little while." Thich Nhat Hahn suggests that no one can listen to others for very long without a good break; he thinks bracketing is our only way to listen.

Zen Buddhism has a great deal to say on this subject, but one must translate for them, because they're fond of being confusing. They're not big fans of the will-yourself-to-greatness school of human development, which Rogers and Peck can be accused of fairly ("just set aside your…"). But Zennies get at a similar result from a completely different angle that can be useful for us liberals. The short version— usually the only version we get from them— is something along the lines of "just sit and listen." We'll do a slightly fleshed-out, hopefully clearer version.

Soto Zen Buddhism has meditation as a centerpiece. There's a boatload of meditation techniques and methods out there; people make noises, they shut their eyes, they open them, they do things with their hands, they walk; they think about certain things, like their nostrils (no, I'm not kidding), they think about nothing. Probably the most common way to meditate, though, can be summed up as sitting and listening. Listening to the wind; listening to trucks going by; noticing what comes up in the mind; "listening" to how a part of your body feels. Thoughts arise naturally, and the common way of describing listening meditation is watching the thoughts come in, and letting them go. Straightforward sounding, right? If you go to a Zen center to meditate as a beginner, that's about all they tell you. Then, they have you sit all day and do it.

If we meditate in that way, though, we notice right away how relentlessly we *stop* listening, without realizing it. We like to stop listening and let our unconscious mind play loops of thought, without consciously willing it. Obviously, though, we're unconsciously willing it; in the earlier metaphor, the unconscious "boss" part of us is doing it's shuck-and-jive, and the secretary part of us is rubber-stamping the boss's will. I've sat in meditation for over ten minutes at a time many, many times, lost in thought, not listening to a damn thing, before waking up to the realization that "I" was off gnawing on some worry, or hope, or fantasy, driven indirectly by my unconscious mind.

Different teachers handle this variously. The old-school Soto Zen masters wander around the room of meditators and whack you with a pretty harmless, loud little stick when you look suspect, or if you're drifting off to sleep. If you don't have a Zen master available, a good technique is to pause when you notice you've drifted off in extended thought, label the thought bubble in a general way ("thoughts about Sara"; "thoughts about work"; "thoughts about my leg pain"), and get back to listening.

I love this technique, because it helps us to treat drifting off as natural and forgivable, while allowing a kind of mental file drawer to be filled with all these little labels. Here's what happens pretty darn quickly, though, to a meditator. When you get up after an hour of meditating, if you peer into that mental file drawer you shoved those labels into, you've filled out a pile of little scraps of paper that look like this:

Thoughts about work	Thoughts about work	Thoughts about lunch
Thoughts about work	Thoughts of leg pain	Thoughts of butt pain
Thoughts about Sara	Thoughts about lunch	Thoughts about Sara
Thoughts of weather	Thoughts about Sara	Thoughts of weather
Thoughts of leg pain	Thoughts of weather	Thoughts about work
Thoughts about work	Thoughts about work	Thoughts about work
Thoughts about lunch	Thoughts about Sara	Thoughts about lunch

If you think I'm exaggerating, you haven't meditated. For most of us, the list would be longer than that in an hour. That's only drifting off and catching myself every three minutes or so; that'd be pretty good.

I wouldn't mind a list with more variety, as if I was experiencing a varied, chosen, interesting set of things: thoughts about the sunlight, sounds, the feel of my clothes, the textures in the wall, a throb of love for my mommy floating through. But look at that list. Repetitive. Dull. Mostly pretty useless. Just like Dr. Peck said it would be, if we don't shed our "prejudices, frames of reference and desires."

If we meditate a little while, it begins to dawn on us that these labels are a kind of epitaph of our life; when we're gone, we can imagine them as a kind of record of what actually happened in our heads during our life. We can't help but shuffle over to that mental file drawer after meditating, to be reminded how dismally simple and boring the arc of our internal existence is. Much of our inventory of thoughts are shown to be involuntary and automatic; which wouldn't be so bad if they were cool, like, I don't know, wondering what it feels like to be an astronaut, or working out new business ventures in villages at the foot of the Andes. Instead, thoughts drift, obsessively and repetitively, back to the same few plots of ground.

We begin to see that the rest of our life isn't much different. We happened to sit down and pay attention, but our internal boss is doing this kind of inane rerouting of thoughts all the time. We may as well be watching the same 2000 reruns of Days of Our Lives over and over, and calling that a life. Our unconscious mind, which Jung taught has no concept of time, has a list of eternal hot button concerns, and it uses our conscious mind to play them out in the same predictable, boring way.

Who are we, then? We realize that we've become more like a misfiring machine than a human who invents their life, who lives it truly voluntarily. A prisoner of banality, looping through the same small thoughts, floating up from the back rooms of our mind. We don't influence the thoughts that drive our lives much— we let the back-room boss choose them for us, and just obey her orders.

Realizing that has been one of the most transformative experiences of my life. I can't even write these words without feeling the grief I've felt many times at what I leave behind in life with uninspired, unaware thinking; what it might've meant— to those I love, or the people I try to help— to spend my time with the possibilities life affords me as it flies by. The waste of living an automatic life continues to motivate me and drive my perspective. I sense an urgency, as my life slips away. I'm not interested in summing up hours and days and decades with involuntary, easily-understood "thoughts about…" lists. Yet that's what happens to our hours if we don't truly live through them. It's what happens to the majority of us: "each present moment is just a repetition of something already seen or experienced."

Listening, then, is the way to refuse the common, banal road, and become an actual, experiencing human. Not that you will ever have "control" over the thoughts coming from your unconscious mind, but that you live a life that is engaged with the outside world. You let the world help create your thoughts and experiences, instead of working from the same, sad set of cue cards endlessly.

We can't grasp fully what reality is, but that doesn't matter; we *can* start with hoping for a list of thoughts that would be, I don't know, interesting, or practical, or insightful, or surprising. *Anything* that isn't 23 variations on worries about how you can't grow a mustache, or what your boss meant with the rude comment last Friday.

There may be something to the notion of exercising will to listen well. But mostly we should think of listening well as a desperate desire to avoid living a script that comes from who-knows-where; from unresolved work pressures, or our sore legs, or an insecurity, or some other involuntary source that drives and defines our life, without us even knowing it, or approving.

If ideology plays a role in our lives, then we have a ton of those banal signals that are coming up for us constantly about ideology, and we're unaware of the vast majority of them. We think we have this lock on reality because we figured out a few things like how bad police brutality is getting; then we want to make sure the world, especially this particular conservative in front of us, gets handed this platter of platitudes of ours that substitutes for a living, breathing sense of the life in front of us now.

While your unconscious boss runs-and-guns her way through your life, with you starring as the secretary, using your face, your vocal cords, and your fingers to get what it wants done.

Autopilot is great some of the time. The rest of the time, it's either dicey or a mess. And we don't get to pick which part of unconscious influence is great and which part is crummy, because being on autopilot means it's a package deal. So let's talk about getting off of autopilot, at least while we listen to conservatives, so that, while they talk, our river of thought runs clearer, and we can actually hear past our own repetitive concerns.

Mechanics and Artists

The mechanical process of listening to someone in most social situations takes about a third of the time they're speaking, on average, depending on the person and subject. That's the amount of time it takes for us to interpret the meaning of the words involved, to string them together into whole ideas in phrases and sentences and paragraphs, match that with body language and tone, and somewhat understand the concepts. The actual science is quite complicated: most of us don't process many of the ideas and words we hear; we burst in and out of the mechanical job of listening in short, unpredictable pieces, even if we listen carefully. We're like a piano player reading and playing music "at the same time," who actually bounces back and forth between playing and reading in short starts and fits. We also play catch up, using a record-rewind-replay trick, so we can think about or do other things.

We kick into the mechanical listening part during and right after key words, phrases, and sentences. The other two-thirds of the time someone is speaking, we spend how we like. We can't think of just anything while someone talks. We can't design a house and listen at the same time. We can only have short bursts of thoughts, or do something that requires little thinking, like dishwashing. But those fleeting moments are actually quite powerful, because human beings can hold a thought in their mind in a given instant that would take over a hundred words to say; we can think very complicated thoughts in those moments, just like we can feel very complicated emotions.

It's almost impossible to think something complicated about a subject outside the conversation topic– not that that's stopped me from trying. But it's *easy* to have involved, interesting thoughts that interweave with each other and what's being said.

If you're asking questions and getting answers for half an hour, and you're understanding what they say perfectly, it means you have about

twenty minutes hidden in there that you can think as deeply as you want about what they're saying. They're giving you twenty minutes for whatever you want, just by talking at you. Figuring out what to do with all that time, all that opportunity— the great majority of the time with the person— is the art of listening. It happens to be the art of living, too. We have complete freedom during that time. What shall we make of those minutes, artiste?

I can tell you what we usually do with it: we think automatic thoughts, just as I did during meditation. If we could slow down a conversation, and track our thoughts perfectly while we're listening, we'd see a third or so of the time taken up with spurts of mechanical interpretation. Then a list like the labels of thoughts during meditation could be created. Let's say I'm listening to a conservative talking about how the minimum wage needs to not go up, or maybe disappear. My list of thoughts might look like this:

> Thought about lunch
> Thought about him being selfish
> Thought about him repeating himself
> Thought about him being whiny
> Thought about lunch
> Thought about how little $1200/mo. is
> Thought about a good retort

That's probably a normal list during one thirty second snippet, during maybe three or four decent-length sentences. He thinks he's talking so that I can consider his thoughts— but what am I doing? I'm on autopilot. Look at that list: there's not a single thought listed that interesting or additive, except maybe the $1200/mo. one; nothing my unconscious mind hasn't passed on to me before, and nothing that adds any useful information to make his ideas worth something to me. I'm not exploring the options; not scanning him for clues on a different way for me to see his arguments; not learning to see beyond what he's saying; to see whoever he is.

That same thirty seconds could look like this in your head instead:

> – What's the actual minimum wage in this state?
> – I remember working minimum wage. It sucked.
> – Can people live on $1,200/mo. gross nowadays here?
> – He looks angry; wonder why.
> – Ask a question about him being a business owner; he talks like an entrepreneur.

Wow, look at you go! That's bringing beer to the party; you're not giving up on your perspective and moral orientation, but you're holding your views more loosely, or you've put them in your pocket for now. You're focused more on getting this fellow, on hearing his clock tick– you're letting what the cat dragged in get some air time in your internal life, instead of playing loops like "Thought about a good retort."

Not genius thoughts; not particularly brilliant stabs at the ether, at what's possible. Definitely not Ghandi; not guru-in-a-box: so what? You're in the game, leaning into his words, free for a time from being a mindless machine. Using 20 seconds of time gifted you to be interested and non-judgmental, to think about him, his approach, and the other places his concepts send you briefly. To interweave your ideas with his uniquely. String together some of those hundred-word fleeting ideas into a bit of foment, or a tiny idea, or the formation of a good question, or a notion that brings this fellow closer somehow. Avoiding half-thoughts, repetitions, and attempts at complicated thoughts that aren't part of the conversation. Walking away with possibilities handed to you by the world.

To me, that imperfect list is what a perfect life look like. You're in the game; you're trying to do something besides work off old scripts; you're not being bossed around by a know-it-all subconscious.

This is exactly the kind of listening technique that's difficult to do when trying to have a give-and-take of ideas at the same time, as our minds fill with inventory about what to say next while the other person is talking. It's much better attempted as a solo, focused, listening effort.

In literature study, there's a notion called "close reading"– taking a short passage and focusing intensely on finding the useful parts of it– that gets at the kind of attention and commitment we should try for, to arrive at meanings and motivations in challenging conversations. Paying attention fully, refusing to be an automaton, is like that. It doesn't imply conversion, or even that you're changed, but it does mean that you are creating the best chance to be *influenced*, usually in some way that has almost nothing to do with their point, like in the above example, where a question about him being an entrepreneur might open a door somewhere. To be having interesting thoughts– to be truly alive. So that the world may look a little different from then on for you. So that the time is *useful*.

There's also a great advantage to them that this approach buys us. Conservatives tend to believe good of people who are kind to them, and to think of them as sharing similar values and opinions,[2] which makes us candidates for having our ideas considered. Technically, it's a combination of anchoring on your good side with what's called the halo effect, where unrelated good traits (like having a full head of hair, or being handsome, or being nice) makes you the master of other traits (having good political ideas). In this case, you get the halo from being pleasant and inquisitive, which makes you into a kind of honorary conservative, worthy of ingroup status.

I've found that supporting conservatives as they speak about their beliefs, especially if you agree here and there, often makes them feel as if I generally agree with them about many other topics. It's such a strong effect that it's often necessary to make the explicit statement that I'm not in agreement with everything they say, or to repeat that I have many liberal views, simply to be honest and clear.

By listening so that you can understand them and their subject from their viewpoint, without heavy judgment, your efforts let them allow you to have different opinions, because you can understand how they feel in their hearts about *something*. They do this among themselves a great deal, too, because they have widely varying views, but they rally around basic principles– ones that you've shown respect for.

Even if you're in the ingroup, they won't likely be open to your political ideas– that depends on many other things, like how political they are, how close their opinion is to yours, and how good your arguments are.

You can mess that tolerance up pretty easily later with a big mouth, as I've done occasionally. But the initial support you may be easily offered is a huge advantage to you in any later political conversations, or when you are simply trying to make a friend.

The big advantage we have in our goal of high-quality listening is that you're planning on doing only enough talking to be supportive and ask questions for awhile. This makes it much easier to avoid one of the big problems we have as listeners: draining away our time, energy, and focus to prepare responses while the other person is talking. You'll still line up counter-arguments in your head even if you're not going to say them, because it's a habit, and because you disagree with their points. But that tendency eventually wears away as you practice this method of listening without thinking about having your say, because you'll end up preferring to use the time to understand them. Listening ends up more interesting and useful.

Most people listen so they can respond (persuade, or argue), not to understand. People can tell the difference nonconsciously which is happening, and they appreciate what you're doing. What you're doing isn't a listening or unfocused meditation, like our Zen example; it's more like *focused attention meditation*, in which you have an object or focus for your thoughts, and you're trying to stay keyed on them. The artistry time of listening, that two-thirds of the time that's not required to mechanically understand what's being said, is plowed back into them.

A very big difference between focused attention meditation and your listening effort, though, is that we need to actively pursue insight from your "object" to truly listen well. There are questions to ask; probably many. Never questions that have a "yeah, but" tinge to them, like "Why do conservatives emphasize spending cuts so much?" We ask questions that actually direct the conversation along productively, like "Conservatives universally believe spending cuts are essential now, don't they?," or "How did you react to yesterday's news about xxx?" or "Did that irritate you?" Questions should also be turned into a kind of compliment when you can, to generate healthy conversation, so that the skids are greased as well as possible, as in "I respect the way conservatives focus on fiscal responsibility– what's your hot button with government spending?" Unless the conservative is from Maine or New Hampshire, that kind of leading statement will typically get them talking.

The other type of question you should be asking is to clarify meaning. If you're not interrupting with a clarifying question occasionally, you're probably not listening well, and you're probably not curious enough. If you're listening well– if you're applying two-thirds of the time to thinking of useful questions and ideas from what she's saying– your mind will get inspired by a particular sentence or idea, and it fouls up your mechanical listening. If I don't miss something someone says every ten minutes or so because of their previous sentence or paragraph, it means I'm not having enough intense follow-on thoughts about what they're saying to get distracted, which isn't good.

These kinds of clarifying questions–"sorry, I was trying to remember what the minimum wage was here in Iowa, and I missed what you just said," or just "hang on, could you say that again?"–are *the most powerful signal you can give that you care about their thoughts*. Strange but true. It's the precise opposite of a normal interruption: you don't want them to shut up, you want them to say it again. Questions like that also sharpen the focus of the other person, not only because you're asking them to be more clear or more specific, but also because they unconsciously understand better that you're paying close attention, so they're less guarded and more dedicated to expressing themselves well.

You should also make a point of asking such questions even when it's not totally necessary, because it's fun and engaging, instead of looking like you're just there to turn a tape recorder on and off. Here's an example from a recent conversation with someone I met in California:

"I've been conservative my whole life–"
"Really? In this town? Even in college?"
"Yep. I was always the outsider."
"That must've been difficult."
"Not really. I've always been pretty independent. There were times when…"

Jump in there! This is the Rule of Yes! as well: a way to propel you both forward somewhere together.

These kind of "poke" questions can lead people away from where they were going– people are easily side-tracked. You can always say "I'm sorry, I interrupted you– you were talking about xxx."

The other tool of listening is affirmation statements you should make for your conversation partner. These phrases allow you to put a shoulder to the wheel for them, so they can get going on an idea, or feel appreciated by you:

– I've never heard it described that way– that's helpful.

– I'm used to thinking about it from the perspective of xxx– it's useful to think of it your way.

– I think you raise a good point that we liberals don't often think about– the idea that xxx. We focus more on xxx.

– That's an unusual perspective.

– I think there's a lot to that.

– I never thought of it that way.

– We see eye-to-eye on that point.

– I can understand why you feel that way: [and state why]

– That's a really [interesting/great/thought-provoking/useful/healthy/different] way to think about it.

– Your approach has the advantage of xxx.

– Well, I learned something here.

– Oh. I see what you mean.

Positive, affirming, and inertia building. Any of these, said in sincerity, can lead to further fruitful conversation. Or you can follow them up with any number of related or unrelated questions– whatever you like– to keep the conversation going in a healthy direction.

Conversations can be started and kept up easily if you are just asking questions and making positive statements. And there's a sort-of-a-question mode, the "Tell me about..." variety. "Tell me about the Tea Party from your perspective, will you? I always hear about it from a certain angle, and I'd like to get your take on it." As she answers, you listen carefully, trying to clear out space in that messy garage of a mind to fit in an image or two, a emotional tone, an idea. You use affirming language naturally, because you're paying strict attention to an interesting viewpoint. You're not swirling off mentally to counterpoints, or sculpting things you want to say, because it's hard enough to understand someone as it is, without all that clutter. Occasionally, you stop them to ask about a term or idea, even if you don't need to. You're on the hunt for a little breakthrough. Not facts- they're mostly a waste of time– but an *insight*. A way of getting something integral about this person– her background, views, or personality. Only listening can buy you such a thing.

Remember how we liberals like new and shiny– how all our wampum goes to that? Well, here's how new happens: we listen, and find it in the wide spaces between what we know and what we can never know, where conservatives and the other oddities of this existence hang out. The curtain's falling on our show, very soon– let's check that place out. Let's tear off a hunk of real life, you and I.

Chapter Eleven

POLITICAL CONVERSATION

My opponent is my teacher.
My ego is my enemy.
                    -Anonymous

W E'RE GOING to lump political conversations in with spousal arguments, challenges at work, and other social difficulties. We'll be weaving in and out of the pure ideological part of the problems we have in those situations, because our working minds don't make a magic distinction between ideological personality traits and the rest of ourselves. Even so, we'll stay within reach of ideology.

How to Avoid Talking about Politics

Political conversation across ideologies can be impossible, even between perfectly good people. Fifteen seconds after a pleasant conversation about their daughter's cute school outfits, five seconds into a response to an innocent question about your views on climate change, you can find yourself forever outed as an idiot, and a morally weak one to boot. Messing it up can be an incredibly fast process.

I don't understand the grinding emphasis on trying. Even when done well with conservatives, it's not very useful. In the end, your instinctive need to preach your moral givens isn't going to make nearly the difference you could make by just being friends, and rubbing off on them subconsciously.

It's much more useful to carry off a fun dual-family barbecue than to master the art of political conversation with them. Having a good barbecue means that you are being productive at something simple with someone who holds quite the different world view— you were able to get past some pretty basic personality differences, some of which might seem in strong opposition, in order to enjoy one another. It might even be the case that your differences complement one another well in unpredictable ways, as happens for many lovers with conflicting ideologies.

You're actually understanding one another ideologically at those times, maybe quite a bit, whether you think you are or not. You can only begin to understand how that happens with an individual conservative through exposure to them over time. The broader reasons for our political ideas show up in how we live our lives, right alongside what we have in common, and what make us human, or talented, or interesting. Examples of real-life problems are the best way of getting across political ideas anyway, because they're clearer than words in conveying ideas.

Those of us who are close to people we regularly argue with unpleasantly about politics should consider that we might have a perfectly normal need to share our political opinions in life, and that may be getting in our way with that person unfairly. If we're built that way, we should recognize that we need people in our lives that can hear and appreciate our heartfelt political and deep moral values, people we can express that side of ourselves with. We should go out of our way to spend time with them and have satisfying political conversations. If we do, we might feel less need to discuss politics with those who can't validate our feelings. We'll also get better at avoiding turning the political conversations we do have into intensive affairs, or into arguments.

Why is it risky enough to talk about politics that we'd want to avoid the subject? The answer is buried within the nature of communication itself. A brilliant linguist named Michael Reddy showed that human language is a teeming mass of metaphors— that, though about 25% of our language allows a pure kind of speech that avoids metaphors, we rarely use those parts, because they're boring, detailed, or legalistic. We communicate almost completely through metaphors. We get *stuck*. We're *seeing* the fellow's point, *going along with* an idea, *taking* a class, or *diving in*.[1]

These simple metaphors, which we don't even notice while we communicate, are used to make simple ideas understood easily— but that kind of direct usage is only the tip of the iceberg. Words like freedom and justice sound to us as if we're talking about specific, concrete things, when they're actually slippery metaphors, Trojan horses. Each person has actually secretly, carefully created a complex, haphazard bundle of meanings for those words. We might think of freedom as a man in a Corvette cruising down the highway in one moment, for instance, but we actually have dozens of different ideas pinned to our notion of being free. Freedom's not just a Corvette: it's more like Corvette being towed by a Nepalese bus, filled with families and their livestock, with their belongings and fathers lashed to the roof and sides, lurching over a mountain pass, with a sketch radiator and bald tires.

We use many kinds of metaphors jumbled together, but they're much more complex metaphors than "paying" in "I'm paying attention." We have gathered to ourselves a very personal set of metaphorical images, other words, personal experiences, and ideas we think are related, and they all connect together to form a complicated notion, far more involved, changeable and mysterious than we think.

Dr. Reddy and his team have shown that we live and speak as if these complex words like freedom and government are simple boxes that we use to contain pure, predictable items, and we give them to other people, to communicate. But between strangers, words can be an unsolvable puzzle, a swamp—a hundred-pound backpack of opportunities to get bogged down, unable to progress.

Let's take a simple example on the facing page, using the word freedom. Version 1 of freedom is a liberal's, who thinks about opportunity a fair amount when she thinks of freedom; version 2 is a conservative's images, metaphors, arguments, and experiences. The ovals are filled with just some of the many tied-in metaphors, images, ideas, and emotions that might play into two people's actual, working definitions of freedom. Each "container" is where the two people pull various references from when they think of freedom after being prompted, like reaching into a tool box labeled "Freedom" and fishing around for just the item you want.

Let's assume, for a moment, that the circle on the top represents your ideas (or metaphors) of freedom, and the circle on the bottom is your conservative friend's freedom metaphor. If that difference is as stark as shown— and it is during many ideological conversations— how successful will you be if you take on the notion of freedom? You don't have a single metaphor of freedom in common. The two of you can nod in tandem at the statement, "We're losing our freedoms," but as soon as you mention problems with equality, or the need to question authority, you immediately enter a world of pain. Even if your friend is inclined to respect those particular views, bringing them up while talking about freedom, which seemed natural to you, can make her very frustrated. She may get annoyed because inequality, which doesn't concern her much, is being incorrectly brought up as an example— she'll feel a need to convey what freedom is really about, like getting out from under excessive government, or crushing Islamofascists.

When we use a word which is a container, with many powerful show-and-tell examples inside, points you make that aren't in the other person's container irritate them. Not only are you bringing up something that's beside the point, but you're also insulting the "real" version of freedom, by talking about things that have nothing to do with it.

Take a look at the two versions of freedom. Do you see any overlap?

Two Versions of the Word Freedom

Version 1

I'm obsessed by my need for privacy

The S&P 500 average CEO making 400 times the average worker.

Anger about wars we started, which I see as murder

Fear of being harassed for my views

Inspiration from Martin Luther King essay, and a speech I saw as a child.

Right to higher education, and quality secondary education

Image of black people in a long unemployment line

I see rebelliousness as a heathy impetus

Version 2

My taxes are so high that it feels like robbery

Image of soldiers in dress uniform on parade

Small business government restrictions helped my business fail

Hard work is getting discouraged in the welfare state.

Moral degradation is ruining this country- everyone can't do what they want all the time.

Strong national security limits risk

I had a strong, good father

Afraid that my children will grow up without having the opportunities I did.

Government is suspect.

You didn't, did you? Neither did I. There's one, sort of: you might be able to commiserate about the conservative concern about her kids not having the chances she did. Other than that, it's just insult and annoyance opportunities from now until you quit trying.

Notice how odd some of these are. Almost all those liberal container items are alien to a conservative, and some even might be strange for you. Then, in the conservative one, what the heck does a "strong father" have to do with freedom? You'd have to ask her; each piece of the puzzle is highly customized to do who-knows-what for her.

If you know how this pattern of misunderstanding works, you hear it in every political conversation, around every issue. When we say deficit, or health care, we are actually wading into a complex metaphor set of theirs that we know little about, and we try to force them to tie other ideas, attitudes, experiences and words into their basket of concepts.

We're not even disagreeing yet; we're just misunderstanding and annoying each other. That's why political conversations between those who disagree are best thought of as two unrelated monologues at the same time: you can't possibly know what's being heard by the other person when you say "capitalism," or thousands of other similarly-charged words. While you use these words, you're creating barriers to true communication– and they're all barriers you can't see.

It's the big political metaphors you especially wish to avoid stepping around in, if you can– defense, freedom, taxes, foreign aid. You want to stick with whether you approve a ceiling height waiver at the planning office. When a political topic comes up, your job is to keep the point small and focused, hopefully on a single person or item, but you can't do that when someone runs right to a deeply abstract statement like "national security is getting worse every day," or "taxes are out of control." In that case, the best thing to do is to gloss over it and move on, hopefully to something useful, like whether there's enough ice on the drinks. Because our individual political words/metaphors are well-developed, mature containers, they feel very real to us– but their true connection to reality is quite willowy, dependent on a certain time in history, a set of attitudes, vocabulary, moral values, and particular experiences.

It's even worse than that. You might say "I like being able to depend on Social Security when I retire." Sounds straightforward enough– except "Social Security spending" might be in that person's "deficit" metaphorical morass, so that your simple statement makes you sound as if you think deficit spending is ok– so it triggers disgust. Even though no one was talking about deficits. They may not even be aware of how they got disgusted, since many of these metaphors are triggered unconsciously. You might say "President Clinton" instead of "Clinton," which may indicate that you respect him more than they feel he deserved, which, in turn, triggers a sensitivity that causes other "mistakes" to be sensed. It's impossible to step in the right place when discussing politics if the field is laden with hidden mines every 6 inches.

It's this unbelievable sensitivity that causes our political enemies to start shaking their head to negate a point of ours before we even get to the third word of the sentence: by then, something mysterious had already happened that ended our chance of communicating– and we rarely even have an idea what it was, because the metaphors we've double-crossed are hidden from view.

Dr. Reddy makes a grand distinction between how we normally think of communication and its true nature. We normally assume it's easy, and any problems are unusual. The actual nature of communication is very difficult, once metaphors have entered into the picture, even without biases and personality differences– it takes time, energy, and a good-faith effort on both peoples' parts. He describes the difference between the easy and hard visions of communication: the easy version he calls the **conduit metaphor**, because we think that using a word like freedom is the same as placing a useful tool in a container, with all the instructions, and sending it through a perfect conduit to a person, who pulls it out and starts using it for the exact same reason as you would. Easy.

Here's the hard, more accurate version of communication– think of the versions of freedom we just covered, and trying to talk about freedom. You receive a tool and a description of the tool via letter from someone in another area, who doesn't use the tool for what you would, who has no idea what you'd use it for, but who assumes you'd use it the exact same way he does, and for the same reasons. There's going to be so many questions that need asking, you won't even know what to ask first– she's sent you this jumble of words and ideas that sounds stupid, or crazy, or random, yet weirdly logical and detailed. You'll ask them to restate, which won't help. You'll ask them to define this or that term, which won't help, either. When you ask them what to do with it, she tells us about how they use it to fetch fruit in the jungle, obviously– but you live on a high-altitude, rock-ridden farm, where there's no trees; you don't even know what "fruit" is. You then think about what you might do with it; you argue here and there, about this and that; and, eventually, decide that a modified version of the tool is just the thing for fetching books off the top shelves in your library. Or you think it's useless, or dangerous, and send it back.

If you think about doing this exchange with a conservative on the fly, about an aspect of freedom that one of you is fascinated with and the other could care less about, you can begin to understand the risk and frustration you're taking on. It's much easier to quit somewhere along the nightmare, and use the fundamental error to proclaim the other fellow excess protoplasm.

That's just one-way communication: one party has a main point they're trying to get across. Trying to do two-way communication, in the sense of both parties trying to get across ideas they care about, is like doubling the confusion of the above scenario, and halving the time and energy available to solve each puzzle. It's no wonder most people end up wandering away from such conversations in frustration, muttering something about how ultimately great their custom tool is, and how hellishly stupid people can be.

We know politics will come up. You'll bring it up, because you can't help yourself; they'll bring it up because it's natural to do so, here or there. Many normal conversations about family, food, church, or work make points that skirt near our political beliefs or land flat on them, so there's a natural dip into political beliefs here and there.

It's one thing to touch upon a political point or two, though, and quite another to have an involved conversation about them. There's an art to dipping in and out of political ideas without getting bogged down in them. The vast majority of the time, the idea is to not get dragged in head-first, but to acknowledge the joke or the comment without elaborating. We want to add extra, related points onto a simple one made in conversation, when most of what is called for is an acknowledgement, a joke in response, or a simple statement— something that doesn't try to build a life of its own. Like liberals, conservatives make little political comments with one another all the time while playing games, or in passing at work, and move on. It's better to fall into that spirit than to decide, on the fly, inattentively, that it's time to make a controversial point, or one that needs a long explanation, just because part of what somebody said might be deceptive or incomplete.

There are four ways out of this jam with conservatives and political talk. The first is to be in so solid with your friend, to get yourself so firmly into the ingroup that you're both safe to wrangle, wrestle, and chuckle your way to an understanding— so that if you're both a little careful to explain yourself and careful to understand, keeping it light, you can have a good experience. This is possible, but rarely—not even with one percent of people, I suspect. I have this relationship myself with a half-dozen conservatives, and it's great: I can break the rules, we have some great, custom-cut shortcuts to understanding. I get mad when I see that the amazing freedom tool I gave him, that we talked about for seventeen hours, is wedging one of his bookshelves up against the wall— but I'm used to it. I'm in their lives more broadly; politics is a tangential sideshow to what we share.

The second way out is to avoid talking about politics– to be satisfied with watching and learning from your conservative friend, and letting them experience your life approach, like normal people would. Talking about political abstractions is much more specialized and much less useful in the real world than we assume. It is the type of conversation where Dr. Reddy's hard conduit metaphor kicks into high gear. Abstinence is a perfectly good, noble path to take. It should be the default if you don't know the person well, or if you're still developing a relationship with the other person.

The third way around the virtual impossibility of communicating is to veer the conversation to the passel of topics that have loosely to do with politics, but that are actually either ideologically neutral or agreed on by almost everybody. This is especially useful as a diversion, when a political conversation has already started against your will– you can keep the topic technically within politics so you don't appear controlling, but steer it to one of these much more neutral topics with a clear, declarative statement that starts with "What I don't understand is…," or "What I get irritated about (concerned about, frustrated with, excited about)." It helps to sigh and seem really concerned/frustrated/excited about it, so you can yank people along with you successfully, away from, say, abortion. You might even have an interesting conversation.

Here's my own quick list to reference before you head to the cocktail party if you like, but if you think a little yourself, you'll likely come up with topics better suited to you.

> Salaries and retirement plans of elected officials are too high.

> Government has an insanely tough time being efficient.

> Social Security is not an "insurance program" that you pay into, it's a tax that covers older peoples' retirement benefits.

> Politicians are too easily influenced, too worried about re-election, and spend way too much time raising money. This might have to do with most of them being extroverted, or naturally oriented toward taking the opinions of others very seriously.

> America's water and electricity infrastructure are not being

maintained safely and adequately.

The tax system is way too complicated.

People don't involve themselves enough in politics– only about half the people even bother to vote, let alone get well informed, or work in other ways to improve politics.

Americans will have to get used to more and more excellent competition in an increasingly global business environment, and be well prepared to deal with it.

Politicians lie, overpromise and exaggerate to look good to prospective voters, and we don't hold their feet to the fire because we expect and tolerate it.

There are over 20 lobbyists in Washington for every elected official working there.

America is still the world's innovator, the largest holder of inventions and patents in the world by far, and we file the most patents annually (closely followed by Japan).

A few of the above are, arguably, too complex to sum up so easily and still be completely true,[2] but if you want to have some agreement on a light, somewhat political topic with a mixed crowd, one that doesn't carry a risk of creating controversy or argument, there are many such topics; they're the easy route. It might even be fun. Ideologues can take such topics and wrench them back to controversial ground instantly, though, so you may need to be prepared to change the subject again to either another neutral point, or a completely apolitical one. (Libertarians, by the way, are the best at turning everything deeply ideological; it has something to do with freedom being their only big, red, button in life. Anything you can say has a freedom angle, it turns out. They can show you where it is).

At this point, I can do that all day pretty well; it's fun, it's not that difficult, and occasionally, it can be productive. It's likely you'll veer off into controversial territory occasionally, though, and not realize immediately what your mouth has done on your behalf. "Oh, it sounds like I've started a rant about climate change; I wonder how I'll shut up." It's ok; murmur an ideological offset in their favor, or straight apologize; no big deal, usually, as long as you're quick.

The final method of having a political conversation is the hardest, but I think the most rewarding with all but those we know very well: it is to have a limited type conversation, where you do the listening, except when you're asking questions, as we covered in the listening chapter. This choice is tough but doable, and it has the advantage of being appropriate for everyone, from strangers to those we know and love well. Let's start with four perfectly good, perfectly achievable goals of the most powerful political conversations:

1. Develop a strong relationship apart from politics.
2. Understand the strong points of their position.
3. Understand the weak points of your own position.
4. Keep the conversation short and focused.

Let's call that the order of importance, as well.

You see what's missing in that list, don't you? I've been trying to hint at this for a hundred pages, but now we need to get explicit: the best way to talk politics with conservatives is to keep your own opinions and strong points out of the conversation, just as we did in the listening chapter.

You're not a spineless traitor to goodness when you push pause on the urge to foist your moral view on others. It doesn't mean you're acknowledging them as better, or that you're buttering them up, or that you're being silent in the face of evil. Remember that learning about conservatives is a kind of cultural anthropology, the study of human culture variation; it doesn't have to be a game of tit-for-tat, centering every three or four minutes on your own cultural beliefs. Cultural anthropologists do not trudge to the caves of Western New Guinea, talk with people, and then cry themselves to sleep every night under their mosquito shroud because they don't feel heard, because the truth about their real lives of Jeopardy reruns and soft pretzels back in the Bronx didn't get expressed that day.

Nobody wants to hear your deep-dish insights about money in politics, anyway. In experiments where conservatives watch scads of political ads all in a row, and they can choose which to watch, they skip over all the Democratic ads and listen to all the Republican ones. You're like a Democratic ad, probably like a lousy one. You should be about the business of figuring out what makes a big slice of America tick. If you're like most of us, you have no idea what you're doing— so do an interview, which makes it fairly possible for you to not screw it up. If it's successful, it will eventually lead to two-way dialogue anyway, if that's what you want– and by then, any dialogue will be much easier and more fruitful, because you will have established yourself as a listener and respecter of opinion, maybe even as a member of the ingroup.

Remember the inflexibility of conservatives that we discussed, that often catches us by surprise– this is not a crowd that handles judgmental liberals well– they don't even handle polite liberals that air their opinions well. Conservatives are famously more black-and-white than you are, and you must respect how hard it is for them to take a liberal seriously, when they know you came through the door with most of your screws loose and your mental shoelaces tied together. They know all about the scrunched-up plan to save the world in your shirt pocket, on the napkin you spilled beer on down at Red's Recovery Room while you thought it up. Put yourself in their shoes as the keepers of the flame, barricaded inside their circle of Truth: they have a *moral* reason to ignore your points. Whenever you open your mouth, there's a risk that your political ideas could infect their thinking. Getting past that obstacle is part Houdini, part Master Po, part Ghandi, and part Freud: if you don't make it, consider yourself normal.

Master Po may be unfamiliar to you. He's from the Kung Fu TV show; he was blind, and caught incoming arrows in his hands anyway. Be that good before you start talking about your brilliant ideas; be Billy Clinton good.

Start out by not trying to wield the Force: simply refuse to drag out your shiny pebbles of truth. Establish trust, and learn a few things about these other Americans. It doesn't mean you're acknowledging their superiority– it means you acknowledge how stupid that clear conduit metaphor of communication is, and how hard even one-way communication really is, especially with a beer in your hand and the TV in the background. It means you're genuinely interested in what her background and makeup causes her to believe, and that you think there's far more to her than any stereotypical, faceless image of conservatives can provide you.

It's a big job just getting one-way to work on sensitive topics! Limit your attempt at two-way miracles to things that matter, like communicating with teenagers, business partners, and life partners.

Like anyone, almost all conservatives get tired of talking about their own view, and they'll eventually ask you a question about your viewpoint. Their first question is usually half-hearted, even if they don't realize it– you will have been sitting there asking questions for so long that it dawns on them for a split-second that they're being self-centered. But then they forget about you again, and you can continue with questions.

You can pick up the baton, if you like: you can start twirling and tossing it; swing your hips a little. This kind of "What about you?" question will usually happen after maybe 90 minutes or so of talking, sometimes after multiple conversations (that's a rough average: a fast girl might go all of two minutes, a slow guy can go five hours, or five months). Before that, they're so pleased to finally be heard that they burble and chortle about and around their view contentedly, usually in a way that's informative and interesting.

I don't usually take the offer to share my opinion seriously early in the relationship, other than maybe making a neutral one from the list above, because I like to plan any liberal idea explanations carefully— I like to know what I'm going to talk about, how I'm going to approach it, and make sure the environment is near-perfect at that moment. Because, remember, the easy version of the conduit metaphor of communication is bullocks.

And I take back that crack about the effort to be accepted requiring that you be part-Houdini— I only mentioned him to be cute. There shouldn't be any sleight-of-hand, trickery, or spying-on-the-bad-guys sense to any of this. You're not trying to burrow in like a tick: you're not getting inside so you can more easily convert/poison them, before they know what happened. Those kind of feelings can come up because we're talking about moral values here, disguised as politics— issues as close to our hearts as any you can name.

But think bigger than that; think about what you can gain from this personally instead. This kind of listening can be one of the best things you've ever done for yourself. In your wildest dreams, any victories you make with them politically might be something like convincing them to vote for a different mayoral candidate, or against a certain bond issue. Well, with respect to the every-little-bit-counts school of political activism: who cares?

And as for fighting the evils that infect conservatism, almost every person you'll talk with will be a good person, unfortunately— you'll look stupid wearing your superhero tights during the conversation. Your mother would be embarrassed. Any errors in their world view are usually, at worst, just that: mistakes. Miscalculations. With a little bias thrown in, of course, same as you. It's not a great evil you're fighting, or willful stupidity, or even closed-mindedness. You're not even fighting at all— you're looking at a guy on a love seat and seeing evil empires, oil tax credits, and back room deals, where you might be able to see a son; a working man; a fellow with an affection for beer and baseball, who has a slobbery dog with too much skin.

As you do it, it becomes fun when ideas come to the fore that you weren't capable of predicting. You learn that there are real, understandable stories behind these "errors"– genuine fears, ideas, and orientations, ones you don't see in your other life, surrounded as you are by liberal friends and family. This is your opportunity to find and truly see one person who breathes the air of the other America, to see and begin to recognize a genuine person instead of a hanger-on, or a symptom of a cause.

In a moment of intensity, with ideas of moral import under foot, it's easy for us to forget that the relationship itself is far more important than any persuasion or accuracy that may happen when talking about politics. You'll make mistakes– I certainly do– because you get overly attached to a contrary view, or you get irritated at something that sounds callous, or you don't stay alert enough. But if you can quickly recognize that you've violated the rule about focusing on building a strong relationship through the conversation, you can steer aright again.

Impossible vs. Seemingly Impossible

There are people you will meet who are quite nice in real life, but they weren't blessed to frame up political abstractions that are a level or three up from the reality in their living room. To some degree, all people have this problem– humans aren't good with abstractions in general, which causes some of our political polarity– but some people are quite bad at it.

Abstraction affects us in many subjects– politics is not a magical exception. Many business owners can't figure out conceptually how to improve their business; parents can't understand how to improve relations with their children; children can't figure out how to put puzzles together. Unfortunately, there's no way for any of us to recognize that we're lousy at abstraction like political thought. There's no reliable feedback loop. Everyone can feel like an expert, like men thinking they're great in bed. This is like the problem of people who are crazy about being music performers but are atrocious. Lack of political sense is worse, because even the most stubborn, mediocre music performer eventually gets the idea that they don't cut it on stage, but politics will never give you enough feedback about how bad you are at it, while you yell at your TV, lecture your kids, read the news, and interpret the nodding of your friends as enthusiastic agreement.

Most of these enthusiastic-but-terrible abstractors are nice, in the sense that you can have a good experience talking politics with them. We're more interested in them as people than any specific political meanderings, anyway. But some of them have a hidden switch that flips to turn them into people who aren't nice in political discussions. If they suddenly get surprisingly rude, hateful, or emotional when they talk politics, they're the switchy kind.

We call these people "flamers" in the business and technical world: in my experience, they comprise about three to five percent of people. Perfectly decent normally, but get just a bit away from their normal lives, into an email system, say, or a set of concepts that are abstract, and they magically turn know-it-all and venomous. This is human, in a way; it's been shown that people would kill others far, far more often if they can push a button or give an order rather than push a person in front of a train or stab them. Abstract is a little further from our hunter-gatherer roots than many of us can handle.

People have different personalities, sometimes very different, depending on whether they're one-on-one, in a group, on the phone, texting, or on email. Anger Management and Alcoholics Anonymous groups are well-populated by people whose personalities turn a corner in certain situations, as if there was another person hiding in there, waiting to get out. If we remember personality is a mask that covers our real selves, we can understand switching it oddly here and there, to express other parts of us.

If you discover you are trying to speak with someone who seems to have actually switched personality while you watched, scamper away immediately. Scoot so quickly away from the subject, toward a barbecue or bathroom, that you leave clothing or bearer bonds behind. These are not people you'll be able to learn from through political conversation: you will end up angry, and so will they. You'll have to find enough in their other personality to enjoy them, and you'll have to work to keep that one there.

One interesting aspect of doing this with them is that there's a part of them that seems to understand, and they often will carry on after a bit of a scene as if nothing happened– as if you didn't pretend to have a family emergency or coughing spell, or as if they hadn't just yelled at you; the sane part of them knows about this part of themselves better than you do, and is used to the slow crawl back to reality they must do to keep jobs, girlfriends, and access into their favorite bar.

Those who are very far right (roughly 5-15% of conservatives, depending on where you are) can seem similarly off-putting to liberals: you can get the same kind of alarm or tingle up your back early in the conversation because they either murder your sacred cow before your eyes, smiling all the while, or they genuflect to one of your Great Satans within the first sentence or two. But if they're being polite, if their face isn't reddening or you haven't been directly insulted, keep going if you can, because many of them are the most thoughtful and moral people you'll meet.

I get upset more quickly than most of them, purely because of their ideas, the standard way that research shows this to be more likely for liberals. The thumb rule that we can comfortably reach about half the distance across the full ideology spectrum shouldn't be ignored, but don't get too easily discouraged by quick, matter-of-fact insults of your ideas by the far-right. If they do upset you, try to re-engage about things other than politics, so that you might have a good relationship anyway.

One of the most interesting and pleasant political conversations I've ever had was with an unfailingly polite lady, quite senior in the national political machinery, who came roaring out of the box with ideas my poor liberal ears curled to hear. I was able to focus on her interesting personality and relax around the ideas that seemed so cruel or simplistic: she was the sweetest bulldog I've ever spoken to: feminine, yet seemingly unable to turn from the course once she'd set her mind to it: driven, yet patient, polite, and confident enough to not be brittle and unyielding. She eventually told me that then-President Obama's ultimate goal was to spend as much as possible so the country would go bankrupt, to "finally implement his secret socialist agenda." I asked her if she was serious: she looked at me, shook her head, and said with a little laugh, "I know. I know." We smiled and shook our heads together a little— not in agreement, but in a shared realization that there was a surreal gulf between us; that the world somehow managed to accommodate us both, and kept turning.

Yet part of it didn't matter in the least. My respect for her skill set, combined with the whole strange line of inquiry, lifted us from our little sub-realities, in a healthy way: we could laugh a little together about a world where people can see things so differently and yet pay tolls on the same Oklahoma roads, and buy shoes from the same fellow. When I think of fervent belief— mine or others— I remember sitting in that Oklahoma City booth with her, and the strange and vital comfort I felt in our ability to like one another, as if I'd found a separate tether to her, apart from her appalling ideas. I've always felt that she and I could hold our strong opinions loosely enough to be good citizens together— to get a park we wanted commissioned, or arrange local disaster relief together. I find great comfort in that. The world can be a bigger place than our opinions.

A common foundation in good couples therapy and mediation works well in political discussion: you repeat what you've heard from the other person, in your own words, to get agreement from them that you understand. We get to avoid that, thankfully— it's extremely slow, and pedantic— but only because you're asking enough questions and following closely enough that real communication is happening. If you're not comfortable that you're understanding something, ask about it, as we discussed in the listening chapter.

And here is the secret: it's very much a two-way conversation to get to the bottom of what one person feels. If you do this right, it doesn't feel as if you've conducted an interview, or acted the psychologist, saying "tell me more about that" every 4 minutes. What I'm asking you to do looks like a conversation and feels like one, because it is one.

The Rule of Yes! Part Two

To repeat: I think the Rule of Yes! is the single most important technique to use when trying to communicate in risky situations like politics. If you're using it adequately, I suspect you'll be using it somewhere between 10% and 30% of the time you open your mouth.

Here are some basic categories of the kind of agreeing you can do, which we'll go over with examples:

> - Agree *partially*: be clear about a piece of what they said.

> – Think through the emotion or value behind what they're saying, and try to *validate* that ("It must be tough to…"; "It's such a frustrating situation").

> – A rephrasing or *mirroring*, either as a statement or question.

> – You can *ask a question* about it, which isn't exactly a Rule of Yes! technique, but it's fantastic anyway sometimes, because you're able to show interest without having to deal with a nasty or controversial opinion directly.

The Rule of Yes! will make your head hurt sometimes, especially if you're feeling a little rebellious about something they've said. For me, for instance, I struggle when someone tells me that rich people are taxed too much; I have to wave away the fog rapidly forming on my mental windshield to see my way forward, and I'm not good at sincerely spitting out "There's no doubt that high taxes cause financial disincentives," which is perfectly true; nor can I say "It's hard to pay taxes" without my jaw clenched, even though that's also obviously true, and a surprisingly effective response. You'll have similar issues as well, but you shouldn't be paralyzed by an emotional response to almost everything they say, or you're not in the spirit of it.

Let's go over a few examples, with a statement and an answer.

> "I believe God created all little children to live out their
> lives, and that abortion is murder."
> "It must break your heart to see so many abortions
> happening in America."

I have said this, and seen them share their deeply-felt grief over the abortions of perfect strangers, driven by the engine of their faith. They knew I didn't believe what they do, but they chose to focus on their own feelings when I made it possible for them, and we ended up bonding over it. Abortion, like almost every other hot-button item in politics, has many different dimensions to it, and each one can and should be discussed *in isolation*, with a minimum of "Yeah, but…" interruptions of emotional perspectives. If I rebuked her for her stance on abortion, it wouldn't make me any more moral, it wouldn't change her opinion, and it would harm our relationship unnecessarily. It would also be intolerant in the same way I fault her for being, for her trying to make abortion illegal: it's no more sensible to do that then to say "your religious beliefs are stupid; you should've changed them a long time ago."

Also, I dislike strongly ideological attitudes that ignore the emotional pain of the other side, simply because our side is supposedly feeling more pain. Our instinct is to ignore or at least discount their pain, in an immature effort to concentrate their attention on our pain. Ironically, bonding over emotional pain is often a bridge to solutions, especially in such intractable problems as abortion, as was shown by creative negotiations done by Essential Partners (whatisessential.org) after killings at abortion clinics.[3]

> "The Democrats think they can spend money we don't
> have, and give everyone a free lunch, and we'll be just fine.
> It's crazy."
> "I wish people paid more attention to financial
> responsibility in the government. I'm really worried about
> it."

I've had versions of this conversation hundreds of times. It sounds like I'm being deceptive, but I'm not. They understand that, as a Democrat, I don't agree with them in particulars on how to spend and how to cut, yet I've *never once* been asked "Well, why are you a Democrat, then?" The reason why is because what they care about is that I value financial responsibility, which is an extension of personal responsibility for them.

That articulated agreement about spending responsibility provides us a bond. It's true that I'm more frightened about our financial situation than many Democrats, and I can comfortably agree with them about disability abuse and government benefit packages, so we can continue to have a fruitful exchange. Sometimes I've successfully expressed my deep reservations about military spending. Once they understand I share their general principle of fiscal prudence, they're not nearly as excited about fighting over the details, though I'm careful to provide details I've prepared, so I don't sound uninformed or unrealistic.

If you don't have that same capability I do to agree with them, there are alternatives that are nearly as useful, like validation of their fears ("You must be worried about last year's deficit, then"; "The debt numbers sure sound high; I don't even know what a trillion dollars means."), restating what they said, or mirroring ("You think the Democrats could really change our financial picture"; "The government spends way more than it takes in, that's for sure."), or asking a question ("What bothers you the most?"; "Do you think it's all the Democrats, or is it corruption, or both parties, or lobbyists, or what?")

"We should've carpet-bombed Syria."
"I have zero idea how to handle that mess over there."

Carpet bombing is insanity, but this fellow was a drug-store manager in Mississippi, so I wasn't too dedicated to changing his mind about his bombing fantasies, since that would save very few Syrians. By focusing on rapport, I'm shaking my head alongside him; we're both looking at Syria together and agreeing, in this odd way: "What a mess. I wish I could help the situation." That validation is what he wants; he doesn't care how many bombs I'd use in the situation, even though it seems by the rules of logic that he would. And what I said was true: I had no idea what the proper response of America was for Syria.

This is a strange and powerful Rule of Yes! method: just agreeing that things are a mess can be bonding, even though you often have very different ideas of how to handle the problem. It's also usually easy to sincerely agree, in this odd way. Notice this, though: what we're *not* saying is just as important as what we *are* saying. I didn't say "that's a stupid opinion," even though he knew I'm a Democrat, and probably thought he was insane. But by not condemning him, I'm saying to him that my relationship with him is more important than his bright idea about murdering the people he wants to save, or whatever carpet-bombing is.

How Does it Go Wrong?

Usually, these conversation veer off course gradually, and you don't recognize it's happening at first. Fortunately, by paying attention, especially to yourself, you can do something about it.

There's a great deal of self-awareness involved in deep-dish listening, but this is not the part where we go Buddhist together, though a background in meditation and relaxation techniques is helpful. This is the temporary kind of self-awareness, the kind you use at the hallway mirror before you open the door to let your date in. You simply need to get used to looking for any deterioration in your attitude during a short conversation, like a third person coming over to check in with you. I picture a white-coated doctor that only I can see and hear: he's bending in a dignified fashion at the waist, to murmur questions in my ear. My guy has a slight northern Indian accent: "Are you comfortable, Scott– tired, cold? Are you starting to lose your concentration– is your mind wandering? Are you getting irritated, impatient?...Oh my, Mr. Scott, that was definitely a blurt. Why don't you excuse yourself now– let's visit those beautiful appetizers. It's been a welly long conwahsation."

There are a thousand uneven paths to stupidity, but keeping this third-party check-in part of the program in play will help you avoid most of them. You can even argue with yourself and disagree about how you're doing– that's fine. But success with conservatives in conversation is best thought of as temporary, for the simple reason that it's hard.

Death Blurts

Conversations aren't usually ruined by anger. Sometimes, it's some kind of irritation you couldn't predict. But for me, the commonest reason has been an automatic response I've made to an idea of theirs that seems wrong to me, that's out of my mouth before I realize it. It can be the result of having an attitude on the subject that's a little like that of a second-grader, one who can't keep his butt in his chair, wiggling and waving to get called upon. Likely, it's at least 15 minutes into the conversation and you're a bit on autopilot, like the fellow on the freeway who looks down and notices he's going 80 instead of 65. It's been going well, but then, you find yourself talking about something you believe in, usually responding to something they've said that you see as wrong or incomplete. You're almost as surprised as they are. You thought you were just supporting your conversation partner, having good rapport, and now you're at least part-way through a two-sentence, shorthand rejection of something she believes.

If you're quick, you can stop yourself and turn it into a cough. You might be able to trail off and say something like "Oh, never mind— wasn't pertinent. Go on, please." Neither of these is my style: I tend to wake up to what I've done just after the two sentence course-correction is handed to them, during the little stunned silence, just after the damage is done, and just before they tell me they have to go now. Gone is half or two-thirds of the good will you'd built up; your ease; their ease; the lack of defensiveness; the easy lope from subject to subject. Welcome to the dueling room— daggers or Derringers, please?

This is the Death Blurt. It results from losing grip on your attentiveness, from a less than fully alert state: your beliefs will betray you in those moments to reveal you as less interested in their outlook at the moment than your own. There's a distinction between bringing up your opinion in contrast, as a polite aside or a point of interest, and doing what I did, which is essentially a "Yeah, but" type of correction.

I met with a kind local businessman in Durango who gave me much of his time and attention. He was sharing his concern about a local problem with long building inspection delays. I remember that it was precisely 24 minutes into the conversation. I should've responded with something akin to this:

"I'm used to thinking of that kind of delay on permits as necessary given all the work the inspectors have to cover with their tiny budgets nowadays, so it's useful to hear about it from your perspective."

That might've gotten a constructive rebuttal about taxes from him, or he might've just moved on, because it would've been quite supportive. He didn't get that. It was 24 minutes in; I'd gotten mentally tired without realizing it. I blessed him with this 'yeah, but' revelation:

"It sounds like taxes aren't covering the costs of doing decent planning. There's no getting around that you get what you pay for."

In other words, I tried to teach *him* about *his* local government; it wasn't unresponsive government, according to me; it was all about taxes being too low. I might as well have told him to work on a campaign to raise taxes, so the guys he was complaining about could get a raise.

It's been years, and I still cringe for that guy. His response was the pause of .7 seconds that's famous among conversation analysts; for polite people, that pause means something between "What did you just say to me??" and "Dude— no. Just no." He let loose a sigh and said, "I should get back to work now." It felt like turning over one of the sucky cards in Monopoly: GO TO JAIL, GO DIRECTLY TO JAIL. It's quite difficult to apologize your way out of it too, by then— you have to have the presence of mind to almost instantly say "No, I see what you mean about the delays killing you."

I have been in this situation many times, and only remember managing a truly successful apology once— a couple of decent splutters a little later that saved some skin and hair, yes, but usually not even that. You'll be a little flustered, as will they, and it'll be tough to kickstart the conversation again.

There's a good reason that there's a rule to keep political conversation short: it's the best way to make certain that both your attention levels will be what they should be throughout the conversation. The main culprit in failures is letting the conversation go on and on. In my experience, one-on-one political conversations of this sort are best limited to 10 or 15 minutes, especially if you're stretching your wings into normal, two-way conversation. If you get along famously— if, by 15 minutes in, they have asked you to be their next child's godmother— go 25 minutes or so. I always pull the plug at 30 minutes, and usually sooner.

The sad truth is that 10 minutes will be too much for some of us, especially men, depending on our ability to buckle down and pay attention, and depending on the conservative. Some people are less interesting than others: some express themselves poorly, or are hard to understand. Others are like sailing directly into heavy swells on a small boat— you get hit with what seems like a fresh, dastardly viewpoint every 10 to 13 seconds, with no letup. It can be like watching a slide show of mass murder scenes. Some people's version of politics makes them like a prize rodeo bull— explosion out of the gate, and no one able to handle a full 8 seconds. But if you're aware of the need to keep it short with conservatives in these early conversations— if you remember it's a kind of numbers game, in that you've only got so many challenges in you to handle well— you'll have a real advantage.

The third-party you should have watching over you, looking for risky deterioration— your version of my neatly-dressed, north Indian doctor— should be invisibly looking inside your head with one of those shiny-light, eye-scope, retina-annoyer thingies, for either of these easy-to-spot signs:

> – The urge to interrupt with a counterpoint, which can be surprisingly hard to see coming.
> – Your mind wandering more than a second or two (which means you're losing grasp of how much is at stake, how difficult this process is).

Catch either of those droops happening and you'll know that you should start looking for a glory-ridden exit to the bathroom, say. Bathrooms should be like Mecca, ideologically speaking. A pause and physical separation of any length allows for an easy change of subject, a chance to breathe a separate air long enough to shrivel the political momentum a little, so both of you can easily turn to something more immediate or personal instead.

Short conversations that you take the initiative to end show your friend you're not living and dying by your political opinions, or hers— that she means far more to you than whatever opinion and abstractions are being cast about.

How to Be Politically Persuasive

As said, many conservatives are a breeze to "persuade", but they're not political, and will almost always switch their opinion back, or forget what they learned from you. It's like arm-wrestling a spaghetti noodle, and roughly as useful, unless you're on a last-minute run in an election.

If you have to try to persuade someone who's political, pick one, single point, of a minor, nearly garden variety to focus on. Then use very personal information, ideally of great import, to get it across. You may have achieved ingroup status, but that just means they like you, or, at best, that they respect your thinking or lifestyle; it usually means little about how receptive they'll be to your smelly political ideas. Don't touch slavery reparations for African-Americans, or why deficits don't matter, or the military budget. With anyone who's political, informed or not, persuasion means a miraculous opening of a 1,200-pound door, with multiple padlocks and voice recognition involved: what you'll need is a combination of the Force and a steel toe you can wedge open the door with as it flickers briefly open— nothing more, nothing less. Plan your one point like a multi-million-dollar robbery: blueprints, rehearsals, custom tools, a secret shop. Start the point with your best friend losing her job, or your husband fighting off a deadly disease, or the Serbian orphan you've adopted; end with an Olympic medal, or a leg lost to a old, forgotten mine. Between the start and finish, blaze through a vividly villainous law or regulation, ideally one they won't know without research is a conservative mistake.

The sign that you succeeded: the conservative will raise an eyebrow, murmur something sympathetic or complimentary, and change the subject. If that happens, you can start planning for another run at persuasion next year.

Let's call the game now. This has been a hard run at the truth, and some of the main bits are lain down. As said, data and wisdom have been leaking furiously across the transom of late, and it has needed to get out. We've sketched out some of the solid theory, and made a stab at what it means across dining room tables. "Getting to yes" and other such concerns with manipulating others well are quite adequately handled by others. You've made the best kind of progress with conservatives by focusing with me on getting along with them, and working well with them.

Go get 'em!

Epilogue

For all that is stained,
lost, or compromised,
we are still the mirror
that shows the face of God.

-Samuel Mills,
"A Postcard from
Grand Central Station"

I'VE ADMIRED, and bested, and been bested by conservatives my whole life. I've cried with and about them, and am not near the end of my affairs with them. I'll never understand them; not fully. In some situations, I don't understand them at all well. It feels a terrible admittance, as we close this effort to encircle and encapsulate and explicate them for you, but there it is.

I yell at conservatives sometimes, usually in public meetings, and usually intend to when I do. Maybe it isn't always right to do so. Unfortunately, there's no law written in the firmament that true kindness and proper humanity entail universal and constant gentleness, or even civility, to every person that has scrambled to a position of authority or power in the modern state or corporation. This is off-putting and seemingly counter-productive, but sometimes I'm happy to pay that cost. Most of my activism is about recruiting the left, center, and maybe a few conservatives, to build a decent-sized minority around an issue, so we can arrive at some influence with it. Contention is just another tactic of activism, like the biggest wrench in the toolbox.

In politics, that ultimate of theaters, there may well be times to sway others with ire or grief, to build a sea change of feelings and facts that can throw a contest our way, against staid, inane conservative impulses, many of which are just there because they always were, or because someone rich would be inconvenienced without them, or because someone in power wants to keep that power at any cost. I don't always see patience as a virtue, and I expect others to agree when we make a clear, persuasive case about injustice or corruption. Other arenas like family, work, and personal conflicts, where these ideological problems appear so predictably, also have similar toolboxes, full of tools with their own tradeoffs.

Mere success or failure itself usually has a great influence with conservatives, apart from the rationale, or justice, or moral aspects of our position. Keying off each other so keenly results in what I see as the regular pattern of how liberals accomplish things when they oppose us:

1. At first, they dismiss without comment; they pointedly ignore, to avoid making a disagreeable point seem worthwhile through a response.
2. They attack (actually, usually a defense), with increasing ferocity.
3. The attack lets off, either because they're being beaten, which in itself influences conservatives, or they begin to see the logic of the counter-argument.
4. They become both silent and unresponsive. This is usually a long period, because it's the time when the notion that it would be wrong to continue with their policy must take hold in a large minority of them.
5. We see evidence of significant, overt disagreement among them in the media. This is usually (not always) a relatively brief period, due to their social nature. Overt argument, even by the minority, becomes less energetic. Ideally, they become more actively involved in the solution's implementation at this stage.
6. Overt support of the old argument disappears, as an extension of the need to conform with their group's beliefs. This is also a very long step, and usually only happens gradually, after the policy has changed.
7. Intermittent and weak but overt support of the new policy begins. This happens alongside the last step.
8. The new policy is embraced by the majority as the right thing to do. This typically occurs long after it becomes policy or law.

These steps are more easily seen in families, at work, and in local and state battles, rather than in the federal government, because the time frames are shorter and the number of people involved are smaller. But the same steps seem to occur at the federal level, such as with the efforts to institute Social Security, the Clean Air Act, civil rights, and the 40-year battle over climate change (where one can argue as of this writing that we're well into the silent stage among the U.S. populace, with the politicians lagging and resisting, as is common for the more ideological strain of conservative). Broad social change is also resisted and them eventually embraced in the same way, like attitudes toward working mothers, or mixed marriages.

If you review those steps, you will easily see the shadows of all the things we've talked about: the emphasis on keeping working processes going, exactly as is; the perspective driven by orderliness, politeness, and low neuroticism; the cavalcade of biases and motivated reasoning that prop up a moral position so avidly; and the ways that social conformity drives them to react in groups, like a flock of starlings at sunset.

Some people may look at this process of change cynically, seeing those steps as unnecessary or evil. That may be, in some theoretical liberal world, but in the real one, where I'd contend that everyone is merely more or less conservative, these steps are a human process, and they have their own logic. I've discussed this process in depth with conservatives, and they don't at all think that that list is a reflection that they're dim-witted, or irresponsible, or weak, or doing anything other than being careful with change. *Something* that looks like a wade through molasses is going to happen when important change has to occur, after all. Think of a 14-year-old young lady with a well-behaved first boyfriend, trying to convince her father to allow them to go (or have him drive them) on a pizza date: something like the steps above may well occur, with the father liable to build obstacles to further progress toward a date at every juncture, in a hope that the impulse will just go away with his resistance.

My perspective on activism is to accept this process of theirs in good faith, but to not at all be accepting of how long they want to take at each milestone. Without pressure, they will stop at each step and start building infrastructure. For a conservative, slowing down change is often their main goal; certainly their manifestos make that claim, and there are fine justifications for that filibustering approach with us. You'll think we've all pulled over on the road to progress to briefly take a leak in the bushes, and they've ordered up heavy equipment to build a full rest area, so the convoy can stay there permanently; they've submitted paperwork to incorporate the rest stop as a town; they've built the nearby town a stadium, and convinced the local government to condemn the next stretch of road until further notice. I want to be able to fairly answer their concerns, in their terms, and then work hard to recruit the mindshare necessary to keep us moving on to the next step. I'm always trying to understand when to be patient, and when to be impatient.

Think about how each step implies very different strategies and tactics, depending on what's trying to be accomplished. I work on the early end of these efforts on issues of militarization, police brutality, and homelessness, where the opposition is massive and entrenched, and the public is removed– so I do civil disobedience, yelling, arm-waving, threatening, emotional messaging, and other divisive tools, to start getting taken seriously. I also try to employ creativity to gain attention, what we call guerilla marketing efforts in the business world. This is the same as the effort to attract "early adopters" in the business world, the influential people who will become loyal to a product early; our efforts are mostly designed to force the right to pay attention and begin or step up their active resistance. These activities of mine are nearly universally off-putting to conservatives, and so I do what I can to make sure I communicate that my efforts aren't personal. My assurances don't do any good in the near-term, but can pay off later in the cycle.

In the more middle steps of change, as a conservative fantasy is in the process of potentially being toppled from an unwarranted throne, the lessons of this guide are much more important. There, we need to work directly with individual conservatives citizens, or family members, or politicians, on powerful persuasion and actual implementation details. These are almost always deceptively complex, and usually underestimated by activists who might've been great at the rabble-rousing and drama, keying off their high neuroticism and compassion. Liberal activism is poor at the front end of a movement (early), but we're even worse at relating to conservative perspectives enough to practically implement a useful change later, when it usually has to be done with conservative support.

In the final steps of change, be it in the family, at work, or in politics, we have a chance to teach the more basic lessons of developing useful openness to those who aren't good at it. Our own efforts are typically helped by their group's partial conversion. Conservatives have a chance to become more used to the idea of useful, uncomfortable change, as we need to in the modern age, accepting ideas that they once fought avidly.

Throughout all those steps, we should keep in mind the wide and real separation between individual conservatives and bad or flawed policies. In both my normal life and as an activist, keeping those two things separate gives me occasional leverage, and it makes life much more fun and informative. I genuinely admire and enjoy working with some of my most bitter enemies, because *they are not their policies*. They're often damn good at what they do, they usually teach me useful lessons about odd, unrelated things, and below it all, they're typically very well-meaning. There are misunderstandings, and dispositions, and circumstance, and a hundred howling vagaries of history that place us across these chasms from one another, communicating with smoke signal and semaphore.

In keeping with what we've learned, after getting the attention of conservatives in activist situations, I try to push morality against the far corner of the room, behind furniture, so we arrive somewhere useful together as easily and quickly as we can.

In the cases where I find myself in the presence of what I call empirical evil, where money, or aggrandized power, or vanity is driving the resistance, another set of skills and techniques come into play. But the methods to counter such things are the same regardless of whether one's enemy is liberal or conservative; covering corruption is afield of our purpose here.

There is a middle ground between empirically evil and good behavior, claimed unwittingly by conservatives in times of high stress, where bias levels and the intense competitiveness of conscientious people lead them to embrace Machiavellian behavior, justifying dishonesty or other immoral behavior in the name of some greater good they perceive themselves serving. In my opinion, that roughly sums up the origins of nearly all the wars America initiated last century. All I will say about that is that the game afoot can shift on us with conservatives, and shift quickly, in moments of import. It may be unwittingly Machiavellian, but it can be just as bad as intentional corruption in outcome, and must be addressed similarly.

It's a grave temptation to fall into that kind of gray area ourselves, but that is a failing, a moral one, entered into with no more logic or justification than schoolchildren debating who started it. Not to attempt a fine point on a messy affair, but we don't have the same psychic motivations or justifications to do such a thing. So far, I've been able to avoid it. Even in my modest pursuits for the good, though, I have gone to the edge of that well and stared down long into it; it's harder for me than for most to condemn the politicians and other powerful people who fall into that habit. It's a strong temptation for people of action, because seemingly small compromises of integrity can deliver great rewards.

But this isn't a philosophical work, nor even a moral one. I'll leave to you the task of wrestling with angels and men for the greater good.

A Separate Viewpoint

The human brain weighs about three pounds. You could hold it easily in your hand; you could ruin it with an easy swipe of a butter knife. Yet every unmeasured mystery of mankind teems within that hand's width of folds and layers. You and I are like people trying to use protractors and calculators to understand and predict the contour and path of a sea wave as it arrives at the shore. We swipe at the sea's movement with tentative, awkward tools, liable to get every tenth thing a bit off, or a great deal off, or even exactly backwards. And all the while, the sea proceeds on its course, aloof to us, its mysteries and flawless movement arising and disappearing a thousand times more quickly than we might model it.

In the same way, our life plunges on, thanks to the brain's effortless confluence and integration of a thousand changing forces, like the waters borne to the sand and out again. We know so little about ourselves.

Both the evidence from what I call exception theory, how each ideology takes inspiration from our respective hemispheres, and the evidence from personality, show a mirrored equivalence between us that I can't reconcile with the world I know. Nothing in these pages, and nothing of the thousands of hours spent preparing them, can remove the terrible tension I feel between the desire I have to understand and work with conservatives, and my knowledge of their danger and error.

When Dr. Sperry accepted the Nobel Prize for work on the brain hemispheres, he called their relationship inherently antagonistic, meaning that the two sides of ourselves get our life done by being at odds in key ways. Maybe a culture needs a similar antagonism: maybe I can only stand on one side of things, forbidden to grasp them fully, designed to be the offset I feel such an urge to provide. Maybe their worth can only be seen or calculated by a culture as a whole.

Two things bring me great comfort in this quandary. Foremost is the love I feel for my conservative family and friends. That emotional connection is mixed with an indescribable admiration and respect, which are the real world's infinitely broader, ineffable expression of the scant principles of this work. I know there are things that drive me to understand them that I can only swipe roughly at here, but that live and breathe and give me great succor within the realm of my unconscious.

Second is my wonder and respect for modern science, and my suspicions about it. Our gains are wonderful, but in the end, our errors and terrific gaps might be even more valuable. They can temper our enthusiasm healthily for the wonderful information pouring forth now about the human mind. I long ago stopped being a smarty-pants about biases, or our cognitive failings; I eventually learned enough respect for our mysteries to edge toward silence as I start to feel sure about some part of us being caricatured by science as primitive. Every tenth swipe at the truth is a bit off, or well off, or exactly backwards. I've ended my attempt to assert what I can see in studies, in conversations, and in behavior as anything like a full measure of who we are, even within the narrow corridors of our ideological selves. I take comfort that there are things we can quaveringly know, but despair of knowing how these, and the many principles still hidden from us, will fit together to make the measure of a particular conservative well.

But there's a delicious backside to all these unknowns, to the grousings of scientists in many fields, like the cosmologists, who have been frustrated for the last half-century that they know virtually nothing about 94% of the "known" universe. Mystery affords us opportunity. It forces us to observe the world with less judgment, and more wonder.

Such is life, thank goodness; such is the education of the human spirit. The occlusions between a man and a woman, a liberal and a conservative, a child and adult, the powerful and powerless— each of these gulfs, and many others, tear at us in their own ways. Yet they yield us balance, in ways we can't even come close to articulating. Each potential melding holds us in thrall. We are terrifically fortunate to live now, as we gain so many inroads into these dualities and tensions.

We can take great comfort at how so many of our neurological and psychological and cognitive postulates, our meditations on our mind's ways, urge us to take unerring shelter under the pavilion of wisdom, within lessons that the more lucky of us learned from caring parents, in a free country, at the feet of inspirational leaders and mentors. In our lifetimes, most of those primeval insights will be largely unadorned by careful hypotheses or double-blind studies. Hopefully, there are many thousands of years left of mankind's investigations, with our poverty of protractors and calculators, to limn and pass on more eagerly to each other the best of the wisdom we've inherited. In this age of materialism, zooming so heedlessly around and beyond the old gods, some of that tradition is winking out, or has gone wholly dark, like species passing to oblivion. Maybe if we're good, and lucky, we might pass on what we've been handed responsibly, or even restore some of the wisdom we've lost, while we add new lessons for the ages. I think my conservative friends would ask us to remember that. I've tried to here, out of respect for them.

In particular, this guide has pointed back to the wisdom of the Golden Rule as a key to success. Nothing will aid a thorough immersion into the mysteries of human behavior more than studying and struggling to incorporate kindness, of which the Golden Rule is a sturdy hallmark. All these things— knowing our biases, listening, rules of yes— are ornaments draped across the ligatures of the greatest human impulse: to be kind to others. That's the unseen path to find, to best live together.

All we can do is approach them in error and humility. Near enough to touch, here and there. To join hands in tragedy certainly, and maybe, if we're fortunate, in times of celebration. Other than that, we two are destined to be at odds a goodly measure of the days we whirl on this world together, stretching our contrasting templates athwart this place, making our own senses of it. Let's not be anxious to miss the beauty and nuance of a separate viewpoint, even when we can't fully know its contours, or justify its ways.

ACKNOWLEDGMENTS

I'd like to thank Mishka's Café in Davis, California, the 806 Café in Amarillo, Texas, Guillermo's in Little Rock, Arkansas, the Charmonte Ranch in Yreka, California, and the Foundation YMCA in Hickory, North Carolina, for allowing me to essentially live there during long stretches of research, interviews, and rumination. To the other 50+ cafes and 2 dozen bars between Santa Cruz and D.C that I closed down with the owner at the end of the night: thank you for letting me get a few more minutes in while you mopped under my legs.

Key parts were written at Phantom Ranch, at the bottom of the Grand Canyon, a fine café and chow hall to write in, though the juxtaposition of Bright Angel creek and a computer felt like a moral compromise to onlookers; the coffee is surprisingly good, and internet access floats between excellent and forbidden, depending on the weather and the green-garbed personage in charge.

Alyssa Pskowski allowed herself to be engaged involuntarily in many helpful early conversations; her close reading and temperate use of silver bullets since then kept scurrilous degeneracies out. My far-flung family helped me sleep however and whenever I could when I was near them, or on the way to some assignment, and, being mostly apolitical, were heroically tolerant of my soapbox moments and odd requests: thanks to Wagners, Woffords, Macraes, Santillis, Jernigans, Malottes, and Feiths.

Steve Messenger provided very helpful commentary throughout; he's a longtime touchstone on every issue that touches on ideological misunderstanding, and is blessed with a remarkable tolerance in the face of distasteful liberal ideas and tendencies. Charles Herz, former chair of the Wyoming Democratic Party, let me extend an interview into a ten-day stay, as my car was repaired in the dead of a Wyoming winter; his encouragement and guidance led to much better clarity in the bias section and ideology appendix. The graphics were enabled by Rod Wenell, who came down from the hill he saw me trying to climb to offer easy and welcome assistance, as well as helpful blank stares when faced with my less lucid insights. For acute mollycoddling and editing, I'm indebted to Karry Walker and Lauren Mackie. Heather Jansen and Michael Houghton of Designed by Monkeys, and Jessica Fillipi did the art and design work, and deserve kudos for tolerating my hands-on involvement with such forbearance.

Over a hundred researchers gave generously of their time and attention via interviews, supporting documentation, and reviews. In particular, Charles Brack first led me to hemispheric dimensions of ideology, through his curations at neuropolitics.com; Dr. Iain McGilchrist provided clarifying adjustment to my hemisphericity ideas; Joe Fried, a conservative writer, started me on this path years ago through a great conversation, and his remarkable collation of various statistics in his book, *Democrats and Republicans: Rhetoric and Reality*. Dr. Stanley Feldman and Dr. Elizabeth Suhay provided a capstone of sorts toward the end through their work on the social aspects of ideology, but also via kind encouragement and tolerance. May there be many more years of their brilliant, insightful contributions.

Dr. Jeff Mondak has been a near-miraculous, kind encouragement throughout, and gently provided steerage, early and late; his work on personality in ideology is a landmark of political psychology, and was an integral reference throughout. Dr. Kurt Gray provided the overall framework of dyadic morality, and helped me integrate it into this work. The Moral Foundations Theory team, particularly Dr. Jon Haidt, who all work hard in the next field over, provided early insights that led to this work's synthetic approach to conservatism through neurology, personality, biases, conformity, and morality. Jon's a tireless advocate of a liberalism that is influenced healthily by tolerance and diversity. He's been exemplary and instructive throughout.

This work wouldn't exist without Dr. Colin DeYoung's research and extensive support; putting up with many years of questions, annoyances, and impertinences, feeding me integral papers, books, and colleagues, and stripping me matter-of-factly of statistical and conceptual fantasies. His work is the foundation of this guide's focus on personality, and he provided a key touchstone early on for calibrating the process-versus-exception approach to ideology that is the heart of this effort.

None of these people are responsible for anything I've written, nor do these pages represent their views. The errors, omissions, conjectures, and assertions are mine.

ABOUT THE AUTHOR

J. Scott Wagner is a writer, management consultant, political activist, and social psychology researcher. He has degrees in sociology and business from SUNY Albany and UC Berkeley. He lives near Sebastopol, California.

APPENDIX A– IDEOLOGY & THE BRAIN

Hemispheric studies is one of the arenas of the social and neurological sciences where there's great support for *antagonistic* models for decision-making or operation, to get things done effectively and minimize errors. This might be, for example, trying to balance between risky and safe ways to do things, or between piecemeal (building from the bottom up, or deductive) and holistic (grasping the big picture, or inductive), or routine and novelty. There are probably dozens of such models, in many fields. Brain hemispheres should be seen as both an iteration or enactor of this type of model, not as the template that stamps them out. Brains could be organized without hemispheres, and we would still have the major issues and general solutions offered up by these basic models.

A sampling is listed below. Most are at least somewhat clear just by looking at the name of the model. None of these radically leverage neurological hemispheric research at this point, though perhaps at some point they might. For each, the first term is associated with the typical/statistical left hemispheric "viewpoint."

Stability-Plasticity	Individual psychology DeYoung
Process-Exception	Ideology Wagner
Exploitation-Exploration	Learning, foraging, visual system Various
Routinization-Novelty	Neurology Goldberg
Conservatism-Openness	Social psychology Schwartz
General-Scout	Neurology Ramachandran
Emissary-Master	Neurology, individual/social psychology, McGilchrist
Accommodation-Assimilation	Developmental psychology Piaget

As one group of neuroscientists said, in a review of hemispheric effects on behavior, "Converging lines of evidence from diverse research domains suggest that the left and right hemispheres play distinct, yet complementary, roles in inferential reasoning."[1] It would be odd, then, if these (mostly behavioral) models didn't have hemispheric dimensionality lodged firmly within their arguments. The behavioral and logical components overlap and repeat themselves across the models, varying with model depth, and very little with model type.

Fortunately, because these models are generalized, we don't have to explain an ideological (individual psychology) iteration of these antagonistic models strictly in terms of neurology. To look into how we approach the problem of ideology from a psychological standpoint, it's best to discuss the concept of a "sub-personality," which is well established in Jungian, Piagetian, and other approaches to individual psychology. The term is commonly used by Jordan Peterson and other theorists in present times as a way to characterize groups of traits or emotions that take over behavior, or even to represent individual strong emotions like anger or jealousy. It should be thought of as a very broad concept, not necessarily just for unusual situations, but also how we operate normally as humans. It gets at the idea that our behavior is done by parts of ourselves, in almost a statistical, not-necessarily-predictable way; that we likely never press our whole selves into activities, instead using specialized pieces of our whole self to get our normal lives done.

Sub-personalities are usually exaggerated or excessive; not just because you're "crazy with jealousy," but more broadly because they are specialists. As specialists, they rely on other sub-personalities that modify, or dampen, or switch them off. So, you can be very angry, and want to throw things, and that can be thought of as a kind of sub-personality; but then another part of you, maybe a part of you that is patient and kind, might combine with a part of you that is orderly enough to think about the future unemotionally, and those two *negotiate* with that furniture-throwing specialist inside, so that the whole you just stands there, glaring at the jerk that made you mad, instead of making big holes in the wall that you'll have to pay for and apologize over.

A hemispheric ideological behavioral model is a relatively straightforward sub-personality model, that isn't comprehensive about personality. It makes the claim that the hemispheres act as sources or, perhaps better stated, inspirations, for two sub-personalities that influence the parts of our personalities that are ideological. The underlying neurological details are completely unknown, other than the very coarse information detailed below about the independent personalities of the hemispheres, as seen in psychological studies of split-brain patients, and the related follow-on work. The model isn't neurological; it's a specialized individual psychology model. It's not designed to provide insight into the neurological substrate involved, nor does it rely on neurological insights beyond what's implied clearly by the psychological tests.

It's easy to disparage popular constructs about brain hemispheres, because it's easy, and accurate, to say that the brain does everything as a unit. Where this logic is wrong is to then assume that executive control, which is largely what a psychological model concerns itself with, is also a self-apparent amalgam of the hemisphere's antagonistic perspectives, the same way it's self-apparent that "the hemispheres always work together on everything." There is no easy elision from antagonism to perfect integration, because those are opposing tasks, the same way it is difficult or impossible in a given instant to be both an enemy and ally in any effort of import.

In other words, at the neurological, psychological, and phenomenological levels, there are highly complex methods necessary to enact effective decisions and perform specialized tasks. While there are loose connections between these levels of analysis, they must be enacted largely independent of one another from a modeling standpoint, and the connections between them are generally ancillary. If the brain hemispheres are antagonistically connected, as Roger Sperry insisted, it implies deep complexity at each of those three levels of analysis, simply because the phenomenological world dictated such a radical, complex approach to biological modeling, for selection purposes.

Yet even neuroscientists are in the habit of cutting off inquiry at both the neurological and psychological levels, based on a simplistic assertion of unitary processing. Meanwhile, the brain is telling us the same story the psychological and phenomenological worlds are telling us about decision-making: that there are at least key situations where radically different perspectives (hemispheres, sub-personalities, political parties) are used, to arrive at a decision that will make one side or the other "miserable" (or unrequited), to perform specialized action that emphasizes one of two competing, antagonistic skill sets.

Below is a list of what might be thought of as sub-personality characteristics of the brain hemispheres, as seen by split-brain studies done since the 1960's, and by many other studies since then, when subjects' hemispheres were interviewed separately. All the traits were discovered after the hemispheres were partially separated, either through surgery or through experiments that temporarily separate the two through freezing. In keeping with our purpose, the explanations for each of the personality traits are in terms of ideology. As this guide shows, our ideological selves seem to reflect a challenge basic to any human life, that goes far beyond politics: to resolve how we take care of important processes in our lives, while still making sure that we allow important exceptions to those processes to be considered and put into action when we should. Each hemisphere can be thought of as a specialist in one of these two conflicting goals. No one yet knows how we end up a whole person, combining any of our sub-personalities healthily. We don't know much about how the hemispheres inhibit each others' tendencies (though hemispheric inhibition is being increasingly highlighted as driving our behavior),[2] or how they "decide" to do something when they might arrive at different decisions alone. Fortunately, it's enough for us now to know that there are negotiations that occur on the way to a human being gaining an integrated perspective when making complicated decisions, and creating our common viewpoints.

The hemisphere's behaviors are described in contrast to what we would see in a normal person; the description is followed by an explanation of the ideological connection in parenthesis.

The Left Hemisphere

1. I make my life more consistent. I become more organized, maybe even a bit fixated on routine. (Conservatives are more dependent on "cognitive closure," or the desire for certainty or complete understanding. They're significantly higher in the personality Big 5 aspect called orderliness, which values consistency and routine.)

2. Legitimate, accepted examples and principles become more important, and I tend to use them more like gospel than I did with both hemispheres working. (Tradition, accepted hierarchy, and orderliness are all more associated with conservatism.)

3. Exceptions and twists on the situation feel less interesting and useful. I might ignore them, or actively oppose accounting for them (see #1.)

4. Decisions are easier, with less variables considered. (Valuing cognitive closure means being more motivated to arrive at decisions quickly. Studies have shown that, statistically, conservatives use fewer variables than liberals when making decisions.)

5. Prioritization is less fine-grained, tending more toward high and low values. (This is an aspect of cognitive closure, orderliness, and boundary-orientation, and is addressed as well in the guide through the notion of thick boundaries, which means to be more black-and-white in decision-making than one would if thinking in terms of shades of gray. Tending toward high and low values is a natural result of being relatively decisive.)

6. I feel more confident. In fact, check me out of the hospital now, please– I feel good, so I'm going to walk home on this one leg. (Conservative higher cognitive closure buys confidence about both oneself and situations: that is one of the major psychological reasons why one values cognitive closure. This is an "approach" characteristic, in

neurological terms, meaning that confidence allows the initial step to action, because of faith in capability; approach has been significantly correlated with left hemisphere brain activity in many studies.)

7. I feel happier, maybe even euphoric. (Conservatives have consistently been shown to be significantly happier than liberals, on average, though it does depend on the stability of circumstances. Happiness is also an approach-related emotion or feeling, correlated significantly with left hemisphere brain activity.)

8. I may be indifferent to my circumstances. (A release from right hemispheric connection results in less safety orientation, a decrease in a basic human value. The ideological considerations of this hemispheric trait are unclear; no evidence exists that conservatives are more or less safety-oriented than liberals, because conservative threat-sensitivity is not the same thing, as addressed in the guide; threat-sensitivity is a tactical orientation, driven by orderliness, to address safety concerns. This indifference to safety could occur because human safety orientation is driven more by the right-hemisphere's "avoid" nature. Some researchers characterize left-hemispheric indifference as "emotional placidity," as a result of the absence of right hemispheric input. It could also be that the euphoria and positive attitude characteristics overwhelm safety considerations within the left hemisphere itself.)

9. I miss more emotional signals in others. My speech has less nuance. I am more matter-of-fact. (Conservatives are not as sensitive emotionally toward others as liberals, as shown in multiple studies. In personality terms, this means that liberals are higher in the Big 5 aspect of compassion, a subset of agreeableness, and in openness, which partially involves sensitivity and interest in emotion. Liberal sensitivity may also reflect higher neuroticism, which can mean higher reactivity to situations in general, including emotional information. Not to say conservatives are relative automatons; in fact, on average, due to higher levels of politeness, they tend to be warmer and friendlier than liberals. But emotional detection and breadth is the province of openness and compassion, and involves much more negative than positive emotion, since emotional variation is much greater in negative than positive emotions.)

10. I make up explanations easily for what I see, and can convince myself that strange explanations make sense. (This is Dr. Michael Gazzaniga's "left-brain interpreter,"[3] and is evidence of being driven by a strong desire for cognitive closure. This also squares with higher observed cognitive bias levels in conservatives, because cognitive bias is essentially the process of convincing ourselves of inaccurate explanations. I believe it to be reflective of a healthy orientation toward approach, neurologically, meaning that inertia toward positive action is benefited through a strong

sense of causation, which allows action to occur more easily. The higher cognitive biases seen in conservatives in certain situations may be a down side of this strength, reflecting a lack of inertial dampening that might be provided by the more "avoid" oriented right hemisphere.)

11. I may anticipate the word, phrase, or idea you might say next, and already be deciding what I'm going to do based on that prediction. (From Dr. Kara Federmeier, though it's related to Gazzaniga's "left-brain interpreter" phenomenon, #10 above; this is more evidence of valuing and operating with strong cognitive closure requirements, higher approach valuation, and lower inertial dampening, all of which lead more easily to the higher cognitive bias levels seen in conservatives in some situations.)

12. I have a hard time following a story. If I'm asked to re-tell it, I mess up the order, clump parts of the story together oddly, and make it more abstract or generic.[4] (This may related to a strong tendency to abstract and categorize information helpfully, which drives orderliness. The right hemisphere appears to provide context for the implementation of order properly, and incorporate emotional information effectively in categorization.)

The Right Hemisphere

1. I may be anxious.[5] (Liberals have been shown to be significantly higher in the Big 5 trait of neuroticism, which includes negative reactivity to stimulus. In multiple Gallup polls, liberals were less than two-thirds as likely as conservatives to characterize their mental state as "excellent." This is almost certainly also relate to the loss of the major hemisphere's control of dominant-side physical control.)

2. I may be more pessimistic. (Again, this may be a partial result of higher neuroticism. Also, less supported explicitly by research, liberal's lower orderliness and lower politeness, from the Big 5 aspects, seem to make it less likely that they leverage the positive attitude possibilities of politeness and industriousness.)

3. I tend to treat even familiar situations as if they were new and unfamiliar. (From Dr. Colin DeYoung. Liberals are much higher in openness, making them much more oriented toward novelty. With lower orderliness, they value proven process or routine less, and are more likely to alter or replace processes than conservatives, more likely to re-engineer an existing process in favor of a novel approach. Test subjects tended to make mistakes over and over, and not be helped by correction. Many neuroscientists assert this as evidence that the right hemisphere anomaly detection and accurate processing mandates preclude systematic

pattern use, as a potential distorting mechanism for grasping reality– too much approach orientation, perhaps. A conjoined brain readily uses pattern processing on the left side.)

4. I have a tough time guessing consequences of events, or my actions. (Figuring out causes is a left hemisphere specialty, essentially the act of cognitive closure, or a tendency toward decision. Liberals have less of a tendency toward cognitive closure than conservatives. This is a great example of where an orientation toward achieving cognitive closure appears to be an advantage, or, better said, a requirement, in inference-making. One can go overboard and create causes or rationales where they don't belong, but the process of leaning into decision-making has to exist, as a fundamental aspect of approach behavior. This seems to indicate that there isn't a cognitive Maginot line between accurate closure and confabulation, but that it occurs along a kind of continuum along a desire toward closure, with dampening (in neurological terms, inhibitory) effects we're not sure of yet that affect the more "pure" process of cognitive closure.)

5. I recognize faces and other complex forms well[6] (This is the "gestalt" advantage, reflecting the right hemisphere connection with visual processing and the processing of individual instances. It fits with the superior emotional interpretation shown by liberals, primarily seen in facial expression studies, as a result of higher neuroticism, higher compassion, and greater openness.)

6. I'm pretty terrible at simple math and word logic (while the left hemisphere's capabilities are near-normal for whole persons. No direct connection to ideology; for instance, liberals are just as good or better at math and other logical efforts. Indirectly, though, I believe this distinction is telling, because the capability mirrors the *emphasis* of the left hemisphere and conservative preference for "local" abstraction, symbolic manipulation, order, and cognitive closure, instead of the right hemispheric emphasis on reading a particular case completely as a novel, unique experience, a "gestalt" with an emphasis on emotional content.)

7. I can't speak, and don't understand language well, but I'm better at interpreting and appreciating music, humor, body language, gestures, and facial expressions (Lack of language capability relates to the physical location of language processing on the left. Language is a direct extension of uniquely left hemispheric skills in abstraction, symbolic manipulation, and order, which are designed for an emphasis on cognitive closure, as opposed to right hemispheric goals such as unique interpretation of the "form" of the situation, and interpretation of emotional content. I believe liberal higher levels of compassion, more interest in emotional information via higher openness, and lower levels of orderliness are the

primary psychological manifestations of the differentiation between two interpretive models of the world: the language- or abstraction-centric, and the visual/immediate- or emotion-centric perspectives. Those overall perspective differences are what shake out as process versus exception in an ideological situation.)

There's clear evidence that the right hemisphere's role is more often and maybe typically unconscious;[7] that, for instance, it provides emotional "prosody" (subtlety) to language expression, even though it's not strong at language itself, injecting interpretation. We grasp the emotion in a face with little conscious processing involved. The left hemisphere is so clearly designed for much of the direct executive action on the world, much of which is overtly conscious, while the right, which is called the "minor" hemisphere in the literature, concerns itself more with qualitative aspects of perception and emotion. I believe that relationship differential to consciousness is also significant with respect to ideology, though I haven't addressed that directly in this work; a perspective that is more conscious is seemingly more oriented around the use of logic, but not in terms of "more logical," more in the sense that it enacts unconscious impulses using logic more aggressively as justification. The less conscious hemisphere seems more comfortable with less overarching logical scaffolding around decisions and actions; this might be thought of in terms of an emphasis on emotional and anomaly processing, as well as a less approach-driven perspective.

The ideological sub-personalities, then, in terms of the five "aspects" of the Big Five that have been reliably shown to be involved, and based on the above psychological results, are:

Liberal: High openness, Low orderliness, low politeness, high neuroticism, high compassion. I would add a *focus* on intellect that doesn't have a strong relative measurement differential, through high openness, per the strong connection between openness and intellect; the intellect is *enacted* differently through high openness.

Conservative: Low openness, high orderliness, high politeness, low neuroticism, low compassion. I would add a *focus* in industriousness, which doesn't have a strong relative measurement differential, through high orderliness, which *enacts* industriousness as its primary function.

Other than the focus points mentioned, this is what's found in individual psychology research, with all of it mirrored in the above patients' psychological results to more or less degree. The "focus" components with intellect and industriousness I've added as a result of qualitative research, and are only lightly supported by very recent quantitative research, and not at all by the split-brain work.

Note that "ideology," is an abused word, as covered in the Introduction and at some length in the Ideology Appendix. Now, though, we can at least define our poor version: for us here, ideology means the orientations that each of these types of people use in their lives, as indicated by the split-brain work and personality research. From my perspective, only a bare minority of the effects of ideology in this sense are political; its effects, as explained at length in this work, are mostly felt outside of politics, particularly socially.

In the spirit of keeping our levels of analysis straight, we should leave the neurological world behind with these findings now, and stick with personality as the expression of these antagonistic impulses. Doing that quickly reveals a primary line of differential: openness versus orderliness. These two are relatively highly negatively correlated for Big 5 constructs. Chapter two deals extensively with this natural personality conflict, along with some (minor) inroads into reconciliation and understanding.

Secondly, compassion, which probably stands in for a broader range of emotional processing and orientation differences. This is explored in Chapter 3 extensively, and plays out across wide swaths of the phenomenological world differential we see between the ideologies in exception-chasing such as victim protection, art, music. It can be thought of as extending openness, as well, either emphasis or de-emphasis.

Politeness naturally aligns with orderliness, in terms of efficiency (politeness is fundamentally efficient in social processes, and can be expected when focus is on industriousness). Neuroticism aligns with an emotion orientation. These two are explored to a lesser degree than the other three sub-personality aspects, because they're less telling, and seem complementary, rather than adding a great deal to the story themselves.

Now that these sub-personalities have been validated independently from the split-brain work, we can use them in their personality trait form to arrive at a better understanding of how naturally antagonistic these approaches are, and begin to explore the potential implications.

There's an interesting controversy in the literature about which hemisphere is "in charge." Michael Gazzaniga asserts that the left hemisphere has executive control, as does V.S. Ramachandran and others. This is contrasted by Iain McGilchrist's contention, following over two decades of psychological and neurological research, that the relatively unconscious right hemisphere is *normatively* (supposed to be) in charge, but that sociocultural conditions have resulted in the "emissary," or left hemisphere, usurping its role at various times in history (like ours).

My own perspectives is a combination; I don't see much difference in the two, since McGilchrist's emphasis on normatives, sociocultural aspects of individual psychology, and the collective unconscious isn't a concern for Ramachandran et al. Moment-by-moment executive control is clearly the province of the left hemisphere, which both camps almost completely agree on (note the dominant hemisphere's control of the dominant body side, and its control of language and many analytical functions). The right hemisphere's *influence* on that executive control is important to develop and support, in the sense that we should be able to balance many dichotomies like: approach vs avoid behaviors and traits; complex (avoid) vs simple (approach) emotion; gestalt versus piecemeal; inductive versus deductive; and orderliness versus openness.

McGilchrist's assertion that the right hemispheric perspective should coordinate and direct the operationally dominant hemisphere, the way a chief executive officer should direct a president, seems a philosophical assertion, not a physiological or even a psychological one. I'm not as anxious to mix is and ought-to-be as he, given my contrasting purpose here. It's especially problematic to do so in the context of this work, because embracing McGilchrist's position would suggest that a self-described liberal's orientation is that of the "master" hemisphere, and the conservative orientation is aligned with the "emissary" hemisphere that has usurped the master's will. That doesn't seem helpful, despite my liberal leanings, even if it is true in some ways. For one thing, asserting primacy doesn't provide any mechanism for it to occur; it provides nothing on the question of influence. Certainly, though, as McGilchrist lays out in detail, there is tremendous historical evidence in support of the notion of mechanistic, inhumane practices being improperly dominant, which, as he suggests, is a left-hemispheric abuse. In that most important way, I completely agree with McGilchrist.

We should keep in mind that hemispheric division is much broader in scope than this ideological dimension. The assertion here is both much more specific (to empirical ideological characteristics) and much coarser (pointing at a few broad, relatively low correlation connections between ideology and personality).

For our purposes, the more pertinent philosophical question is the practical notion of determining not who's the boss, but how these two antagonistic viewpoints can possibly work together for decision-making, framed primarily through openness versus orderliness, and secondarily through emotional characteristics. In that sense, the question of who's in charge is a straw man, the same way that a strong executive team emphasizes relative strengths and excellent communication, not the hierarchical particulars.

The neuroscientist Lisa Feldman Barrett likens the effort of a proper life to the Avengers taking on an evil foe, with our various thought types acting like superhero teammates, providing somewhat interchangeable strengths to the task of decision-making. In that model, there's no real leader, though, again, in an antagonistic model, something must win out or dominate at any given time, and we likely develop well-worn patterns for doing that. Dr. Barrett's claim of an utterly flexible, democratic process that balances internal forces dynamically and optimal, sounds reasonable in many situations, but it doesn't sound like any human being I know under stress; her model may be how the Avengers play penny-ante poker, but stress channels us into more trenchant patterns. Even so, Dr. Barrett's may be a better framing than trying to figure out who's the default boss, which is a coarse question. In a work designed to help liberals to understand and work well with conservatives, it doesn't do any good to know whether one is supposed to be in charge or not, especially if it's not clear what that means in a given situation.

There may be counter-evidence the initial studies and follow-on scientists missed; we may be painting the picture with too few colors, or misunderstanding the evidence, or cherry-picking. But that's always true of any set of psychological studies. Ideology doesn't have to have its stamp all over hemispheric differences, nor does it need to be a perfect fit. Our main purpose is to make a powerful case that ideology is here for only a few fundamental reasons, and we should pay attention to them.

The hemispheres also have many similarities and seeming redundancies. In this guide, we've shown extensively how we are cognitive misers, yet here we see evidence of what would appear to be quite expensive cognitive redundancies, as evidenced by the patients in the original split-brain studies, who were able to do many of the same tasks using either decoupled hemisphere's cognitive capabilities. One reason for that inefficiency may be how necessary it is to keep particular modules or sectors separated for decision-making or compare-and-contrast purposes. Redundancies may be necessary in the case of antagonistic viewpoints, to work off models that provide value through their fundamental separateness, or soup-to-nuts distinctiveness.

In any case, the robust capabilities, redundancies, and unintuitive interdependencies we see in the hemispheres are incredibly well-developed and complex. That can only be for essential reasons. If that wasn't the case– if they were just designed to work on everything together, or through tightly-coupled sharing of tasks– when the primary network between hemispheres was severed, a more integrated brain would've been reduced to uselessness, the same way any complicated software would collapse if data couldn't be shared between large portions of the program. Inherent in the high-level cognitive schema for humans, then, is a remarkable degree and mix of independence, dependence, and interdependence in these two clumps of modules–something more like how our two hands divvy up work, appropriately enough, not the two halves of a car engine. To violate a narrow view of cognitive efficiency so blatantly cannot be either accidental or ancillary.

Knowing that an argument is about a negotiation between a process and an exception is very powerful strategically. It can help us abandon trying to communicate the issue in our own terms, by convincing us how useless or worse that would be for an antagonistic viewpoint. It allows us to do our best to recognize and reframe for another person their take on their process or exception, which can help soften the edges of the argument and lead to breakthroughs, or increased tolerance. We can see why the arguments are built up the way they are, and which pieces are lynchpins. It lets us understand arguments as supportive of something usually largely hidden from our own perspective, that we can address more directly through both better education and better communication. That conflict is not based on unfocused ill will. Accepting the conflict as naturally and necessarily antagonistic forces the parties to admit that they should focus their respective communication efforts on the awkward, unnatural side of the argument that they aren't advocating for.

Most helpfully, it allows us to focus on personality as the tactics to express our faithfulness to either exceptions or processes, and to neglect the other. That provides a manageable, practical set of dimensions to the conflict, while allowing us an excuse to skirt morality as much as possible as we resolve conflicts.

APPENDIX B– IDEOLOGY

There may be a strongly inherited component to you being a liberal,[1] or a heavy influence from your fetal development, or childhood, or maybe you've been influenced greatly since then[2]. Everyone is a product of these major influences. But we tend to ignore that about ourselves. When we discuss subjects we care about, we usually convince ourselves that we're approaching the topic with a fresh, open mind, when we are doing no such thing. Like the ghost of Jacob Marley's clanking chains in "Ebenezer Scrooge," we drag our unseen genetic and personal histories with us into every conversation.

If our ideological variation results mostly from personality differences, neither liberals nor conservatives can possibly be the emissaries of a complete political Truth. The whole notion of a single political ideal is highly questionable. One group may be right most of the time, sure; or they may be right on certain subjects, or because of chance occurrences that ended up making them correct–or at least making them look correct, if you cross your eyes and tilt your head a little. But all the time? No way. I'm a dedicated liberal, but running as fast as you can with your one solution for mankind about anything at all– freedom, religion, democracy, even ways to achieve honesty or limit corruption– is highly suspect, solely because the complexities introduced through all these personality differences zinging around guarantee that you're wrong. So if you assume that you and your "team" have the only true grasp of all American political solutions, you have to fantasize that your team's personality type is the only one qualified for correct political thought; that with enough time and emphasis on their bad ideas, everyone would finally see that the other guys' ideas are poison. In other words, our society should ignore the people with important personality variations from ours. Which would imply a justification for some very big changes around here--so hear, hear! Due to their various unfathomable illogicisms, conservatives may stay citizens, but they are to give up their voting rights effective immediately, as well as their public offices. Here is a list of personality changes they'll need to accomplish prior to reinstatement into the democratic process, and a list of the liberal homes that will take in their children to raise them properly…congratulations to all! Let the healing of society begin.

The Secret Costs of Ideology

Liberals and conservatives rarely argue about actual, tangible differences. We **purposefully** remove politics from reality– lift it to the level of abstraction, to the level of principles, to design the correct approach toward Equality, or National Security, or Justice, or any number of other noble concepts. We do this abstraction to have patterns that can be useful across broad portions of reality, but they are such broad ideas that the distance from specifics builds inaccuracies into the process. We proceed enthusiastically anyway. We call our collection of beliefs about abstractions a political "ideology," because it's our collection of *ideas* that explain how things best work politically, from our personality's standpoint. As we build or adopt our ideology, many of us get our approach toward life and our personality all wrapped up in the ideas so thoroughly that there is often little difference between the strength of our political ideology and the strength of a faithful Christian's belief in their God.

The word "ideology" can refer to the manner of thinking of a group, social class, or individual. That's the definition I like– calm, measured, specific, neutral. No mention of truth. But that's the second dictionary definition. The first definition makes explicit that we tend to define ideology narrowly as *political* ideology, even though there are ideologies in most social and physical science fields, or groups of overarching ideas about how those fields work. In these other subjects, it is usually obvious to participants that an ideology does not refer to Truth with a capital T, but an accepted, tentative group of ideas. But because politics, like religion, is an expression of some of our most sacred personal values, lodged deep in our personalities, we naturally think of our ideology as Truth. In reality, **a political ideology is a loose, changing collection of useful ideas** that we develop as we go along, almost always with other like-minded people.

Ideology is a tool humans use to act out our *psychological essentialism*, which is a way we dumb down the world to be able to understand it. It's a vital tool we use as children to understand the world: we lump people and ideas together in vats, so that we can talk about them together. Saying "poor people," for example, or "brilliant," conjures in our mind an *essence* about people that we run with to decide truths, to categorize and reason. This may not be a terrible thing– after all, our minds are very limited, and we have to put things in such buckets to be able to talk about them at all. But we do it religiously, and take these essences way too seriously, long after when, as children, it helped us begin to make sense of the world.

For example, now that we've grown up, most of us have a sense that there have been many volumes written about what poor people are like,; that there's a whole set of social sciences that roil about on the subject, and argue, and admit that much that is basic about poor people– like how we become poor, or how we stop being poor, or how we stay healthy while poor, or how we help and hinder the poor– is a grand mix of clear, controversial, and mysterious among scholars. The same is also true about being lazy, which gets at part of what it means to be industrious, in personality terms, which, in turn, has puzzled and captivated scholars for hundreds of years. We clomp around in abstract reality with such ideas anyway, as if we were describing eating an apple.

One way of thinking about this is that we categorize the things around us, and use those categories to make decisions, instead of being more tentative, in a world that is more fluid and mushy in its relationships than we like to admit. Tentative is no fun for us humans. Worse: we usually see the categories as very different from each other (lazy versus hard-working), and we won't let things leave their categories in our minds (lazy people are just that way).

Another way of thinking about our essentialism is as stereotyping, which we know can be very good, if we're careful, but that we tend to overuse, or misuse.

Ideology is a perfect expression of our psychological essentialism, because: it's in the business of categorizing: the categories are usually seen as permanent and in opposition: and there's usually only two categories, which makes fights simple. And it's true that every principle of politics can be countered with at least one other principle that should get used in opposition part of the time, as we see with the pairs here:

Care for the poor	Personal Responsibility
Consumer Protection	Deregulation
Equality	Unlimited Opportunity
Transparency	Confidentiality
Peace	Security

There are many others, and even these can be varied greatly. This natural, healthy, somewhat-opposed set of abstractions, or principles, is how humans think, and reflects something fundamental and true about our world, as we explored in Chapter One, and in the Hemisphere Appendix.

All fine. But then we grab one "essence" or the other, and keep that frozen, simple category that we like away from the other, and emphasize their opposition as if we're talking about a football game. But a society that runs exclusively with either the left column or the right is a fundamentally dangerous society. That danger is the exact problem that separation of government powers, and other checks and balances mandated by the Constitution were designed to address. That's why when I hear conservatives talk about freedom, or a Marxist talk about revolution, I cringe; they almost always want to talk about exactly one side of something that's already way too crude as a two-sided affair.

Principles exist *in tension* with other principles. Every single principle listed above has aspects that any thinking political participant should consider. Because we are liberals, we tend to focus on the principles we know best, or that we seen beat down the most in our society from our standpoint. If you're like most active liberals, you are somewhat knowledgeable about the principles in the left column, and feel they are under-emphasized. You can address some of those points fairly well. But you are likely far worse at doing the same for the principles in the right column: even if you can, you will often do so with a short, vague sentence that has a comma and a 'but' in the middle, as in "Sure, deregulation can reduce cost and help business profit, but it usually leads to disaster because of greed or carelessness."

This is the "yeah but" treatment: it is an especially arrogant and dangerous habit because only the principles in the left column come naturally to us, so we stick with them almost exclusively. Yet we need liberals to also become more knowledgeable about the principles in the right column while we fight for principles in the left column. That way, the real issues that we know are there can be addressed at least a little bit by each of us, to allow for a powerful, well-informed, balanced argument on how competing principles co-exist.

Finding the correct tension between competing goals is the true task of the American political system. But here's the main complication: having an awareness of the importance of balance between competing principles doesn't at all mean you're a centrist, or a moderate– it doesn't mean every principle needs an equivalently loud voice at any given time. Centrists are not necessarily more useful than radicals on the left or reactionaries on the right; most people who consider themselves centrist or non-partisan aren't paying attention, and are using the word centrist like you or I would use the words lazy or inattentive, as in "I'm not taking a side, because I'm lazy."

Being truly balanced can look quite crazy to those around us. In 2011, the urge for balance prompted Tamchoe Sangpo and about 20 other Tibetan Buddhists to light themselves on fire publicly, because China violates human rights with totalitarian excess in their isolated country. They felt the need to highlight that lack of balance between principles so strongly that they gave up their lives, in a most painful way, just to potentially bring the world's attention to the problem. The need for balance also prompted the Boston Tea Party, an illegal, deceptive act of wanton destruction. My personal activism against our recent wars has no doubt appeared unbalanced, unpatriotic, or downright evil to many onlookers. Working to achieve a better balance between useful principles does not place one in the center of every argument, asking everyone to get -along, to give a little. There's plenty of that kind of work to do, of course--but for some, today may be a good day to die in the service of an ideal.

Recognizing balance as essential, as the goal, is only the first step toward achieving it: for a given person, there is a whole spectrum of possible appropriate actions. That's why the need to understand conservatives should have nothing to do with how leftist we are, and it's why being "influenced" by them, whatever that means, should not be about becoming moderate, or centrist, or agreeing or disagreeing with them. It's about other stuff: understanding their arguments; understanding the principles you're weaker at representing; incorporating their ideals as well as you can, given your own moral constraints; and figuring out their weaknesses, and what to do about them.

Let's take a concrete, small example from within a common, actual political conflict, as opposed to the faraway federal ones pundits fixate on. Liberals usually want everyone to have a fair chance to participate in society, while conservatives tend to be more focused on ensuring there are no unfair blocks to individual success. We typically view these two values as opposites. A battle between the haves and the have-nots. And though it's true that the two positions can clash, if that's all you see, you've settled for a simplistic viewpoint.

For example, a building regulation can be so expensive that it stops someone from opening a shop that would be a good addition to downtown. Now, that fact, in itself, doesn't tell you enough to decide whether the regulation should be enforced or not. Not really– it depends on the particular regulation, doesn't it? On the problems caused if it isn't enforced. That's true whether we're conservative or liberal– at least it should be. We should expect strong differences of opinion about, say, whether we are required to build a handicap ramp for business access that doubles our opening costs, as happened to a friend. Even bringing fire protection up to code can be controversial, if there's evidence that the extra expense is not that helpful, and the entrepreneur has to think seriously about whether or not they can afford to risk the business. So– there's a conflict based on principles, but it's a reasonable one to have, and looking into the conflict may help us arrive at the best outcome, by everyone paying close attention to the competing principles together.

There are many other times when there's virtually no real ideological conflict, only what appears to be one from one side or the other. A matter of bad management, or integrity, or bureaucracy, or even a simple error that causes injustice. For instance, after a longer delay than represented, the planning department rules that a door turns out to be 2" too skinny per the building code, and you are forced to delay your advertised grand opening and take on high unexpected costs (also a true story). That kind of unanticipated delay and risky expense shouldn't be fair, no matter what your ideology is. Or the planning commission approves using a building for public meetings or parties, when the last building inspection was clearly incomplete– the building's wiring was old and potentially dangerous. Again, ideology wasn't integrally involved: public safety was at stake, but too much focus on a particular good thing– having a local community gathering place– led to a lack of balance between a competing need for safety and unbiased due process.

Dr. Christian Duncker, perhaps the world's leading researcher on ideology, calls the abandonment of balance the core characteristic of ideology. We see things as a battle for our own sacred principles against wrong ideas. He has proposed a definition of ideology as a "system of ideas that rises from the explicit or implicit claim to **absolute Truth,"** and refers to our "deformed" consciousness that thinks all Truth about a particular situation can be captured by one set of principles,[3] or essences. When we take on the role of bearer of Truth, we become a bearer of inflexibility. Usually, we think that inflexibility is a small price to pay to get a handle on the Truth, but it is actually quite expensive. "Deformed" is an excellent choice of words to describe what ideology does to us: being principled but inflexible secretly deforms how we think, how narrowly we approach problems, and how poorly we perceive other people's real characteristics.

We're usually convinced that we need to believe in "the Truth" to be properly motivated. But a mere strong belief is enough to set the world on fire. After all, the two positions are **both** beliefs: one just happens to be masquerading as knowledge. It is this masquerade as unassailable Truth, this deformation, that makes all the difference. If you can let a doubt sneak in here or there, or get a slightly different perspective– and especially if you can see a way to satisfying competing goals without making a large sacrifice to your own– you may find better solutions to society's problems than the ones you had in mind.

If you are a normal liberal, you likely think we are mostly talking about conservatives when we talk about inflexible Bearers of Truth. But we're talking about you. We liberals have many sneaky ways of hiding our weaknesses around flexibility from ourselves. I assume you agree with me intellectually about the need for flexibility with competing principles, because I can't recall a liberal ever disagreeing with me about needing flexibility– we're proud of how flexible we are. Even so, in a little while you're going to get up and go right on doing what your conservative brethren do: without realizing it, you will keep those political ideas and tools of yours locked in the Truth circle, instead of moving them to the half-empty toolbox where they belong.

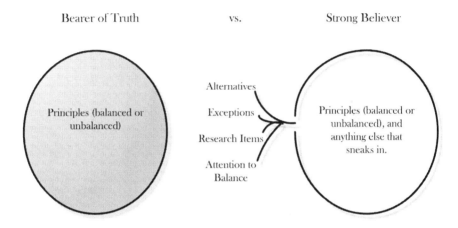

Bearer of Truth   vs.   Strong Believer

Principles (balanced or unbalanced)

Alternatives

Exceptions

Research Items

Attention to Balance

Principles (balanced or unbalanced), and anything else that sneaks in.

Why would you do such a narrow-minded thing? Well, because of one huge advantage: the closed circle on the left cannot be pierced with any ideas outside one's personal ideology. That's the point, actually, of being a political Truth Bearer: there's danger in taking input, because it can confuse you from doing what's right. It's not just that other ideas are dangerous, either: it wastes time, and makes you lose your focus on the best (true) way of acting. Everything you need to do anything politically is already inside the circle.

The opening in the circle on the right makes all the difference: it connects the outside with the inside. Borrowing a technique from the mathematics branch of topology, the opening makes the inside and outside "equal," or accessible to each other, no matter how small we consider the opening. There's no necessary difference between outside and inside the circle for a tiny idea, say, ambling around on your 2-D political reality: it can get in there, and it can leave. It's not like the closed, safe version on the left, which provides comfort and clarity: any idea, like an odorless, colorless gas, could potentially get in and muck things up for us, or help us out. We have to look at that list in the middle of the illustration and decide whether we **need** any of those things to make their way in, and whether we should **risk** getting other things in that we don't want. Sure, you say– of course I want the little hole there– to not have one would be inflexible, and call me what you will, I'm a liberal: I am not inflexible.

That is a response many conservative might see as foolish, because of the strengths their world outlook buys them. Because look at what happens to us as soon as we allow input to sneak across the membrane. The first thing that becomes obvious is that we're busy people, and can't let everything through for serious consideration, no matter what our belief system is– that's completely impractical. So we have some limits to set up– not one simple one, like "No dumb conservative points," which provides little guidance on how to strain ideas– probably a flurry of limits actually, ones like: "don't listen to Uncle Al, Ann Coulter, the preacher,…"; and "give Tim at work a listen when he's got a point that he seems to want to get across." Or we create a new routine for ourselves: we have a certain conservative commentator we start reading; we start reading the nutjob stuff mom is emailing us. We might pick up a Ronald Reagan biography, or select a few subjects to work on from the thousands we could research, as in 'I need to find out whether natural gas fracking problems are isolated incidents or a general rule'.

What a giant bother all that is! Wait– you were thinking that the little hole in your circle entails just talking with your friends in your celebrated, "open" liberal way about controversies? Pfft. Dop. That's inside-the-circle stuff; ideas and people you already accept as truth-saturated. We're talking about **real**, minor-league openness, as in considering letting into your sacred circle conservative (heretical, embarrassing, and maybe even immoral) possibilities, the kinds your friends might be horrified to hear you're considering. Ones that are against your principles, as in: you protested a war that seems as if it might've ended up working out well; or a certain kind of beloved tax might actually be a terrible idea; or an alternative energy subsidy you voted for has completely flopped because of dumb-dumb moves by your heroes, and maybe because the idea was just bad in the first place.

I know: horrible, unrealistic, risky stuff. You don't have to swallow that eventuality all at once now, though; I just wanted to introduce the idea. Let's move on.

After we've arranged for gatekeeping somehow to control as best we can what gets in, we now have to wade through the mostly-worthless ideas, exceptions, etc. that we let in for consideration, from that Reagan biography, say, alongside our sacred principles. This creates an enormous amount of extra pain for us. It's hard, annoying mental work, because you have to wade through half-arguments, incendiary statements, and statistics now, all thanks to that teeny hole in your worldview. Most of what we take in is said in an offensive or careless way, because that's the conservative way; you have to translate as you go along, just to see if there's any truth in it. And while you're doing all this, you do it fully aware that it's mostly wrong information, or at least misleading.

You're finally rewarded– you'll learn something practical from the other side– usually something small, not particularly helpful. A new outlook on sales taxes, say, or a new appreciation for how much welfare fraud is out there. Good for you– a minor concession in the interest of bipartisanship. Makes me feel a bit saintly when that happens. A month later, you find another good, minor conservative point, and add it to your worldview– another minor concession. This keeps happening, which seems like good news– but is it? Because, at some point, I guarantee you that you'll have to consider changing an actual principle, not just adding a new, minor one– and even *considering* doing that is quite arduous psychically. It makes you uncomfortable, and liberal or conservative, we're not fans of uncomfortable.

That's not the worst of it. Along about the 5th or 6th good little point, you buy into another one of the little exceptions to your viewpoint that came through the hole– and you discover quite late that it was wrong– you were fooled. It usually happens because everyone likes to tell exactly half the story, and you heard a good half-argument. You let in what turned out to be a germ instead of a nugget or harmless stupidity. Maybe it's affected you. Maybe some of those other little insights were also distortions. Now, you're *really* uncomfortable.

And why are you doing all this anyway, exactly? To get a few facts, at the price of being regularly duped dangerously by cleverly worded, well-lit Republican ideas? Don't be naïve– don't think that mistakes like that won't happen sometimes, thanks to this risky perforation in your worldview: it will. If you're open to input you'll make many mistakes, because there a whole asteroid field of energetic, distorting ideas out there desperately trying to get through to you through that hole.

Is this openness really worth that risk? You've been agreeing a little with people you feel uncomfortable with generally, people who argue bitterly with your friends. This is not the political experience you enjoy. You like putting your shoulder to the wheel with the good guys, against bad guys. Sacrificing that, in itself, is quite a price to pay– but now, this dribble of mistakes calls the whole business suddenly into question. Maybe you should close the little hole down, for at least awhile. Take a break. Reassess.

(The whole time this business of yours with a hole is going on, the Truth Bearer within is muttering over and over, in a vaguely scriptural tone, "this hole maketh us impure; yea, we wander in the wilderness and wasteth time, and just in general becometh less and less useful and more and more confused, because of this compromise in integrity, this hole that lets my lovely ideology be tainted with all this deceptive, extraneous information which, behold, is hella unpopular with my friends, full of bias, and mostly annoyingly stupid.")

So– inject a bunch of on-the-other-hands, unpopular ideas, and mostly-wrong pundit ideas from conservatism into your life? Where people might see? You know you're going to be right at least 99% of the time by just following your principles. The little bit of detail you'd miss with that hole being closed has to be inconsequential, right?

So I'm calling your bluff. If you **actually** agree with me about principles in tension– if you're not interested in just stopping where most of us liberals do, at the nod-in-agreement stage: great! Understanding and working with conservatives will happen much better, and more naturally, as part of working to understand, no matter what our political beliefs are, that our own ideology is a half-empty box of tools. Not an effulgent Ark of The Covenant, cradling glowing documents that translate God's sacred wishes, or Gaia's, or anybody else's.

My sympathies. And good luck.

APPENDIX C–
TEN CONSERVATIVE PRINCIPLES
By Russell Kirk

Adapted from *The Politics of Prudence* (ISI Books, 1993). Copyright ©
1993 by Russell Kirk. Used by permission of Annette Kirk and the Estate
of Russell Kirk, with no commentary.

Being neither a religion nor an ideology, the body of opinion termed
conservatism possesses no Holy Writ and no Das Kapital to provide
dogmata. So far as it is possible to determine what conservatives believe,
the first principles of the conservative persuasion are derived from what
leading conservative writers and public men have professed during the
past two centuries. After some introductory remarks on this general
theme, I will proceed to list ten such conservative principles.

Perhaps it would be well, most of the time, to use this word
"conservative" as an adjective chiefly. For there exists no Model
Conservative, and conservatism is the negation of ideology: it is a state of
mind, a type of character, a way of looking at the civil social order.

The attitude we call conservatism is sustained by a body of sentiments,
rather than by a system of ideological dogmata. It is almost true that a
conservative may be defined as a person who thinks himself such. The
conservative movement or body of opinion can accommodate a
considerable diversity of views on a good many subjects, there being no
Test Act or Thirty-Nine Articles of the conservative creed.

In essence, the conservative person is simply one who finds the
permanent things more pleasing than Chaos and Old Night. (Yet
conservatives know, with Burke, that healthy "change is the means of our
preservation.") A people's historic continuity of experience, says the
conservative, offers a guide to policy far better than the abstract designs
of coffee-house philosophers. But of course there is more to the
conservative persuasion than this general attitude.

It is not possible to draw up a neat catalogue of conservatives'
convictions; nevertheless, I offer you, summarily, ten general principles; it
seems safe to say that most conservatives would subscribe to most of these
maxims. In various editions of my book The Conservative Mind I have
listed certain canons of conservative thought—the list differing somewhat
from edition to edition; in my anthology The Portable Conservative
Reader I offer variations upon this theme. Now I present to you a
summary of conservative assumptions differing somewhat from my
canons in those two books of mine. In fine, the diversity of ways in which

conservative views may find expression is itself proof that conservatism is no fixed ideology. What particular principles conservatives emphasize during any given time will vary with the circumstances and necessities of that era. The following ten articles of belief reflect the emphases of conservatives in America nowadays.

First, the conservative believes that there exists an enduring moral order. That order is made for man, and man is made for it: human nature is a constant, and moral truths are permanent.

This word order signifies harmony. There are two aspects or types of order: the inner order of the soul, and the outer order of the commonwealth. Twenty-five centuries ago, Plato taught this doctrine, but even the educated nowadays find it difficult to understand. The problem of order has been a principal concern of conservatives ever since conservative became a term of politics.

Our twentieth-century world has experienced the hideous consequences of the collapse of belief in a moral order. Like the atrocities and disasters of Greece in the fifth century before Christ, the ruin of great nations in our century shows us the pit into which fall societies that mistake clever self-interest, or ingenious social controls, for pleasing alternatives to an oldfangled moral order.

It has been said by liberal intellectuals that the conservative believes all social questions, at heart, to be questions of private morality. Properly understood, this statement is quite true. A society in which men and women are governed by belief in an enduring moral order, by a strong sense of right and wrong, by personal convictions about justice and honor, will be a good society—whatever political machinery it may utilize; while a society in which men and women are morally adrift, ignorant of norms, and intent chiefly upon gratification of appetites, will be a bad society—no matter how many people vote and no matter how liberal its formal constitution may be.

Second, the conservative adheres to custom, convention, and continuity. It is old custom that enables people to live together peaceably; the destroyers of custom demolish more than they know or desire. It is through convention—a word much abused in our time—that we contrive to avoid perpetual disputes about rights and duties: law at base is a body of conventions. Continuity is the means of linking generation to generation; it matters as much for society as it does for the individual; without it, life is meaningless. When successful revolutionaries have effaced old customs, derided old conventions, and broken the continuity of social institutions—why, presently they discover the necessity of establishing fresh customs, conventions, and continuity; but that process is painful and slow; and the new social order that eventually emerges may be much inferior to the old order that radicals overthrew in their zeal for the Earthly Paradise.

Conservatives are champions of custom, convention, and continuity because they prefer the devil they know to the devil they don't know. Order and justice and freedom, they believe, are the artificial products of a long social experience, the result of centuries of trial and reflection and sacrifice. Thus the body social is a kind of spiritual corporation, comparable to the church; it may even be called a community of souls. Human society is no machine, to be treated mechanically. The continuity, the life-blood, of a society must not be interrupted. Burke's reminder of the necessity for prudent change is in the mind of the conservative. But necessary change, conservatives argue, ought to be gradual and discriminatory, never unfixing old interests at once.

Third, conservatives believe in what may be called the principle of prescription. Conservatives sense that modern people are dwarfs on the shoulders of giants, able to see farther than their ancestors only because of the great stature of those who have preceded us in time. Therefore conservatives very often emphasize the importance of prescription—that is, of things established by immemorial usage, so that the mind of man runneth not to the contrary. There exist rights of which the chief sanction is their antiquity—including rights to property, often. Similarly, our morals are prescriptive in great part. Conservatives argue that we are unlikely, we moderns, to make any brave new discoveries in morals or politics or taste. It is perilous to weigh every passing issue on the basis of private judgment and private rationality. The individual is foolish, but the species is wise, Burke declared. In politics we do well to abide by precedent and precept and even prejudice, for the great mysterious incorporation of the human race has acquired a prescriptive wisdom far greater than any man's petty private rationality.

Fourth, conservatives are guided by their principle of prudence. Burke agrees with Plato that in the statesman, prudence is chief among virtues. Any public measure ought to be judged by its probable long-run consequences, not merely by temporary advantage or popularity. Liberals and radicals, the conservative says, are imprudent: for they dash at their objectives without giving much heed to the risk of new abuses worse than the evils they hope to sweep away. As John Randolph of Roanoke put it, Providence moves slowly, but the devil always hurries. Human society being complex, remedies cannot be simple if they are to be efficacious. The conservative declares that he acts only after sufficient reflection, having weighed the consequences. Sudden and slashing reforms are as perilous as sudden and slashing surgery.

Fifth, conservatives pay attention to the principle of variety. They feel affection for the proliferating intricacy of long-established social institutions and modes of life, as distinguished from the narrowing uniformity and deadening egalitarianism of radical systems. For the preservation of a healthy diversity in any civilization, there must survive orders and classes, differences in material condition, and many sorts of inequality. The only true forms of equality are equality at the Last Judgment and equality before a just court of law; all other attempts at levelling must lead, at best, to social stagnation. Society requires honest and able leadership; and if natural and institutional differences are destroyed, presently some tyrant or host of squalid oligarchs will create new forms of inequality.

Sixth, conservatives are chastened by their principle of imperfectability. Human nature suffers irremediably from certain grave faults, the conservatives know. Man being imperfect, no perfect social order ever can be created. Because of human restlessness, mankind would grow rebellious under any utopian domination, and would break out once more in violent discontent—or else expire of boredom. To seek for utopia is to end in disaster, the conservative says: we are not made for perfect things. All that we reasonably can expect is a tolerably ordered, just, and free society, in which some evils, maladjustments, and suffering will continue to lurk. By proper attention to prudent reform, we may preserve and improve this tolerable order. But if the old institutional and moral safeguards of a nation are neglected, then the anarchic impulse in humankind breaks loose: "the ceremony of innocence is drowned." The ideologues who promise the perfection of man and society have converted a great part of the twentieth-century world into a terrestrial hell.

Seventh, conservatives are persuaded that freedom and property are closely linked. Separate property from private possession, and Leviathan becomes master of all. Upon the foundation of private property, great civilizations are built. The more widespread is the possession of private property, the more stable and productive is a commonwealth. Economic levelling, conservatives maintain, is not economic progress. Getting and spending are not the chief aims of human existence; but a sound economic basis for the person, the family, and the commonwealth is much to be desired.

Sir Henry Maine, in his Village Communities, puts strongly the case for private property, as distinguished from communal property: "Nobody is at liberty to attack several property and to say at the same time that he values civilization. The history of the two cannot be disentangled." For the institution of several property—that is, private property—has been a powerful instrument for teaching men and women responsibility, for

providing motives to integrity, for supporting general culture, for raising
mankind above the level of mere drudgery, for affording leisure to think
and freedom to act. To be able to retain the fruits of one's labor; to be
able to see one's work made permanent; to be able to bequeath one's
property to one's posterity; to be able to rise from the natural condition
of grinding poverty to the security of enduring accomplishment; to have
something that is really one's own—these are advantages difficult to
deny. The conservative acknowledges that the possession of property
fixes certain duties upon the possessor; he accepts those moral and legal
obligations cheerfully.

Eighth, conservatives uphold voluntary community, quite as they
oppose involuntary collectivism. Although Americans have been attached
strongly to privacy and private rights, they also have been a people
conspicuous for a successful spirit of community. In a genuine
community, the decisions most directly affecting the lives of citizens are
made locally and voluntarily. Some of these functions are carried out by
local political bodies, others by private associations: so long as they are
kept local, and are marked by the general agreement of those affected,
they constitute healthy community. But when these functions pass by
default or usurpation to centralized authority, then community is in
serious danger. Whatever is beneficent and prudent in modern
democracy is made possible through cooperative volition. If, then, in the
name of an abstract Democracy, the functions of community are
transferred to distant political direction—why, real government by the
consent of the governed gives way to a standardizing process hostile to
freedom and human dignity.

For a nation is no stronger than the numerous little communities of
which it is composed. A central administration, or a corps of select
managers and civil servants, however well intentioned and well trained,
cannot confer justice and prosperity and tranquility upon a mass of men
and women deprived of their old responsibilities. That experiment has
been made before; and it has been disastrous. It is the performance of our
duties in community that teaches us prudence and efficiency and charity.

Ninth, the conservative perceives the need for prudent restraints upon
power and upon human passions. Politically speaking, power is the ability
to do as one likes, regardless of the wills of one's fellows. A state in which
an individual or a small group are able to dominate the wills of their
fellows without check is a despotism, whether it is called monarchical or
aristocratic or democratic. When every person claims to be a power unto
himself, then society falls into anarchy. Anarchy never lasts long, being
intolerable for everyone, and contrary to the ineluctable fact that some
persons are more strong and more clever than their neighbors. To

anarchy there succeeds tyranny or oligarchy, in which power is monopolized by a very few.

The conservative endeavors to so limit and balance political power that anarchy or tyranny may not arise. In every age, nevertheless, men and women are tempted to overthrow the limitations upon power, for the sake of some fancied temporary advantage. It is characteristic of the radical that he thinks of power as a force for good—so long as the power falls into his hands. In the name of liberty, the French and Russian revolutionaries abolished the old restraints upon power; but power cannot be abolished; it always finds its way into someone's hands. That power which the revolutionaries had thought oppressive in the hands of the old regime became many times as tyrannical in the hands of the radical new masters of the state.

Knowing human nature for a mixture of good and evil, the conservative does not put his trust in mere benevolence. Constitutional restrictions, political checks and balances, adequate enforcement of the laws, the old intricate web of restraints upon will and appetite—these the conservative approves as instruments of freedom and order. A just government maintains a healthy tension between the claims of authority and the claims of liberty.

Tenth, the thinking conservative understands that permanence and change must be recognized and reconciled in a vigorous society. The conservative is not opposed to social improvement, although he doubts whether there is any such force as a mystical Progress, with a Roman P, at work in the world. When a society is progressing in some respects, usually it is declining in other respects. The conservative knows that any healthy society is influenced by two forces, which Samuel Taylor Coleridge called its Permanence and its Progression. The Permanence of a society is formed by those enduring interests and convictions that gives us stability and continuity; without that Permanence, the fountains of the great deep are broken up, society slipping into anarchy. The Progression in a society is that spirit and that body of talents which urge us on to prudent reform and improvement; without that Progression, a people stagnate.

Therefore the intelligent conservative endeavors to reconcile the claims of Permanence and the claims of Progression. He thinks that the liberal and the radical, blind to the just claims of Permanence, would endanger the heritage bequeathed to us, in an endeavor to hurry us into some dubious Terrestrial Paradise. The conservative, in short, favors reasoned and temperate progress; he is opposed to the cult of Progress, whose votaries believe that everything new necessarily is superior to everything old.

Change is essential to the body social, the conservative reasons, just as it is essential to the human body. A body that has ceased to renew itself has begun to die. But if that body is to be vigorous, the change must occur in a regular manner, harmonizing with the form and nature of that body; otherwise change produces a monstrous growth, a cancer, which devours its host. The conservative takes care that nothing in a society should ever be wholly old, and that nothing should ever be wholly new. This is the means of the conservation of a nation, quite as it is the means of conservation of a living organism. Just how much change a society requires, and what sort of change, depend upon the circumstances of an age and a nation.

Such, then, are ten principles that have loomed large during the two centuries of modern conservative thought. Other principles of equal importance might have been discussed here: the conservative understanding of justice, for one, or the conservative view of education. But such subjects, time running on, I must leave to your private investigation.

The great line of demarcation in modern politics, Eric Voegelin used to point out, is not a division between liberals on one side and totalitarians on the other. No, on one side of that line are all those men and women who fancy that the temporal order is the only order, and that material needs are their only needs, and that they may do as they like with the human patrimony. On the other side of that line are all those people who recognize an enduring moral order in the universe, a constant human nature, and high duties toward the order spiritual and the order temporal.

APPENDIX D–
COMMON COGNITIVE BIASES

A sample of common cognitive biases and heuristics (decision-making shortcuts) allowed by the "gateway" biases, the objectivity bias (or assumption) and the fundamental attribution error. Some of these biases are involved for almost all of us in our everyday lives. None of these get to be skipped by being smart or alert; some of them are made worse by being smart, and a few are made much worse with intelligence (think of being smart as being a way to be able to figure out all kinds of optional, clever tricks to avoid reality to your short-term advantage, or to find ways to express your motivated reasoning). They should give you a sense of how removed from actual reality we try to be in our lives, thanks to:

- our limited minds (cognitive misers),
- our desire for certainty and simplicity (motivated reasoning), and
- our inability to ever share the minds of others.

You can't rid yourself of these biases; you can only work to reduce their effect, by being conscious you have them, and by learning to recognize them, mostly through focusing on controlling the gateway biases we'll cover, and by listening to other people use them. Hopefully, as you read on, you can see these in yourself: you'll certainly be able to see them in others.

Some of Your Social/Political Biases

False Consensus Bias– The tendency to think your belief is more common than it is, or that there is a consensus on your belief.

Information Bias– Assuming the other guy has bad information, so that there will be easy persuasion to your side when all facts are included.

Representative Heuristic– If something (person, situation) is similar to one we know of, it's thought of as just like the one we know.

Authority Figure Bias– If a respected authority figure (parent, pundit, political or religious leader) believes it, it must be true. And the opposite: if Jerry Falwell or Ann Coulter said it, it must be false. Unless they agree with you, in which case you can say, "Even Ann Coulter knows the war in Afghanistan was a mistake!"

Availability Heuristic– We think something is more likely if it's easy to think of an example (because it's vivid, or dramatic, or has to do with a friend, or we saw it on TV). The latest of several examples is usually the most vivid, too, so we depend on the latest information this way.

Disinterested Judge Bias– You believe that a neutral 3rd party would side with you.

Hostile Media Bias– The belief that the media purposely spread lies about the truth, infecting innocent people's opinions with falsehood.

Personal Flaw Bias– When someone has personal flaws that bother you, everything they say about anything is probably wrong.

Introspection Bias– "I'm being introspective, so I can't be biased." (studies show that belief about one's introspection has no affect on how biased we are).

Self-interest Bias– If it does you good to believe something, you underestimate how important that belief is to you, as your unconscious mind grinds away in the background, getting you to vote hard for what's good for you.

Hindsight Bias– gives you the belief that an appropriate decision (aligned with your belief) was obvious at the time, when it was not.

Planning Fallacy– The belief that a person or a group can or will accomplish a task much more easily than they can. Studies show that tasks usually take longer than the worst-case estimate.

The Halo Effect– Seeing a person as beautiful makes us think they're intelligent; if something's large, we think it's heavy; if it's heavy, we think it's important.

Trait Ascription Bias– You see yourself as more variable in actions, personality and mood than others (it helps us be prejudiced to think of people as simple and predictable).

Nonconscious Mimicry– Imitating the behavior or beliefs of others that we admire. Less well known: we imitate those who have bested us or been shown to be superior, whether we like them or not.

External Agency Bias– If a negative event happens, it is caused by something outside of us. If it is positive, we caused it.

Conjunction Fallacy– You view a scenario described with a great deal of detail as more likely than the same thing with less detail. This bias is used by salespeople, and in politics. Think of the power of story.

Thin Slicing– the tendency to make decisions extremely quickly based on very limited, even unknown (subconscious) information. Studies have shown this to be surprisingly accurate, but only under certain conditions.

Base Rate Fallacy– Making assumptions based on common math mistakes, where the proper answer is a little more complicated to figure out, and way different.

Overconfidence Effect– You are much more confident that you are accurate than you actually are. Especially if you're male.

OK. I'm going to stop now, a little early. That was a lot to handle about yourself, when you're so open, so sensitive and caring. You should do what I did when I found all this out– get a massage, and do a little retail therapy. Chant up your self-worth in the mirror.

Hopefully, you can recognize examples of these in yourself and others, so that these feel alive and authentic. If not, you might want to get yourself checked out, because you're probably conservative…kidding, kidding.

INDEX

NOTES

Introduction

[1] There turned out to be some political psychology involved, but it mostly entailed evolutionary psychology, cultural anthropology, general social psychology, personality neuroscience, cognitive neuroscience, linguistics, philosophy, evolutionary genetics, analytical psychology, communication theory, marketing/sales, theater, information theory, and mediation studies.

[2] As in many fields, political ideology can be modeled as one kind of person (we're all just more or less conservative), two kinds (liberal/conservative), three kinds (liberal/social conservative/economic conservative), four (social liberal/conservative and economic liberal/conservative), and maybe more. As quality analysis includes more distinct kinds of people (or, in math terms, variables), it becomes a better model, more and more useful, until we've found all the right ones (which we probably haven't yet). But even the simplest model explains important parts of what's going on; and sometimes, the most important lessons are provided best by the simplest models.

[3] This means, only somewhat subjectively, that the studies or surveys were careful and large. Depending on the context, "large" may mean as few as 190 subjects, or 160,000. If they were small studies, which are common in neurological work, the study quality is evaluated carefully, because neurology is full of goofy study design and small samples, a deadly combination. People tend to construct better studies when they're larger, because they're expensive and difficult, and there are usually more experts involved in the construction: it's not one professor or institute man, making a favorite point. "Careful" means that, as a quantitative and liberal arts-educated fellow, schooled in both qualitative and quantitative analysis, I respected the study as well controlled and well planned.

[4] Evaluating study quality is an important aspect of any graduate-level science study, and it is not a trivial skill, particularly in more complex and sociological settings. I had assistance by independent scientists in the field occasionally to pass judgment on study design, to supplement my own review. Typically, in rejected studies the sample sizes were small. Other studies were poorly designed, poorly executed, or containing conclusions designed more for dissemination than explanation. I used very little foundation/institute research, because most of it was either bad science or obviously grinding an axe. If any basic information about the study like demographics, location, or sample size were not publicized, it was not used, if for no other reason that basic factors being overlooked in the writeup is, in my experience, a strong signal of bad science.

Another common weakness of sociological studies is the tendency to skew the sample population with uncontrolled variance, for convenience– to build in detailed forms of biases by using, say, a Mongol horde of 1) 21 year old 2) college students, ones that 3) complete the study for money as a funding strategy for the Friday night frat party, all of whom were apprised of the study through ads in a 4) liberal college's 5) social sciences building, or from their 6) sociology friends who just love the 7) great professor and/or his 8) cute assistant. These kind of biases, if uncontrolled for, are a great way to show, as has been done, that all liberals are smarter and dumber, better and worse informed, nicer or meaner, with both larger and smaller body and brain parts than conservatives, to a 95% confidence level. QED.

5 Lee Jussim, Jarret T. Crawford, Rachel S. Rubinstein, "Stereotype (In)Accuracy in Perceptions of Groups and Individuals," Current Directions in Psychological Science, Vol. 24(6) 490-497, 2015.
6 Robert Frost, "There are Roughly Zones," in *A Further Range*, Holt, 1936.

Chapter 1

1 Carney, C., Jost, J., Potter, J, The Secret Lives of Liberals and Conservatives: Personality Profiles, Interaction Styles, and the Things They Leave Behind, Political Psychology, Vol. 29, No. 6, 2008, pg. 807-840. Sports data from the General Social Survey 1993-1996 (Sports Illustrated, by the way, did a 2007 survey of race car drivers that showed 59% were Republicans, and not a single one was a Democrat). Dogs and cats info from neuropolitics.org, as reported by the Washington Monthly 3/5/2006; the olfactory survey is a good, large sample one, albeit done over the internet, and was also conducted by neuropolitics.org, who have done a good job of presenting serious, interesting science for many years now along these lines. Conservatives used sports teams to decide where to live in a 2,000+ person survey conducted by the team at yourmorals.org: it wasn't a big factor for them—but the liberals couldn't have cared less about the local teams. Fast food statistic from hunch.org, from a very large sample.
2 See *The Righteous Mind: Why Good People are Divided by Politics and Religion*, Jonathan Haidt, 2012, Pantheon.
3 Seth C. McKee, Jeremy M. Teigen, "Probing the reds and blues: Sectionalism and voter location in the 2000 and 2004 U. S. presidential elections," Political Geography 28 (2009) 484–495. See also Ian McDonald, "Migration, Polarization, and Sorting in the Congressional Electorate". American Politics Research May 2011. v.39(3). pp. 512-533.
4 Motyl, M., Iyer, R., Oishi, S., Travalter, S, and Nosek, B., "How Ideological Migration Geographically Segregates and Polarizes Groups, 10/7/12, available at SSRN.com
5 Andrew Luttrell, Richard E. Petty, Pablo Briñol, Benjamin C. Wagner, "Making it moral: Merely labeling an attitude as moral increases its strength," Journal of Experimental Social Psychology, Volume 65, July 2016, Pages 82–93.
6 This work is fiercely American, for two reasons. First, although liberal and conservative differences exist in virtually every society, the cultural differences play out enormously in how those underlying emphases are expressed. Secondly, we're going to be looking at almost exclusively American research; much of it doesn't translate cleanly to other countries. Though Euro types will see many parallels, fewer will be obvious in the Middle East, or the Far East.
7 Not every statement of this kind is footnoted: if it's not a very well-known effect or tendency, there'll be a reference in the notes. If it's a well-known tendency or effect, and there's no reference, it generally means you should be able to look it up and see detail on the web without being a genius.
8 Lee Jussim, Jarret T. Crawford, Rachel S. Rubinstein, Stereotype (In)Accuracy in Perceptions of Groups and Individuals, Current Directions in Psychological Science, Vol. 24(6) 490-497, 2015.
9 Joseph B. Hellige, Hemispheric Asymmetry: What's Right and What's Left,, Harvard University Press, 1993.
10 Timothy Crow, attr. By Iain McGilchrist in "The Master and his Emissary".
11 Steven M. Miller, Guang B. Liu, Trung T. Ngo, Greg Hooper, Stephan Riek, Richard G. Carson, John D. Pettigrew, "Interhemispheric switching mediates perceptual rivalry," Current Biology 10:383-392 2000
12 Elkhonon Goldberg, "The Wisdom Paradox: How Your Mind Can Grow Stronger As

Your Brain Grows Older,*" NY: Penguin, 2005. The tendency toward becoming more conservative as one grows older, which is a long-known phenomenon in social science, probably reflects this statistical migration of hemispheric dependence, perhaps related to a shift in dependence from fluid or innate intelligence to crystallized intelligence, the latter of which is more like what you've put in your hard drive and use from experience.
[13] See the Brain Hemispheres Appendix for more detailed information, including an expanded set of ideological connections from more recent research.
[14] Marinsek, N, Turner, BO, Gazzaniga, M., Miller MB., "Divergent hemispheric reasoning strategies: reducing uncertainty versus resolving inconsistency." *Frontiers in Human Neuroscience.* 8: 839.
[15] To see a detailed description, along with a great deal of other insights into the machinery of our perception and how we use it, see VS Ramachandran, The Evolutionary Biology of Self-Deception, Laughter, Dreaming and Depression: Some Clues from Anasognosia, Medical Hypotheses (1996), 47, 347-362.
[16] In the context of defense mechanisms, he went on to say, « Of course, when I speak of a 'general' in the left hemisphere or that the right hemisphere is required for "paradigm shifts," I am being strictly metaphorical. But the use of metaphors is quite permissible in a field such as ours, that is still in its infancy, so long as one recognizes their tentative status and does not take them too literally. After all, even the notion of a gene or an electron as a 'particle' was once a metaphor, useful only as an approximation until more accurate accounts could be formulated. What is exciting to me, however, is that one can even begin to experimentally approach such questions as self-deception or Freudian psychology at a neurological level."
[17] Another very useful metaphor of brain hemispheres, by the neuroscientist and psychiatrist Iain McGilchrist, has the conservative side as the "emissary" to the "master" hemisphere. Not as cool for them.
[18] A minority of left-handers have these hemispherical relationships flipped, and very few right-handers. But the hemispheric specialization still seems to occur similarly. Hemispheric talk of the left doing this and the right doing that is heavily dumbed-down from the rather snarly statistical results, because brains are incredibly varied in structure. Virtually all the statements about the brain in this chapter are stereotypes, statistical composites.
[19] Russell Kirk's "Ten Conservative Principles," which is in the Appendix of the same name, with kind permission from Mrs. Kirk and kirkcenter.org.
[20] Try not to think in terms of actual brain processing as we talk about hemispheric this-and-that. For instance, if you could miraculously track brain processing accurately and in real-time (which is very difficult), you'd see very little correlation between novelty and the right hemisphere, even though that's a very well-founded connection, because only the parts of novelty related to the philosophical idea of novelty, or the initiations of processing it, originate there. Processing to get anything done might be spread anywhere in the brain, especially when one considers that much of what's going on in the brain electrically is inhibitory, i.e., activity to get highly specific circuits and processes shut down or de-emphasized. The split-brain studies this guide is based on were psychological, not neurological studies. The evidence is solely based on clues from behavior. For our purposes, actual brain processing is irrelevant.
[21] Politico.com, 6/21/16, "House GOP dodges vote to block Harriet Tubman from $20 Bill"
[22] Raymonde Carroll, *Cultural Misunderstandings: The French-American Experience*, University of Chicago Press, 1990.

23 We'll be discussing *instrumental* values, which are how we want to behave, not *terminal* values, which are what we are trying to achieve in life. We focus this way because the analysis is simpler and ties back directly to our fundamental hemispheric perspectives. It's not always best to ignore terminal values, but we get to them well enough through our later discussion of personality and morality.

24 This list is from the hemispheric studies, but it was also necessary to conform with an amalgam of several different political psychological theories, combined with my own qualitative research with conservatives in the Midwest and South. It is too early in political psychology to posit a final, clear model of conservative psychology, as the great minds of the effort haven't resolved on one yet; but they're overlapping and converging. I've tried to do a compromise between what's out there as of October, 2016 and my own research, but this list is best thought of as a practical combination of strategic (safety, order, certainty) and more tactical (strong boundaries, consistency, simplicity, hierarchy, loyalty) values/goals, for the practical purpose of understanding conservative behavior. The first of the theories used is from applicable parts of Schwartz's 10 universal human values theory; next is Xu et al's DiGI theory of political ideology formation, which speaks in terms of goals instead of values, and extends the "conservatism" Schwartz values somewhat (X.Xu, J.E. Plaks, J. Peterson, "From Dispositions to Goals to Ideology: Toward a Synthesis of Personality and Social Psychological Approaches to Political Orientation," Social and Political Psychology Compass 10/5, 2016, pp 267-280); and finally, the work of Gary Lewis and Timothy Bates on personality and ideology, in the form of moral foundation theory's "binding foundations" mediating the relationship between ideology and personality (G.J. Lewis, T.C. Bates, "How the Personality System Allows Basic Traits to Influence Politics Via Characteristic Moral Adaptations," British Journal of Psychology, August 2011, pp. 546-558.) My own additions are the integration of boundaries as the central tactic of orderliness, and the modest use of boundary theory from psychoanalysis: this also allows dragging simplicity in along with the other values/goals, as a fallout of boundary-based valuation of simplicity, via the concomitant goal of breaking down categories into discrete "pails" that are simple, or unitary.

25 Safety isn't seen as a distinguishing high relative value of the left hemisphere; it is the only value listed that didn't arise directly out of observed left hemisphere values. The other two values that are part of Conservation in the Theory of Basic Values can be easily seen in the hemispheric studies as left-side values. Security is a conservative value because it's a human one. The isolated left hemisphere is noted for its lack of care. It's not clear why safety isn't revealed in the left hemisphere like the other values, though a sense of safety is clearly overridden by repressions and confabulations that are designed to keep patterns or processes consistent and certain. Valuing safety greatly may require communication with the right hemisphere, or perhaps the right hemisphere drives part of the logic needed to focus on safety considerations.

26 John Duckitt, "A Dual-Process Cognitive-Motivational Theory of Ideology and Prejudice," Advances in Experimental Social Psychology, 33:41-113, December 2000.

27 The main Schwartzian value related to hierarchy might be fairly thought of as centered around social conservatism, which concerns itself most with morality; that value is called Conformity, and is explained by Dr. Schwartz as "restraint of actions, inclinations, and impulses likely to upset or harm others and violate social expectations or norms". In Schwartz's model, the values nearest conformity may also involve a love or use of hierarchy. In Schwartzian value terms, then, the love of hierarchy is a mélange of Conformity, Achievement (personal success through demonstrating competence according to social standards), Power (social status and prestige, control or dominance

over people and resources), and Benevolence (Preserving and enhancing the welfare of those with whom one is in frequent personal contact, i.e., the "ingroup.")

[28] Freedom is a tricky, two-faced concept. This version refers to the concept of negative freedom, meaning "don't tread on me," which most conservatives and all libertarians are very fond of. Positive freedom is associated more with liberals, and concerns people having similar chances to succeed by removing unfair barriers to success for some people. These are typically viewed as in natural conflict, and, though they do conflict sometimes, there are important ways that they don't. Negative vs positive freedom is another way of stating the natural conflict between the Schwartzian Self-enhancement and Self-transcendence families of values, i.e., Achievement and Power vs Universalism and Benevolence. Libertarians think of positive liberty as mostly oppression, a violation of natural human rights; liberals feel the same way about negative liberty.

[29] Stanley Feldman, Christopher Johnston, "Understanding the Determinants of Political Ideology: Implications of Structural Complexity," Political Psychology, Vol. 35, No. 3, 2014.

[30] Hierarchy and authority is such a useful handle on conservatives that the linguist and political strategist George Lakoff bases his approach for communicating with conservatives on what he terms their "strict father" viewpoint on life, versus the "nurturant parent" approach of liberals. This approach, while limited due to its emphasis on hierarchy, is remarkably powerful anyway in helping divine conservative thinking in many settings, because order is expressed so often through hierarchical thinking. Hierarchy or conformance emphasis is mixed via hemispheric studies, much less clear than the orderliness-related values. Patients can lose their normal obedience, and similar to their attitude about safety, will override conforming preferences in a powerful, fantasy-driven attempt to keep patterns in place and consistent. Patients commonly deny they are ill, try to check themselves out of the hospital when they're not even mobile, or argue that their limbs aren't paralyzed. Yet other forms of conformance are still evident through their execution of patterns they obsess on, like following rules of games and other aspects of authority that are integral to an ordered existence.

[31] For example, this took the form of a fascination with simple patterns, which were often repeated endlessly, in very good humor.

[32] Jacob B. Hirsh, Colin G. DeYoung, Xiaowen Xu, and Jordan B. Peterson, Compassionate Liberals and Polite Conservatives: Associations of Agreeableness With Political Ideology and Moral Values, Personality and Social Psychology Bulletin 36(5) (2010), pgs. 655–664. Conscientiousness, one of the Big 5 factors of personality, is generally positively correlated with conservativism, but the correlation is through one of two aspects of this factor, Orderliness (which includes rigidity), while we're yet unclear that there's a correlation with the other aspect, industriousness. To understand the two aspects better as defining conscientiousness, see Colin G. DeYoung, Lena C. Quilty, Between Facets and Domains: 10 Aspects of the Big Five, Journal of Personality and Social Psychology, Vol. 93/5 (2007), pgs. 880–896.

[33] Safety shouldn't be considered being evident as a higher value from split-brain studies' findings about the left hemisphere—it's not—but is at the foundation of all human values, such as Maslow's hierarchy of needs and other psychological indicators of value. It's not clear that conservatives actually value safety any more than liberals do; what's important to recognize is that it is a primary values, and that they *express* that value through emphasizing certainty, consistency, and order (which are all indicated as much more important for the left hemisphere). That perspective helps greatly later when we look at their approach to personal safety, sanctity/purity, policing, national defense, and imperialism.

[34] Eviatar Zerubabel, *The Fine Line: Making Distinctions in Everyday Life*, Free Press, 1991; an entertaining and somewhat philosophical treatment. Boundary Theory is a little-known field of social psychology that has great currency in ideological issues, expressing either 'thick' or 'thin' boundary orientation as an important personality trait. The current Big 5 personality theory seems to mostly ascribe boundary issues to the traits of personality related to orderliness, closely tied to hierarchical thinking. See also Ernest Hartmann, *Boundary in the Mind: A New Psychology of Personality*, Basicbooks, 1991.

[35] Michael Gazzaniga, "The Split Brain Revisited," Scientific American 2002.

[36] The listed asterisked values that conservatives consciously hold align perfectly with Schwartz's list of universal human values, a popular and well-researched list of 10 universal human values; they are the three values that make up the "conservation" category of values, which are tradition, safety, and conformity (conformity, one can argue, is a kind of synonym, in this context, of hierarchy). Safety isn't found to be a documented left hemisphere relatively high value; if anything, it's more important for the right hemisphere. Of course, conservatives value many more than these listed items, as all humans do; and all humans value these things, to some degree. See Schwartz, S.H., "Universals in the content and structure of values: Theoretical advances and empirical tests in 20 countries" Advances in Experimental Social Psychology, M. Zanna, San Diego: Academic Press, 1992.

[37] While it's true that order is mentioned only occasionally explicitly, with many very conservative people, whole conversations can sometimes be interpreted fairly as various takes on order: desired order, poor order, disorderly people, how order is fun, etc.

[38] The footage is available on youtube.com by searching for "Esa Wroth".

[39] The problem the solo right hemisphere has with logic in split-brain patients is complex and not fully understood. One known part of it is that the relatively straightforward logic-handling needed to create and especially run the learned routines of our lives is normally provided by the left hemisphere, in a classic share of roles in which a kind of handshake agreement happens on what a routine is; the two hemispheres normally then work together to agree on and build usable routines. In the brain-damaged patients, though, those left-side logic facilities weren't available, so the right hemisphere is weak on certain aspects of mathematical or symbolic logic on its own.

[40] Damage to the left hemisphere language and logical processing areas render these patients mute or often confused, as well, which is very stressful, and may contribute even more to suicidal thoughts or depression, or be part of a cascading group of causes. Individual cases vary much more widely than many of the other statistical effects covered in this guide.

[41] L.I. Benowitz, K.L. Moya, D.N. Levine, Impaired Verbal Reasoning and Constructional Apraxia in Subjects with Right Hemisphere Damage, Neuropsychologia, Volume 28, Number 3, 1990, pp 231-241.

[42] The equivalent of this book for conservatives will be much tougher to write, for many reasons; one way of sensing the challenge is to recognize how much easier it is for anybody to understand what the brain's left hemisphere does for a living.

Chapter 2

[1] There isn't a single accepted definition of personality. One reason why is a wide, friendly disagreement on what personality is; another is that different aspects of what people consider personality are separate scientific fields. Though personality can be a bit of a weasel word, this definition works for us because we'll be focusing on its role in expression of underlying impetus, which gets us around a lot of the concerns about theory

validity. This particular ("rough") version of personality, like a lot of trait theories, is missing any reference to attitudes, biology, cognition, morality, or direct emotions, which in some circles are felt to be needed to be analyzed quite independently of value expression to explain personality. That's one reason why we're addressing those things separately: so they're not missed. Our definition also assumes that personality doesn't explain values, that it just expresses them– that personality isn't explanatory, but descriptive– a common modern assumption.

Personality is also viewed by some reputable psychologists as poorly represented through trait theory because of observed relatively low correlations to predicted behaviors, some evidence of non-stability (impermanent), and serious questions about both the statistical and scaling (testing) assumptions behind trait theories. All of these issues have been addressed exhaustively by trait theorists, but not to some scientists' satisfaction. My position is that: 1) trait theories are as good as we have right now, so we should use them; 2) my field work provided powerful indication that, at least in the realm of the ideological personality considerations, there is a) considerable stability (people tend to keep the same personality characteristics over long periods of time), b) considerable behavioral predictive power, despite relatively low correlation, and c) a strong relationship to political choices, independent of social considerations; and 3) trait theorists acknowledge many of the weaknesses of their critics, and try to be judicious about conclusions drawn. These per

[2] Technically, values are expressed through personality, not personality traits: it can be argued that personality traits cannot capture values completely, because they don't capture all dimensions of personality. The Big 5 Theory of personality that we use here, for instance, doesn't include honesty, gender, religiosity, or some other morality-inflected aspects, some of which one might argue are important if you're talking about trying to understand a person's whole personality. Some of the differences in personality theory are about what's a trait and what isn't.

Trait studies into personality are viewed by most personality scientists as capturing a very large portion of personality, and, since almost all useful studies on personality are trait-based, they'll have to do as a proxy for full personality evaluation. I think the point stated here, that conservative values are expressed through personality aspects of the Big 5 Theory, is an excellent assumption, as this discussion tries to show.

[3] This argument owes much of its spirit and some of its content to Daniel Nettle's excellent overview, *Personality: What Makes You the Way You Are*, OUD Oxford, 2007.

[4] P. Fischer, T. Greitemeyer, A. Kastenmüller, D. Frey, S. Oßwald, "Terror salience and punishment: Does terror salience induce threat to social order?," Journal of Experimental Social Psychology, Volume 43, Issue 6, November 2007, Pages 964–971. There are many other studies that show the same effect.

[5] Colin DeYoung, Lena Quilty, Jordan Peterson, "Between Facets and Domains: 10 Aspects of the Big 5," Journal of Personality and Social Psychology, Vol. 93, No. 5, 880–896.

[6] Mondak, Jeffrey J., *Personality and the Foundations of Political Behavior*, Cambridge University Press, 2010.

[7] George Allan, *The Importances of the Past: A Meditation on the Authority of Tradition*, State University of New York Press, 1985.

[8] The Pew 2014 U.S. Religious Landscape Study is based on telephone interviews with more than 35,000 Americans from all 50 states. The story is even more dramatic, because African-Americans are much more religious than the average liberal, and they skew the liberal numbers higher. As we discuss in the "On Politics" chapter, African-Americans

can be considered quite conservative in terms of the most common, personality-centric definition of ideology, with a strong historical/situational impetus to be liberal now.
9 This is a very well-replicated finding. There is one very good answer to part of the happiness difference, and that is that it's a bit patriotic for conservatives to be happy, so there's a natural bias toward saying "yes, I'm happy" for conservatives. But I think the entire quite significant difference can't nearly be explained adequately by that bias.
10 Graham, Jesse, Brian A. Nosek, and Jonathan Haidt. "The moral stereotypes of liberals and conservatives: Exaggeration of differences across the political spectrum." *PloS one* 7.12 (2012): e50092. Section 3b in the Results section showed liberals underestimating their "binding foundations" emphasis dramatically; it was the largest misperception finding in a wide-ranging study about ideological perceptions of people's personal ideology or others. The binding foundations (valuing respect for authority, sacredness, and loyalty) don't map directly with industriousness– they can be thought of as valuing a broader mix of conscientiousness (which includes both industriousness and orderliness) and politeness (which is half of Agreeableness) but there's a great deal of overlap with industriousness alone, since it's the personality's home for loyalty, working with authority efficiently, and group goal orientation.
11 Ozer, D.J., & Benet-Martinez, V., Personality and the prediction of consequential outcomes. Annual Review of Psychology, 57 (2006), pgs. 201–221
12 Christopher J. Boyce, Alex M. Wood, Gordon D.A. Brown, The dark side of conscientiousness: Conscientious people experience greater drops in life satisfaction following unemployment, Journal of Research in Personality, Volume 44, Issue 4, August 2010, Pages 535-539.
13 That's the far-left commentators talking. The centrists and center-left version is more like, "Hey, if I had to distance myself from the problems of the world to be happy, I'd rather be a little less happy." A somewhat muffled implication hangs in the air that they'd sacrifice some happiness for the world to be improved, but the amount of the sacrifice is left nebulous. The radicals are all in on the point, though: the more personal misery, the better, if the world is improved. This raises the implicit notion that liberals easily assume we must buy efficacy in the world with the coin of happiness; that the world is more zero-sum in the happiness arena, in that anyone's happiness likely comes at the cost of the happiness of another who isn't being adequately taken care of. This is an extension of a world view with thinner boundaries, or more interdependencies. The conservative mindset doesn't see happiness as zero-sum at all; though they believe in heroic sacrifice that can potentially cause great personal harm to the hero, they tend to think that they can be happy, and other people's happiness can increase easily at the same time; that tradeoff's aren't necessary. Both of these coarse ideological assumptions are naïve.

Chapter 3

1 Colin G. DeYoung, Jordan B. Peterson, Daniel M. Higgins, Sources of Openness/Intellect: Cognitive and Neuropsychological Correlates of the Fifth Factor of Personality, Journal of Personality 73:4, August 2005
To be unduly, technically clear, the two Aspects are conjoined as one Factor because the statistics determine it, because the Big 5 was derived through statistical analysis, after creating the traits based on lexical studies. This study is trying to get at the why of it, but the actual Factor is a purely statistical construction, like all the other Big 5 Factors, that most theorists don't even try to explain; they just use it. The statistical analysis that derived the Big 5 Factors computationally forces them to accept the groupings determined by the math. Not that people haven't tried to separate the two in less

scientifically-derived personality theories, to make logical sense of the affair. But many replications have validated that openness and intellect are related, even if we have a tough time conceptualizing why.

2 The researchers that theorize this continuum call it a "paradoxical simplex," because it is sets of traits that correlate positively with their neighbor traits all along it, while some traits have negative correlation with one another: it is a simplex (a continuum), but it has an important paradox because parts of the "simplex"/continuum are negatively correlated. For a good, more detailed treatment, see Dr. Scott Barry Kaufman's explanatory article at creativitypost.com, "Must One Risk Madness to Achieve Genius?"

3 Another example of a useful, enlightening generality with some great exceptions. Here are some conservative comedians who are very, very funny, broadly so, or in any other sense one cares to name; though most lean toward the libertarian end, and many use a lot of profanity and anger, which messes with the stereotype a little bit, since many of them are more popular with liberals: Lenny Bruce, Adam Corrolla, Doug Stanhope, Bill Burr, Dennis Miller, Joe Rogan, Jackie Mason, and Vince Vaughan. Perhaps 90% of the top 100 comedians are overtly liberal or their politics is unclear, I'd estimate. But also let's be clear that humor is more about what listeners gravitate to, and who are comedy fans: those are more important than the politics of the deliverers. I don't know of any polls of ideology for listeners of Larry the Cable Guy, but I don't think a poll is necessary.

4 Schmidt, G.L., DeBuse, C.J., Seger, C.A., "Right hemisphere metaphor processing? Characterizing the later alizarin of semantic processes," Brain and Language, 2007, 100(2), 127-141.

5 Mitch McConnell on Charlie Rose, June 1, 2016.

6 This is a way of saying that there's collinearity, or correlation, between orderliness and openness. They're significantly negative correlated, which makes sense, given all the factors we're discussing.

Collinearity of the Big 5 is a subject unto itself. For our purposes, I'm assuming at least a little simplistically, as most personality research does, that the Big 5 are orthogonal (uncorrelated), meaning you could be strong in all 5, or weak in all 5– having more of one factor doesn't mean anything about how you use the other factors. The correlation of individual traits across different factors can technically be allowed with orthogonal Big 5 factors, but more than a little is quite problematic, requiring unrealistic assumptions. For our purposes, it's OK to assume some correlations between Big 5 factors or the aspects (the 10 that are the 5 split in two); it's a theoretical problem for the theory's validity, shared by nearly every trait theory of personality, that just means it's incomplete, or unclear. For a detailed treatment, see S.V. Paunonen, D. Jackson, "What is Beyond the Big Five? Plenty!," Journal of Personality, 68:5, October, 2000.

7 Martin Bäckström, Fredrik Björklund, Magnus R. Larsson, "Five-factor inventories have a major general factor related to social desirability which can be reduced by framing items neutrally," Journal of Research in Personality 43/3, 6/2009, Pages 335–344.

8 Michael Weiss' life is dramatized in the 2011 independent film "Puncture".

9 This comes quite close to Jung's notion of libido, which is quite different from Freud's. Jung likened libido to linked pools of water at different levels, pouring into one another; personality can be thought of as the way that humans enact libido, or life energy: pools that dynamically filled, disbursed, and then mysteriously filled again from whatever propels our humanity.

10 Conservatives do this same bouncing along the openness/intellect continuum to express their intelligence; they just do a relatively muted version. Often, all the bouncing or variation one will see with a conservative is either still in the intellect family of traits, or

it includes only some of the 'early' openness traits, those with a strong correlation to intellect, like cleverness and ingenuity. In my experience, the openness traits that are more negatively correlated with openness are relatively rare to see in conservative personalities, perhaps because of how they tend to conflict with orderliness traits.

Chapter 4

[1] Jacob B. Hirsh, Colin G. DeYoung, Xiaowen Xu, and Jordan B. Peterson, Compassionate Liberals and Polite Conservatives: Associations of Agreeableness With Political Ideology and Moral Values, Personality and Social Psychology Bulletin 36(5) (2010), pgs. 655–664.
[2] A "strong" effect in personality registers as a medium, or even medium-low correlation, because personality effects typically register low in correlation studies. This has been addressed by researchers many times, and I've had the same experience. One of the personality aspects we talk about, neuroticism, is a tiny correlation in normal terms, but I find it to be a powerful effect anyway.

I think a good way of explaining this is to think about how even a small difference in directions followed on a road trip can make a huge difference in where you go, or how long you get there. How a two-degree error in a plane ride can put you hundreds of miles away from where you were going. A seemingly small or occasional insertion of a personality trait into a situation makes a big difference in personal relationships.
[3] I don't have a statistics degree, but it sounds funnier than psychology degree.
[4] Danny Osborne, Liz W. Wootton, and Chris G. Sibley, "Are Liberals Agreeable or Not? Politeness and Compassion Differentially Predict Political Conservatism Via Distinct Ideologies," Social Psychology 44, 2015, pp. 354-360.
[5] Cicone, Michael, Wendy Wapner, and Howard Gardner. "Sensitivity to emotional expressions and situations in organic patients." *Cortex* 16.1 (1980): 145-158. The initial portion of this study is a balanced overview of some of the clear evidence on the point.
[6] Jacob M. Vigil, "Political leanings vary with facial expression processing and psychosocial functioning,"
Group Processes & Intergroup Relations 13(5) 547–558
[7] Joseph Fried, *Democrats and Republicans: Rhetoric and Reality*, Angora Publishing, 2008.
[8] By Stanley Feldman, unpublished.
[9] The trait tranquility, part of neuroticism, is negatively correlated with openness/intellect, meaning that being high in neuroticism affects a person more if they're also high in openness/intellect, like most liberals. See Colin G. DeYoung, Lena C. Quilty, Jordan B. Peterson, "Between Facets and Domains: 10 Aspects of the Big Five" Journal of Personality and Social Psychology, 2007, Vol. 93, No. 5, 880– 896.
[10] Caitlin M. Burton, Jason E. Plaks, Jordan B. Peterson, "Why Do Conservatives Report Being Happier Than Liberals? The Contribution of Neuroticism," Journal of Social and Political Psychology, 2015, Vol. 3(1).

Chapter 5

[1] These three are, in order, termed biased information search, biased assimilation, and identity-protective cognition; the last creates strong excuses, often out of thin air, purely to reduce cognitive dissonance.

Motivated reasoning is a useful way of looking at many political biases, but we'll concentrate on certain biases that are essentially tactical versions of motivated cognition.
[2] This is the idea of the political metaphorical complex, which is loosely rooted in a neurological setting by George Lakoff in his books. A more academic treatment is Lakoff, G. "The Contemporary Theory of Metaphor," Metaphor and Thought, Ed. Athony Ortony. Cambridge 1993: Cambridge University Press. 202-251.
[3] Thomas Gilovich, Dale W. Griffin, Daniel Kahneman, *Heuristics and Biases: the Psychology of Intuitive Judgment*, Cambridge University Press, 1992, page 9.
[4] Pronin, Emily; Matthew B. Kugler, "Valuing thoughts, ignoring behavior: The introspection illusion as a source of the bias blind spot". Journal of Experimental Social Psychology (Elsevier) 43 (4): 565–578, July, 2007.
[5] Ibid; see also Dr. Pronin's earlier work for a clearer treatment. The blind spot also impacts the actor side of the actor/observer asymmetry, an important examination of how we view our own motivations and actions different than we do other's.
[6] There is an important exception to this rule, with biases that we come to embrace, or perceive as a virtue. One way to understand ethnic cleansing, or a Klu Klux Klan member's racism, both of which have their roots in common biases, is as complexes of biases that have grown over the wall between the unconscious and the conscious mind, so that genocide or racism is now embraced as a virtue.
[7] Don't worry, there'll be other cases when liberal ideas are the heroes. We have to take turns– sorry.
[8] K. Lewin, "Übergang von der aristotelischen zur galileischen Denkweise in Biologie und Psychologie" (Transition from an Aristotelian to a Galileian Way of Thinking, in Biology and Psychology). Erkenntnis 1931.
[9] I'm including character in with personality. Many modern personality models consider honesty, patience, and other things we think of as character to be personality traits. That approach serves us well here.
[10] The two most common names of this bias are the Fundamental Attribution Error and the Correspondence Bias, but it's also called by many other equally unclear and confusing names, such as the Fundamental Error of Attribution, the Attribution Error, the Correspondence Biases (this latter because the "bias" is technically at least 4 different biases riding around in the same jitney), and Lay Dispositionism. The wide spread of names of this bias is common for many of the biases we'll review, because there is a great deal of disparate research on the biases among many fields, and they sometimes conflate two or more into what's considered one bias in other fields. For our purposes, which, it turns out, are relatively simple and specialized, I was able to tiptoe through most of the controversy to deliver you fairly agreed-upon biases. But you should be aware that my terminology is a bit tentative or non-standard here or there, simply because there are as yet few standards in bias study. There are also many other biases besides the ones in this book, some of which may be related or identical to ones in this treatment.

I will usually call this bias the fundamental error, so you'll remember that it's almost always the foundation of your political communication problems. "The Fundamental Attribution Error" is a precise name, but the precision comes at the cost of clarity. The bias is much more general than is explained here for our political purposes: it describes the tendency to over-value dispositional or personality-based explanations for the observed behavior of others while devaluing situational (historical and/or instructional) explanations for those behaviors. Saying it this less specific way shows that the error also shows up in situations in which the people agree with each other, i.e., the agreement is due to their wonderful personality, not situational circumstance. There are four primary ways the bias is manifested, and they're all useful and interesting, but going into all that here would make your head hurt way too early.

Some of the 'stand-alone' biases we treat in the next chapter are actually either aspects of this fundamental error, or they're a mixture of the Fundamental Attribution Error and one or two other biases. Because the field is not standardized yet, I have had to clump biases in ways that work for this particular political world. The list of biases would look different in other applications. Fortunately, politics is not as tough as other high bias situations, like trial law or general sales.

[11] Duncan, B. L. (1976). "Differential social perception and attribution if intergroup violence: Testing the lower limits of stereotyping of Blacks". Journal of Personality and Social Psychology 34 (4): 75–93.

[12] Miller, A.G., Jones, E.E., & Hinkle, S. (1981). A robust attribution error in the personality domain. Journal of Experimental Social Psychology, 17, 587-600.

[13] We typically fall into a bias we'll discuss in the next chapter, because our first assumption when we disagree with someone is often that the person is ill-informed, and we can cure them of ignorance: if they appear informed but still in disagreement, we will then either choose intelligence flaws or personality flaws, depending on our observations. We often settle on a combination of the two as an explanation. Psychologists don't normally consider "intelligence flaws" and "personality flaws" to be separate problems, maybe because they consider intelligence as part of the personality. But I've found the distinction helpful in a political situation because the assumption of intelligence defects is a persistent liberal bias, and is often as demonstrably false as this kind of thing can be. Discussion around this "intelligence defect" bias is often productive with some liberals intellectuals, who have a narrow range of acceptable **personas** of intelligence, i.e., George W. Bush is "obviously" not smarter than John Kerry (when actually, Bush's IQ is higher).

[14] Even when we can see that we lost the debate, there are psychological payoffs and mitigants similar to those of sports events: revenge fantasies or martyrdom (took one on the chin for the good guys).

[15] Tobina A. Marks I, Dar R. Advantages of bias and prejudice: an exploration of their neurocognitive templates. Neuroscience Biobehavior Review 1999 Nov;23(7):1047-58.

[16] Oftentimes the conscious mind helps in our support of the hidden biases, but usually with strong subconscious assistance, and not often in the dominant position. For instance, when Ann Coulter strikes out with great venom and creativity, she employs a rather remarkable set of conscious skills to support a statement that may be somewhat deceptive, or partial, or exaggeratory, but one that expresses an unconscious bias. Her efforts help her feel more certain of the biased viewpoint, and the conscious mind is artfully helping to reinforce the bias.

[17] This is an oversimplification. Some high-quality, recent work makes a strong case that the "newer" stages of the brain and consciousness in general are not new, but vastly developed of late. Although it's an important distinction in some arenas, it doesn't seem to impact ours much, so I've stuck with the more common perception among cognitive neuroscientists.

[18] There are many examples of partially cognitive roots to moral hazard and unlawful behavior throughout cognitive, legal and psychological literature. One representative, interesting case is the discrimination example in Krieger, L. The Content of Our Categories: A Cognitive Bias Approach to Discrimination and Equal Employment Opportunity. Stanford Law Review, vol. 47, No.6, July 1995 pg. 1161.

[19] This metaphor is expounded powerfully in Dr. Jonathan Haidt's book "The Happiness Hypothesis: Finding Modern Truth in Ancient Wisdom", 2006, Basic Books

[20] Joseph Henrich, The Secret of our Success, Princeton University Press, 2015

[21] Henry Kissinger was an American Secretary of State, and a longtime diplomat for the United States. He is a war criminal, as defined by international statute, but due to America's influence internationally, has never been arraigned or prosecuted for his crimes. Among other crimes, he's responsible for the deaths of many thousands of civilian Cambodians during a secret, massive bombing campaign in that country, as well as the assassination of Chile's head of state, which led to the long reign of terror by the ultra-right General Augusto Pinochet.

[22] Pew Research Center IAT, 2/2/2015 – 4/2/2015

Chapter 6

[1] Actually, research shows that it's totally possible to persuade people of political ideas, but only people who flop around with every idea, and who typically could care less about politics. This is how a conservative can feel they've handily persuaded their liberal date to vote for lower taxes. Ideological people have been shown to be impossible to convince in these kinds of conversations, especially if they're smart and knowledgeable.

[2] Model Tiane, L. Lee, Susan T. Fiske, Not an outgroup, not yet an ingroup: Immigrants in the Stereotype Content, International Journal of Intercultural Relations 30 (2006) pp. 751–768.

[3] In the famous original study, Drs. Kahneman and Tversky asked the question "Was it more or less than 10%?, then asked people to estimate. If they asked "Was it more or less than 65%?" before asking for an estimate, guesses were 20% higher, on average. See Tversky, A. & Kahneman, D. (1974). Judgment under uncertainty: Heuristics and biases. *Science*, 185, 1124-1130.

[4] Based on work by Arthur Asch in 1946 at the New School for Social Research, as explained in "Forming Impressions of Personality," which has been replicated and extended by others.

[5] Joseph Henrich, *The Secret of Our Success: How Culture is Driving Human Evolution, Domesticating Our Species, and Making us Smarter*, Princeton University Press, 2015

[6] Kahan, D., "Ideology, motivated reasoning, and cognitive reflection," Judgment and Decision Making, Vol. 8, No. 4, July 2013, pg. 417. As of this writing, there's a great deal of confusing and conflicting evidence with regards to ideological aspects of motivated reasoning, though the preponderance of evidence and general agreement in the academy is for relative conservative attachment to cognitive closure the way we've described here, leading to higher levels of bias.

[7] Sukhwinder S. Shergill, Paul M. Bays, Chris D. Frith, Daniel M. Wolpert, "Two Eyes for an Eye: The Neuroscience of Force Escalation," Science, Vol. 301, pg. 187, 7/2003. The extrapolations to social science are mine.

[8] Research has demonstrated that we're very good at doing certain kinds of tasks without bias, to be properly influenced by reality. But abstract discussion of politics is not one of them.

Chapter 7

[1] Karen Stenner, "Three Kinds of 'Conservatism'," Psychological Inquiry, 20: 142–159, 2009, has evidence for a third type, which she names "status quo conservatives," different than my use here. More recently, Feldman and others have excellent statistical evidence for two conservative types instead of three like Stenner: using their work, Stenner's third type is likely akin to my version of status quo conservative here, meaning conservatives of both stripes that aren't high in authoritarianism or SDO.

[2] This treatment mostly depends on Karen Stenner's work, but takes a cue from Stanley Feldman, who makes a distinction between social conservatives and authoritarians. I believe labeling social conservatives authoritarian as a group, as Stenner did, is deceptive; "high in authoritarianism" for both Feldman and Stenner is answering positively on parenting preferences that effectively pit individualizing and binding foundation values against each other; this inevitably and intuitively gathers people who engage in authoritarian behavior in the same tent as most conservatives, which, notwithstanding a great deal of hand-wringing on the part of researchers, is problematic and deceptive with such nomenclature. While the correlation between healthy child-rearing preference choices and authoritarianism is extremely helpful in some ways, using that connection indiscriminately is no different than the kind of thinking that would keep black people off police forces because they're statistically more violent and less educated as an ethnic group. Dr. J.J. Ray termed authoritarianism "directedness," in an early attempt to give it a reasonable name; Stenner said she would prefer to simply call it "difference-ism". Authoritarianism is an accurate term in the sense of advocating for strong authority and the ingroup to guide society, but the name is associated with Nazism, and it obfuscates the fact that, statistically, it simply refers to a person forced, one-point landing on one half of a continuum that, in Stenner's words, is "marked at one end by preference for uniformity and insistence upon group authority and at the other end by preference for diversity and insistence upon individual autonomy." The name implies a set of behaviors and beliefs, when it is referring merely to a much broader statistical concept. As a result, for clarity, I've deviated from some of the literature by limiting my use of the term authoritarian to those who engage in things like racism, rather than referring to people high in authoritarianism, i.e., merely located statistically on the group authority side of the continuum. I've done this to pull us out of the statistical clouds, and limit the misunderstanding and liberal prejudice that is inevitable when using such a pejorative term in a scientific context.

[3] Kim R. Holmes, "The Closing of the Liberal Mind," Encounter Books, 2016, pg. 245.

[4] Feldman S., "Enforcing social Conformity: A Theory of Authoritarianism," Political Psychology, Vol. 24, No. 1, 2003, pg. 58-61.

[5] Jeffrey Mondak, "The Trump Draw: Personality Traits as Predictors of Candidate Support," in press.

[6] Matthew MacWilliams, "The One Weird Trait That Predicts Whether You're a Trump Supporter," politico.com, January 17, 2016

[7] Thanks to professor Jennifer Mercierca, a political rhetoric scholar, for most of this information. The quotes can easily be found and verified online.

[8] Ashbrock F., Sibley C., Duckitt J., "Right-Wing Authoritarianism and Social Dominance Orientation and the Dimensions of Generalized Prejudice: A Longitudinal Test," European Journal of Personality, 24: 324–340 (2010)

[9] Nate Silver, "The Mythology Of Trump's 'Working Class' Support," fivethirtyeight.com, 5/3/2016

[10] A great treatment of psychopathy at work, or the kind of neurosis I believe SDO entails, is Babiak, P., Hare, R., "Snakes in Suits: When Psychopaths Go to Work," HarperBusiness, 2006

[11] Stanley Feldman, Christopher Johnston, "Understanding the Determinants of Political Ideology: Implications of Structural Complexity" Political Psychology, Vol. 35, No. 3, 2014, pg. 349. "The confused" refers to groups 1 and 3 on that page that self-affiliate as conservative, even though their positions are mostly liberal. Most scholars suspect this occurs commonly because liberalism has a poor reputation in a lot of the country, supposedly stemming from events of the 60s. I think it's more about our fundamentally conservative natures as human beings, that makes the word itself attractive to us, particularly if we have strong family ties, or if we're religious.

[12] Elizabeth Suhay, "Explaining Group Influence: The Role of Identity and Emotion in Political Conformity and Polarization," Political Behavior (2015) 37:221–251

[13] See for example Herbert C. Kelman, "Interests, Relationships, Identities: Three Central Issues for Individuals and Groups in Negotiating Their Social Environment," Annu. Rev. Psychol. 2006. 57:1–26. Harvard's Dr. Kelman refined this theory for over a half-decade. John Turner's "Self-Categorization Theory" is a purely cognitive version of SIT's social influence approach. There are both competing and complementary views as well, and 6 X 4 matrices, and a whole painful lexicon involved. But these issues we covered seem to be in relative agreement among the psychologists, political scientists, and neurology/anthropology/evolution people involved.

[14] This is a well-known rule in publishing. Simple, intense books that sell liberalism as stupid and evil are the most popular sub-category of American political book. And it's not a conspiracy. Liberals buy fewer such books, and the ones they do buy are more focused on comedy, as a kind of extension of the Daily Show, probably because we're not as socially sensitive or orderly.

I also have a sneaky reason to mention the "Makers and Takers" book; it's actually quite informative, with mostly decent research, and it provoked much thought for me. We shouldn't be overly sensitive about our strengths and weaknesses, as I've said elsewhere; sometimes they sketch us rather well.

[15] This isn't the forum for a lengthy treatment of how one should define ideology. The short version is that looking at it by issues and by personality are both helpful and deceptive, depending on the context of analysis. Personality-as-ideology arguably became the lens of primacy upon ideology with Jost et al in 2003 (Jost JT, Glaser, J, Kruglanski AW, Sulloway FJ, "Political conservatism as motivated social cognition" Psychol Bull 2003 May;129(3):339-75). But strains of the similar thinking go back over half a century. Personality correlates via the Big 5 are only medium-strength with ideology, though, so cultural and objective issue dimensions almost certainly play large roles in ideology.

[16] Jost JT, Glaser, J, Kruglanski AW, Sulloway FJ, "Political conservatism as motivated social cognition" Psychol Bull 2003 May;129(3):339-75. This may be the most cited paper in political psychology, but this little-known part of the paper may end up being the most important aspect of their findings. The strongly-embedded connection between personality (or disposition) and ideology seems to be the first place where scholars made the claim that personality better defines a person's ideology than beliefs. That precedence is very strongly posited through metanalysis.

[17] Imbens, Guido, Gelman, Andrew, "The Great Society, Reagan's Revolution, and Generations of Presidential Voting," working (unpublished) paper, 6/5/2014.

[18] Even personality is at least partially socially-constructed, since a rough-edged estimate of heritability is about 50%; it's not as if personality is "over here," and social/cultural influences are "over there". How the non-purely genetic portion of our personalty

(whatever that means) is formed is a great mystery, but much of the answer to, say, why Eastern Germany conservative personality is the way it is may well be related to generations of cultural influence, moving high orderliness, Low openness conservative personalities away from where they might've landed before communism.
19 John Duckitt, Kirstin Fisher, "The Impact of Social Threat on Worldview and Ideological Attitudes," Political Psychology, Vol. 24, No. 1, 2003.

Chapter 8

1 The rest of this discussion is an attempt to thread our way usefully through moral theory that is still controversial and partial, but that has many agreed-upon, very practical points for those of us trying to get to bed tonight knowing how to not lose it with conservatives. As we'll see, morality is a messy affair, with its tentacles wrapped around emotions, values, right and wrong, ideology, religion, and strong cultural influences. It shouldn't be surprising that achieving "parsimony," or brief simplicity in explaining morality, would be a little like asking economics or physics or relationships to be summed up quickly. The good news–great news, actually– is a tremendous amount of creative, informative, and revolutionary research since the turn of the century, providing deep insights into useful overall frameworks, the influence of ideology, the role of emotion, and neurological clues into related psychological processes. We'll be following a contructionist approach to morality overall, threading initially through insights afforded us using dyadic morality; we'll then turn to the deep view into ideological and cultural morality differentiations provided by Moral Foundation Theory.
   Probably the largest crux of controversy between dyadic and moral foundations theorists is in the relationship between morality and disgust: here, I've mostly ducked the theoretical clashes by pulling it a bit out of the morality sphere so we can understand it more tactically in an ideological setting.
2 Ditto, P. H., & Liu, B. (2011). Deontological dissonance and the consequentialist crutch. In M. Mikulincer & P. R. Shaver (Eds.), The social psychology of morality: Exploring the causes of good and evil (pp. 51–70). Washington, DC: American Psychological Association.
3 Honesty and self-discipline are technically candidate moral foundations as of this writing. They're acknowledged by moral psychologists as important moral values. Both of them can be thought of as individualizing or binding foundations, depending on the context. Freedom is also a bit of a hybrid, in that it can be seen as binding or individualizing in different situations.
4 W. Hofmann, D Wisneski, M. Brandt, L. Skitka, "Morality in everyday life," Science, 12 Sep 2014: Vol. 345, Issue 6202, pp. 1340-1343
5 A full treatment of Moral Foundation Theory is beyond our scope here, and this is a specialized version of the overall approach. I encourage you to take a test to determine your moral approach at yourmorals.org, and get a sense of how you stack up against others. There are many useful links on that site to related information about morals and how they play out in our political lives.
6 Jesse Graham, Brian A. Nosek, and Jonathan Haidt, The Moral Stereotypes of Liberals and Conservatives: Exaggeration of Differences across the Political Divide, 1/1/2011. Available online.
7 The notion of biological sex is assumed to be binary, with male and female the only choices. Human sexuality is often best thought of as a continuum, both biologically and cognitively. Biology is a broader topic than genitalia; urges and wiring are also biological,

as are hormonal and other distinctions that impinge on the notion of biological sex. For more, see isna.org.

But most transgender activists see biological sex as irrelevant to the issue, and feel that it's inappropriate to think of gender, especially in the context of bathrooms, as more than a social construct; further, that the notion of biological sex cannot be used as a legal concept, so it cannot be used to distinguish who uses a given bathroom. While this idea appeals to many liberals, it tends to sidesteps the argument about who is harmed or potentially harmed when people use bathrooms, by assuming conservatives can't be harmed when transgender people use a restroom. Hopefully, the clarification of morality here helps show that argument as at least worthy of exploring. Who uses what bathroom is an excellent conversation to have now in America, because there are principles in tension that need to be resolved, for practical purposes.

[8] The evolutionary roots of our sense of sanctity and purity are thought by evolutionary biologists and evolutionary psychologists to be in avoiding poisonous food and disease, which is why Group Safety is lined up with the moral foundation of Sanctity. It has since evolved in us into a spiritual notion of becoming tainted through, say, wrong living– but can still be argued to reflect a need for group safety and success.

[9] Jonathan Haidt, *The Righteous Mind: Why Good People are Divided by Politics and Religion*, Pantheon, 2012. This book is a development of this statement.

[10] G.J. Lewis, T.C. Bates, "How the Personality System Allows Basic Traits to Influence Politics Via Characteristic Moral Adaptations," British Journal of Psychology, August 2011, pp. 546-558.

[11] This difference between conservatives and liberals in parenting styles is so marked that George Lakoff has developed a useful metaphor for ideological difference through contrasting parenting styles, though without this Moral Foundations Theory overlay used here: many references to his thoughts can be found online and in his books. His work emphasizes how liberal causes can be more successful in the political marketplace by understanding ourselves through parenting styles.

[12] Graham, Jesse, Brian A. Nosek, and Jonathan Haidt. "The moral stereotypes of liberals and conservatives: Exaggeration of differences across the political spectrum." *PloS one* 7.12 (2012): e50092.

[13] Yoel Inbar, David Pizarro, Ravi Iyer and Jonathan Haidt, "Disgust Sensitivity, Political Conservatism, and Voting," Social Psychological and Personality Science 2012 3: 537 originally published online 6 December 2011.

[14] JK MacCormick, JA Lindquist, "Bodily Contributions to Emotions: Schacter's Legacy for a Constructionist View on Emotion," Emotion Review, In Press. Examples are given of Japanese reactions to situations that register strong anger in America that register different emotions, and/or register radically different affective response. This is also commonsensical, in the sense that people with different makeup, faced with similar situations, can face strong shame, or strong anger, or strong frustration, or disgust, or so little that they're not sure what they're feeling.

[15] Ahn WY, Kishida KT, Gu X, Lohrenz T, Harvey A, Alford JR, Smith KB, Yaffe G, Hibbing JR, Dayan P, Montague PR., "Nonpolitical images evoke neural predictors of political ideology." Curr Biol. 2014 Nov 17;24(22):2693-9. Epub 2014 Oct 30.

[16] C. Daryl Cameron, Kristen A. Lindquist, and Kurt Gray, "A Constructionist Review of Morality and Emotions: No Evidence for Specific Links Between Moral Content and Discrete Emotions," Personality and Social Psychology Review 1–24, 2015.

Chapter 9

[1] Tina Fey, *Bossypants*, Reagan Arthur / Little, Brown; Reprint edition (January 29, 2013).

Chapter 10

[1] M. Scott Peck, *The Road Less Traveled*, Touchstone, 1998, 2nd Ed.
[2] LaMarre, Landreville, Beam, "The Irony of Satire: Political Ideology and the Motivation to See What you Want to See in the Colbert Report," The International Journal of Press/Politics April 2009 Vol. 14 no. 212-231 . This was a careful study that showed conservatives unusually prone to think Colbert, the liberal comedian, is conservative in real life: conservatives don't usually miss the satire, but they don't view Colbert as strongly negative about their ideology (as liberals might assume they would). This study covers a related point to mine in the text, but it doesn't address the broader point, the conservative tendency to award you ingroup status easily, and allow you to keep it until you lose it by making an important error.

Chapter 11

[1] M.J. Reddy, "The Conduit Metaphor: A Case of Frame Conflict in our Language about Language," In A. Ortony (Ed.), *Metaphor and Thought* (pp284-310), Cambridge: Cambridge University Press.
[2] Government has been shown to be very efficient, due to economies of scale, in certain ways. In other ways, especially when close monitoring is involved, or if we include the waste that happens through poor regulation or badly-written laws, government service can be very wasteful.
   Though the tax system is very complicated, it became so by trying to address certain social goals, such as helping the poor with children, making home ownership feasible, or making sure that certain ailing or sensitive industries received special treatment. The tax system essentially provides subsidies to people or businesses that the government decided deserves them. If we want a less complicated system, we have to give up the ability to grant those specific subsidies, or find some other (complicated) way to provide them.
   SSI is still technically an insurance program, with actuarial tables and a structure like insurance– it's just heading into the red so quickly that it can be interpreted as a tax that just pays present retirees with present worker payments. 2010 was the last year that payments covered benefits paid.
[3] See whatisessential.org, "An Overview of Public Conservation's Work on Abortion".

Appendix– Hemispheres

[1] Nicole Marinsek, Benjamin O. Turner, Michael Gazzaniga, Michael B. Miller, "Divergent hemispheric reasoning strategies: reducing uncertainty versus resolving inconsistency," Frontiers in Neuroscience, 8:839
[2] A recent breakthrough model of inhibition may be quite helpful in making progress: see Grimshaw, Carrhel, "An asymmetric inhibition model of hemispheric differences in emotional processing," *Frontiers in Psychology*, May, 2014, 5:489.
[3] Marinsek N, Turner BO, Gazzaniga M, Miller MB, "Divergent hemispheric reasoning strategies: reducing uncertainty versus resolving inconsistency." Frontiers in Human Neuroscience, 8:839.

[4] David O'Neil, "Hand and Mind: What Gestures Reveal about Thought," University of Chicago Press, 1992, pgs. 345-352.

[5] Sackeim, H. A., Greenberg, M. S., Weiman, A. L., Gur, R., Hungerbuhler, J. P., & Geschwind, N. 1982. Hemispheric asymmetry in the expression of positive and negative emotions. Archives of Neurology, 39, 210-218.

[6] Levy, Trevarthen, Sperry, "Perception of Bilateral Chimeric Figures Following Hemispheric Deconnexion," *Brain*, 1972, 95, 61-78.

[7] Gonzalo Munevar, "The Myth of Dual Consciousness in the Split Brain: Contrary Evidence from Psychology and Neuroscience," from proceedings of the Brain-Mind Institute, 2012.

Appendix– Ideology

[1] Besides variation in the amount of genetic influence, etc., combinations of factors can create unpredictability, the impossibility to evaluate these factors with individuals, because genetic and environmental influences are not separate. Genetic influences depend greatly on environmental factors. As a simple example, certain inherited traits, such as a mild propensity toward depression, may not even be evident through some circumstances, but if your life contains an unusual amount of high stress, this propensity may have a critical impact in your life. There are many other more complicated examples, such as genetic factors that arise or go quiescent at a certain time in life, or others that are triggered by a single catalytic event but not in a predictable direction.

[2] For any individual, there can also be important interrelationships between these factors due to chance, and changes from genetics and our environment that occur over time. We also have wide variation in what makes us liberal– for many of us, our personality doesn't even play in that much. It's important to think of these as statistically useful stereotypes, but we are far from understanding a single person well enough to understand them completely in this way.

[3] Duncker, C., Kritische Reflexionen des Ideologiebegriffes: Zur Bedeutung der Ideologien für den Menschen ("Critical Reflections on the Concept of Ideology: On the Importance of Ideology for the Public"), London: Turnshare Ltd. 2006, pg. 34

RIGHT
LEARNING
ADJUSTING
ANXIETY & PESSIMISM
INDECISIVE
TAKES PICTURES
3-D CAPABILITY
UNDERSTANDS STORIES
VISUAL PROCESSING
EMOTION

LEFT
MANAGING
FOLLOWS LEARNED RULES
MAKES CATEGORIES
PUTS EVENTS IN CONTEXT
LOGICAL

ORDERLINESS

INDUSTRIOUSNESS